NATIONAL GEOGRAPHIC
Reach™

Language • Literacy • Content

Program Authors

Nancy Frey

Lada Kratky

Nonie K. Lesaux

Sylvia Linan-Thompson

Deborah J. Short

Jennifer D. Turner

NATIONAL GEOGRAPHIC LEARNING | CENGAGE Learning®

Literature Reviewers

Carmen Agra Deedy, Grace Lin, Jonda C. McNair, Anastasia Suen

Grade 3 Teacher Reviewers

Sandy Cano
Case Manager/Special Education Teacher
Pasteur Elementary School
Chicago, IL

Sina Chau-Pech
Elementary ELD Lead Teacher
Folsom Cordova Unified School District
Sacramento, CA

Ana Sainz de la Peña
Director, ESOL and Bilingual Programs
The School District of Philadelphia
Philadelphia Allentown, PA

Griselda E. Flores
Bilingual Instruction Coach
Chicago Public Schools
Chicago, IL

Lisa King
District Lead ESOL Teacher
Polo Road Elementary School
Columbia, SC

Janie Oosterveen
Bilingual Teacher Specialist
San Antonio Independent School
District
San Antonio, TX

Cristina Rojas, MS. Ed.
District Program Specialist, EL Programs
Hacienda La Puente Unified School
District
Hacienda Heights, CA

Jennifer Skrocki Eargle
*District Elementary Language Arts Specialist
& Contract Employee*
Galena Park Independent School District
Houston, TX

Acknowledgments
Grateful acknowledgment is given to the authors, artists, photographers, museums, publishers, and agents for permission to reprint copyrighted material. Every effort has been made to secure the appropriate permission. If any omissions have been made or if corrections are required, please contact the Publisher.

Illustrator Credits:
Front Cover: Joel Sotelo

Acknowledgments and credits continue on page 646.

For product information and technology assistance, contact us at
Customer & Sales Support, 888-915-3276

For permission to use material from this text or product, submit all requests online at **www.cengage.com/permissions**
Further permissions questions can be emailed to
permissionrequest@cengage.com

National Geographic Learning | Cengage Learning
1 Lower Ragsdale Drive
Building 1, Suite 200
Monterey, CA 93940

Cengage Learning is a leading provider of customized learning solutions with office locations around the globe, including Singapore, the United Kingdom, Australia, Mexico, Brazil, and Japan. Locate your local office at **www.cengage.com/global**.

Cengage Learning products are represented in Canada by Nelson Education, Ltd.

Visit National Geographic Learning online at **NGL.Cengage.com**
Visit our corporate website at **www.cengage.com**

Printed in the USA.
Quad/Graphics, Versailles, KY

ISBN: 978-13054-93513
ISBN (CA): 978-13054-94572

Printed in the United States of America
18 19 20 21 22 23 24
13 12 11 10 9 8 7 6 5 4

Contents at a Glance

Table of Contents

Happy to Help

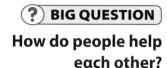
BIG QUESTION

How do people help
each other?

Read More

 = Comprehension Coach    = Interactive Whiteboard   = NGReach.com

Unit **1**

SOCIAL STUDIES
▸ Individual Actions

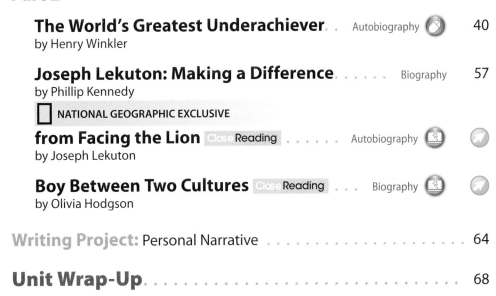

Table of Contents

Nature's Balance

? BIG QUESTION

What happens when nature loses its balance?

Read More

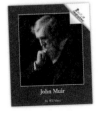

 = Comprehension Coach    = Interactive Whiteboard   = NGReach.com

Unit 2

SCIENCE
▸ Ecosystems

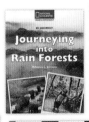

Table of Contents

Life in the Soil

? BIG QUESTION

What is so amazing about plants?

Read More

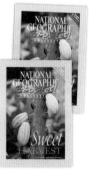

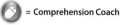 = Comprehension Coach    = Interactive Whiteboard   = NGReach.com

Unit 3

SCIENCE
▸ Plant Life Cycles
▸ Plant Diversity

Table of Contents

Let's Work Together

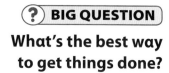
BIG QUESTION

What's the best way to get things done?

Read More

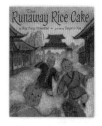

 = Comprehension Coach    = Interactive Whiteboard   = NGReach.com

x

Unit 4

SOCIAL STUDIES
▸ Community

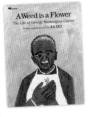

Table of Contents

Mysteries of Matter

? **BIG QUESTION**

What causes matter to change?

Read More

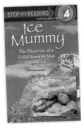

 = Comprehension Coach    = Interactive Whiteboard   ➜ = NGReach.com

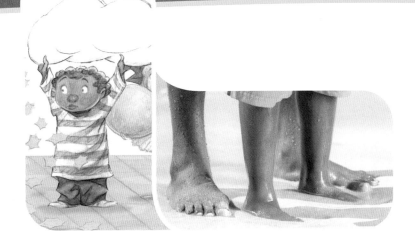

Unit 5

SCIENCE
▸ Matter

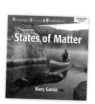

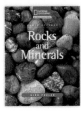

Table of Contents

From Past to Present

(?) **BIG QUESTION**

How can we preserve our traditions?

Read More

 = Comprehension Coach   = Interactive Whiteboard   = NGReach.com

Unit 6

SOCIAL STUDIES

▸ Cultures and Traditions

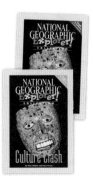

Table of Contents

Blast! Crash! Splash!

BIG QUESTION

What forces can change Earth?

Read More

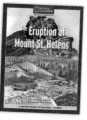
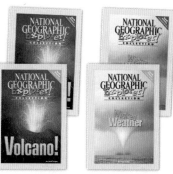

 = Comprehension Coach    = Interactive Whiteboard   = NGReach.com

SCIENCE

▸ Forces of Nature

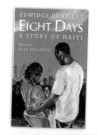

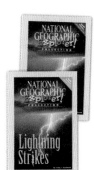

Table of Contents

Getting There

? **BIG QUESTION**

What tools can we use to achieve our goals?

Read More

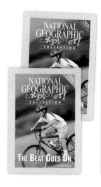

 = Comprehension Coach    = Interactive Whiteboard    = NGReach.com

Unit 8

MATH AND SOCIAL STUDIES

▸ **Planning and Perseverance**

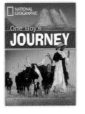

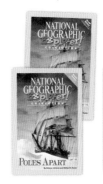

Genres at a Glance

Fiction

Poetry

Drama

Nonfiction

📱 = Interactive Whiteboard   ➤ = NGReach.com

Happy to Help

BIG Question

How do people help each other?

Unit at a Glance
▶ **Language:** Retell a Story, Make Comparisons, Social Studies Words
▶ **Literacy:** Plan and Monitor
▶ **Content:** Helping

Unit
1

Share What You Know

Do It!

I can read to my little sister.

❶ **Think** about the people you know. Who could use some help?

❷ **Draw** yourself helping the person.

❸ **Tell** the class your idea. How does it make you feel?

Build Background: Watch a video about helping.
NGReach.com

Retell a Story

Listen to Tanya's story. Then listen to her friend
Sonia retell the story. Use **Language Frames** to tell a new story.
Have a partner retell the story to you.

Chant (((MP3)))

A Friend Helps Out

Tanya:

The day my puppy ran away
I searched everywhere.
Sonia helped me find him.
He was right under the stairs.

Sonia:

First, the puppy ran away.
Next, Tanya searched around.
Then, I came by to help my friend.
Finally, the pup was found!

Key Words

action

difference

gift

problem

receive

solution

Key Words

Look at the pictures. Use **Key Words** and other words
to talk about **actions** that make a **difference**.

Friends see the **problem**.

They have a **solution**.
They fix the house.

**A Gift
of Kindness**

Thank you!

She **received** help from her friends.

Talk Together

Think of a time when you helped someone in your community. Use
Language Frames from page 4 and **Key Words** to retell the story.

Plot

When you tell a story, you tell the events in order.

- The beginning is what happens first.
- The middle is what happens next.
- The end is what happens last.

All these events are called the **plot**.

Look at these pictures. They tell a story about Tanya.

Map and Talk

You can use a story map to show the plot of a story. Here's how you make one.

The beginning goes in the first box. The middle goes in the second box. The end goes in the last box.

Story Map

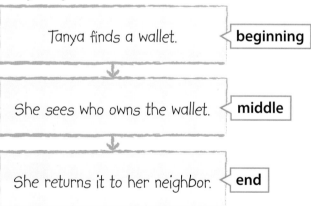

Tanya finds a wallet. — beginning

She sees who owns the wallet. — middle

She returns it to her neighbor. — end

Talk Together

Tell a partner a story about someone you know who needs help. Your partner makes a story map.

More Key Words

Use these words to talk about "Those Shoes" and "Guardian Angel."

kindness
(**kīnd**-nus) *noun*

You show **kindness** when you are nice to someone. Teddy shows **kindness** to his mom.

need
(**nēd**) *verb*

When you **need** something, you cannot live without it. People **need** to drink water.

understand
(un-dur-**stand**) *verb*

When you **understand** something, you know what it means.

value
(**val**-yū) *verb*

When you **value** something, you care about it. The girl loves and **values** her dog.

want
(**wawnt**) *verb*

To **want** something is to hope or wish for it. He **wants** to get a guitar like this one.

Talk Together

Make a Vocabulary Example Chart for the **Key Words**. Then compare your chart with a partner's.

Word	Definition	My Example
Kindness	a nice act	My friend helped me fix my bike.

Add words to My Vocabulary Notebook.
 NGReach.com

Learn to Plan and Monitor

Look at the picture. The text does not say how Tanya will help, but you can look for details in the picture. This is called **previewing**. Then you can make a guess about what will happen next. This is called **predicting**.

When you read a text, you can **preview** and **predict**. This helps you decide on a purpose for reading.

How to Preview and Predict

👁	**1.** Read the title. Look at the pictures. Think about what you will read.	I read _____ . I see _____ .
💭	**2.** Make predictions as you read.	I predict _____ .
👁	**3.** Read on to check whether your predictions are correct or incorrect.	My prediction _____ .

Talk Together

Read Tanya's story. Read the sample prediction.
Then use **Language Frames** to make and confirm
predictions. Tell a partner about them.

Story

A Puppy Problem

I **received** a puppy for my birthday. It was
the **gift** I really **wanted**. I named him Riley.

Riley was almost perfect. He was always
happy, and he barked all the time. There was just
one **problem** about that.

Our neighbor Mrs. Perry said that Riley was
too loud. I didn't **understand**. All puppies bark.
Right?

Mom said, "Mrs. Perry **needs** rest and
quiet. I really **value** her friendship. Let's teach
Riley not to bark so much." Then we took Riley to
doggy school. He was in a class with many other
puppies. ◀

In just a few weeks, Riley learned not to bark
so much. That made a big **difference**.

Riley and I went to visit Mrs. Perry. "Thank
you for your **kindness**," she told me. She gave ◀
Riley a pat on the head. Now she really likes my
puppy, too!

Sample Prediction

"I read the title. I see a
puppy in a box.

I predict that someone
gets a puppy.

My prediction is
correct. Tanya gets a
puppy."

◀ = A good place to make a prediction

9

Read a Story

Genre

A story that tells about events that could really happen is **realistic fiction**.

Characters

Characters are the people in the story. This story is told by a character named Jeremy. He uses words like *I*, *me*, and *my* to tell his story.

Jeremy

Grandma

Antonio

Those Shoes

by **Maribeth Boelts**

illustrated by **Noah Z. Jones**

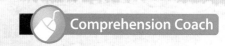
Comprehension Coach

▶ **Set a Purpose**
Jeremy **wants** new shoes, but there's
a **problem** . Find out what it is.

I have dreams about those shoes. Black **high-tops**.
Two white stripes.

"Grandma, I **want** them."

"There's no room for 'want' around here,"
Grandma says. "What you **need** are new boots
for winter."

In Other Words
high-tops sports shoes

Brandon T. comes to school in those shoes. He says he's the fastest runner now, not me. I was always the fastest runner before **those shoes came along**.

Next, Allen Jacoby and Terrence **each get a pair**.

In Other Words

those shoes came along Brandon T. got those shoes

each get a pair get the same shoes

Then one day, in the middle of kickball, one of my shoes **comes apart**.

"Looks like you could use a new pair, Jeremy," Mr. Alfrey, the **guidance counselor**, says. He gives me a pair of shoes with a cartoon animal on it.

In Other Words
comes apart tears
guidance counselor adult who helps students solve **problems**

When I come back to the classroom, the only kid not laughing is Antonio Parker.

At home, Grandma says, "How kind of Mr. Alfrey." I nod and **turn my back**. I'm not going to cry about any dumb shoes.

In Other Words
turn my back turn away

▶ **Before You Move On**

1. **Clarify** Why can't Jeremy get the new shoes he **wants**?
2. **Character's Motive** Why does Jeremy **want** the black high-tops?

▶ **Predict**
What will Jeremy do to get the
new black shoes?

On Saturday Grandma says, "Let's **check out** those shoes you're wanting so much. I got a little bit of money **set aside**. It might be enough—**you never know**."

In Other Words
check out look at
set aside saved
you never know you might be surprised

At the shoe store, Grandma turns those shoes over. She **checks the price**. When she sees it, she sits down **heavy**.

"Maybe they wrote it down wrong," I say.

Grandma shakes her head.

In Other Words

checks the price looks to see how much the shoes cost

heavy in a sad way

Then I remember the **thrift shops**. We ride the bus to the first one. There's every kind of shoe **except the ones** I want.

We ride the bus to the second thrift shop. Not a pair of those shoes **in sight**.

In Other Words
thrift shops stores that sell used clothes
except the ones but not the shoes
in sight anywhere

High-tops.
Perfect shape. $2.50.
THOSE SHOES.

Around the corner is the third thrift shop. I see something in the window.

I shove my foot into the first shoe. Grandma feels for my toes at the end of the shoe.

"Oh, Jeremy," she says. "I can't **spend good money** on shoes that **don't fit**."

"They're okay," I say, curling my toes. Then I buy them with my own money.

In Other Words

spend good money use money I worked so hard to save

don't fit are too small

A few days later, Grandma puts a new pair of snow boots in my closet. She doesn't say a word about my **too-big feet shuffling around in my too-small shoes**.

"Sometimes shoes **stretch**," I say.

In Other Words

too-big feet shuffling around in my too-small shoes shoes that are too small

stretch get bigger

▶ **Before You Move On**

1. **Confirm Prediction** What **actions** did Jeremy take to get the black shoes? Was your prediction correct?
2. **Character** How do Jeremy's **actions** show what kind of person he is?

▶ **Predict**
What will Jeremy do with the
too-small shoes?

I check every day, but those shoes don't stretch. I have to wear **my Mr. Alfreys** instead.

One day during Math, I **glance** at Antonio's shoes. One of them is **taped up**, and his feet look smaller than mine.

In Other Words
my Mr. Alfreys the shoes Mr. Alfrey gave me
glance look quickly
taped up held together with tape

I'm not going to do it!

That night, I am awake for a long time thinking about Antonio.

When morning comes, I run across the street to Antonio's apartment. I put the shoes in front of his door. I push the doorbell—and run.

At school, I feel happy when I look at
Antonio's face and mad when I look at my
Mr. Alfrey shoes.

Later, snow is everywhere.
Then I remember what I have in my
backpack. New black boots.

Standing in line to go to recess, Antonio leans forward.

"Thanks," he says.

I smile and give him a **nudge**. "Let's race!" ❖

▶ **Before You Move On**

1. **Confirm Prediction** What did you think Jeremy would do with the small shoes? Was your prediction correct?

2. **Character** How does Jeremy feel about helping Antonio? How do you know?

Think and Respond

Key Words

action	receive
difference	solution
gift	understand
kindness	value
need	want
problem	

Talk About It

1. Name two **realistic** events that happen in the story.

    One realistic event in the story is _____ .

    _____ was also like real life.

2. How would Antonio retell this story? Work with a partner to **retell the story** as if you are Antonio.

    First, _____ . Next, _____ . Then, _____ . Finally, _____ .

3. Compare how Jeremy feels about the black high-tops and the shoes from Mr. Alfrey. Which does he **want?** Which does he **need?** Why?

    Jeremy wants _____ , because _____ .

    Jeremy needs _____ , because _____ .

Learn test-taking strategies.
🌐 NGReach.com

Write About It

Imagine you are Antonio. Write a sentence to tell how you felt when you **received** Jeremy's **gift.** Use **Key Words**.

> When Jeremy gave me the shoes,
> I felt _____ because _____ .

Plot

The events of a story are called the **plot**. Create a story map to show the main events in "Those Shoes."

Story Map

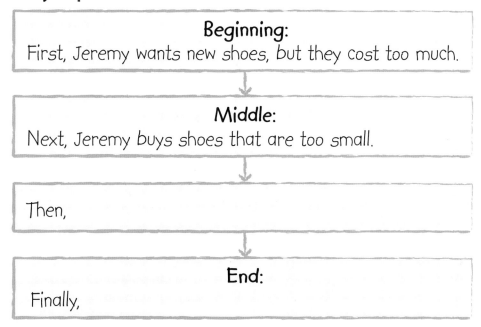

Beginning:
First, Jeremy wants new shoes, but they cost too much.

↓

Middle:
Next, Jeremy buys shoes that are too small.

↓

Then,

↓

End:
Finally,

Now use your story map to sequence and summarize the plot's main events for a partner. Use time-order words and **Key Words**. Record your summary.

First, _____ .
Next, _____ .
Then, _____ .
Finally, _____ .

Fluency Comprehension Coach

Use the Comprehension Coach to practice reading with expression. Rate your reading.

Talk Together

How can one act of **kindness** make a **difference**? Draw a picture. Use **Key Words** to tell your class about the picture.

Alphabetical Order

The words in a dictionary follow the same order as the letters of the alphabet. To look up words, you need to know **alphabetical order**.

> These words are in order by the first letter of each word.

action
change
difference

> If the words begin with the same first letter, look at the second letter.

need
nice
now

> If the words begin with the same first and second letters, look at the third letter.

sunlight
supply
surface

sunlight
(**sun-līt**) *noun*
Sunlight is the light that comes from the sun.

supply
(**su-plī**) *verb*
When you **supply** something, you give it what it needs or wants.

surface
(**sur-fis**) *noun*
The **surface** is the outside part of something.

the surface of the Moon

Try It Together

Answer the questions.

1. **Which word comes before want in a dictionary?**

   A **w**ait

   B **w**hat

   C **w**ave

   D **w**ater

2. **Which word comes after receive in a dictionary?**

   A **r**ace

   B **r**ead

   C **r**ealistic

   D **r**estaurant

Guardian Angel

by **Francisco X. Alarcón**

illustrated by **Josée Masse**

when I felt so sad
and all alone

wanting to cry
in the classroom

In Other Words
Guardian Angel A Kind, Helpful Person

▶ **Before You Move On**

1. **Ask Questions** What questions do you have about the speaker of the poem?
2. **Predict** What do you think will happen to help the speaker feel better?

29

the girl seated
   next to me

suddenly
   held my hand

and with the darkest
and most tender eyes

I have ever seen—
told me without a word:

"don't worry
you're not alone"

In Other Words

most tender kindest

without a word without talking

don't worry do not feel sad

▶ **Before You Move On**

1. **Confirm Prediction** What happened to change the speaker's feelings?

2. **Character** What is the girl like? How do her **actions** help the speaker?

Respond and Extend

Compare Genres

A story like "Those Shoes" and a lyrical poem like "Guardian Angel" are different forms of writing, or genres. How are the two genres different? How are they the same? Work with a partner to complete the checklist chart.

Checklist Chart

Think about each characteristic.

	Story	Poem
It is arranged in lines.		✔
It has paragraphs.	✔	
It is usually long.		
It is usually short.		
It expresses the writer's feelings.		
The words sound like music.		

Write check marks to show whether the characteristics describe a story, a poem, or both.

Talk Together

How do people help each other? Think about the characters in the story and the poem. How do their **actions** help others? Use **Key Words** to talk about your ideas.

Complete Sentences

A sentence expresses a complete thought. A **complete sentence** has two parts.

Grammar Rules Complete Sentences

• The subject tells whom or what the sentence is about.	Grandma The boys
• The predicate tells what the subject is, has, or does.	shakes her head want those shoes
• To make a complete sentence, use both a subject and a predicate.	Grandma shakes her head. The boys want those shoes.

Read Sentences

Read this passage from "Those Shoes." Which group of words is a complete sentence?

> I have dreams about those shoes. Black high-tops.
> Two white stripes.

Write Sentences

Choose a picture from pages 12–15. Write a sentence to tell what is happening. Be sure to include a subject and a predicate. Read your sentence to a partner.

Make Comparisons

Listen to Kemal's song. Then use **Language Frames** to tell how you changed something that helped other people.

I Am Feeling Good

Song

I am feeling good.
I have helped to clean my street.
First I picked up all the trash,
Then I gave it a good sweep.
Oh, before, the street was messy,
But now, it is clean and neat.
And I'm feeling good!

Tune: "Do Your Ears Hang Low?"

34

Social Studies Vocabulary

Key Words

improve

individual

neighborhood

offer

volunteer

Key Words

Look at the graphic organizer to learn **Key Words**.

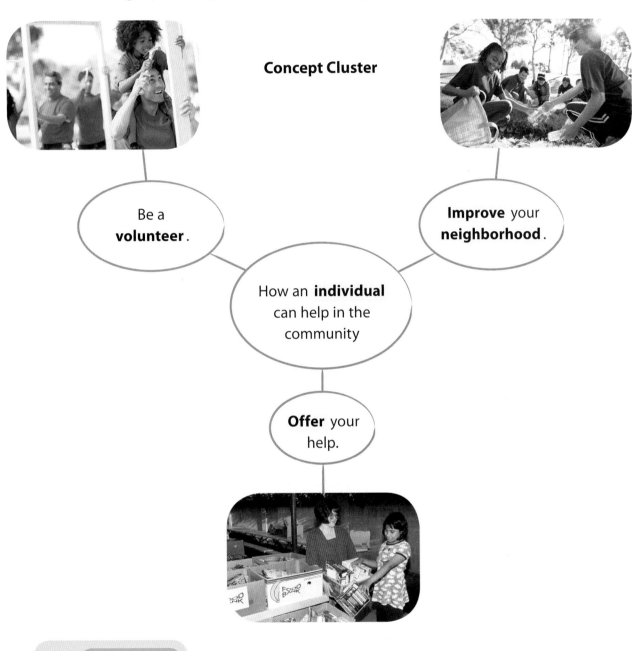

Concept Cluster

Be a **volunteer**.

Improve your **neighborhood**.

How an **individual** can help in the community

Offer your help.

Talk Together

How have you helped in your community? How did things change? Try to use **Language Frames** from page 34 and **Key Words** to make comparisons for a partner.

35

Make Comparisons

You **make comparisons** to show how two things are alike and different, or to show how something has changed. When you talk about something that has changed over time, use:

- *before* and *then* to tell about the past

- *now* and *after* to tell about the present

Compare the pictures. How has the area near the tree changed?

Map and Talk

You can make a comparison chart to show how something has changed.

Comparison Chart

Before	Now
There were weeds and trash around the tree.	There are flowers around the tree.

Tell a partner about something that has **improved**. Tell what it was like before and what it is like now. Your partner makes a comparison chart.

More Key Words

Use these words to talk about "The World's Greatest Underachiever" and "Joseph Lekuton: Making a Difference."

benefit
(**be**-nu-fit) *noun*

A **benefit** is something that is helpful. One **benefit** of rain is that it helps flowers grow tall.

duty
(**dü**-tē) *noun*

When you do your **duty**, you do what you are supposed to do.

identify
(ī-**den**-tu-fī) *verb*

When you **identify** something, you tell what it is. She wants to **identify** a type of bird.

impact
(**im**-pakt) *noun*

What you do has an **impact** on things. The children have a positive **impact** on the park.

learn
(**lurn**) *verb*

To **learn** means to find out how to do something. You can **learn** to play music.

Talk Together

Make a Study Card for each **Key Word**. Then compare your cards with a partner's.

> learn
>
> **What it means:** to find out
>
> **Example:** I learn about horses from my uncle.
>
> **Not an example:** I don't know anything about dogs.

Add words to My Vocabulary Notebook.
NGReach.com

Learn to Plan and Monitor

Look at the round picture of Kemal and his friend. Ask yourself a question about what you see. To find the answer, look more closely at the round picture or look at the big picture.

When you read, check, or **monitor**, yourself to make sure you understand everything. Ask questions to **clarify** the parts you do not understand.

How to Monitor and Clarify

👁	**1.** Read the text carefully.
❓	**2.** Ask yourself: What does this mean?
👁	**3.** Reread the text or read on. Look for facts and details to answer your questions.

I read _____ .

I ask myself:
_____ ?

I find out _____ .

Talk Together

Read Kemal's letter with a partner. Read the sample.
Then use **Language Frames** to monitor and clarify. Tell your
partner how you checked your understanding of the text.

Letter

March 14, 2010

Dear Opal,

This week I **learned** something important. I learned
that one **individual** can make a big difference. Let me tell
you how.

It had been raining hard all week. Then last night, it became
a flood. Mr. Ruiz **identified** the problem right away. The flood
wall in our **neighborhood** was about to burst! Everyone started
to fill and stack sandbags. But the water was rising fast.
More **volunteers** were needed, so I **offered** to help.

We stacked hundreds of sandbags. But the situation didn't
improve. The water kept going higher and higher. Nobody gave
up, though. We all did our **duty** and kept working hard.

Finally, the rain stopped. We all cheered. Our neighborhood
was saved!

Boy, was I tired, but I felt good, too. My help made an
impact, and we all understood the **benefit** of working together.

Your friend,

Kemal

Sample

"I read that Kemal learned something.

I ask myself: What did he learn?

I find out that he learned something because of a flood."

◀ = A good place to monitor and clarify your reading

Read an Autobiography

Genre

An **autobiography** is the true story of a person's life written by that person.

First-Person Narrator

The person who tells the story is the narrator. A first-person narrator uses **first-person words** to tell what happens to him or her.

I studied **my** spelling words in my apartment in New York City. Somehow, during the time it took **me** to walk the block from my apartment to my school, the words vanished.

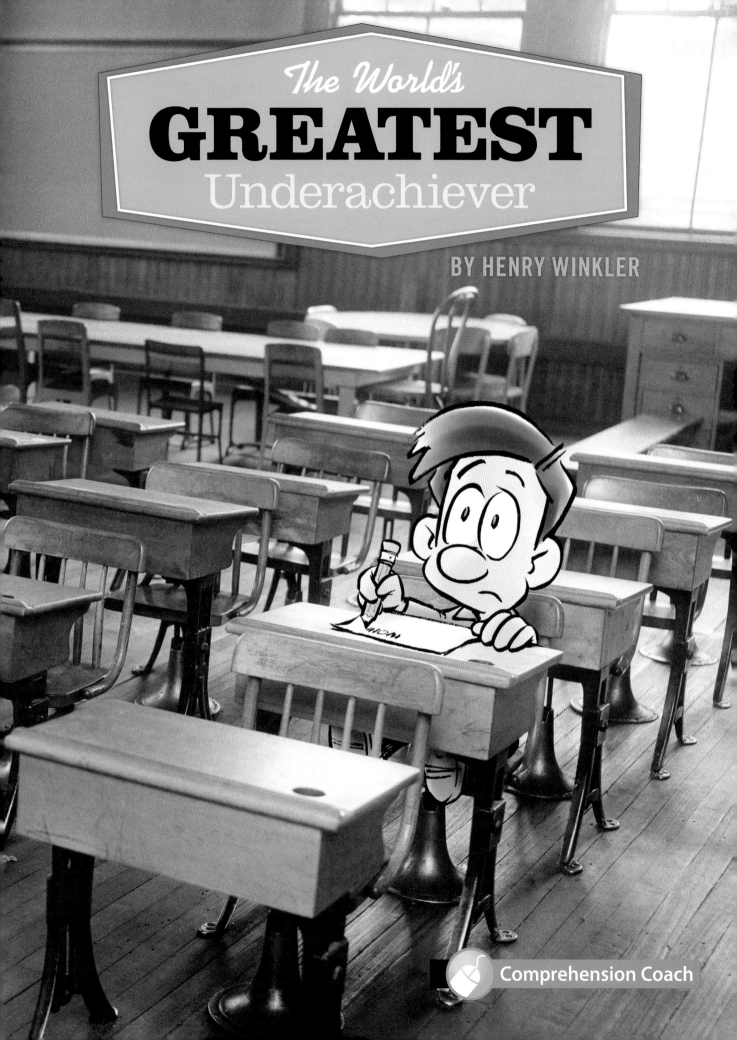

HENRY WINKLER is best known for **playing** "The Fonz" on the TV show *Happy Days*. Today, he **is the co-author of a series** of children's books. Winkler also visits schools to talk to students and share his story.

▲ Winkler is an actor, director, producer, and co-author of children's books.

◄ Winkler when he was nine years old

In Other Words

playing being a character called

is the co-author of a series works with another person to write a group

▶ **Set a Purpose**
Henry has trouble in school.
Find out what the problem is.

All through grade school, I **was tutored**. If I got a D, I was **in heaven**. If I got a C-minus, I had **achieved greatness**. A's and B's were a **kingdom I could never enter**.

▲ Winkler with his classmates at school

In Other Words

was tutored got extra help with schoolwork

in heaven very happy

achieved greatness done a great job

kingdom I could never enter goal I could never reach

I studied my spelling words in my apartment in New York City. Somehow, during the time it took me to walk the block from my apartment to my school, the words **vanished**.

In Other Words
vanished disappeared

My teacher, Miss Adolf, had given me a list of ten spelling words.

My mother and I **went over** the list until I *knew* those words. I felt **terrific**. I thought, *Wow! This time, I'm going to* **pass**.

In Other Words

went over studied
terrific great
pass get a good grade

▶ **Before You Move On**

1. **Clarify** What does Henry mean when he says "the words vanished"? How is this a problem at school?
2. **Point of View** Who is telling the story? How do you know?

▶ **Predict**
Henry studied his spelling words.
Will his spelling improve on the test?

The next day, I went into the classroom and took out a sheet of paper. Then Miss Adolf gave us the words. The first word was *carpet*. I wrote that one down: *c-a-r-p-e-t*. I was feeling **pretty confident**.

PUBLIC SCHOOL 87 MAN.

▲ **A school building in Manhattan**

In Other Words
pretty confident sure that I would do well

Then came *neighbor*—I wrote down the letter *n*. Then *rhythm*—I knew there was an *r*. *Suburban*—I wrote *s-u-b*.

My heart sank. I had gone from **100 percent to maybe a D-minus**. Where did the words go?

1. carpet
2. n
3. r
4. sub
5.
6.
7.
8
9.

In Other Words

My heart sank. I became very unhappy.

100 percent to maybe a D-minus good to bad

Some people talk about **information sliding off the blackboard of your brain.** That was my life. I was called "stupid," "lazy." **My self-image was down around my ankles.**

In Other Words

information sliding off the blackboard of your brain forgetting things you know

My self-image was down around my ankles.
I did not feel good about myself.

The one thing **I had going for me** was my **sense of humor**. It sure didn't get me any A's, though. It got me a trip to the principal's office.

No matter what I did, it didn't seem to **make a difference**.

In Other Words

I had going for me that helped

sense of humor way of making people laugh

make a difference help

▶ **Before You Move On**

1. **Confirm Prediction** Did Henry's spelling **improve** on the test? Explain.
2. **Goal/Outcome** What does Henry want?

▸ **Predict**

What will help Henry **learn** to feel good about himself?

wish I'd known then what I know now: I have **dyslexia**. My brain learns differently. When my stepson, Jed, was in the third grade, we had him tested for learning differences. As they explained dyslexia to him, I thought, *That's me!*

▼ **A person with dyslexia might see** *the* **as** *teh.* **He or she might see** *was* **as** *saw,* **and** *bird* **as** *brid.*

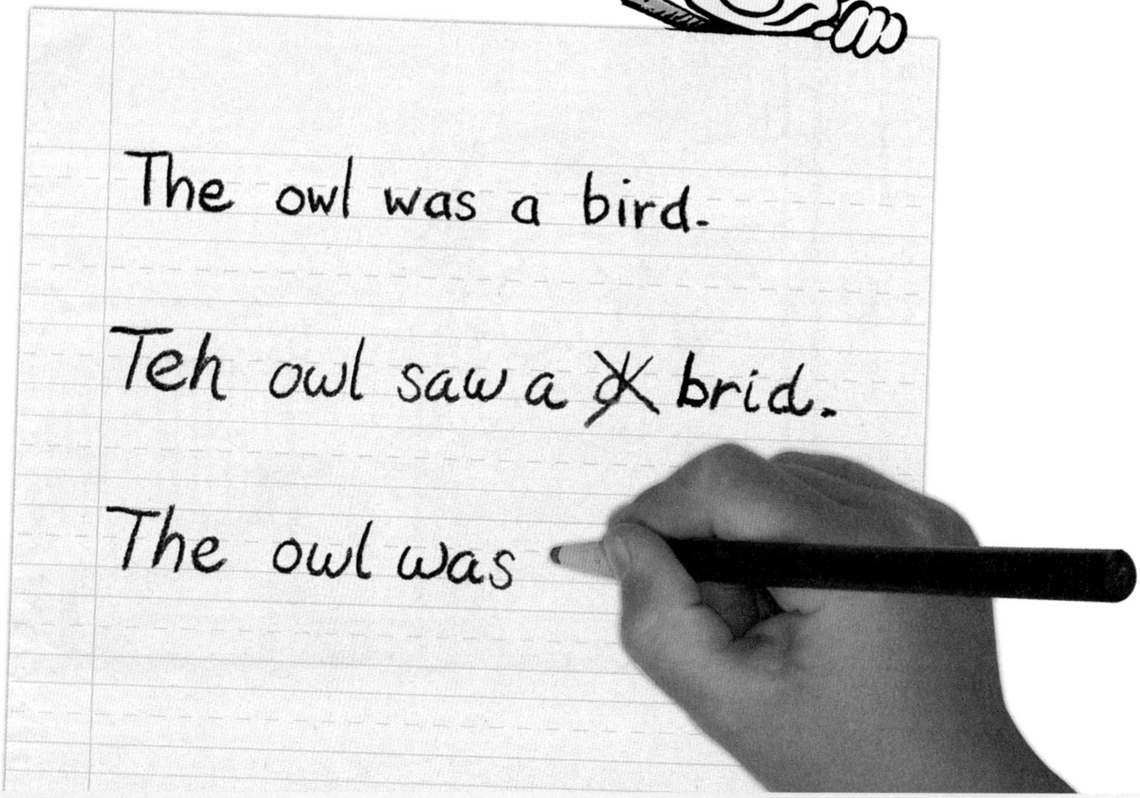

The owl was a bird.

Teh owl saw a ⚡ brid.

The owl was

In Other Words

dyslexia a **learning** problem that makes it hard to read, spell, write, and do math

50

A learning disability can really **affect** the way you feel about yourself. Now I know that even if a person learns differently, he or she can still **be filled with greatness**.

▼ Winkler became famous when he grew up. Here he is as "The Fonz."

In Other Words
affect change
be filled with greatness do wonderful things

Today when I visit schools, I tell children that everyone has something special **inside**. It's our job to **figure out what that is**. Dig deep, get it out, and give it to the world as a gift. ❖

▲ Winkler helps young people. He shares his story with them.

In Other Words

inside that people cannot always see at first

figure out what that is find what makes us special and great

▶ **Before You Move On**

1. **Confirm Prediction** How does Henry **learn** to feel good about himself? Was your prediction correct?

2. **Goal/Outcome** What goal does Henry have for the young people he meets today?

Henry Winkler

Even though school was hard for him, Henry Winkler graduated from high school. He then went on to college and got a master's degree in drama from Yale University.

Mr. Winkler's difficulties in school inspired him to write. His popular children's books are about a character named Hank Zipzer. Like Mr. Winkler, Hank has a learning disability. In his stories, Mr. Winkler uses the real names of two teachers. One of them is Miss Adolf!

Winkler with some of his Hank Zipzer books. ▶

Writer's Craft ✏

Henry Winkler uses words that sound like him. He writes using his own voice. Write a sentence to describe how you feel about going to school. Use words that sound like you. Read the sentence aloud. Does it sound like something you would say?

Key Words

benefit	individual
duty	learn
identify	neighborhood
impact	offer
improve	volunteer

Talk About It

1. How do you know that "The World's Greatest Underachiever" is an **autobiography**?

   I know that it is an autobiography because _____ .

2. **Compare** how the author felt about himself when he was young to how he feels now.

   Before, Henry felt _____ .

   Now, he feels _____ because _____ .

3. Why do you think Henry calls himself an underachiever in school?

   Henry calls himself an underachiever because _____ .

Learn test-taking strategies.
NGReach.com

Write About It

Henry helps children. Write a letter thanking him. Tell him what you **learned** from his story. Then share how you can have a positive **impact** on people's lives. Use **Key Words**.

_____ , 20_____

Dear Mr. Winkler,

Thank you _____ . I learned _____ .

Your friend,

_____

Make Comparisons

Create a comparison chart to show how Henry changed in "The World's Greatest Underachiever."

Comparison Chart

Before	Now
1. Henry had trouble spelling.	1. He writes books.
2. He didn't like school.	2.

Use your comparison chart to compare things about Henry's story for a partner. Use the sentence frames and **Key Words**. Record your discussion.

> Before, Henry _____.
> Now, he _____.

Fluency  Comprehension Coach

Use the Comprehension Coach to practice reading with intonation. Rate your reading.

Talk Together

How do adults help students in school? With a partner, brainstorm a list of ways. Use **Key Words**. Share your list with the class.

Determine Meanings

When you read an unknown word, you can find its meaning in a dictionary or glossary. In a dictionary, words are listed in alphabetical order.

Look at the following example of a dictionary entry.

The definition tells you the meaning of the word.

This part tells you how to pronounce the word.

ben•e•fit (be-nu-fit) *noun* A benefit is something that is helpful or useful.

This tells you what kind of word it is.

Try It Together

Use the dictionary entries to answer the questions.

im•prove (im-prüv) *verb* To improve something is to make it better.
in•di•vid•u•al (in-du-vi-ju-wul) *noun* An individual is one person.

1. **What kind of word is improve?**
   - **A** verb
   - **B** noun
   - **C** adverb
   - **D** adjective

2. **What does individual mean?**
   - **A** noun
   - **B** improve
   - **C** something
   - **D** one person

NATIONAL
GEOGRAPHIC
EXCLUSIVE

Connect Across Texts Read about a man who tries to help others in Kenya, Africa.

Genre A **biography** tells the story of someone's life. The author uses words like *he* and *him* to give information about the person.

Joseph Lekuton:
Making a Difference
BY PHILLIP KENNEDY

Joseph Lekuton was born in Kenya, a country in Africa. Joseph and his family **are Maasai**. Many of the Maasai take care of **cattle**.

△ Joseph Lekuton

Kenya — AFRICA

In Other Words

are Maasai belong to a group of people in Kenya who live and work together

cattle cows

▶ **Before You Move On**

1. **Identify Details** What group does Joseph's family belong to? What work do most of the people do?

2. **Ask Questions** What questions do you have about Joseph?

57

An Important Decision

Every Maasai family has to send one child to school. So Joseph's father sent one of Joseph's brothers. But his brother didn't like school. He hid in a **hyena hole** and didn't go to class!

▲ **Lekuton's village**

hyena

In Other Words

Decision Choice

◄ **hyena hole** hole where a wild animal called a hyena lives

Joseph wanted to go to school. He **volunteered** to go instead of his brother. When Joseph was older, he went to schools in far-away parts of the country. One school was **600 miles** away.

▲ **Original photo of Lekuton with his school soccer team**

In Other Words

600 miles very far; about 965 kilometers

▶ **Before You Move On**

1. **Clarify** Find sentences that tell you that Joseph wanted to go to school and his brother did not.

2. **Point of View** Does the author tell the story or does Joseph? How do you know?

A Challenge

Keeping Joseph in school was **difficult**. His family sold a lot of their cattle to pay **his school fees**. Joseph was also far from home. He couldn't always help his family care for their cattle.

▲ **A Maasai boy takes care of cattle.**

In Other Words

Challenge Hard Job

difficult not easy

his school fees the money it cost to go to school

A Way to Help Others

When Joseph grew up, he became a teacher. He helped build schools in Maasai communities. He also **helped create scholarships**. Joseph's work has made a difference. Now it is a little easier for Maasai children to go to school.

"The more children we can **educate**, the fewer problems we'll have in Africa," Joseph says. ❖

▲ **a school in Kenya**

In Other Words

helped create scholarships
  made it possible for more
  children to go to school

educate teach

▶ **Before You Move On**

1. **Make Comparisons** What was Joseph's life like before he went away to school? How did it change after he went to school?

2. **Details** How has Joseph helped to **improve** his community?

61

Key Words

benefit	individual
duty	learn
identify	neighborhood
impact	offer
improve	volunteer

Compare Points of View

An autobiography and a biography have different points of view. A point of view is the way a story is told. Who tells the story in an autobiography? Who is the narrator in a biography?

Look at the beginnings of the selections.

Now write the name of each author next to the correct description below. Then explain to a partner the difference in point of view between a biography and an autobiography.

Tells the story of his or her own life: _____

Tells the story of another person's life: _____

Talk Together

How do people help each other? Think about the people in the autobiography and the biography. How do they help others? Use **Key Words** to talk about your ideas.

More Subjects and Predicates

The **verb**, which is the most important word in the predicate, must agree with the subject of the sentence.

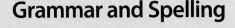

Grammar Rules Subject-Verb Agreement

Verbs in the Present	
• Use **-s** at the end of an action verb if the subject is **he**, **she**, or **it**.	Henry **reads** a spelling word. He **reads** a spelling word.
• Do not use **-s** for **I**, **you**, **we**, and **they**.	The words **slide** off his brain. They **slide** off his brain.
• Use **am** for **I**.	I **am** a fan of Hank Zipzer.
• Use **is** for **he**, **she**, and **it**.	He **is** a funny character.
• Use **are** for **you**, **we**, and **they**.	The books **are** in the library. They **are** in the library.

Read Sentences

Read these sentences from "The World's Greatest Underachiever." Identify the subjects and the verbs.

> Today, he is the co-author of a series of children's books. Winkler also visits schools.

Write Sentences

Write two sentences about Henry Winkler. Make sure the subjects and verbs agree. Read your sentences to a partner.

63

Write About Yourself

Write a Personal Narrative

Tell about a time when someone in your school helped you, or when you helped someone. You can add your story to a class book.

Study a Model

A personal narrative is a true story. The author uses words like *I, me,* and *my.*

Open House

by Emilio Campos

Last August, I was a Student Guide for an Open House at my school. My job was to help new students and their parents get used to our school. I handed out school maps and answered questions.

When I saw a mom and her son looking nervous and confused, I went up to help them. The mom started talking in Spanish. Emilio to the rescue! I'm Mexican, so I said in Spanish that I'd show them around.

They both looked so happy! I knew how it felt to be in an unfamiliar place. So, it felt great to help them feel better about being there.

The **beginning** tells what the narrative is about.

The **middle** tells more about the event. The author uses an informal style and words that sound like him.

The **end** tells what happened last and why the experience was important.

Prewrite

1. **Choose a Topic** What will you write about? Talk with a partner. Choose an event from your life that was important to you.

Language Frames

Tell Your Ideas	Respond to Ideas
_____ helped me once when I had a problem.	Was _____ really important to you? Tell me why.
I remember when my friend needed help and I _____ .	I'd like to know more about what happened when _____ .
The nicest thing anyone ever did for me was _____ .	_____ doesn't sound very special. Do you have another idea?

> Use sentences like these to help you choose your topic.

2. **Gather Information** Think about the event. What happened at the beginning, in the middle, and at the end?

3. **Get Organized** Use a story map to help you organize your thoughts.

Story Map

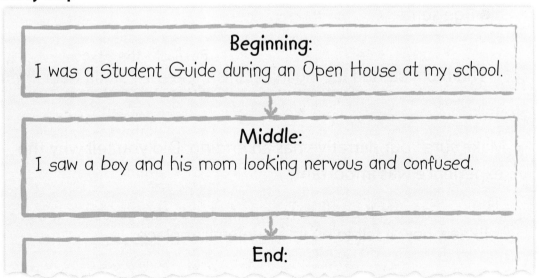

Beginning:
I was a Student Guide during an Open House at my school.

Middle:
I saw a boy and his mom looking nervous and confused.

End:

Draft

Use your story map to write your draft. Use informal words that sound like you. Tell why the experience was important to you.

Revise

1. **Read, Retell, Respond** Read your draft aloud to a partner. Your partner listens and then retells the story. Next, talk about ways to improve your writing.

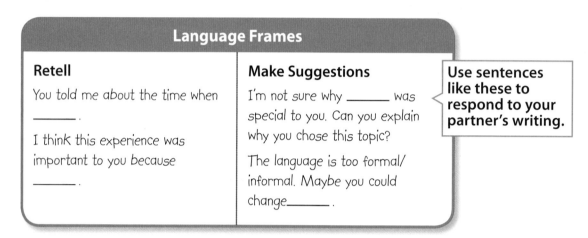

Language Frames		
Retell	**Make Suggestions**	Use sentences like these to respond to your partner's writing.
You told me about the time when _____ . I think this experience was important to you because _____ .	I'm not sure why _____ was special to you. Can you explain why you chose this topic? The language is too formal/informal. Maybe you could change_____ .	

2. **Make Changes** Think about your draft and your partner's suggestions. Then use the Revising Marks on page 573 to mark your changes.

- Do your words and sentences sound like you? If not, change some.

> Emilio to the rescue!
> The mom started talking in Spanish. ~~I knew I could help them~~.
> ^

- Make sure your narrative has an ending. Did you tell why the experience was important?

> So, it felt great to help them feel better about being there.
> I knew how it felt to be in an unfamiliar place.
> ^

Edit and Proofread

Work with a partner to edit and proofread your personal narrative. Be sure the subject and verb agree in each sentence. Use the marks on page 574 to show your changes.

Use the marks on page 574

> **Spelling Tip**
>
> ✓ When you use the present tense, put **-s** at the end of an action verb if the subject is **he**, **she**, or **it**.

Publish

1. **On Your Own** Make a final copy of your personal narrative. Choose a way to share it with your classmates. You might read one another's narratives or sit in a circle and take turns telling your experiences.

Presentation Tips	
If you are the speaker…	**If you are the listener…**
Make eye contact with your listeners. Look up even if you are reading your story.	Nod or smile to show the reader that you are listening attentively.
Keep your expression friendly as you tell about your experience.	Think about why the event was important to the speaker.

2. **In a Group** Collect all the personal narratives. Bind them into a book called "Helping Others." Tell your family and friends about the book. They might want a copy!

BIG Question

How do people help each other?

In this unit, you found lots of answers to the **Big Question**.
Now, use your concept map to discuss the **Big Question** with the class.

Concept Map

give others
something
they need

How people
help
each other

Write a Plan

Review the ideas on your concept map. Choose your best
idea. Then write a plan to tell how you can help others.

68

Share Your Ideas

Choose one of these ways to share your ideas about the **Big Question**.

Do It!

Draw a Self-Portrait

How do you feel when you do something nice for someone? Draw a picture of yourself to show this feeling. Post your picture in a class Portrait Gallery.

Talk About It!

Form a Panel

With three other classmates, sit in a row of chairs in front of the class. Discuss ways you can help your teachers or other students in school. Afterward, answer questions from the audience.

Write It!

Write a Mini-Biography

Work with a partner. Write about someone you know who has helped others. Tell who the person is and how the person's actions made a difference in other people's lives.

Do It!

Role-Play Workers

Think of workers in your community who help others. Choose a job to role-play. Have your classmates guess your job and tell how you help others.

Nature's Balance

BIG Question

What happens when nature loses its balance?

Unit at a Glance
▶ **Language**: Ask and Answer Questions, Give and Carry Out Commands, Science Words
▶ **Literacy**: Ask Questions
▶ **Content**: Ecosystems

Unit 2

Share What You Know

① **Draw** a place where plants and animals live, such as a fish tank or a field.

Do It!

Fish might get sick in dirty water.

② **Imagine** that something changes in this place. Does the fish tank get dirty? Does rain flood the field?

③ **Display** your drawing. Tell what could happen to the plants or animals because of the change.

Build Background: Watch a video about ecosystems.
NGReach.com

Ask and Answer Questions

Language Frames

- Who is _____ ?
- What is _____ ?
- Where is _____ ?
- The _____ is _____ .

Listen to the dialogue between Linda and Mike.

Then use **Language Frames** with a partner. Ask and answer questions about something in nature.

Dialogue (((MP3)))

1.

Nice garden. Who is your gardener?

My mom. Gardening is her hobby. See that hole near the tulips? It's a gopher hole. Gophers live there.

2.

What is a gopher?

It's an animal that eats plants. We have too many gophers. Mom set out a trap, but the gophers won't go near it.

3.

The trap is in the middle of the tulip bed.

Where is the trap?

4.

I like tulips.

So do the gophers!

Key Words

Key Words

amount

behavior

decrease

increase

supply

Look at this example. Use **Key Words** and other words to talk about bird **behavior**.

What happens when the **supply** of birdseed **increases**?

What happens when the **amount** of birdseed **decreases**?

Talk Together

With a partner, talk about balance and the supply of bird food. Use **Language Frames** from page 72 and **Key Words** to ask and answer questions.

73

Compare and Contrast

Sometimes you tell how things are alike and how they are different. When you do this, you **compare and contrast**.

Look at the pictures. How are the animals alike and different?

squirrel

acorn

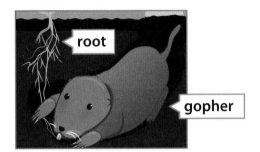

root

gopher

Map and Talk

You can make a Venn diagram to compare and contrast.

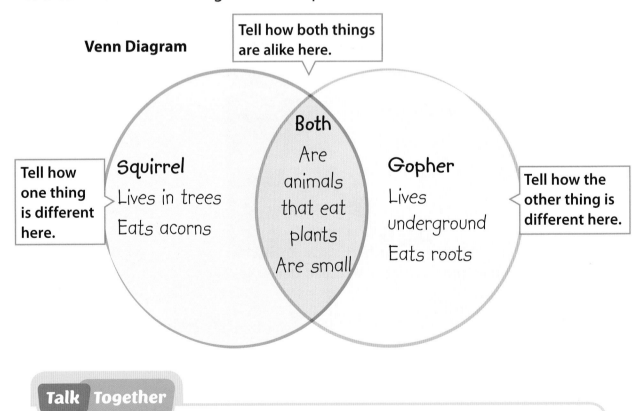

Venn Diagram

Tell how both things are alike here.

Tell how one thing is different here.

Tell how the other thing is different here.

Both
Are animals that eat plants
Are small

Squirrel
Lives in trees
Eats acorns

Gopher
Lives underground
Eats roots

Talk Together

Compare and contrast what you see in the pictures on page 73. Tell a partner. Your partner makes a Venn diagram.

More Key Words

Use these words to talk about "When the Pigs Took Over" and "Animals, More or Less."

balance
(**ba**-luns) *noun*

The two sides of the scale are in **balance**.

control
(kun-**trōl**) *verb*

To **control** means to make a person or thing do what you want. What do the boys **control**?

interact
(in-tur-**akt**) *verb*

To **interact** means to act together. The students **interact** with each other to do a science project.

react
(rē-**akt**) *verb*

When things happen, you usually **react** to them. The child **reacts** to the snowball.

scarce
(**skairs**) *adjective*

When something is **scarce**, it is hard to find or get.

Talk Together

With a partner, take turns telling a story. Use the **Key Words**.

> Jim did not control his bike on the hill.

> He lost his balance!

Add words to My Vocabulary Notebook.
 NGReach.com

75

Learn to Ask Questions

Look at the picture. Do you understand what Linda and her cat are doing? **Ask** yourself **questions** about what you see. Look more closely at the picture to find the answers.

As you read, **ask questions**. The answers to some questions can be found in the text. Read to find the answers. This will help you understand the text better.

How to Ask Questions

1. Ask a question.

2. Look for the answer. You might find the answer in the text. Or you might have to think and search.

3. Think about the answer. Read on and ask more questions.

I wonder: _____?

I read _____.
So _____.

Now I wonder: _____?

Language Frames

?   I wonder:
     _____ ?

👁   I read _____ .
     So _____ .

💭   Now I wonder:
     _____ ?

Talk Together

Read Linda's fable with a partner. Read the sample questions. Then use **Language Frames** to ask and answer questions to check your understanding.

Fable

The Gopher and the Squirrel

One day Squirrel met Gopher in a garden. She wasn't sure how to **interact** with a gopher. So she spoke politely. "Good day," she said. "May I collect the acorns in this garden?"

"No! Go away!" said Gopher.

This was a rude way to **react** to a polite request. But Squirrel tried again. "You see, the trees didn't get enough rain this year. Nature is out of **balance**. Acorns are **scarce**."

"I can't **control** the weather," said Gopher. "But I control this garden, and all the acorns are mine."

"But you have roots to eat," Squirrel protested.

"So what? The acorns are mine, too!" Gopher replied.

Then Squirrel asked, "Is that little wire shed near the fence yours, too?"

"What little wire shed?" asked Gopher. He came out of his hole to take a look. The shed was just the right size for a gopher. A few carrots were on the floor. Gopher ran inside to get the carrots. Slam! Down fell the cage door. He was trapped.

Squirrel laughed. "Looks like I'm in control now!"

Moral: If you are selfish, you might lose everything.

◄ = A good place to ask a question

Sample Questions

"I wonder: Why is Gopher so rude?

I read that Gopher doesn't want to share the acorns. So I know that he is greedy.

Now I wonder: Will Gopher give Squirrel some acorns?"

Read a Humorous Story

Genre

A **humorous story** has funny characters and events.

Setting

The setting is where and when a story happens.

This story happens one day in a small village.

When the Pigs Took Over

by **Arthur Dorros**

illustrated by **Diane Greenseid**

▸ **Set a Purpose**

Don Carlos wants more food for his restaurant. Find out what he and his brother, Alonzo, get.

Alonzo was little. Don Carlos was big. He was Alonzo's big brother—much older and much, much bigger.

Alonzo had one hat. Don Carlos had seven, and he wore them all at once. "***Más***," said Don Carlos as he found three more.

Oh no, thought Alonzo. More.

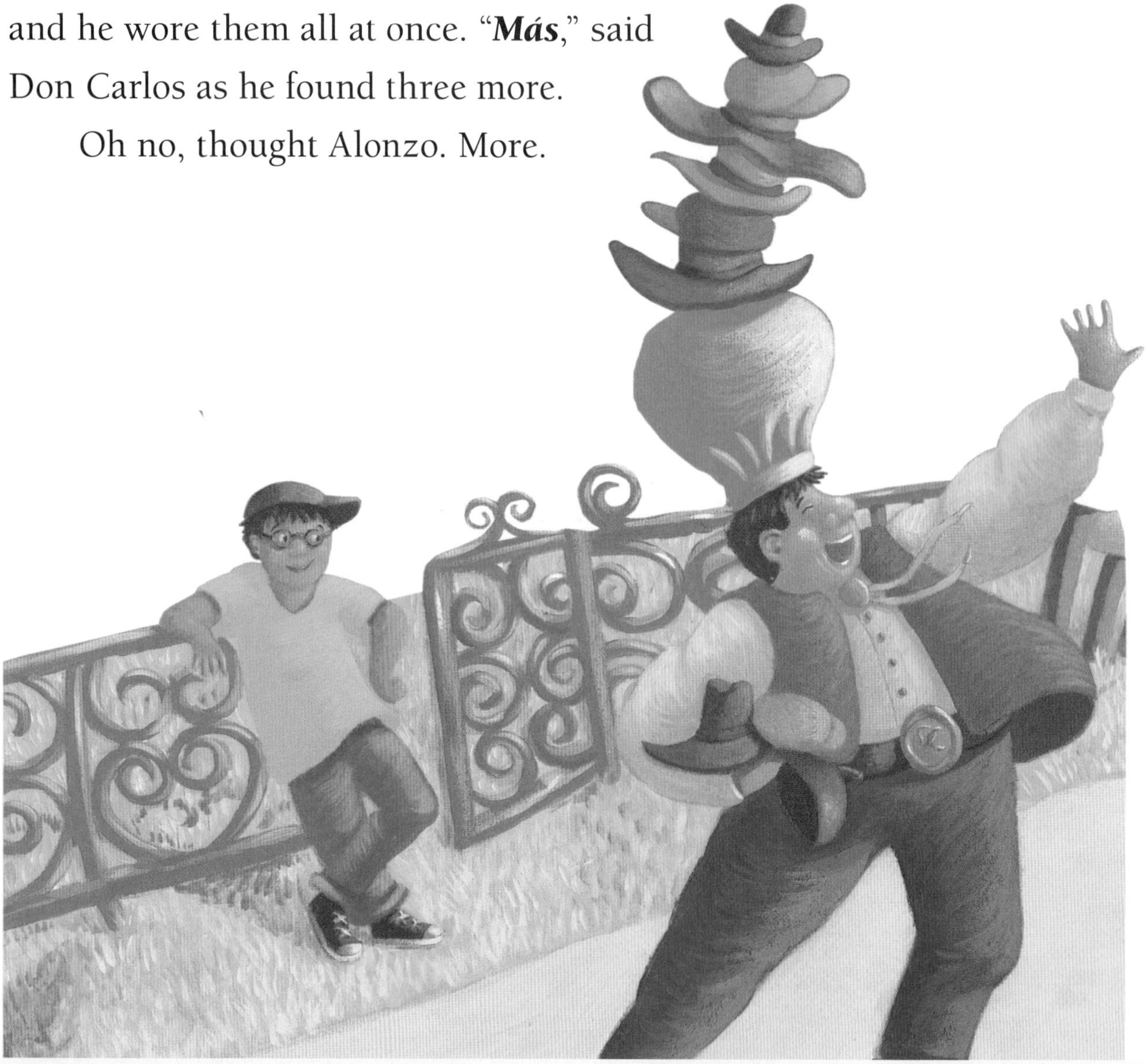

In Other Words
Más More (in Spanish)

Don Carlos had lots of ideas about "more," especially at his restaurant. Don Carlos had the only restaurant in the **village**. He served huge, **sizzling, steaming** plates of food, bowls of food, **platters** of food that people liked eating.

"¿*Más?*" Don Carlos always asked.

In Other Words
village small town
sizzling, steaming hot
platters big dishes

Alonzo liked playing his violin at the restaurant.

"*¡Magnífico!*" villagers cheered. Of all the villagers, none could play music as well as Alonzo.

"*Más*," said Don Carlos.

People were happily listening to the music and eating. But Don Carlos was thinking about more foods that he could add to the **restaurant menu**.

In Other Words

¡Magnífico! Magnificent! Wonderful! (in Spanish)

restaurant menu list of food the restaurant has for people to eat

Alonzo read that in a big, fancy restaurant in the city, people ate snails.

"¡*Caracoles!*" said Don Carlos. Snails!

There were lots of snails in the village. Alonzo helped gather snails. Soon there were pails of snails, baskets of snails, **wheelbarrows** of snails.

"*Más*," said Don Carlos.

They looked for more snails.

◀ **wheelbarrow**

In Other Words
¡*Caracoles!* Snails! (in Spanish)
wheelbarrows small carts

▶ **Before You Move On**

1. **Cause/Effect** What food do Don Carlos and Alonzo get for the restaurant? Why?

2. **Ask Questions** Think about Don Carlos or Alonzo. Ask yourself a question about the character. Look for the answer as you read.

▶ **Predict**
Look at the pictures. How will the brothers stop the snails?

Snails crawled out of baskets, pails, and wheelbarrows in the restaurant kitchen. The snails were looking for food.

The snails ate and ate— and ate. They ate every **blade** of grass, every plant and flower in the village.

"*¿Qué hacemos?*" the villagers cried, wondering what to do.

In Other Words
blade piece
¿Qué hacemos? What do
    we do? (in Spanish)

"*¡Pájaros!*" Alonzo said. Birds! He had seen birds eat snails. He threw corn and **bread crumbs to attract birds**. At first only a few birds **landed**.

"*Más,*" said Don Carlos.

The villagers tossed more crumbs. Birds flapped in tree branches, fluttered on rooftops, even landed on people's heads.

In Other Words

¡Pájaros! Birds! (in Spanish)

bread crumbs to attract birds small pieces of bread to make birds come

landed came

The birds started to eat snails. They raced across roads, finding snails to eat.

Soon there were no snails. But birds were everywhere, **squawking and screeching and scratching**. SCRAA, KEEYAA, CRIC CRAC.

Birds and what they dropped covered everything.

"*¿Qué hacemos?*" cried the villagers.

In Other Words

squawking and screeching and scratching making loud noises

"*¡Puercos!*" said Alonzo. Pigs! He had seen pigs chase birds away. Alonzo and the villagers **rounded up pigs**. Pigs ran, **snorting and grunting**, at the birds. GARUMPF, ERRR, ERRR, ERRR. But the birds kept flapping through the village.

"*Más*," said Don Carlos.

In Other Words

¡Puercos! Pigs! (in Spanish)
rounded up pigs brought pigs to the town
snorting and grunting making noises

▶ **Before You Move On**

1. **Confirm Prediction** How do the brothers stop the snails? Was your prediction correct?
2. **Details** What does Alonzo think the pigs will do?

Alonzo asked Don Carlos if he was sure he wanted more.

"*¡Sí, más!*" Don Carlos said.

Large pigs, small pigs, pigs with spots and pigs with none, were brought from **the nearby countryside**.

The pigs **snuffed and snapped and squealed**. They scared away the birds and then began to eat.

In Other Words

Sí Yes (in Spanish)

the nearby countryside farms near the town

snuffed and snapped and squealed
     made a lot of noise as they looked for food

They ate everything in front of their **snouts**. Pigs **clattered into kitchens, trotted** into Don Carlos's restaurant, tipped over tables, **tore up** the village looking for more.

Don Carlos began to jump and shout, trying to chase away the pigs. But the pigs were everywhere.

"*¿Qué hacemos?*" Everyone wondered what to do.

In Other Words

snouts noses

clattered into kitchens, trotted bumped into things in kitchens and then ran

tore up destroyed

▶ **Before You Move On**

1. **Confirm Prediction** What was your prediction? Was it correct? Explain.
2. **Setting** Describe how the village was different after the snails, birds, and pigs came.

▶ **Predict**
Look at the pictures. How will
the villagers make the pigs leave?

"**¡Música!**" Alonzo said. Music! He had heard
a story about a boy who played music and led rats out of
a village. Alonzo played his violin.

The villagers brought other **instruments**. SCRIC,
SCRONK, KABLOM, PUM-PAM, PUM-PAM. Terrible
sounds came from the instruments. The sounds were
bad, they were awful, they were horrible.

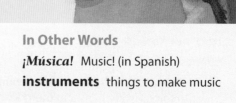

In Other Words
¡Música! Music! (in Spanish)
instruments things to make music

The pigs kept running wild.

Don Carlos put his hands over his ears. The music was more than even he could **stand**. "¡No más!" he cried.

"¡Más!" Alonzo shouted to the villagers.

The villagers marched through the streets, playing louder and louder.

In Other Words
stand listen to

Hearing the terrible sounds, pigs tried to get away. The pigs ran fast and far, until **there was not a pig in sight**.

Don Carlos uncovered his ears. He looked at how much the village had been destroyed.

"*¡No más!*" he said sadly. He **realized** that more was not always better.

"*¡Sí, más!*" said Alonzo. He wanted more . . .

In Other Words

there was not a pig in sight all the pigs were gone

realized understood

. . . practice for the band.

So in the evening, in a **cozy** village restaurant
that serves a lot but does not serve snails, a band
can be heard playing—or **practicing**—more. ❖

▶ **Before You Move On**

1. **Confirm Prediction** How do the villagers
   make the pigs leave? Was your prediction
   correct?

2. **Compare/Contrast** Compare what Don
   Carlos says at the beginning of the story
   and at the end. What does he learn?

Talk About It

1. What is the funniest part of this **humorous story**? Tell your opinion.

> To me, the funniest part _____ .

2. Think of a question that Alonzo might ask Don Carlos at the end of the story. **Ask and answer** the question.

> Alonzo asks, "_____ ?"
> Don Carlos answers, "_____ ."

3. How does Don Carlos change at the end of the story? Why does he change?

> Don Carlos _____ .
> He changes because _____ .

Learn test-taking strategies.
NGReach.com

Write About It

Imagine that your own community gets out of **balance**. What could make it get out of balance? How would people **react**? Write two sentences. Use at least one **Key Word**.

> When a lot of _____ , things get _____ .
> People _____ .

Compare and Contrast

Make a Venn diagram for "When the Pigs Took Over." Use the pictures and the text to compare and contrast the brothers.

Venn Diagram

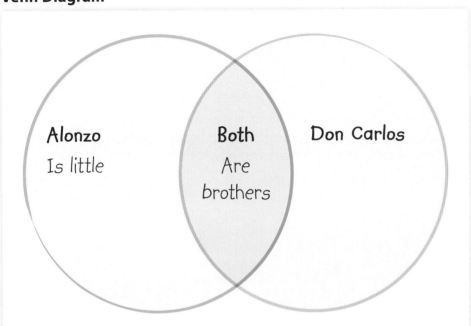

Alonzo
Is little

Both
Are
brothers

Don Carlos

Use your diagram to tell a partner how the brothers are alike and different. Use the sentence frames and **Key Words**. Record your comparison.

They are alike because _____.
Alonzo _____, but Don Carlos _____.

Fluency  Comprehension Coach

Use the Comprehension Coach to practice reading with expression. Rate your reading.

Talk Together

What happens to the town when nature loses its **balance**? Describe the town before and after. Use **Key Words**.

Syllables

In a dictionary, a word may be divided into **syllables**, or word parts.

Look at this example of a dictionary entry. How many syllables does **supply** have?

> **This part shows how to divide the word into syllables.**

sup•ply (su-**plī**) *noun* A supply is the amount you have of something.

Try It Together

Use the dictionary entries to answer the questions.

in•ter•act (in-tur-**akt**) *verb* To interact means to act together.
scarce (**skairs**) *adjective* When something is scarce, it is hard to find or get.

1. How many syllables does <u>interact</u> have? **A** one **B** two **C** four **D** three	**2. Scarce is a one-syllable word. How can you tell?** **A** It is hard to say. **B** It is not divided. **C** It is an adjective. **D** It has only six letters.

Connect Across Texts Read about more silly things that could happen when nature is out of balance.

Genre A **riddle** is a question that has a funny answer. The answer may have playful language, such as words within words, rhyming words, or words that sound alike but mean different things.

Animals, More or Less

by Mike Thaler * illustrated by Jared Lee

What do you call too many pigs on the same road?

SORRY!

WATCH OUT!

HEY!

Hint:

Too many cars on the same road is called a traffic jam.

a ham jam

Word Play

ham meat that comes from pigs

▶ **Before You Move On**

1. **Identify** What kind of playful language does this riddle use?

2. **Apply** Using one or two words from this page in a playful way, make up a riddle of your own. Try it on a partner.

What can too many rabbits in the air cause?

hare pollution

Hint:

Too many poisons in the air can cause air pollution.

Word Play

hare another name for a rabbit

What does one lonely buffalo do when it sees other buffalos?

HELLOOOO....

It tries to be herd.

Hint:

A <u>herd</u> of animals is noisy. It can be <u>heard</u> as it runs across the plains.

Word Play

herd animals grouped together

heard listened to

▶ **Before You Move On**

1. **Identify** What kinds of playful language do the riddles on pages 98–99 use?

2. **Apply** Find words on the page that have multiple meanings. Use one or two of them to make up your own riddle.

What happens when too few acorns fall from the trees?

Hint:
Acorns are nuts that squirrels like to eat.

The squirrels go nuts!

Word Play

go nuts act in a strange or silly way

What happens when there are too many frogs on a baseball team?

They catch all the flies.

Word Play

flies insects; high balls in baseball that when caught count as outs

▶ **Before You Move On**

1. **Identify** What kind of playful language do the riddles on pages 100–101 use?

2. **Apply** Find the multiple meaning words in the riddle. Then use them to make up your own riddle. Share it with the class.

Key Words

amount	increase
balance	interact
behavior	react
control	scarce
decrease	supply

Compare Genres

"When the Pigs Took Over" is a humorous story. "Animals, More or Less" has riddles. How are a humorous story and a riddle alike? How are the two genres different? Complete the checklist chart with a partner.

Checklist Chart

Think about each description.

	Humorous Story	Riddle
funny	✔	✔
usually long		
short		
playful language		
paragraphs		
questions and answers		

Write check marks to show whether the words describe a humorous story, a riddle, or both.

Talk Together

What happens when nature loses its **balance**? Think about the story and the riddles. Use **Key Words** to talk about your ideas.

Grammar

Kinds of Sentences

There are four kinds of sentences.

Grammar Rules Kinds of Sentences

• Use a **statement** to tell something.	I'm in the village**.**
• Use an **exclamation** to show strong feeling.	The snails will eat all the plants**!**
• Use a **command** to tell someone to do something.	Please play the violin**.** Catch that pig**!**
• Use a **question** to ask something. Some **question words** are: *Is, Are, Do, Does, Who, What, When, Where.* Some answers have **contractions**.	**Is** the restaurant open**?** No, it **isn't**. **What** is that**?** **It's** a wheelbarrow. **Do** you like the town**?** Yes, I do.

Read Sentences

Read this passage about the story. How many kinds of sentences can you find? Tell a partner about the sentences.

> The birds eat the snails. Soon they're all gone. Now there are too many birds! What will the villagers do?

Write Sentences

Write three questions about your town. Your partner writes answers. Are there contractions in any of the answers?

103

Give and Carry Out Commands

Listen to Rico's song. Then pretend you are somewhere outside, such as by a pond or in a forest. Use **Language Frames** with a partner to give and carry out commands.

Watch Out!

Watch out! Keep away from the water.
Watch out! Keep away from the water.
Point to the clams, but don't get close.
Watch out or you'll slip in the water.

Song ((MP3))

A crab, and a snail, and a
    starfish, too,
All of them live in the
    tidepool zoo.
Show me the clams and
    anemones.
But do not touch them.
    Be careful, please!

Tune: "Boom! Boom! Ain't It Great!"

clam

sea snail

starfish

crab

sea anemone

Key Words

drought

ecosystem

food chain

level

river

Key Words

Look at these pictures of two **ecosystems**. Use **Key Words** and other words to talk about each place.

Bears catch fish in a **river**. If the bears eat too many fish, it will affect the **food chain**.

In a **drought**, the water **level** falls. Elephants have less water to drink.

Talk Together

Imagine that you and your partner are by the water in the pictures. Use **Language Frames** from page 104 to give and carry out commands. Then use **Key Words** to discuss how an ecosystem can lose its balance.

Cause and Effect

A **cause** makes something happen. An **effect** is what happens. When you identify causes and effects, what you read, see, or hear becomes clearer.

Look at these pictures. Read the captions.

Water gets trapped in rocks.

A tide pool forms.

Map and Talk

You can use a cause-and-effect diagram to show what happens and why it happens. Here's how you make one.

A cause goes in the first box. The effect goes in the second box.

Cause-and-Effect Diagram

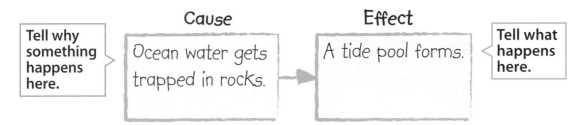

Cause

Effect

Tell why something happens here.

Ocean water gets trapped in rocks.

A tide pool forms.

Tell what happens here.

Talk Together

Look back at page 105. Find a cause and an effect. Make a diagram to show what happens, and why. Explain your diagram to a partner.

More Key Words

Use these words to talk about "When the Wolves Returned" and "Megafish Man."

competition
(kom-pu-**ti**-shun) *noun*

A **competition** is a contest or struggle between two or more people or animals.

nature
(**nā**-chur) *noun*

Nature means things like rivers, trees, and animals. She likes to study **nature**.

negative
(**ne**-gu-tiv) *adjective*

Something that is **negative** is bad. Screaming at someone is a **negative** action.

positive
(**pah**-zu-tiv) *adjective*

Something that is **positive** is good for you. Exercise is a **positive** activity.

resources
(**rē**-sors-uz) *noun*

Resources are things that you can use. A library has many **resources**.

Talk Together

Work with a partner. Make a Word Web of examples for each **Key Word**.

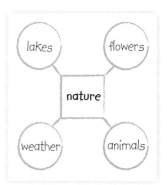

Add words to My Vocabulary Notebook.
NGReach.com

Learn to Ask Questions

Do you want to know more about this picture? If so, **ask** yourself **questions**. To figure out the answers, take a closer look at the picture, or think about what you know about ecosystems.

This photo shows a tiny ecosystem.

As you read, **ask questions**. You can find the answers to some questions in your head. Think to come up with answers. This will help you understand the text better.

How to Ask Questions

?	**1.** Ask a question.
☁	**2.** Think about your experiences and what you know. Think about what the author is trying to tell you.
☁	**3.** Think about the answer. Read on and ask more questions.

I wonder: _____?

I know _____. The author _____.

So _____. Now I wonder: _____?

Language Frames

? I wonder:
_____ ?

☁ I Know _____ .
The author
_____ .

☁ So _____ .
Now I wonder:
_____ ?

Talk Together

Read Rico's report with a partner. Read the sample questions. Then use **Language Frames** to ask and answer questions to check your understanding. Tell a partner about them.

Report

What Makes an Ecosystem?
by Rico Borelli

An **ecosystem** is made up of living and nonliving things. Each thing interacts with everything else in the system. An ecosystem needs **resources** . These resources include soil, sunlight, and water. Dead plants and other wastes play a **positive** part, too. They put nutrients into the soil.

Plants take nutrients from the soil. Plant-eaters eat the plants. Predators eat the plant-eaters. This **food chain** keeps the ecosystem in balance. That means there is never too much or too little of any one thing.

Prey and predators eat to stay alive. So there is always **competition** for food in an ecosystem. Sometimes one kind of animal eats too many of another kind. This will have a **negative** effect. It throws the system out of balance.

There are many different ecosystems in **nature** . Some are large, like forests and deserts. Others are as small as a crack in a tree. But every one of them is part of the largest ecosystem of all: planet Earth.

Sample Questions

"I wonder: What are the resources?

I Know that water, sun, and soil are important. The author probably means those resources.

So I learn that I'm right. Now I wonder: What do dead plants do in an ecosystem?"

◄ = A good place to ask a question

109

Read a Science Article

Genre

A **science article** is nonfiction. It can explain why certain things happen in nature.

Text Feature

A **time line** shows a sequence of important events. It tells about each event and when it happened.

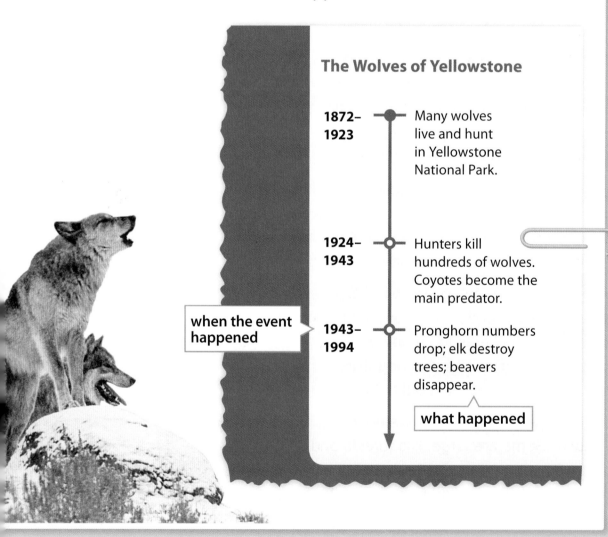

The Wolves of Yellowstone

1872–1923 — Many wolves live and hunt in Yellowstone National Park.

1924–1943 — Hunters kill hundreds of wolves. Coyotes become the main predator.

when the event happened

1943–1994 — Pronghorn numbers drop; elk destroy trees; beavers disappear.

what happened

WHEN THE WOLVES RETURNED

adapted from a book by **DOROTHY HINSHAW PATENT**

photographs by **DAN HARTMAN AND CASSIE HARTMAN**

Comprehension Coach

▶ **Set a Purpose**
Find out why wolves are an
important part of an **ecosystem** .

THE FIRST NATIONAL PARK

Where would you go to see some of Earth's
natural wonders? You might go to a place
called Yellowstone. In Yellowstone, **geysers
shoot steam** high into the air and waterfalls
flow into colorful canyons. All kinds of wildlife
roam the land. Luckily, this special place
became the world's first **national park** in 1872.

Yellowstone National
Park is in Wyoming.

Steam rises from a geyser.

Yellowstone has many waterfalls.

In Other Words

geysers shoot steam hot water
   comes up from under the ground

national park protected area of
   land

112

TROUBLE WITH WOLVES

The purpose for making Yellowstone a national park was to protect its natural wonders for visitors. People enjoyed seeing animals in the park, too, like elk and deer. But wolves **fed on** them. So, hunters were paid to kill the wolves. **Park officials** did not understand that killing the wolves would **throw nature out of balance**.

The Wolves of Yellowstone

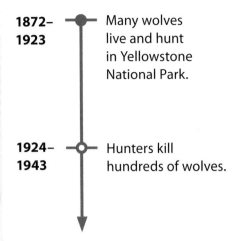

1872–1923 — Many wolves live and hunt in Yellowstone National Park.

1924–1943 — Hunters kill hundreds of wolves.

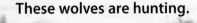
These wolves are hunting.

In Other Words
fed on killed and ate
Park officials People in charge of Yellowstone
throw nature out of balance change the way animals usually live and die

▶ **Before You Move On**
1. **Cause/Effect** Why did the United States make Yellowstone a national park?
2. **Explain** Tell why wolves were a problem when Yellowstone first opened. Use your own words.

▲ The wolves disappeared. More and more elk filled the park.

YELLOWSTONE WITHOUT WOLVES

By 1926 the wolves were all gone. Without wolves to hunt them, the number of elk increased. To control the elk population, **rangers** trapped them and sent them to other parks. Rangers also had to shoot and kill the elk to keep their numbers down.

fox

In Other Words
rangers park workers

▲ coyote

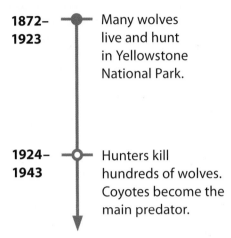

The Wolves of Yellowstone

1872–1923 — Many wolves live and hunt in Yellowstone National Park.

1924–1943 — Hunters kill hundreds of wolves. Coyotes become the main predator.

Coyotes also increased in number. Without wolves at the top of the **food chain**, they became Yellowstone's **main predator**. Coyotes eat everything from elk **calves** to insects. But mostly they eat small animals like ground squirrels. So coyotes made it harder for other small predators, like foxes, to find food.

In Other Words

main predator top killer

calves babies

▶ **Before You Move On**

1. **Cause/Effect** The wolves disappeared. What were the effects of that event on the **food chain**?

2. **Ask Questions** What questions might visitors have asked the park rangers in 1926?

PRONGHORNS IN DANGER

Coyotes in Yellowstone also fed on newborn pronghorns. They became experts at finding pronghorn **fawns**. With so many coyotes in the park, pronghorn numbers dropped. Every year, fewer pronghorn fawns survived. Park managers worried that pronghorns might disappear completely.

▲ pronghorn fawn

In Other Words
Pronghorns Animals That Look Like Deer
fawns babies

NEW PLANTS DON'T GROW

Even the trees and shrubs **suffered** because the wolves were gone. The elk ate **young shoots** and bark. Young trees and shrubs could not grow fast enough to replace the old ones that died. Soon, the birds that **nested** in the trees and bushes became **rare**.

The Wolves of Yellowstone

1872–1923 — Many wolves live and hunt in Yellowstone National Park.

1924–1943 — Hunters kill hundreds of wolves. Coyotes become the main predator.

1943–1994 — Pronghorn numbers drop; elk destroy trees.

Elk eat tree bark.

An elk eats young shoots.

In Other Words

suffered hurt
young shoots new plants
nested made their homes
rare fewer in number

▶ **Before You Move On**

1. **Ask Questions** Ask a question about the pronghorns or elks in Yellowstone. Tell a partner how you plan to find the answer.
2. **Sequence** What happened that led to some birds becoming rare in Yellowstone? Tell the events in order. Use your own words.

117

BEAVERS DISAPPEAR

Beavers use their teeth to cut down trees. They **store** the trees to eat during the winter. They also use the trees to build **dams**. Beaver dams create ponds that provide homes for ducks and other animals.

Without trees, the beavers could not survive. They were almost gone from part of the park by the 1950s.

A beaver builds a dam.

In Other Words
store save
dams walls that hold back water

A SOLUTION

Many of the problems in the park began soon after the wolves were **eliminated**. Scientists predicted that bringing wolves back would help. Wolves could control the numbers of coyotes and elk. This would **allow** plants and other animals to live and grow.

The Wolves of Yellowstone

1872–1923 — Many wolves live and hunt in Yellowstone National Park.

1924–1943 — Hunters kill hundreds of wolves. Coyotes become the main predator.

1943–1994 — Pronghorn numbers drop; elk destroy trees; beavers disappear.

squirrel

In Other Words
eliminated killed
allow make it possible for

▶ **Before You Move On**

1. **Cause/Effect** When the beavers left, other animals in Yellowstone lost their homes. Why?

2. **Summarize** What have you learned so far about wolves? How do they affect the balance of **nature** in Yellowstone?

THE WOLVES RETURN

Wolves from Canada were brought to Yellowstone in 1995 and 1996. Seven groups of wolves were set free in the park. Each **pack** lived in a wide area called a territory. It didn't take long for the wolves to **feel at home**. There were a lot of animals, especially elk, for them to hunt.

Year by year, the number of wolves in Yellowstone grew. When a pack became too big, it broke into smaller packs. These groups slowly filled the park. Now, about twelve wolf packs live in Yellowstone. There are usually around 150 wolves in the park.

young wolves

In Other Words
pack group of wolves
feel at home enjoy living in Yellowstone

The Wolves of Yellowstone

1872–1923 — Many wolves live and hunt in Yellowstone National Park.

1924–1943 — Hunters kill hundreds of wolves. Coyotes become the main predator.

1943–1994 — Pronghorn numbers drop; elk destroy trees; beavers disappear.

1995–1996 — Wolves return to Yellowstone.

▶ **Before You Move On**

1. **Use Text Features Make Inferences**
   What probably helped the wolf packs from Canada grow in Yellowstone?
2. **Evaluate** Was it a good idea to return wolves to Yellowstone? Use facts from the text to support your answer..

NATURE'S BALANCE RETURNS

Wolves saw the coyotes as **competition**. They killed coyotes or chased them out of their territories. Now, with fewer coyotes hunting them, pronghorn and other animals survive more easily. Foxes, owls, and other animals also **benefit**. There are fewer coyotes to **compete** with them for the same food.

Without wolves, elk **lingered along the streams** in the park. They ate young trees before they had a chance to grow. Now the elk must keep moving. This makes it harder for wolves to find them. Because the elk are moving, trees can grow again.

▲ Elk keep moving. They want to stay away from wolves.

In Other Words
benefit do better
compete fight
lingered along the streams stayed near the small **rivers**

The Wolves of Yellowstone

1872–1923	Many wolves live and hunt in Yellowstone National Park.
1924–1943	Hunters kill hundreds of wolves. Coyotes become the main predator.
1943–1994	Pronghorn numbers drop; elk destroy trees; beavers disappear.
1995–1996	Wolves return to Yellowstone.

▲ **A wolf chases a coyote.**

▶ **Before You Move On**

1. **Cause/Effect** How do wolves help pronghorn survive?
2. **Details** What do elk do to stay safe from wolves?

beaver

owl

BEAVERS COME BACK

The animals that need the trees are also coming back. For example, in 1996 only one **beaver colony** lived in the northern part of the park. By 2003, there were nine. Scientists hope that birds that hunt from trees, like owls, will also **become more common**.

In Other Words
beaver colony group of beavers
become more common increase in number

A BALANCED ECOSYSTEM

Returning the wolf is helping to make Yellowstone **whole again**. Scientists hope that as the years go by, even more plants and animals will come back. Today, Yellowstone is becoming a healthy system again, thanks to the wolves' return. ❖

The Wolves of Yellowstone

1872–1923	Many wolves live and hunt in Yellowstone National Park.
1924–1943	Hunters kill hundreds of wolves. Coyotes become the main predator.
1943–1994	Pronghorn numbers drop; elk destroy trees; beavers disappear.
1995–1996	Wolves return to Yellowstone.
1997–today	Wolf packs continue to increase. Nature's balance improves.

In Other Words

whole again a balanced **ecosystem**

▶ **Before You Move On**

1. **Details** Name two animals that need the trees in Yellowstone.
2. **Author's Purpose** What is this article about? Why did the author write it?

Talk About It

Key Words

Key Words	
competition	nature
drought	negative
ecosystem	positive
food chain	resources
level	river

1. What did you learn about animals in this **science article**? Give two facts.

   I learned _____ . I also learned _____ .

2. Imagine you work at Yellowstone Park. What might a visitor ask you about the history of wolves in the park? **Ask and answer** the question.

   Why were wolves _____ . Wolves were _____ . because _____ !

3. Wolves, coyotes, and elk are part of the **food chain** in Yellowstone. Explain how this part of the chain works. What does each animal eat?

   Wolves eat _____ , and coyotes eat _____ . Elk eat _____ .

Learn test-taking strategies.
NGReach.com

Write About It

In folk tales and other stories, wolves are often **negative** characters. Why do you think this is so? Do you think it is fair? Write two or three sentences to explain your thoughts. Use **Key Words**.

Wolves are often negative characters because _____ .
I think/do not think this is fair because _____ .

Cause and Effect

Complete a cause-and-effect diagram for "When the Wolves Returned."

Cause-and-Effect Diagram

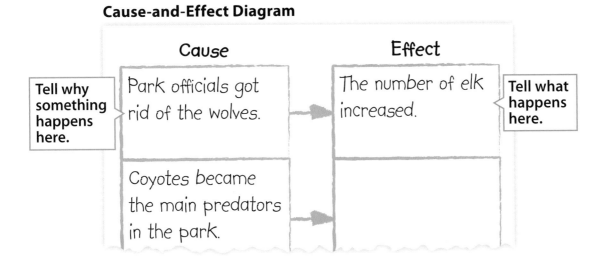

Cause		Effect
Park officials got rid of the wolves.	→	The number of elk increased.
Coyotes became the main predators in the park.	→	

Tell why something happens here.

Tell what happens here.

Now use your diagram to retell the information in the article to a partner. Tell each cause. Then use the sentence frame to tell the effect. Use as many **Key Words** as you can. Record your retelling.

This happened, so _____ .

Fluency  Comprehension Coach

Use the Comprehension Coach to practice phrasing as you read. Rate your reading.

Talk Together

How did **nature** lose its balance in Yellowstone? Summarize the events for a partner. Use **Key Words**.

Pronunciation

Suppose you are unsure about how to say a word. You can use a dictionary to determine the **pronunciation**.

Look at these examples from a dictionary.

> This part tells you how to pronounce the word. The heavy type tells you to stress the first part of the word.

na•ture (**nā**-chur) *noun* Nature means things like rivers, trees, and animals.

Pronunciation Key:

h**a**t   c**ā**ke   f**ah**ther

b**o**x   g**ō**t   fr**ü**t

> You can look up a mark, like **ā**, in the pronunciation key. The mark **ā** tells you to say the **a** in **nature** the same way you say the **a** in **cake**.

Try It Together

Use the dictionary entries to complete the items. For the second item, look at the pronunciation key above, too.

com•pe•ti•tion (kom-pu-**ti**-shun) *noun* A competition is a contest or struggle between two or more people or animals.

pos•i•tive (**pah**-zu-tiv) *adjective* Something that is positive is good for you.

1. **When you say competition, you stress the _____ part.**
   - **A** first
   - **B** third
   - **C** fourth
   - **D** second

2. **You say the o in positive the same way you say the a in _____ .**
   - **A** hat
   - **B** cake
   - **C** father
   - **D** nature

NATIONAL
GEOGRAPHIC
EXCLUSIVE

Connect Across Texts Now read about an explorer who works to keep a **river ecosystem** healthy.

Genre A **human interest feature** gives facts about someone. It tells what the person does and cares about.

Megafish Man

*by **Michael Sandler***

▲ **Zeb Hogan [*on left*] with a river stingray**

The telephone rang. Zeb Hogan got the news. A fisherman in Cambodia had caught a giant **river** stingray. Soon, Zeb was **headed** there by plane. "These catches are so **rare**, I don't want to miss out on any of them," he says.

In Other Words

Megafish Man A Man Interested in Very Large Fish

headed on his way

rare special; unusual

▶ **Before You Move On**

1. **Ask Questions** What questions do you have about Mr. Hogan? How will your questions help you as you read on?
2. **Use Text Features** What helps you figure out what a stingray is?

Monsters of the Mekong

Zeb is an **aquatic ecologist**. He is always searching for megafish. Megafish are aquatic monsters that grow to at least 6.5 feet (2 meters) or 220 pounds (100 kg). He studies the megafish that live in the Mekong River in Southeast Asia. Many megafish live in this river and the smaller rivers that **flow** into it.

▲ **The Mekong River flows through Southeast Asia.**

Megafish

giant skeetfish

giant stingray

giant carp

In Other Words

Mekong Mekong **River**

aquatic ecologist scientist who studies water animals and how they live

flow go

130

Why is Zeb so interested in megafish? By studying megafish, we can learn a lot about the health of an aquatic **ecosystem**. "If you still have these giant fish **species** in the river, it's a good **indication** that the river is healthy," he says.

For centuries, the Mekong's fish of all sizes **thrived** in clean water. There were so many fish, Cambodians often said, "Where there is water, there are fish."

◀ People in Cambodia fish in the Mekong River.

In Other Words
species types
indication sign
thrived lived well

▶ **Before You Move On**

1. **Make Inferences** What details in the text help the reader understand whether these "aquatic monsters" are helpful or harmful?

2. **Clarify** What do **levels**, or numbers, of megafish tell about the health of a **river**?

131

A River in Trouble

Today, however, fewer and fewer big fish are found in the Mekong. To Zeb, it's a warning. Something is **out of balance**.

Overfishing is one cause of fewer fish. **Pollution** is another. Soon there may be fewer smaller fish, too. This will hurt people who need the fish for food.

A woman sells fish at the market. ▶

▼ People weigh a giant catfish. There are few left.

In Other Words
out of balance not right
Overfishing People taking too many fish from the **river**
Pollution Dirty water

▲ **Zeb Hogan** (*on left*) **looks at a stingray. It was caught by a fisherman.**

Zeb wants to make Mekong waters healthy again. In Cambodia, he **set up a program**. When fishermen catch megafish, they give them to Zeb. He lets the fish go and **tracks their movements**.

This program **benefits** both the fishermen and the fish. It also helps Zeb learn how to better protect megafish, and the river so many people and animals **depend on**. ❖

In Other Words

set up a program made a plan

tracks their movements watches where they go

benefits is good for; helps

depend on need to help them live

▶ **Before You Move On**

1. **Cause/Effect** Why are fewer big fish found in the Mekong **River** today than in the past?

2. **Goal/Outcome** What is Mr. Hogan's goal? What has he done to try to reach that goal?

Compare Ecosystems

Key Words

competition	nature
drought	negative
ecosystem	positive
food chain	resources
level	river

List five facts about the **ecosystem** in
"When the Wolves Returned" or "Megafish Man."
Look back at the selection to locate facts about:

- where the ecosystem is

- what the natural features are

- what animals live in the ecosystem

- why it was or is out of balance

Find a partner who wrote about the other ecosystem.
Use your lists to create a comparison chart.

Comparison Chart

Yellowstone Park	Mekong River
Is in the United States	Is in Cambodia

Now discuss your chart. What is different about the two
ecosystems? What is the same?

Talk Together

What happens when ecosystems lose their balance? Think about
the article and the feature. Use **Key Words** in your discussion.

Compound Sentences

You can use the words *and*, *but*, or *or* to put two sentences together. When you make a **compound sentence**, put a comma (**,**) before *and*, *but*, or *or*.

Grammar Rules Compound Sentences

• Use **and** to join two ideas that are alike.	The wolves hunt coyotes **, and** the coyotes hunt squirrels.
• Use **but** to join two ideas that show a difference.	The fox is little **, but** the bear is big.
• Use **or** to show a choice between two ideas.	We can visit a national park **, or** we can go to the beach.

Read Compound Sentences

Read these sentences about Yellowstone Park. Identify two compound sentences. Point to the word in each sentence that joins the ideas.

Yellowstone is a special place. Geysers shoot steam up into the air, and waterfalls spill over rocks. You can look at these natural wonders, or you can watch the animals.

Write Compound Sentences

Look at the picture of the beaver on page 118. Write a compound sentence to go with the picture. Read your sentence to a partner.

135

Write as a Recorder

Write a Summary

Write a summary of something you read about the balance of nature. Add your summary to a class nature magazine.

Study a Model

In a summary, you present the most important ideas about something you have read or learned in another way.

Without Wolves

by Jessie Landon

Officials at Yellowstone Park once thought wolves were killing too many of the other animals. So they paid hunters to kill all the wolves.

Park officials quickly learned that this was a mistake. Without the wolves, animals like elk and coyotes grew in number. Soon they were out of control.

The elk destroyed trees and shrubs. As a result, many birds and beavers could not survive. Meanwhile, the coyotes ate food that smaller animals needed to live.

Scientists finally figured out what to do. They brought wolves back to Yellowstone, and the ecosystem got better.

The **title** gives the focus of the summary.

The summary contains only the most **important ideas**. All the ideas in the article are about the same topic.

The summary has a beginning, a middle, and an end. The writing is complete.

Prewrite

1. **Choose a Topic** What are the most interesting things you have learned about the balance of nature? Talk with a partner to choose one set of ideas to summarize.

Language Frames	
Tell Your Ideas	**Respond to Ideas**
The most interesting thing I learned this week was _____ .	Will you be able to summarize _____ in just a few sentences?
I never knew _____ before.	_____ doesn't sound very interesting. Maybe you should choose a different topic.
I'd like to write about _____ because _____ .	

2. **Gather Information** Reread the information you want to summarize. What are the important ideas? Look at the title, headings, and topic sentences.

3. **Get Organized** Use a chart to help you list the most important ideas. For this article, a cause-and-effect diagram works well.

Cause-and-Effect Diagram

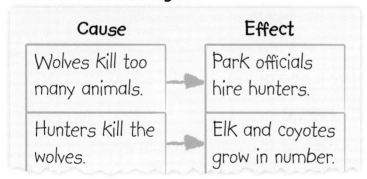

Draft

Use your cause-and-effect diagram to write your draft.

- Include only the most important ideas.

- Make sure all the ideas go together.

Revise

1. **Read, Retell, Respond** Read your summary aloud to a partner. Your partner listens and then retells the important ideas. Next, talk about ways to improve your writing.

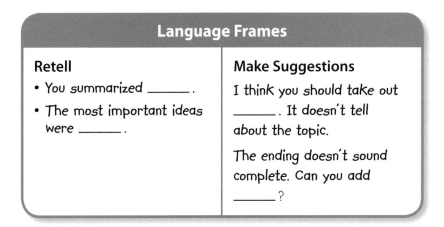

Language Frames	
Retell	**Make Suggestions**
• You summarized _____. • The most important ideas were _____.	I think you should take out _____ . It doesn't tell about the topic. The ending doesn't sound complete. Can you add _____ ?

2. **Make Changes** Think about your draft and your partner's suggestions. Then use the Revising Marks on page 573 to mark your changes.

   • Delete information that doesn't tell about the topic.

   > Without the wolves, animals like elk and coyotes grew in number, ~~and rangers sent many of them to other parks~~.

   • Does your writing have a beginning, a middle, and an end? Make sure it is complete.

   > Scientists finally figured out what to do. They brought wolves back to Yellowstone. *and the ecosystem got better.*

Edit and Proofread

Work with a partner to edit and proofread your summary. Punctuate compound sentences correctly. Use the marks on page 574 to show your changes.

Punctuation Tip

✔ Put a comma (,) before **and**, **but**, or **or** in a compound sentence.

Publish

1. **On Your Own** Make a final copy of your summary. Present it as a short oral report.

Presentation Tips	
If you are the speaker…	**If you are the listener…**
In a summary, every word is important. Be sure to speak slowly and clearly.	Think about whether the summary was clear to you. Did anything seem to be missing?
Repeat any parts of your summary that you say too fast or incorrectly.	Think about what you could learn about summarizing from the example you heard.

2. **With a Group** Illustrate your summary. Then work with your classmates to create a magazine called "Nature Out of Balance." You and your classmates may want to donate the magazine to your school library.

139

?
BIG
Question

What happens when nature loses its balance?

In this unit, you found lots of answers to the **Big Question**. Now, make a concept map to discuss the **Big Question** with the class.

Concept Map

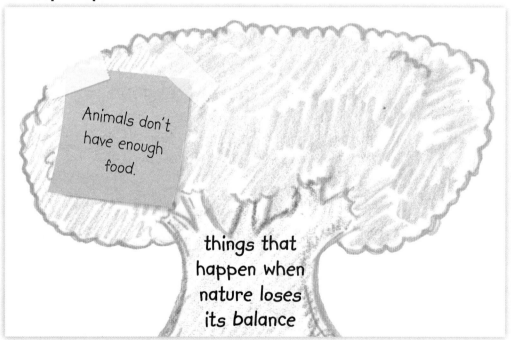

Animals don't have enough food.

things that happen when nature loses its balance

Write a Description

Select one thing on your concept map that can happen when nature is not in balance. Write a description of it.

Share Your Ideas

Choose one of these ways to share your ideas about the **Big Question**.

Write It!

Trade Cards

On a slip of paper, write something that could make an ecosystem lose its balance. Trade slips with a partner. Draw an example of your partner's ecosystem. Share and discuss your drawings.

Talk About It!

Share Pictures

Find a picture of a forest, pond, or other ecosystem. Decide whether the place is in balance or out of balance. Explain your picture to the class.

Do It!

Create a Riddle

Create a riddle with a partner. Write about something in nature. Then find another pair of partners. Ask them your riddle. Try to guess theirs!

What did the dog say to the wolves? (Woof! Woof!)

Write It!

Perform a Skit

Write a skit about an ecosystem. The characters are the animals, plants, water, and so on. What do they say about their home? Do they use formal or informal language? Present your skit to the class.

RIVER: It rained. I am full of fresh, clean water!

Life in the Soil

? **BIG** **Question** What is so amazing about plants?

Unit at a Glance
- **Language**: Give Information, Define and Explain, Science Words
- **Literacy**: Make Inferences
- **Content**: Plants

Unit
3

Share What You Know

Do It!

My plant grows without much water.

❶ **Think** of the most amazing plant you know. Draw it.

❷ **Display** all the class drawings. Don't tell which is yours!

❸ **Say** an amazing thing your plant does. Can your class guess which plant is yours?

Build Background: Use this interactive resource to learn about plants.
NGReach.com

Give Information

Listen to Marco's song. Then use **Language Frames** to give information about a plant you know.

Song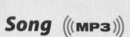

flower

leaf

stem

seed pod

My Big, Strong Plant

A big, strong plant lives in my yard.
Its stem is thick and wide.
Its leaves are nearly two feet long.
I'm glad it lives outside!

Chorus:

My big, strong plant!
It grows against my wall.
It has flowers in the summer
And seed pods in the fall.

Tune: "Oh! Susanna"

Key Words

blossom

cycle

root

seed

soil

sprout

Key Words

Look at this diagram. Use **Key Words** and other words to talk about the life **cycle** of a pea plant.

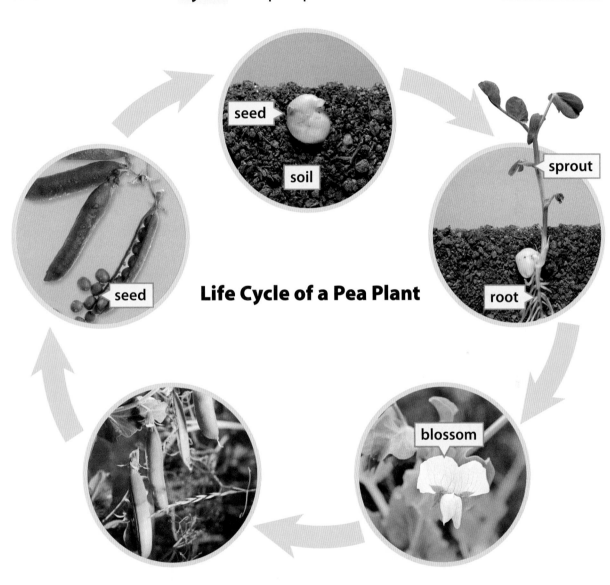

Life Cycle of a Pea Plant

seed

soil

sprout

root

blossom

seed

Talk Together

What is amazing about a pea plant's life cycle? Use **Language Frames** from page 144 and **Key Words** to give information to a partner.

145

Sequence

When things happen in a certain order, they are in **sequence**. When you talk about sequence, you can use:

- time-order words: *first, next, then, finally*
- names of days, months, seasons: *Monday, May, summer*

Look at the pictures of a growing plant.

 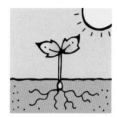  

Map and Talk

You can use a sequence chain to show when events happen. Here's how you make one.

Each event goes in a box in the sequence chain. The first event goes in the first box. The second event goes in the second box, and so on.

Sequence Chain

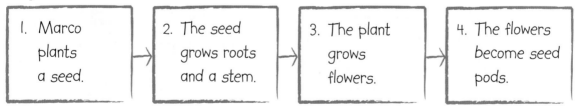

1. Marco plants a seed. → 2. The seed grows roots and a stem. → 3. The plant grows flowers. → 4. The flowers become seed pods.

Talk Together

Tell your partner the steps of a plant's life **cycle**. Your partner makes a sequence chain.

More Key Words

Use these words to talk about "Two Old Potatoes and Me" and "America's Sproutings."

characteristic
(kair-ik-tu-**ris**-tik) *noun*

A **characteristic** is how something looks or what something does. A **characteristic** of this plant is white flowers.

conditions
(kun-**di**-shunz) *noun*

When **conditions** are right, good things happen. Clear skies and wind are good **conditions** for sailing.

depend
(di-**pend**) *verb*

To **depend** means to need something or someone for support. A baby **depends** on its mother.

growth
(grōth) *noun*

The **growth** of something is how much bigger it gets.

produce
(pru-**düs**) *verb*

To **produce** means to make something. This factory **produces** cars.

Talk Together

Use a **Key Word** to ask a question. A partner uses a **Key Word** to answer.

> What is a characteristic of some plants?

> Some plants produce fruit.

Add words to My Vocabulary Notebook.
NGReach.com

Learn to Make Inferences

Look at the cartoon. The text does not say how Marco and his mom feel. Look at their expressions to figure out, or **make an inference** about, their feelings.

When you read, you have to **make inferences**, too.

How to Make Inferences

👁	**1.** Look for details in the text.	I read _____.
☁	**2.** Think about what you already know about the details and the topic.	I know _____.
🧩	**3.** Put your ideas together. What else can you figure out about the details?	And so _____.

Talk Together

Read Marco's "Gardener's Journal." Read the sample inference. Then use **Language Frames** to make inferences. Tell a partner about them.

Journal

Gardener's Journal

June 15:   I love my big plant! I water it every day. It is in a sunny place, so it has all the right **conditions** to grow.

June 20:   My plant bloomed today! The **blossoms** are bright orange. The color is a **characteristic** of this plant. Tomorrow, I go to Grandma's house for a long visit.

July 10:   I just got back from Grandma's house. My plant looks terrible! I expected a lot of **growth**, but its stem is bent over. I watered it, but I'm so worried.

July 11:   This morning I checked my plant again. It looks fine! The stem is strong and straight. The **soil** is damp and cool.

August 1:   Oh, dear! My plant is in trouble again! It looks like someone has put little holes in its leaves.
What can I do? My plant **depends** on me! ◄

August 2:   Dad told me to wash each leaf with dish soap. That sounds crazy!

August 8:   The soap worked! My plant looks great. ◄

September 1: This week my plant **produced** giant pods. I'll plant the **seeds**. Next summer I'll have more big, strong plants!

Sample Inference

"I read that Marco was gone and the plant looks terrible.

I know that some plants need water every day.

And so the plant must need water."

◄ = A good place to make an inference

149

Read a Story

Genre

Realistic fiction is a story that sounds as if it could be true. The characters, plot, and setting all seem real.

Characters

Characters are the people in the story.

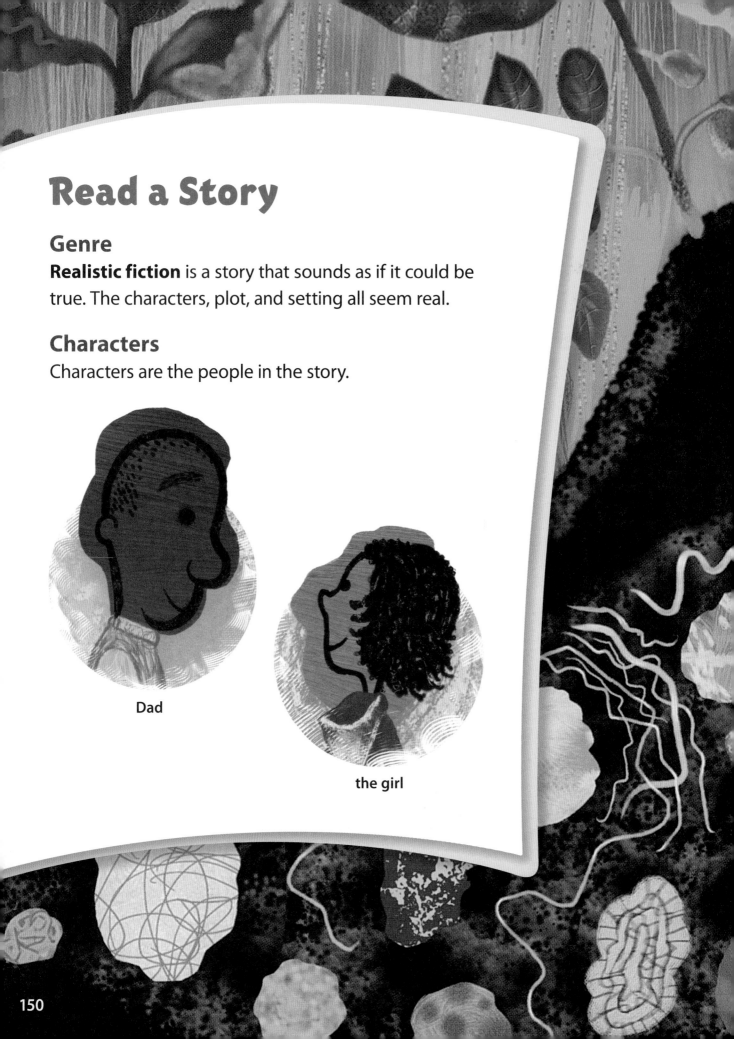

Dad

the girl

Two Old Potatoes and Me

by **John Coy**

illustrated by **Carolyn Fisher**

Comprehension Coach

▶ **Set a Purpose**
A girl finds two **potatoes**.
Find out what she does with them.

Last spring at my dad's house, I found two old potatoes in the back of the cupboard. They were so old, **sprouts** were growing from **their eyes**.

"Gross." I tossed them in the trash.

"Wait," Dad said. "I think we can grow new potatoes with those. I'll call your grandpa. He'll know."

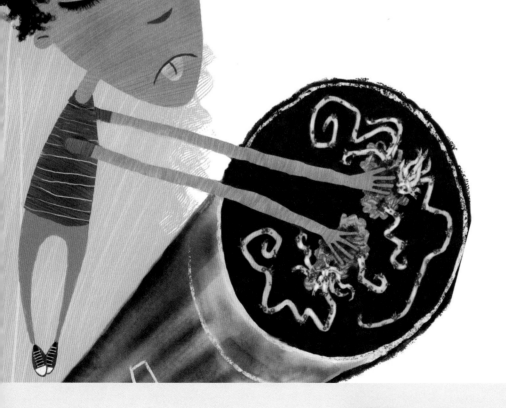

In Other Words

◀ **potatoes** vegetables that grow below the ground

their eyes spots on their skins

152

Dad and I talked with Grandpa. Then we took the potatoes to the sunniest spot in the garden. We dug. We picked out rocks. We raked the **soil** smooth.

Dad **carefully** cut the potatoes into nine **pieces**. I made sure each piece had one yellow sprout. Dad dug nine small holes. I put a piece of potato, with the eye facing up, in each hole. Then I covered them with dirt to make little hills.

Dad got the hose and I watered **gently**.

In Other Words
carefully slowly
pieces parts
gently with care

▶ **Before You Move On**
1. **Sequence** What do the girl and her dad do with the potatoes? Explain each step.
2. **Make Inferences** Why do the characters put the potato **sprouts** facing up?

In May, green plants poked up like caterpillars unfolding. We got down on our knees and picked weeds. We **shoveled compost onto** each hill.

"Won't that **smother** the plants?"

"No. They'll grow through it."

"Are we really going to get new potatoes from old potatoes?"

"I think so," said Dad.

In Other Words

shoveled compost onto put a special kind of **soil** on

smother keep air from

In June, the plants grew bigger. Violet flowers **blossomed** , and we added more compost. When we watered, **I accidentally sprayed my dad** with the hose. He laughed and sprayed me back.

blossoms

In Other Words

I accidentally sprayed my dad I made a mistake and got my dad wet

In July, when the plants were as tall as my waist, we picked potato beetles off the leaves. I dropped them into a pail of soapy water.

"Gross."

"We have to do this," Dad said. "**Otherwise**, the bugs will eat the leaves and the potatoes won't grow."

potato beetle

In Other Words
Otherwise If we don't

In August, some of the plants **turned brown and withered**.

"Are they dead?"

"No," said Dad. "The potatoes are growing **underground**."

"Are you sure?"

"I hope so. That's what your grandpa said."

We weeded.

We watered.

We waited.

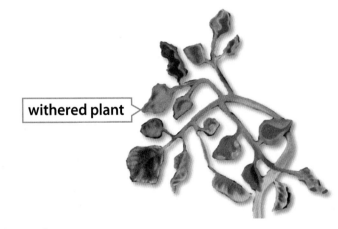

withered plant

In Other Words

turned brown and withered became brown and dry

underground below the surface of the earth or **soil**

▶ **Before You Move On**

1. **Confirm Prediction** Was your prediction correct? Tell what happens during this part of the plant's life **cycle**.

2. **Character** Do the girl and her dad get along well? How do you know?

▶ **Predict**
How many new potatoes will the
old potatoes **produce**?

Now, on a cool September day, Dad and I sit on the bench in the yard. Soon we get up and walk to the garden.

"What's your favorite way to eat potatoes?" Dad asks.

"Mashed, with lots of butter and a **sprinkle of nutmeg** for good luck."

"Mmmmmm, that's my favorite, too. Let's see what's under these hills."

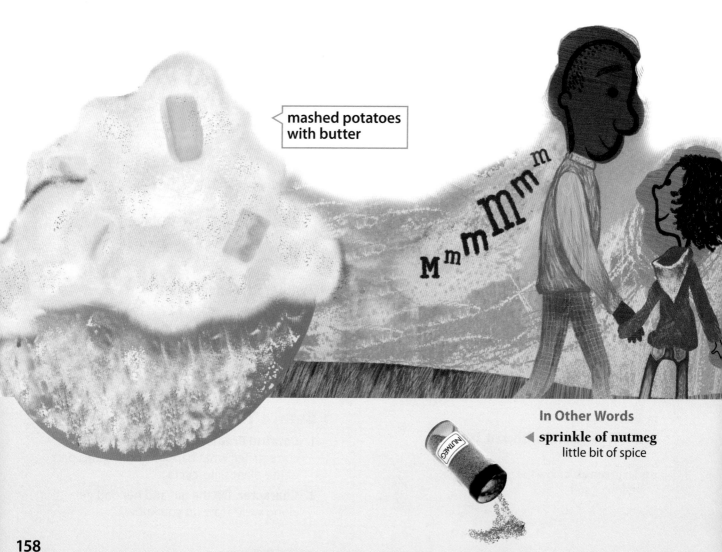

mashed potatoes with butter

In Other Words
◀ **sprinkle of nutmeg**
little bit of spice

Dad gets the garden fork from the **shed** and I carry the big bucket. Dad digs at the first hill. Nothing but dirt. He digs again. More dirt.

"After all that work," I say.

Dad **hands** me the fork. "You try."

I dig deep. I lift the fork and see seven golden shapes. "Potatoes!" I shout.

"Look at those **spuds**," Dad says.

In Other Words

shed little building where we store things

hands gives

spuds potatoes

I bend down and pick up a potato. I rub the dirt off its skin and set it in the bucket.

One potato, two potatoes, three potatoes, four.

Five potatoes, six potatoes, seven potatoes, more.

Each hill has lots of potatoes. Some are small. Some are big. Some have funny faces.

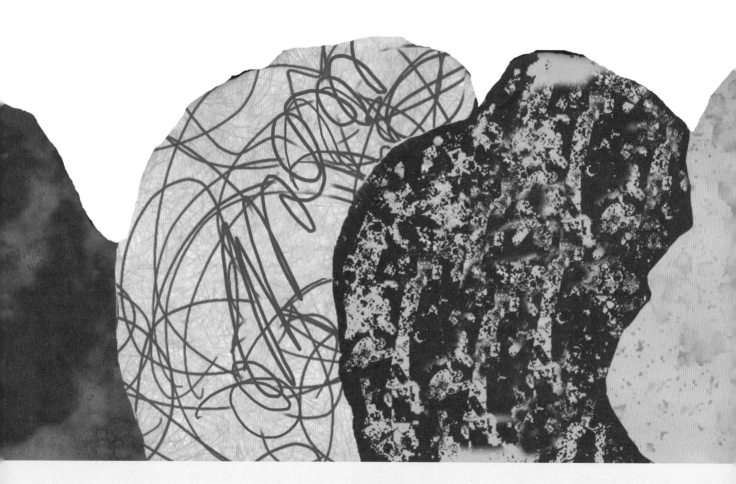

51 potatoes, 52 potatoes, 53 potatoes, 54.

55 potatoes, 56 potatoes, 57 potatoes, more.

I count sixty-seven, and our bucket is overflowing.

"All this from two old potatoes."

"Yes." Dad rubs my head.

"Ready to **dig into** the potatoes you grew?"

"Yeah, I'm hungry." ❖

In Other Words

dig into eat

▶ **Before You Move On**

1. **Confirm Prediction** How many potatoes did you think the plants would **produce**? Did the number surprise you?

2. **Point of View** Who tells the story? How do you know?

John Coy

When John Coy was eight he wrote a poem about an ice chunk! But now he writes about many different subjects.

Once, when Mr. Coy shared a big crop of his potatoes, a friend suggested he write about them. "Normally, when people suggest a topic I should write about, nothing comes of it," says Mr. Coy. "But the next day, I set my other work aside and started writing about potatoes."

How does he eat potatoes? He loves to mash them up with butter and a lot of milk, of course!

Carolyn Fisher drew John Coy using the same style as her drawings in the book. ▶

Writer's Craft 🖊

Find places in the story where John Coy helps you see and feel what is happening. Then write your own sentences. Describe the way your favorite plant looks and feels.

Think and Respond

Talk About It

Key Words	
blossom	produce
characteristic	root
conditions	seed
cycle	soil
depend	sprout
growth	

1. What seems **realistic** about the story? Give two examples.

   The story is realistic because _____ .

2. Imagine you are the dad. **Give information** to the girl about the life **cycle** of a potato plant.

   First, the plant has _____ . Next, _____ . Then, _____ .

3. Think about the potatoes that the girl dug up. What were some of their **characteristics?**

   All the potatoes _____ .
   Some potatoes _____ . Others _____ .

Learn test-taking strategies.
NGReach.com

Write About It

The girl worked with her dad to grow potatoes. What do you think the girl learned about the **growth** of a potato plant? Write two sentences. Use **Key Words** to explain your thinking.

I think the girl learned that _____ .

Sequence

Make a sequence chain to show what happens in "Two Old Potatoes and Me." Notice that some of the events in the sequence influence future events.

Sequence Chain

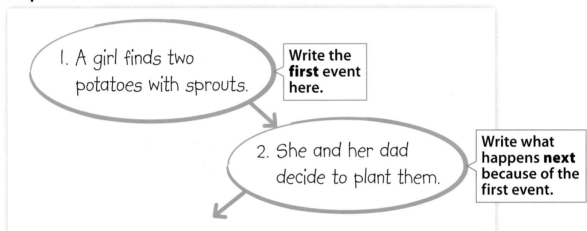

1. A girl finds two potatoes with sprouts.

Write the **first** event here.

2. She and her dad decide to plant them.

Write what happens **next** because of the first event.

Now use your sequence chain as you retell the story to a partner. Use time-order words and **Key Words**. Record your retelling.

First, _____ .
Next, _____ .
Then, _____ .

Fluency ■ Comprehension Coach

Use the Comprehension Coach to practice reading with expression. Rate your reading.

Talk Together

What is amazing about how a potato plant grows? Draw a picture. Use **Key Words** as labels. Share your picture with the class.

Multiple-Meaning Words

Some words have more than one meaning. You can use context, or the words near the word, to figure out the correct meaning.

Roots is a **multiple-meaning word**. Compare these examples.

The plant has long **roots**.
Meaning: the plant part that grows underground

The crowd **roots** for its favorite team.
Meaning: cheers for

Try It Together

Read the sentences. Then answer the questions.

We live in the country. New homes sprout up every year. We sell carrots, bean sprouts, and other vegetables to our new neighbors.

1. **What does sprout mean in the second sentence?**

   A a new young plant

   B to appear suddenly

   C to grow shoots or buds

   D a plant part you can eat

2. **Which word helps you understand the meaning of sprouts in the third sentence?**

   A year

   B homes

   C neighbors

   D vegetables

Connect Across Texts Read poems about potatoes and other amazing foods.

Genre A **haiku** is a poem that has three lines. The first line has five syllables. The second line has seven syllables. The last line has five syllables. How many syllables do you count in each poem?

America's Sproutings

by Pat Mora

Papaya

Chewing your perfume,

We taste your leafy jungle.

Yum! Juicy tropics.

In Other Words
perfume good smell
tropics warm place

▶ **Before You Move On**

1. **Make Inferences** Based on the poem, where do you think papayas grow? Explain.
2. **Describe** Name two **characteristics** of papayas, based on words in the poem.

Potato

Underground magic.

Peel brown bundle, mash, pile high.

Salt and pepper clouds.

In Other Words

Peel brown bundle Take off
the skin

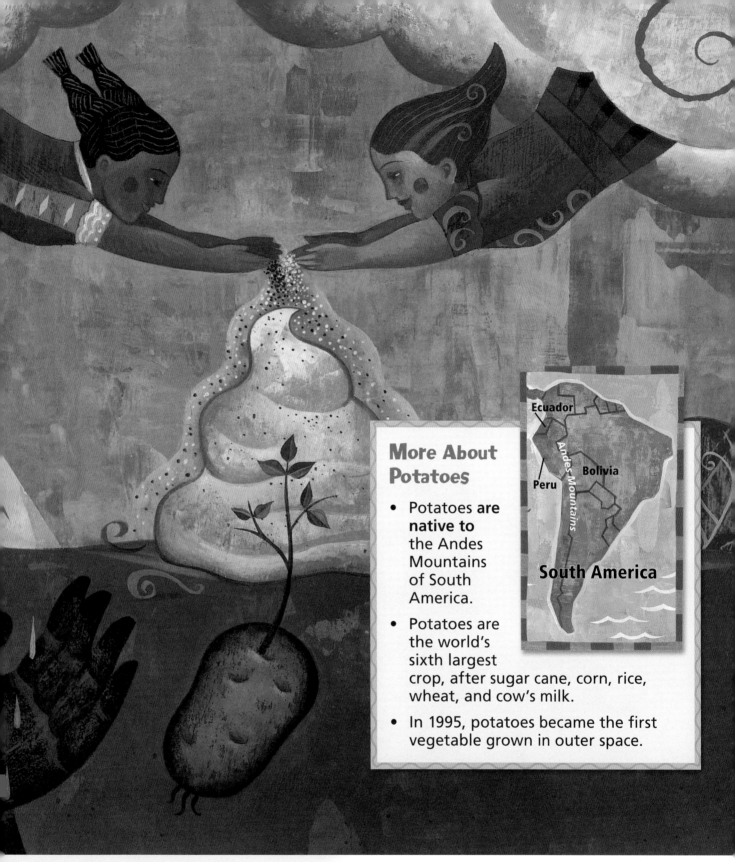

More About Potatoes

- Potatoes **are native to** the Andes Mountains of South America.

- Potatoes are the world's sixth largest crop, after sugar cane, corn, rice, wheat, and cow's milk.

- In 1995, potatoes became the first vegetable grown in outer space.

Ecuador

Andes Mountains

Peru

Bolivia

South America

In Other Words

are native to grow naturally in

▶ **Before You Move On**

1. **Make Inferences** Why are potatoes "underground magic"?

2. **Details** List two facts about potatoes that you learned by reading the information on page 169.

Corn

Leaves sprout silk-snug house.

Smell grits, tortillas, corn bread.

Pass the butter, please.

In Other Words

silk-snug house a soft place for the
corn to grow

grits cereal made of corn

tortillas thin, round pieces of bread
made of corn

More About Corn

- In the 1600s, Native Americans made hills of **soil** where they planted corn **seeds**.

- Pueblo Indians of the southwestern United States planted corn of **various** colors, including blue corn.

- Today, **the starch from** corn is used to make things like crayons and chalk.

In Other Words

various many different

the starch from one part of the

▶ **Before You Move On**

1. **Imagery** What words help you see, smell, and feel things in the poem?

2. **Details** Name two things **produced** from corn that are not food.

Key Words

blossom	produce
characteristic	root
conditions	seed
cycle	soil
depend	sprout
growth	

Compare Genres

A story and a haiku are different forms of writing, or genres. What about the two genres is the same? What about them is different? Work with a partner to complete the Venn diagram.

Venn Diagram

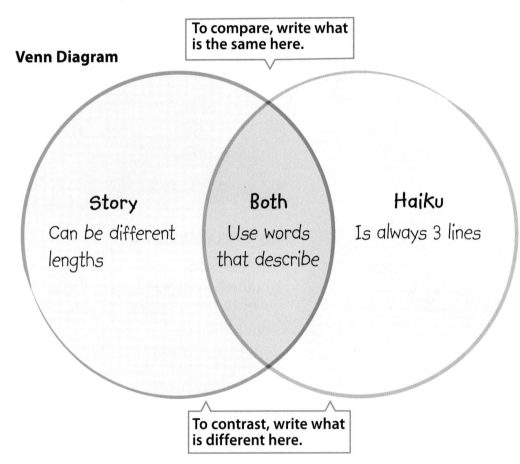

To compare, write what is the same here.

Story
Can be different lengths

Both
Use words that describe

Haiku
Is always 3 lines

To contrast, write what is different here.

Talk Together

What is amazing about how a plant grows? Think about the story, the haiku, and the facts about plants. Use **Key Words** to talk about your ideas.

Plural Nouns

A noun names a person, place, thing, or idea. A **singular noun** shows "one." A **plural noun** shows "more than one."

Grammar Rules Plural Nouns

	singular noun	plural noun
• Add -**s** to most nouns to show more than one.	cycle flower	cycle**s** flower**s**
• Add -**es** to nouns that end in **x**, **ch**, **sh**, **ss**, **z**, and sometimes **o**.	bush tomato	bush**es** tomato**es**
• For most nouns that end in **y**, change the **y** to **i** and then add -**es**. For nouns that end with a vowel and **y**, just add -**s**.	berr**i**y̸ famil**i**y̸ boy day	berri**es** famili**es** boy**s** day**s**

Read Plural Nouns

Read this passage. What plural nouns can you find?

> I found two old potatoes in the back of the cupboard. They were so old, sprouts were growing from their eyes.

Write Plural Nouns

What do you see on pages 168–169? Tell your partner what you see. Then write a sentence for your partner. Use a plural noun.

Define and Explain

Listen to Lily and Nico's dialogue. Then use **Language Frames** to define and explain. Talk about places where plants live.

Dialogue ((MP3))

1.

What does desert mean?

2.

Desert means a place where there is very little rain. Plants in the desert are unusual.

3.

They can store water. For example, this cactus fills its stem with water when rain falls.

4.

They can change to survive. For example, this plant drops its leaves when it is dry.

Key Words

Look at the pictures. Use **Key Words** and other words to talk about ecosystems, or different places where plants live.

Key Words
city
desert
rainforest
vine
weed

city

weed

In cities, plants grow through cracks and in open areas around buildings.

desert

cactus stem

Many plants in deserts have thick stems that can store water.

rainforest

tall tree

vine

broad leaf

In rainforests, broad leaves, tall trees, and climbing vines collect sunlight.

Talk Together

What is amazing about where plants can grow? Talk with a partner. Try to use **Language Frames** from page 174 and **Key Words** to define words and explain your ideas.

Main Idea and Details

When you explain something, start with the most important idea. This is called the **main idea**. Then give **details** to add more information.

Look at the pictures of interesting **desert** plants. Read the text.

This cactus can store water.

This plant drops leaves to survive.

Map and Talk

You can use a main idea and details diagram to organize information. Here's how you make one.

The main idea goes in the top box. Each detail is listed under the top box.

Main Idea and Details Diagram

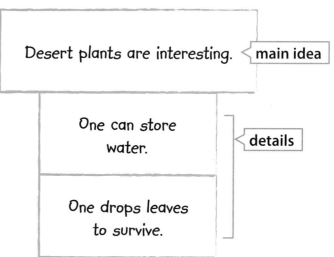

Desert plants are interesting. ◁ main idea

One can store water.

One drops leaves to survive.

◁ details

Talk Together

Look back at page 175. Make a main idea and details diagram with this main idea: **Rainforest plants are unusual**. Tell your partner about your diagram.

More Key Words

Use these words to talk about "A Protected Place" and "Rosie's Reports."

diversity
(du-**vur**-su-tē) *noun*

Diversity means a lot of different people or things.

environment
(in-**vī**-run-munt) *noun*

Your **environment** is the kind of place where you live. This is a hot, dry **environment**.

organism
(**or**-gu-ni-zum) *noun*

insect

leaf

An **organism** is a living thing. This leaf and insect are both **organisms**.

protect
(pru-**tekt**) *verb*

spine

You **protect** something when you keep it safe. Sharp spines **protect** the plant from animals.

unique
(yoo-**nēk**) *adjective*

Unique things are different from other things. The yellow flower is **unique**.

Talk Together

Make a Vocabulary Study Card for each **Key Word**. Write the word on the front. On the back, write the meaning and a sentence. Use the cards to quiz your partner.

protect

to keep safe
A fence protects my garden.

Add words to My Vocabulary Notebook.
NGReach.com

Learn to Make Inferences

Look at the picture. It does not show the complete plant. Look at the details to figure out, or **make an inference** about, what this plant is like.

When you read, you have to **make inferences**, too.

How to Make Inferences

👁	**1.** Look for details in the text.	I read _____ .
💭	**2.** Think about what you already know about the details and the topic.	I know _____ .
🧩	**3.** Put your ideas together. What else can you figure out about the details?	And so _____ .

Read Nico's report, "So Many Plants!" Read the sample inference. Then use **Language Frames** to make inferences. Tell a partner about them.

Report

So Many Plants!
by Nico Lutz

This summer, my family drove to our new home. Along the way, we saw many different **environments**. Our country has such a **diversity** of plants!

In my old home, the ground is covered with sidewalks and streets, but there are still different kinds of plants. People grow plants in pots. Some plants sprout in open areas around buildings.

In another place we saw, there are tall trees all around. Small, leafy plants grow around them. It's a good environment for **organisms** like snails.

Sample Inference

"I read that the ground is covered with sidewalks and streets. I know that cities are like this. And so they must have lived in a city."

The plants are so different in our new home! The cactuses are **unique**. For example, some have round stems. Others have long, thin branches. We have to **protect** ourselves from their sharp spines!

◀ = A good place to make an inference

179

Read a Science Article

Genre

A science article is **nonfiction**. It gives facts about a topic in nature.

Text Features

Look for **photographs with captions**. They help you understand the text better.

photograph

caption

◀ **An okapi eats leaves.**

A Protected Place

by Elizabeth Sengel

A Special Place

The Okapi (ō-**kɑh**-pē) Reserve is an amazing place, full of amazing plants. It is in the northeastern corner of Congo and is part of a tropical **rainforest** called the Ituri Forest. The reserve covers 5,200 square miles of land.

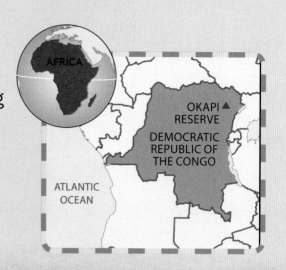

▲ The tops of trees create a cover over the Ituri Forest.

If you flew over the reserve in a plane, all you would see is a thick, green cover. But plant life fills the forest. From top to bottom, it is a tangle of roots, branches, and leaves. The forest **is so dense** that very little sunlight **seeps in**.

In Other Words

is so dense has so many plants

seeps in enters

▶ **Before You Move On**

1. **Main Idea and Details** Give two details about the Okapi Reserve that support the idea that it is an amazing **environment**.
2. **Make Inferences** What would the **environment** of the Okapi Reserve be like?

A Variety of Plants

One amazing thing about the Okapi Reserve is its **diversity** of plants. There are hundreds of **native species of plants** in the reserve. **Vines** **dangle** from trees. The leaves of giant ferns curve like dinosaur tails. Tall trees reach toward the sky and make a roof with their thick leaves.

▼ A strangler fig grows around another tree in the forest.

giant fern

vines

In Other Words

native species of plants different kinds of plants that grow naturally

dangle hang

184

▼ An okapi runs through the woods.

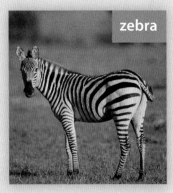
zebra

horse

The Purpose of the Reserve

The Okapi Reserve was created in 1992. The purpose of the reserve is to **protect** the rich diversity of plants and animals.

The reserve's name comes from one of those animals—the okapi. This strange-looking animal has the stripes of a zebra and the neck of a horse. But guess what? **It's related to** the giraffe!

giraffe

In Other Words

It's related to It is in the same animal family as

▶ **Before You Move On**

1. **Use Text Features** How do the photographs help you understand the text?
2. **Make Inferences** Why was it important to create the reserve?

185

A Leafy Home

Many different animals, such as elephants, duikers (**dī**-kurz), and pottos (**pɑh**-tōz), depend on the forest. Some of the animals make their homes in trees.

yellow-backed duiker

potto, or tree bear

▼ **An elephant eats plants in the forest.**

Many animals also rely on plants for food. Remember the okapi? It eats the leaves of plants that grow well in the **dim** light of the forest. It has a long tongue that rips the leaves off the branches. The Okapi Reserve has plenty of leaves for okapis to **munch**!

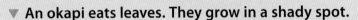
▼ An okapi eats leaves. They grow in a shady spot.

In Other Words
dim low, weak
munch eat

▶ **Before You Move On**

1. **Make Connections** How does the okapi's long tongue help the animal survive?
2. **Details** Name two ways the plants in the reserve meet animals' needs.

A Home for Humans

People make their home in the Okapi Reserve, too. **Mbuti Pygmies** have been living in the **rainforest** for hundreds of years. According to one **botanist**, Mbuti Pygmies are "walking dictionaries of nature." They understand everything about the forest, and they rely on it for food, shelter, and clothing.

▼ A **Mbuti Pygmy** child fishes.

In Other Words

Mbuti Pygmies A group of native people

botanist scientist who studies plants

Mbuti Pygmies travel from place to place to hunt and fish. They don't just catch **game**, though. They also collect insects, seeds, fruit, and honey to eat. They make nets, arrows, and other **necessities** from forest materials like wood, bark, mud, and leaves.

▼ Mbuti Pygmies made these huts from forest materials.

In Other Words
game wild animals to eat
necessities things
    that they need

▶ **Before You Move On**
1. **Make Inferences** Why do you think Pygmies know so much about the **rainforest**?
2. **Details** Name three things that Pygmies do in the forest.

A Brave Botanist

Corneille Ewango (kor-**nā**
ē-**wahn**-gō) is a botanist who
works on the reserve.
He loves the forest and its
plants and animals.

In 1996, something terrible
happened. A war **broke out** in
Congo. Soldiers **invaded the
forest**. They **destroyed** plants
and killed animals.

Many of the workers on the
reserve ran away, but Ewango
wouldn't leave. He knew he
had to save the forest. "I was
afraid," he says, "but I didn't
have a choice."

Soldiers march
during the war. ▶

In Other Words
broke out started
invaded the
forest came into
the forest with force
destroyed ruined

▲ This bridge is important to Ewango. He hid under it once during the war.

Ewango rushed to save what he could. He grabbed computers and buried **data files** in the forest. He packed thousands of **plant samples** in boxes. Friends kept the plants safe.

Ewango hopped on a bicycle and carried other plants into a neighboring country.

Because of Ewango, **unique** and valuable plants were saved. They would continue to grow again after the fighting stopped in 2002.

In Other Words

data files computer files
with information

plant samples
different kinds
of plants

▶ **Before You Move On**

1. **Details** Why did Ewango stay in the **rainforest** during the war?

2. **Make Inferences** How do you know that Ewango is a brave person?

The Future of the Reserve

Today, the Okapi Reserve still faces **threats**. Sometimes people destroy animals' homes. They chop down trees. Yet Ewango and other people work every day to solve these problems.

▼ People sometimes sneak into the Okapi Reserve. They cut down trees.

In Other Words
threats problems

192

Ewango believes that Congo needs more scientists to study its forests. He is working hard to **train a new generation of students**.

He wants young people to understand and protect the Okapi Reserve and other rainforests in Congo. ❖

▲ Ewango

▼ Ewango wants to train young people. He wants to help protect forests in Congo.

In Other Words

train a new generation of students
teach children about plants

▶ **Before You Move On**

1. **Details** Name two problems that the Okapi Reserve has today.

2. **Paraphrase** What does Ewango believe about Congo? How is he helping?

193

Talk About It

1. Give two facts about nature from the **science article**.

   The first fact ____ . The second fact ____ .

2. **Define** the word *reserve* **and explain** the purpose of the Okapi Reserve.

   Reserve means ____ . The purpose of the Okapi Reserve is ____ .

3. How do you think the author of the article feels about the Okapi Reserve **environment**?

   I think the author ____ . I can tell because ____ .

Learn test-taking strategies.
NGReach.com

Write About It

The photographs in the science article help you understand the ideas. Write a caption to explain the photograph on page 181. Use at least one sentence and at least one **Key Word**.

This is ____ .

Main Idea and Details

Make a main idea and details diagram for "A Protected Place."

Main Idea and Details Diagram

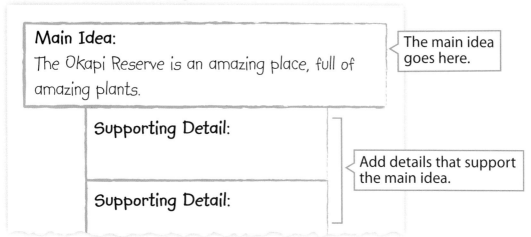

Main Idea:
The Okapi Reserve is an amazing place, full of amazing plants.

> The main idea goes here.

Supporting Detail:

> Add details that support the main idea.

Supporting Detail:

Now use your diagram as you summarize "A Protected Place" for a partner. Use the sentence frames and **Key Words**. Record your summary.

> The main idea is _____.
> A supporting detail is _____.

Fluency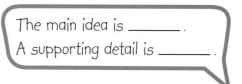

Use the Comprehension Coach to practice reading with phrasing. Rate your reading.

Choose a photograph from "A Protected Place." Use **Key Words** to tell a partner what the photograph shows about an amazing plant.

Suffixes

A **suffix** is a word part. A suffix comes at the end of a word. It changes the word's meaning.

Look at this example. How does the word **weed** change?

The suffix **-y** means "full of."

| weed | + | -y | = | weedy |

Weedy means "full of weeds."

Try It Together

Read each item. Choose the correct answer.

1. **The suffix -less means "without." What does vineless mean?**

   A with vines

   B full of vines

   C without vines

   D the state of vines

2. **The suffix -ness means "state of." What does uniqueness mean?**

   A in a unique way

   B full of unique things

   C without anything unique

   D the state of being unique

Connect Across Texts Read this blog to learn more about the plants of the Okapi Reserve.

Genre A **blog** is a site on the Internet where you can post your thoughts about a topic for others to read.

About Rosie's Reports

http://ngreach.com

Rosie's Reports

MAIN SCREEN | ABOUT THIS BLOG | PICTURES | REGISTER | SIGN IN

About Rosie's Reports

*Rosie Ruf works at the Okapi Reserve. One of her jobs is to take care of several okapis. The okapis are kept in a special **breeding station**. Every day, workers gather fresh leaves for the okapis' food.*

Search All Posts

GO!

BLOG ARCHIVE
November
September
May
February
January

POSTS BY CATEGORY
okapi
Africa

In Other Words

breeding station place where they can have babies

▶ **Before You Move On**

1. **Make Inferences** How does Rosie probably feel about okapis? Why do you think this?

2. **Predict** What do you think this blog will be about? Explain why you think that.

197

MAIN SCREEN | ABOUT THIS BLOG | PICTURES   REGISTER | SIGN IN

Category: Okapi | Date: November 8

Collecting Leaves

It is early in the morning. Baya and Apomau are already preparing their **machetes**. They will walk 45 minutes to reach the place where they will cut the leaves for today. In the afternoon, some of the leaves will be fed to the okapis.

◀ **Apomau and Baya have collected and bundled their leaves. It took them less than three hours.**

It is amazing how well they and the other workers know the forest! They are able to find the right amount of leaves every day.

POSTED BY: Rosie

7 COMMENTS   LINKS TO THIS POST

Search All Posts

GO!

BLOG ARCHIVE
November
September
May
February
January

POSTS BY CATEGORY
okapi
Africa
Okapi Reserve

MOST POPULAR KEYWORDS
protected
rainforest

November						
S	M	T	W	T	F	S
	1	2	3	4	5	6
7	8	9	10	11	12	13
14	15	16	17	18	19	20
21	22	23	24	25	26	27
28	29	30				

<<October

In Other Words
machetes knives

Preparing Leaves

The workers bring the leaves to a special building. The next step is to prepare 1,536 bundles of leaves! These are the leaves that the okapis will eat in the afternoon and the next morning.

▲ A worker gets ready to wrap a bundle of leaves. The bundle will hang in an okapi's pen.

POSTED BY: Rosie

4 COMMENTS   LINKS TO THIS POST

▶ **Before You Move On**

1. **Make Inferences** Why do you think Baya and Apomau know the **rainforest** so well?

2. **Steps in a Process** Tell the steps the workers follow to feed the okapis.

Compare Text Features

A science article and blog postings both have captions. What other text features do they both have? What different text features do they have? Work with a partner to complete the comparison chart.

Comparison Chart

"A Protected Place"	"Rosie's Reports"
Feature: captions **Example:** An okapi runs through the woods.	**Feature:** captions **Example:** A worker gets ready to wrap a bundle of leaves.
	Feature: Date line **Example:** Date: November 8

Talk Together

What is amazing about the plants in the Okapi Reserve? Think about the science article and the blog postings. Use **Key Words** to talk about your ideas.

More Plural Nouns

Count nouns are nouns that you can count. They change in different ways to show the plural.

Noncount nouns are nouns that you cannot count. They have only one form for "one" and "more than one."

Grammar Rules Plural Nouns

Count Nouns		
• Add **-s** or **-es** to make most nouns plural.	tree	▶ tree**s**
	lunch	▶ lunch**es**
• For a few nouns, use special forms to show the plural.	tooth	▶ teeth
	child	▶ children
Noncount Nouns		
• Use the same form to name "one" and "more than one."	corn	▶ corn
	sunshine	▶ sunshine

Read Plural Nouns

Read these sentences based on "A Protected Place." What plural nouns can you find? Can you identify a noncount noun?

> The forest is a tangle of roots and branches. It is so dense that very little sunlight seeps in.

Write Plural Nouns

Make a list of the things you see on pages 192–193.
Compare your list with a partner's.

Write Like a Scientist

Write an Article ✏️

Write an article that explains what you think is so amazing about plants. Add your article to a class science magazine to share with others in your school.

Study a Model

An article includes facts and details about a topic. Read this article that Mariah wrote about plants.

Plants Are Everywhere

by Mariah Ruiz

Plants are amazing because they can grow in so many different places. We know that plants grow in soil, but they pop up in other places, too. Did you know that seeds can sprout in tiny cracks on sidewalks? Some daisies, for example, grow big enough to break the pavement!

Other plants, like seaweed, live completely underwater. There are even plants, like mistletoe, that grow on other plants!

So, the next time you're outside, take a look around. You might see a plant or two growing in the most unusual place!

The **topic sentence** tells the main idea.

Each **fact** or **detail** supports the main idea. The writing is focused.

The **concluding sentence** connects all the ideas. It makes the writing complete.

Prewrite

1. **Choose a Topic** What topic will you write about in your article? Talk with a partner to choose the best one.

Language Frames

Tell Your Ideas

- Plants can _____ . That might be a good topic.

- I know a lot about _____ , so I'll write about that.

- My favorite plant is _____ . I would like to tell more about it.

Respond to Ideas

- I think/do not think that is a good topic because _____ .

- _____ sounds interesting. Tell me more.

- I like that plant, too. I would like to read about _____ .

---

2. **Gather Information** Find all the facts and details you'll need for your article. Do they all tell about the same topic?

3. **Get Organized** Use a main idea and details diagram to help you organize what you'll say.

Main Idea and Details Diagram

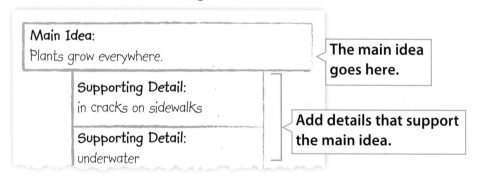

Draft

Use your main idea and details diagram to write your draft.

- Turn your main idea into a topic sentence.

- Turn your details into sentences that tell more about the main idea.

Revise

1. **Read, Retell, Respond** Read your draft aloud to a partner. Your partner listens and retells what your article is about. Next, talk about ways to improve your writing.

<table>
<tr><td colspan="2" align="center">**Language Frames**</td></tr>
<tr><td>**Retell**

• The topic is _____ .
• Most of the facts and details tell about _____ .</td><td>**Make suggestions**

• The detail about _____ does not tell about _____ . Can you take out that detail?
• I like the examples you used to tell about _____ .</td></tr>
</table>

2. **Make Changes** Think about your draft and your partner's suggestions. Then use the Revising Marks on page 573 to mark your changes.

   • Delete details that don't tell about the topic or support the main idea.

   > Did you know that seeds can sprout in tiny cracks on sidewalks? ~~There are many plants near my house~~.

   • Add details or examples that support your main idea and keep your writing focused.

   > Some daisies, for example, grow big enough to break the pavement!
   > Did you know that seeds can sprout in tiny cracks on sidewalks?

Edit and Proofread

Work with a partner to edit and proofread your article. Check the spelling of plural nouns. Use the marks on page 574 to show your changes.

Publish

1. **On Your Own** Make a final copy of your article. Then choose a way to share it with your classmates. You might want to read your article aloud, or you can just retell it from memory.

Presentation Tips	
If you are the speaker...	**If you are the listener...**
Speak slowly and clearly.	Take notes to help you understand and remember.
Provide more details if your listeners do not understand what you thought was amazing.	Make inferences based on what you know.

2. **With a Group** Work with your classmates to put all the articles into a science magazine. Make several copies to share with others in your school. You can post your magazine online, or turn it into a series of Web pages.

Talk Together

In this unit, you found lots of answers to the **Big Question**. Now, use your concept map to discuss the **Big Question** with the class.

Concept Map

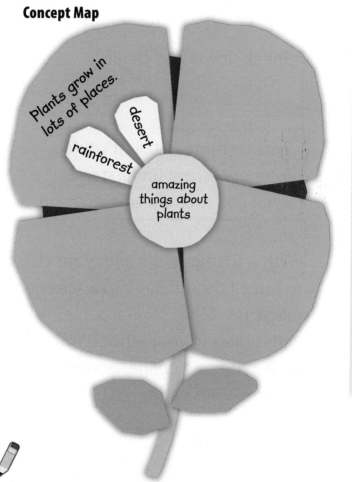

Plants grow in lots of places.

rainforest

desert

amazing things about plants

Write a Journal Entry

Choose one amazing thing about plants from your concept map. Write a journal entry about it.

Share Your Ideas

Choose one of these ways to share your ideas about the **Big Question**.

Write It!

Make a Cartoon

Draw a cartoon about an amazing plant. Write a caption to show what is so amazing about the plant. Explain your cartoon to the class.

This plant eats bugs!

Talk About It!

Talk Show

Choose classmates to talk about each selection in this unit. Each guest on the talk show gives amazing information they have learned about plants. Use formal language.

Do It!

Perform a Skit

Write a skit about people who work with plants. Show why the people think plants are amazing. Decide whether to use formal or informal language. Perform your skit for the class.

Write It!

Plant Poem

Think about your favorite plant. Write a haiku about it. Count the syllables in each line. Then read your poem aloud to a partner.

Let's Work Together

? BIG Question

What's the best way to get things done?

Unit at a Glance
▶ **Language**: Express Needs, Wants, and Feelings; Persuade, Social Studies Words
▶ **Literacy**: Determine Importance
▶ **Content**: Working Together

Unit
4

Share What You Know

Do It!

❶ **Sketch** people doing a job. Put your pictures face down in a pile.

❷ **Take** turns drawing a picture. Begin to pantomime the job.

❸ **Have** classmates join in, one by one, to help pantomime the job. The rest of the class can try to guess the job at any time.

washing a car

Build Background: Watch a video about people working together.
🌐 NGReach.com

Express Needs, Wants, and Feelings

Listen to Noah's song. Then use **Language Frames** to express needs, wants, and feelings of your own.

Song

Everyone Helps

Oh, let's celebrate with a great big cake.
We'll play music on the trumpet and the drum.
But I need some help when I decorate
With flowers and balloons for everyone.

Everyone, everyone,
I want everyone to come.
If we work to help each other
We can celebrate together.
I feel sure that our big party will be fun!

Tune: "Polly Wolly Doodle"

Congratulations, Team!

balloon

trumpet

drum

Key Words

advertisement
buyer
market
money
pay
seller

Key Words

People go to a store or a **market** to buy food, party supplies, and other things they need. Use **Key Words** and other words to talk about the market in the picture.

How much does this cost?

You can **pay** me $3.50.

buyer

money

seller

advertisement

Buy fresh fruit at Joe's Market!

Talk Together

What's the best way to get things you need? Talk with a partner. Use **Key Words**. Then use **Language Frames** from page 210 to express your needs, wants, and feelings about the topic.

211

Theme

A **theme** is the main message you get from a story or a situation. How do you figure out a theme? You use clues from the people, place, and events.

Look at these pictures of Noah's party. Read the text.

An Extra Guest

My sister Marty wants to join our party.

Let's make space for her.

Welcome, Marty!

Thank you! This is fun.

Map and Talk

A theme chart can help you paraphrase a theme, or tell it in your own words. Here's how you make one.

Write details, or clues, in the squares. Use the clues to help you write a theme sentence.

Theme Chart

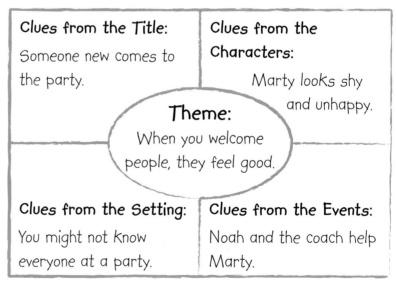

Clues from the Title:
Someone new comes to the party.

Clues from the Characters:
Marty looks shy and unhappy.

Theme:
When you welcome people, they feel good.

Clues from the Setting:
You might not know everyone at a party.

Clues from the Events:
Noah and the coach help Marty.

Talk Together

Tell your partner a story. Your partner makes a theme chart.

More Key Words

Use these words to talk about "Mama Panya's Pancakes" and "Ba's Business."

accomplish
(u-**kom**-plish) *verb*

To **accomplish** means to finish something that you want to do. What did she **accomplish**?

cooperation
(kō-ah-pu-**rā**-shun) *noun*

Cooperation is when people work together. It takes **cooperation** to row the boat quickly.

plenty
(**plen**-tē) *noun*

When you have **plenty** of something, you have a lot of it. The picture shows **plenty** of fruit.

purpose
(**pur**-pus) *noun*

A **purpose** is the reason for doing something. What is the **purpose** of writing a letter?

reward
(ri-**word**) *noun*

A **reward** is a gift or prize for doing something well. He gives the dog a **reward**.

Talk Together

Tell the meaning of a **Key Word** to a partner. Your partner uses the word in a sentence. Switch roles.

Plenty means a lot of something.

I have plenty of friends.

Add words to My Vocabulary Notebook.
NGReach.com

213

Learn to Determine Importance

Look at the picture. Which parts mean the most to you? When you figure out what is important to you, you **determine importance**.

When you read, you **determine what is important to you**, too.

How to Determine Importance

🗨	**1.** Identify what the text is about.	This part is about _____ .
🗨	**2.** Decide on a purpose for reading.	I want to know more about _____ .
👁	**3.** Focus on your purpose. Look for details that tell you what you want to know.	When I read _____ , I learn _____ .

Talk Together

Read the personal narrative. Read the sample determination. Then use **Language Frames** to determine what is important to you. Explain your thinking to a partner.

Personal Narrative

Balloons for Food

Our Little League team is planning a food drive. The **purpose** is to aid the homeless people in our city. We are working in **cooperation** with the **sellers** at the Farmer's **Market**. Many people have already bought food from the sellers to give to the drive. That will help us **accomplish** our goal of feeding the homeless.

"Will the donors get a **reward**?" asked Marty.

"What kind of reward?" asked Coach. "We can't **pay** a lot of **money** for rewards."

"Balloons!" said Marty. "You could order printed balloons that say 'Farmer's Market Food Drive' and give information about it."

Coach agreed. He paid ten dollars for 200 printed balloons. "That should be **plenty**," he said.

On the day of the drive, he asked Marty to hand out the balloons. Marty untied the first balloon, and an entire bunch escaped! A dozen balloons sailed up into the air.

Coach just laughed. "Look at that!" he said, pointing to the bright spots in the sky. "Maybe we'll get more donors this way."

He was right. People found the balloons and brought more food to the drive.

Sample Determination

"This part is about a food drive.

I want to know more about the food drive.

When I read that the team is working with a farmer's market, I learn more about how the food drive will work."

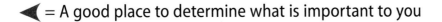

◄ = A good place to determine what is important to you

215

Read a Village Tale

Genre

This story tells about something that could really happen in a village in Kenya. It is **realistic fiction**.

Third-Person Narrator

The person who tells a story is the narrator. A third-person narrator uses the words *he, she,* and *they* to describe the action in the story.

Mama Panya sang as she kicked sand with her bare feet, **dousing** the breakfast fire.

"Adika, hurry up," she called cheerfully. "Today, we go to **market** ."

"Surprise! I'm one step ahead of you, Mama." Adika stood in the doorway, dressed in his finest shirt and cleanest shorts. "I'm ready."

Mama Panya's Pancakes

a village tale from Kenya

by **Mary and Rich Chamberlin**   illustrated by **Julia Cairns**

▶ **Set a Purpose**
Find out what happens when Mama
Panya and her son go to buy food.

Mama Panya sang as she kicked sand with her bare feet, **dousing** the breakfast fire.

"Adika, hurry up," she called cheerfully. "Today, we go to **market**."

"Surprise! I'm one step ahead of you, Mama." Adika stood in the doorway, dressed in his finest shirt and cleanest shorts. "I'm ready."

Now Mama Panya had to hurry.

In Other Words
dousing putting out

After **storing** her pots, gathering her bag and slipping her feet into her sandals, Mama Panya called, "I'm ready too, Adika. Where are you?"

"Here I am, Mama—two steps ahead of you." He sat under the baobab tree, Mama Panya's walking stick in hand.

"Why, yes you are." She **accepted** the stick and led them down the road.

"What will you get at the market, Mama?"

"Oh, a little bit and a little bit more."

In Other Words
storing putting away
accepted took

"Are you making pancakes today, Mama?"

"You are a smart one. I guess I can't surprise you."

"Yay! How many pancakes will you make?"

Mama **fingered** two coins folded in the cloth tied around her waist. "A little bit and a little bit more."

In Other Words
fingered touched

Rounding the corner, they saw Mzee Odolo sitting by the river. *"Habari za asubuhi?"* Mama asked softly, so she wouldn't chase away the fish.

Adika **blurted out**, "We're having pancakes tonight, please come."

"Adika," Mama whispered in his ear.

Mzee Odolo waved back, saying, *"Asante sana*—I'll be there."

In Other Words

Rounding Turning

Habari za asubuhi? (ha-**bar**-ee zah ah-suh-**boo**-ee) What's new this morning? (in Kiswahili)

blurted out said quickly

Asante sana (uh-**sahn**-tay **sahn**-ah) Thank you (in Kiswahili)

Mama **quickened her pace**.

"We had to invite Mzee," Adika said, "he's our oldest friend."

"Hurry up, you're a few steps behind," Mama **replied**.

"Look, Mama, it's Sawandi and Naiman." Adika's friends **tapped long reeds** against the thighs of their cattle, moving them along. "I'll be just a few steps ahead."

"Wait, Adika!" Mama called.

Mama hadn't gone too far before he returned.

"They'd be happy to come," Adika **panted**.

In Other Words
quickened her pace walked faster
replied answered
tapped long reeds softly hit with thin sticks
panted said while he was breathing hard

Mama Panya frowned, thinking about the coins in her wrap.

"Ohhh! How many people will that be?"

"Let's see. Sawandi, Naiman, you and me," Adika counted. "And Mzee Odolo, that's only five."

"**Aiii!** How many pancakes do you think I can make today, son?"

"**I'm one step ahead of you**, Mama. You'll have a little bit and a little bit more. That's enough."

In Other Words

Aiii! Oh no! (in Kiswahili)

I'm one step ahead of you I already thought of that

▶ **Before You Move On**

1. **Make Inferences** How does Mama Panya feel about cooking for everyone? How can you tell?

2. **Point of View** Is the narrator a character in the story? How do you know?

▶ **Predict**

What will happen when Adika sees
more friends at the **market**?

At the market, there were many **buyers** and **sellers**.
Adika saw his friend Gamila at her **plantain** stand. "Mama,
pancakes are her favorite."

"Now, now—don't you . . ." and before she could finish
he ran to greet her.

Mama tried to catch up, arriving just in time to hear,
"You will come, won't you?"

"Of course," Gamila replied.

Mama **shot a stare at Adika** and quickly
grabbed his hand, **whisking** him away.

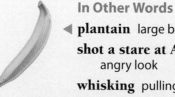

In Other Words
plantain large banana
shot a stare at Adika gave Adika an
    angry look
whisking pulling

224

"Mama, we'll be able to **stretch the flour**."

"**Ai Yi!** How much do you think I can stretch flour, son?"

Adika waved his hand. "Oh, a little bit and a little bit more."

At the **flour stand** Mama said, "Adika, you sit here."

After greeting Bibi and Bwana Zawenna, Mama asked, "What can you give me for my **money**?" She offered a coin to Bibi Zawenna, who **scooped some flour** onto a piece of paper.

In Other Words

stretch the flour make many pancakes from a little flour

Ai Yi! Oh no! (in Kiswahili)

flour stand place to buy flour

scooped some flour took some flour out of a box and poured it

Adika **popped up**. "Mama's making pancakes today. Can you come?"

"Oh, how wonderful! I think we can give a little more for that coin." Bwana Zawenna put more flour on the paper, then tied it up with string. "We'll see you later."

Mama **tucked** the package into her bag. "**Ai-Yi-Yi!** You and I will be lucky to share half a pancake."

"But Mama, we have a little bit and a little bit more."

In Other Words
popped up jumped up to talk
tucked put
Ai-Yi-Yi! On no! (in Kiswahili)

"Come Adika. We may have just enough left for a small chili pepper."

"Leave it to me, Mama. I'll get a good one."

"No Adika!" she cried out, but he ran ahead to Rafiki Kaya's spice table.

Mama got there just in time to hear, "Mama's making pancakes tonight, can you come?"

"I'd love to!" Kaya exclaimed. She took Mama's coin and **replaced it with the plumpest pepper**. "Thanks for inviting me."

Mama just **sighed**.

In Other Words

replaced it with the plumpest pepper
  gave Mama the biggest pepper

sighed let out a short breath

▶ **Before You Move On**

1. **Confirm Prediction** What did Adika do at the **market**? Was your prediction right?

2. **Determine Importance** Which details about what happened at the **market** are important? Why?

227

▶ **Predict**
Will Mama Panya have enough
food to feed all the people?

They **headed** home.

"How many people did we invite for pancakes tonight?"

Adika, skipping two steps ahead, sang his reply, "All of our friends, Mama."

Mama piled small twigs and sticks into the firepit.

Adika ran to **fetch a pail** of water.

Mama crushed the chili pepper in a pot, while Adika added some water. She stirred in all the flour. Mama poured a **dollop** into the oiled pan on the fire.

In Other Words
headed went
fetch a pail get a bucket
dollop small amount

Sawandi and Naiman were the first to arrive. They carried two **gourds** filled with milk and a small bucket of butter. "Mama Panya, we have extra from our cattle."

Mzee Odolo came soon after. "**Old-man river has given us three fish today.**"

Gamila arrived with a bunch of bananas. "They go very well with pancakes."

Bibi and Bwana Zawenna brought a package of flour and handed it to Adika. "**Store this away** for later."

◄ **gourd**

In Other Words

gourds containers

Old-man river has given us three fish today.
    I caught three fish in the river today.

Store this away Keep this

229

When Rafiki Kaya arrived, she brought handfuls of salt and **cardamom spice**, along with **her thumb piano**.

And the feast began, as they sat under the baobab tree to eat Mama Panya's pancakes.

Afterward, Kaya played the thumb piano and Mzee Odolo sang **slightly off key**.

Adika said with a gleam in his eyes, "I know you will make pancakes again soon, Mama."

She smiled. "Yes, Adika, you're one step ahead of me." ❖

In Other Words

cardamom spice seeds for flavor

her thumb piano a small musical instrument ▶

slightly off key badly

▶ **Before You Move On**

1. **Confirm Prediction** Was your prediction about the food correct? Explain.
2. **Theme** What is the theme of the story? Give details from the story to support your ideas.

Julia Cairns

Julia Cairns was born in Oxfordshire, England, and traveled to Africa after college. The beauty of Botswana's landscape and its joyful people inspired her to paint.

Cairns recently returned to Botswana to visit the friends who inspired her art. "The skies are still vast, with rich sunsets . . . just as I remembered it," says Cairns.

Cairns' artwork appears on many products, including calendars, quilts, and postage stamps. But, Cairns takes the greatest pride in teaching children about life in Africa through her book illustrations.

▲ **Julia Cairns designed postage stamps for Botswana.**

Writer's Craft ✏️

The authors use dialogue to help you understand Adika and Mama Panya. Imagine that Adika wants to have another party. What would he say to Mama Panya? Write his dialogue. Use words that sound like something Adika would say.

AWARD WINNER

231

Talk About It

1. Compare this story to another **realistic** story you know. How are they the same?

   They are the same because _____ .

2. Adika invites many people to have pancakes. Pretend you are Mama Panya. **Express needs**, **wants**, **and feelings** about the situation.

   I need _____ . I want _____ . I feel _____ .

3. Adika and his mother say "a little bit and a little bit more." What do they mean? What happens to show they are right?

   When they say "a little bit and a little bit more," they mean _____ . This is shown in the story when _____ .

Learn test-taking strategies.
NGReach.com

Write About It

Why do you think there was so much **cooperation** at the feast? Write two sentences to explain why the guests brought things to share. Use **Key Words** to help explain your response.

The guests brought things because _____ .
They _____ .

Theme

Make a theme chart for "Mama Panya's Pancakes." Locate details, or clues, in different parts of the story. Then use the clues to help you write, or paraphrase, a theme sentence.

Theme Chart

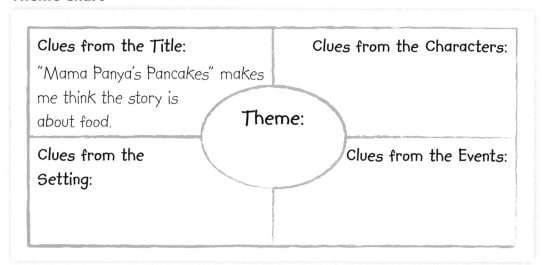

Clues from the Title:
"Mama Panya's Pancakes" makes me think the story is about food.

Clues from the Characters:

Theme:

Clues from the Setting:

Clues from the Events:

Work with a partner. Discuss your theme sentence and the details that support it. Use the sentence frames and **Key Words**. Record your discussion.

This clue _____ .
This clue _____ .
So the theme is: _____ .

Fluency Comprehension Coach

Use the Comprehension Coach to practice reading with intonation. Rate your reading.

Talk Together

What's the best way to plan a party? Write what Adika would say. Use at least one **Key Word**. Read Adika's words to a partner.

Prefixes

A **prefix** is a word part that comes at the beginning of a word. A prefix changes the meaning of the word.

How does the word **market** change? Look at this example.

The prefix **super-** means "larger than" or "superior to."

super- + market = supermarket

A **supermarket** is a very large market.

Try It Together

Read the sentences. Then answer the questions.

> We did not have to wait in line at the movie. We had <u>prepurchased</u> our tickets. When we got popcorn, my friend paid for me. "I'll <u>repay</u> you tomorrow," I said.

1. **The prefix pre- means "before" or "in front of." What does prepurchased mean?**

   A purchased a lot

   B purchased after

   C purchased before

   D purchased quickly

2. **The prefix re- means "back" or "again." What does repay mean?**

   A pay back

   B pay after

   C pay more

   D pay before

Connect Across Texts Read to find out more about how working together can have good results.

Genre This story tells about events that could really happen. It is **realistic fiction**.

Ba's Business

*written and illustrated by **Grace Lin***

Ba was selling *daan taht* at the **street fair**. Hannah and Rose knew that their father's sweet egg tarts were delicious, but no one stopped at the **booth**.

"Business is very bad today," Ba sighed and shook his head sadly.

In Other Words
Ba Dad (in Chinese)
street fair outdoor **market**
booth table where they sold food

▶ **Before You Move On**

1. **Point of View** What words tell you this story has a third-person narrator?
2. **Clarify** What does *daan taht* mean? What clues help you understand the meaning?

235

"Maybe we can make it better," Hannah whispered to Rose.

So Hannah made a large sign and Rose **offered free samples**.

People lined up to try the small pieces of *daan taht*.

"This is delicious!" everyone said. "I have to buy some for my family!"

FREE Samples daan taht

In Other Words
offered free samples gave people free pieces of *daan taht* to try

By the end of the day, Ba had sold **every last** *daan taht*.

"Business was very good today!" Hannah and Rose said to Ba.

Ba nodded and **grinned** at his daughters.

"With your help," he said, as he put an arm around each girl, "our business will be good every day." ❖

In Other Words

every last all of the
grinned smiled

▶ **Before You Move On**

1. **Determine Importance** Look back at the text. What part of the story is most important to you? Why?

2. **Theme** What is the theme of the story? Use details from the text to support your ideas.

Compare Characters

Key Words

accomplish	pay
advertisement	plenty
buyer	purpose
cooperation	reward
market	seller
money	

In the stories, both Mama Panya and Ba change. What are the characters like when the stories begin? How do they act at the end? Make a comparison chart with a partner.

Comparison Chart

	Beginning of Story	End of Story	Why does the character change?
Mama Panya	She is worried about having enough food.		
Ba			

Now use your chart to describe the interactions of the characters, or how they act with one another. What does Mama Panya learn from her guests? How do Ba and his daughters act? What is their relationship?

Talk Together

What is the best way to have a meal together or to sell food? Look back at the selections. Use **Key Words** to talk about your ideas.

Grammar and Spelling

Skills Trace: ▶ Present-Tense Action Verbs
▶ Present-Tense Verbs: *am, is, are*
⏵ **Present-Tense Action Verbs; Agreement**

Present-Tense Action Verbs

A **present-tense action verb** tells about an action that is happening now. The verb must agree with the subject.

Grammar Rules Present-Tense Action Verbs

• Use **-s** at the end of an action verb if the subject is **he**, **she**, or **it**.	Adika **waves** to his friend. He **waves** to his friend. Mama **buys** some flour. She **buys** some flour. The fire **crackles** under the pan. It **crackles** under the pan.
• Do not use **-s** for **I**, **you**, **we**, or **they**.	I **cook** with my dad. We **wash** the dishes together.

Read Present-Tense Action Verbs

Read these sentences about Mama Panya and Adika. Identify three action verbs. Spell the verbs. Name the subjects.

> One morning Mama grabs her bag. She calls to Adika. They walk to the market.

Write Present-Tense Action Verbs

Write two sentences about the characters. Use present-tense action verbs. Make sure the verbs agree with the subjects. Read your sentences to a partner.

Persuade

Listen to Clara's chant. Then use **Language Frames** to persuade classmates about an idea you have.

A Healthy Idea

Chant

We must eat our vegetables—
Three vegetables a day.
So we should grow a garden here.
Let's do it right away!

We could plant this plot of dirt
With vegetables and herbs.
All those vitamins and minerals
Will make us feel superb!

You should plant a garden, too.
It's a healthy thing to do.

Social Studies Vocabulary

Key Words

agriculture

crop

farmer

field

harvest

plow

Key Words

Look at the pictures. Use **Key Words** and other words to talk about **agriculture**.

Farmers plow the land.

They plant seeds in their **fields**.

They water the plants.

They **harvest** their **crops**.

Talk Together

What's the best way to do the work on a farm? Use **Language Frames** from page 240 and **Key Words**. Try to persuade your partner to agree with you.

Opinion and Evidence

When you give an **opinion**, you tell what you believe about something. You might say:

- In my opinion, _____ .
- I think _____ .

Read Clara's opinion and supporting reasons, or **evidence**.

Map and Talk

You can use an opinion chart to record an opinion and the evidence that supports it. To make one, write the opinion in the top box. List each piece of evidence under the top box.

Opinion Chart

> **Opinion:**
> I think we should plant our own vegetables.

> **Evidence:**
> Our vegetables will taste fresher.

> **Evidence:**
> They will cost less money.

> **Evidence:**
> Gardening is good exercise.

Talk Together

Tell your partner an opinion of your own. Give supporting reasons. Your partner makes an opinion chart.

More Key Words

Use these words to talk about "A Better Way" and "The Ant and the Grasshopper."

alternative
(awl-**tur**-nu-tiv) *noun*

An **alternative** is another choice. An apple is a healthy **alternative** to candy.

conservation
(kon-sur-**vā**-shun) *noun*

Conservation means the opposite of waste. **Conservation** of water is important.

future
(**fyū**-chur) *noun*

The **future** is what will happen tomorrow or sometime after that. My birthday is in the **future**.

method
(**me**-thud) *noun*

A **method** is a way of doing something. Is using your fingers to count a good **method**?

sustain
(su-**stān**) *verb*

To **sustain** means to keep something or someone alive or in existence.

Talk Together

Write a sentence for each **Key Word**. Use context clues. Put a blank for the **Key Word**. A partner fills in the word.

> We give the plants food to _____ them.

Add words to My Vocabulary Notebook.
⬤ NGReach.com

Learn to Determine Importance

Look at the picture. What does it show? Determine which parts are important. Then think of a sentence or two to briefly tell, or **summarize**, what the picture shows.

Basil

Peppermint

When you read, you can **summarize**, too.

How to Summarize

💭	**1.** Identify the topic.	This part is about _____ .
✏️	**2.** Take notes as you read. Jot down important details.	I should remember _____ .
💬	**3.** Use your notes to retell the important ideas in your own words.	This part _____ .

Read the speech. Identify what Clara wants the reader to do. Then read the sample summary. Use **Language Frames** to summarize parts of the text.

Persuasive Speech

Window Dressing

This week, my mom and I planted two herb boxes outside our kitchen windows. I think everyone should have herb boxes. They have so many benefits. Today, I'm going to tell you what some of those benefits are.

First, herb boxes are tiny gardens. They are easy to plant and to **sustain**. All you need is a container full of planting soil, seedlings, sunlight, and water. You don't need much water either. These tiny gardens are great for water **conservation**.

Also, fresh herbs are great for cooking. Mom's spaghetti topped with basil sauce is the best! Freshly grown herbs give cooks a wonderful **alternative**. They are always handy. Sure, you can buy herbs in a bottle. But these are never as fresh as the herbs you grow yourself. It's the best **method**.

Finally, herb gardens smell wonderful! Sweet, sharp smells float on the air. Herb gardens look pretty, too. Imagine all those tiny green leaves outside your window.

As I prepared this speech, I hoped that I could persuade you to plant herbs. I really hope that each of you has your own herb garden in the **future**.

Sample Summary

"This part is about planting an herb garden. I should remember the things you need. This part says that you just need soil, seedlings, sunlight, and a little water for an herb garden."

◀ = A good place to summarize

245

Read a Persuasive Article

Genres

A **persuasive article** states an opinion about an issue and gives evidence to support it.

Text Features

Text is divided into parts called **sections**. A **section heading** tells what a section is about.

section heading

A New Solution

section

Paola Segura and Cid Simões, who live in Brazil, have a different solution. They agree that we need to help save trees. But they believe that we need to help people, too. They think that the way to help the Earth and the farmers is to use a way of farming. It is called "sustainable agriculture."

A Better Way

by **Juan Quintana**

Comprehension Coach

▶ **Set a Purpose**
Learn about a **method** of farming
that helps both the land and people.

Losing Trees

Every year, many **acres** of Earth's precious forests are cut down.
Sometimes people cut down the forest for wood. Other times,
they cut it down to make room for **cattle** or large farms. Often,
poor **farmers** burn a small area of forest to **clear it of** trees. In
the cleared area, they plant **crops** to feed their families. This is
called **slash**-and-burn **agriculture** .

Slash-and-Burn Agriculture

1. Farmers cut down trees.

2. Farmers burn the dry trees to clear the land.

3. Farmers plant crops. When the land wears out, they clear new land.

In Other Words
acres large areas
cattle cows
clear it of get rid of the
slash cut

For all of these reasons, forests have been disappearing. Some people blame humans. They think farming is the problem. To them, the solution is clear. People should stay out of the forest. **Farming must be limited!**

▼ crops planted in a forest

▶ **Before You Move On**

1. **Summarize** In your own words, retell the important ideas in this section.

2. **Steps in a Process** What is the second step in slash-and-burn **agriculture**? Point to where you found the information.

A New Solution

Paola Segura and Cid Simões, who live in Brazil, have a different solution. They agree that we need to help save trees. But they believe that we need to help people, too. They think that the way to help the Earth and the farmers is to use a way of farming. It is called "sustainable agriculture."

BRAZIL

SOUTH AMERICA

▲ Segura and Simões were named "Emerging Explorers" by the National Geographic Society. The Society wanted to thank them for their work.

Segura and Simões met in Costa Rica at Earth University. There they studied sustainable agriculture. They believe that farmers can earn money from a small piece of land. They can live there and **raise** their families. They can have healthy land and a community that **lasts**.

Using sustainable agriculture, farmers use the same small piece of land over and over again to grow crops. That way they don't have to find new land and cut down more forests.

Simões and Segura check plants in a greenhouse. ▶

In Other Words
raise take care of
lasts stays together for a long time

▶ **Before You Move On**

1. **Use Text Features** Does the heading on page 250 give you a good idea of what this section is about? Explain.

2. **Summarize** Tell a partner the most important ideas on this page.

Helping Farmers

Today, Segura and Simões teach farmers about crops that grow well in the forest. Fruit trees and flowers can provide a good **income**. Fruit trees don't have to be replanted every year. Their deep roots help keep water and healthy nutrients in the soil. Some flowers, such as orchids, grow on less land than other crops. Farmers can sell their flowers to markets around the world.

People like to buy beautiful flowers. These are orchids. ▶

▲ Inside the fruit of a cocoa tree are seeds. The seeds can be sold to make chocolate.

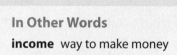

In Other Words
income way to make money

Branching Out

To make a difference, many farmers need to grow crops this way. Segura and Simões use a special plan to teach more farmers. It is called the 5 x 5 System. First, they teach one family how to grow crops that don't ruin the land. Then that family teaches five new families what they learned. Each new family teaches five more families. Think of all the land that could be saved in the **future**!

5 x 5 System

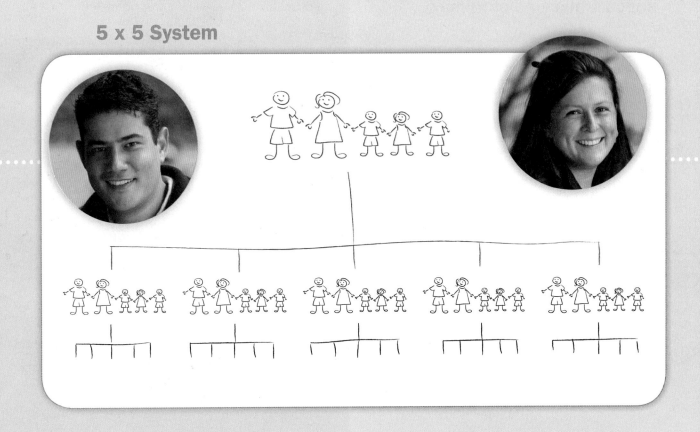

▶ **Before You Move On**

1. **Details** What are two types of sustainable crops for a forest?

2. **Summarize** Explain briefly in your own words how the 5 x 5 System works.

Let's Help Farmers Save Land!

Sustainable agriculture is good for the farmer. It is also good for the land. Here are three reasons why you should **support** this kind of farming.

First, sustainable agriculture lets farmers grow crops on the same land year after year. This is much better than slash-and-burn agriculture. When farmers stay on the same land, they build strong communities.

Palm hearts like these can grow on the same tree year after year. ▶

In Other Words
support help

Soybeans are a
high-value crop. ▶

▲ Orchids grow naturally in the forest.

Secondly, sustainable agriculture is better for the forest. Farmers don't need to clear new land every year. Instead, they can grow **high-value crops**. That way, they can make money from a small amount of land. Some crops grow right in the forest. Farmers don't have to clear any land at all!

In Other Words

high-value crops crops that are grown easily that people will always buy

▶ **Before You Move On**

1. **Opinion/Evidence** What is the author's opinion about slash-and-burn **agriculture**? How do you know?
2. **Use Text Features** Look at the photos. Name two plants that help save land.

Finally, sustainable agriculture **keeps farmers farming**. Every year, many poor farmers leave the land. They move to the city. This causes problems, such as **unemployment**. It also leaves the land without people to care for it.

▲ **If they can't farm, some farmers have to move to the city to find work.**

To save forests and help farmers, we must support people like Paola Segura and Cid Simões. We must be part of the sustainable way of farming. What can you do to help?

◀ **unshelled Brazil nuts**

▲ **Brazil nuts can be a sustainable crop .**

▶ **Before You Move On**

1. **Author's Purpose** What is the author's purpose for writing the article? How do you know?

2. **Cause and Effect** According to the text, what can happen when farmers are not able to keep farming?

Key Words

agriculture	future
alternative	harvest
conservation	method
crop	plow
farmer	sustain
field	

Talk About It

1. Do you think this was a strong **persuasive article**? Give two reasons to support your opinion.

   It was/was not strong because _____ .

2. Imagine you are a **farmer**. What is the best farming **method**? **Persuade** another farmer. Use evidence from the article.

   The best method is _____ because _____ .

3. What kind of people are Paola Segura and Cid Simões? Tell about their personalities and ideas.

   Segura and Simões are _____ . They _____ .

Learn test-taking strategies.
NGReach.com

Write About It

Segura and Simões teach farmers about an **alternative** farming method. What are some benefits of this kind of farming to the whole community? Write two sentences. Use **Key Words** to explain your ideas.

One benefit is _____ .
Another benefit is _____ .

258

Opinion and Evidence

Make an opinion chart for pages 254–257 in "A Better Way."
Identify what the author is trying to persuade people to think or
do. List the supporting reasons, or evidence.

Opinion Chart

Opinion: Sustainable agriculture is good for the
farmer and good for the land.

Evidence: It lets farmers grow crops
on the same land year after year.

Now use your opinion chart to explain
the author's opinion and evidence to a
partner. Use the sentence frames and
Key Words. Record your explanation.

The author thinks _____ .
One piece of evidence is _____ .
Another reason is _____ .

Fluency 🖱 Comprehension Coach

Use the Comprehension Coach to practice phrasing as you read.
Rate your reading.

Talk Together

What's the best way to grow **crops**? Give a persuasive talk to
a group of classmates. State your opinion and give at least two
reasons to support it. Use **Key Words**.

259

Classify Words

You can group, or **classify**, words that tell about the same topic. This gives you a deeper understanding of the topic.

Look at this example. How does classifying help you understand the topic better?

Word Web

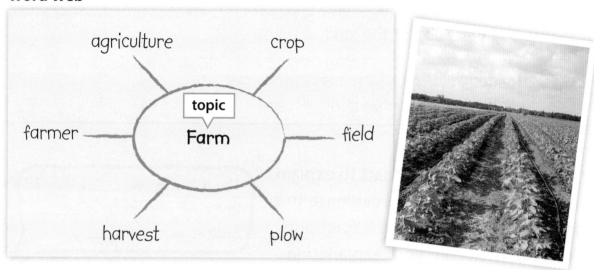

Try It Together

Read each item. Choose the correct answer.

1. **Which word does NOT belong in a group of words for the topic agriculture?**

   A land

   B seed

   C plant

   D ocean

2. **For the topic crop, add a word to this group of words: beans, nuts, _____ .**

   A fire

   B markets

   C potatoes

   D community

The Ant and the Grasshopper

an Aesop fable

retold by **Shirleyann Costigan**
illustrated by **Pablo Bernasconi**

fiddle

One sunny day, a **merry** grasshopper was dancing to his fiddle. "**Watch your step!**" came a voice at his feet. It was an ant carrying **an enormous kernel** of corn.

◀ corn

▲ kernel

In Other Words

merry happy

"Watch your step!" "Be careful where you walk!"

an enormous kernel a big piece

▶ **Before You Move On**

1. **Ask Questions** What do you want to find out as you read? If you don't understand something, what will you do?

2. **Character** What is the grasshopper like? How do you know?

261

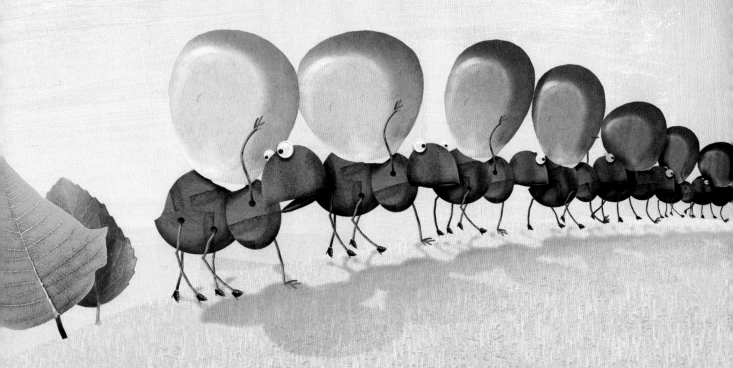

"Come dance with me!" **urged** the grasshopper.

"No time, no time," the ant answered without stopping. "I must gather food for winter. Why aren't you gathering food? It's a bad idea to wait until it snows."

"**Nonsense**," said the grasshopper. "Winter is a long time away."

"**Suit yourself**," said the ant, and she **staggered forward** under her heavy load.

In Other Words

urged said

Nonsense That's silly

Suit yourself Do what you want

staggered forward walked with difficulty

▶ **Before You Move On**

1. **Summarize** Reread this page. Tell the ideas in your own words.
2. **Character** How do you think the ant and the grasshopper would describe each other? Explain.

Soon winter came, and snow covered the land. Not a kernel of food could be found. "Oh!" **lamented** the grasshopper. "I'm so hungry I **must surely** die!"

"Hey, Grasshopper!" cried a voice at his feet. It was the same ant. She was carrying another kernel of corn.

"I warned you this day would come," said the ant.

"Yes, you did," **admitted** the grasshopper sadly. "And if I live to see another year, I will **heed your warning**."

"You'll live," said the ant, and she dropped the kernel in the snow. The grasshopper gratefully picked it up and began to eat.

And ever after Grasshopper remembered the tiny ant's lesson, and was never hungry again.

Moral: *When someone tells you to save for the future, listen.*

In Other Words
admitted said
heed your warning listen to you
And ever after From then on

▶ **Before You Move On**

1. **Character** How does Ant help Grasshopper? How does Grasshopper change?

2. **Theme** Use your own words to tell the fable's moral, or lesson. Is the story a good example of the lesson? How?

Compare Purposes

An author has a reason, or purpose, for writing. An author might write to:

- inform
- express feelings
- entertain
- persuade

What is the author's purpose in each selection? Make a comparison chart with a partner. Write the topic of each selection. Then locate the text in each selection that helps you understand the author's purpose. List the purpose. Can you write more than one purpose for each author?

Comparison Chart

Title: "A Better Way" by Juan Quintana	Topic: sustainable agriculture	Author's Purpose:
Title: "The Ant and the Grasshopper" by Shirleyann Costigan	Topic:	Author's Purpose:

Discuss the chart together. Do the authors share any purposes? Which purposes are different?

Talk Together

What's the best way to have enough land or food in the **future**? Think about the article and the fable. Use **Key Words** to talk about your opinions.

Grammar

Skills Trace:
- ▶ Modals: *can, could, should*
- ▶ Modals: *may, must*
- ▶ Forms of *be, have*; Subject-Verb Agreement

Forms of *be, have*

The verbs *be* and *have* have irregular forms. The subject and verb must agree. Look at the present-tense forms.

Grammar Rules Forms of *be/have*

	be	**have**
• Use for **I**:	*am*	*have*
• Use for **you**:	*are*	*have*
• Use for **he**, **she**, and **it**:	*is*	*has*
• Use for **we**:	*are*	*have*
• Use for **they**:	*are*	*have*

Read Forms of *be/have*

Read this passage based on "A Better Way." Find present-tense forms of *be* and *have*. Identify the subjects.

> A farmer has a small piece of land. He practices sustainable agriculture. It is a good farming method.

Write Forms of *be/have*

Choose two pictures on pages 250–251. Write a sentence for each picture. Use a present-tense form of *be or have*. Read your sentences to a partner.

Write as a Citizen

Write a Persuasive Essay ✏️

Write an essay about the best way to do something at school or in your neighborhood. You can present your opinion as a speech, then share it in a book or blog.

Study a Model

In a persuasive essay, you state your opinion and then give evidence to support it.

Plant a Garden!

by Nick Wojtek

What's the best thing to do with an empty lot? In my opinion, you should make a neighborhood garden!

A neighborhood garden is a great idea for many reasons. First, it's a chance for neighbors to get to know each other.

Second, the garden gives people of all ages something to do. A garden always needs watering and weeding. Even little kids can help with that!

Finally, the garden is something everyone can enjoy. Flowers bloom all summer long. If you plant vegetables, you can eat them as they ripen.

So, if there's an empty lot in your neighborhood, plant a garden! You'll be happy that you did.

The first paragraph includes the writer's **opinion**.

Evidence supports the opinion and develops the writer's ideas. The ideas are worthwhile and interesting.

The **end** restates the opinion. The writing feels complete.

Prewrite

1. **Choose a Topic** What do you want to persuade people to do? Talk with a partner to choose the best topic.

Language Frames	
Tell Your Ideas	**Respond to Ideas**
I think the best way to _____ .	Why do you think _____ is the best way?
I think people should _____ .	I agree/disagree because _____ .
I really believe _____ .	Let me see. You're saying _____ .

2. **Gather Information** What evidence, or reasons, can you give to support your opinion? What details or examples might help?

3. **Get Organized** Use an opinion chart to organize your ideas.

Opinion Chart

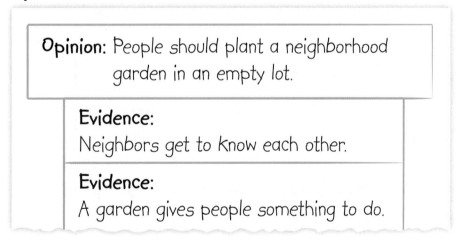

Opinion: People should plant a neighborhood garden in an empty lot.

Evidence:
Neighbors get to know each other.

Evidence:
A garden gives people something to do.

Draft

Use your opinion chart to help you write your draft.

- State your opinion in the first paragraph.

- Put each piece of evidence in a new paragraph.

- Explain your reasons with details and examples.

Revise

1. **Read, Retell, Respond** Read your draft aloud to a partner. Your partner listens and retells your opinion and evidence. Next, talk about ways to improve your writing.

Language Frames	
Retell	**Make Suggestions**
Your opinion is _____ . The reasons you give are _____ .	I think you should state your opinion _____ . Can you give a detail or example to help support _____ ?

2. **Make Changes** Think about your draft and your partner's suggestions. Then use the Revising Marks on page 573 to mark your changes.

   - Make sure you include your opinion in the first paragraph.

   > What's the best thing to do with an empty lot?
   > ~~Neighborhood gardens are nice.~~ ⋀ In my opinion, you should make a neighborhood garden!

   - Do you develop your ideas with important details and examples? If not, add text.

   > Second, the garden gives people of all ages something to do. ~~Gardens take a lot of work.~~ ⋀ A garden always needs watering and weeding.

Edit and Proofread

Work with a partner to edit and proofread your persuasive essay. Pay special attention to subject-verb agreement. Use the marks on page 574 to show your changes.

Publish

Use the marks on page 574

1. **On Your Own** Make a final copy of your persuasive essay. Present it as a speech to your classmates or to younger students. Ask them to share their responses when you are done.

Presentation Tips	
If you are the speaker…	**If you are the listener…**
Remember, you are persuading others. Keep your tone firm and confident.	Listen attentively for the speaker's opinion. Make sure you understand what it is.
Make eye contact to make sure your audience is listening.	Listen for the reasons and details the speaker uses to support his or her opinion.

2. **With a Group** Share your advice with others. Collect all the essays. Bind them into a book, and think of a good title for it. You could also start a weekly advice blog.

What's the best way to get things done?

In this unit, you found lots of answers to the **Big Question**. Now, use your concept map to discuss the **Big Question** with the class.

Concept Map

work together

What's the best way to get things done?

Write a Description

Choose one of the ways on your concept map. Write a description of people using that method to get something done.

Share Your Ideas

Choose one of these ways to share your ideas about the **Big Question**.

Write It!

Write a Skit

Write a skit with a partner. Tell about a great way to protect trees or another part of nature. Decide whether to use formal or informal language. Perform your skit for the class.

Talk About It!

Be a Reporter

Have a partner pretend to be a character or person from the unit. Think of something you want to do, such as plant a vegetable garden. Use formal language to interview your partner about the best way to do this. Switch roles.

Do It!

Do a Chore Together

Think of a classroom chore, such as washing desk tops. Have a group discussion to figure out the best way to do the chore. Ask questions and make comments. Then do the job!

Write It!

Write a Letter

Pretend that you have visited a city that recycles. Write a letter to a leader in your city. Tell how you think your community should recycle.

April 5, 20____

Dear Mr. Reyes,

I have just visited a city that recycles everything! I think our city should do that, too.

273

Mysteries of Matter

? BIG Question

What causes matter to change?

Unit at a Glance
▶ **Language**: Describe Actions and Places, Science Words
▶ **Literacy**: Make Connections
▶ **Content**: Matter

Unit
5

Share What You Know

Do It!

① **Put** one ice cube in a bowl on a table.

② **Watch** what happens to the ice. How long do you think it will take to melt?

③ **Draw** what you see. Describe your drawing to a partner.

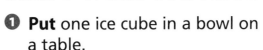
This is how the ice cube changed.

Build Background: Use this interactive resource to learn how matter changes.
🔘 **NGReach.com**

Describe Actions

Listen to Amita and David. Then use **Language Frames** to describe what you do in different kinds of weather.

When It Is Hot!

Dialogue

1. When the weather is hot, I eat ice cream!

2. When it is cold, I eat ice cream, too.

3. You like ice cream when the weather is cold?

4. Yep! When it is cold, I can finish the ice cream *before* it melts!

5. When the weather is cold, I drink hot cocoa.

6. Me, too! It warms me up so I can eat more ice cream!

Key Words

Key Words
form
freeze
liquid
melt
solid
temperature
thermometer

Look at the pictures. Use **Key Words** and other words to talk about **forms** of water.

Solid water **melts** when the **temperature** is warmer than 32°F.

Liquid water **freezes** at 32°F.

thermometer

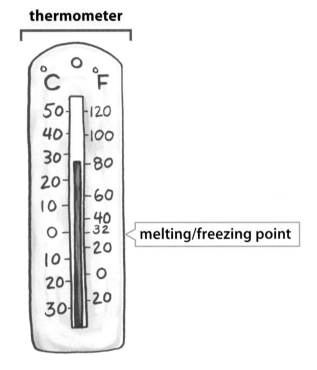

melting/freezing point

Talk Together

Tell a partner what causes water to change its form. Use **Key Words**. Then use **Language Frames** from page 276 to describe fun things you can do with water in different kinds of weather.

Character and Plot

When **characters** speak, you can find out:

• what the characters are like

• what is happening in the **plot**

Amita and David made up a skit about building a snowman. Look at the pictures and read the dialogue.

David builds the best snowmen!

Thanks for your help, Amita!

It takes a lot of work to be the best!

Map and Talk

You can make a chart that shows what characters say and what the words tell about the characters and the plot.

Character-Plot Chart

Character	What the Character Says	What This Shows About the Character	What This Shows About the Plot
Amita	"David builds the best snowmen!"	Amita values other people's work.	David is building a snowman.
David	"Thanks for your help, Amita!"	David accepts other people's help.	Amita is helping.

Talk Together

Plan and act out a short skit with a partner. Then use the characters' words to help you create a character-plot chart.

More Key Words

Use these words to talk about "Melt the Snow!" and "Saved in Ice."

alter
(**awl**-tur) *verb*

When you **alter** something, you change it. She **alters** the dress to make it shorter.

occur
(u-**kur**) *verb*

When something **occurs**, it happens. A sunrise **occurs** every morning.

state
(stāt) *noun*

The **state** of a person or thing is the way it is at a certain time. He is in a happy **state**.

substance
(**sub**-stuns) *noun*

Substance is the material that something is made of. Snow is a cold **substance**.

trap
(trap) *verb*

To **trap** something means to catch it and not let it go. Spiders **trap** insects with webs.

Talk Together

Work with a partner. Make a Word Web of examples for each **Key Word**.

Word Web

hair — clothes — alter — recipe — math answer

Add words to My Vocabulary Notebook.
NGReach.com

Learn to Make Connections

Look at the cartoon. Does it make you think of something in your own life? **Make connections**, or compare what you see in the picture to your own experiences.

People feel better when the weather is warmer.

When you read, you **make connections**, too.

How to Make Connections

	1. As you read, think about what is happening in the text.	This is about _____ .
	2. Ask yourself, "What is this like in my own life?"	I think of _____ .
	3. Think about how this connection helps you understand the text.	Now I understand _____ .

Talk Together

Read "A Change of Weather." Read the sample connection. Then use **Language Frames** to make connections. Tell a partner about them.

Story

A Change of Weather

Amita felt happy. It was her family's first picnic of the year. She didn't mind the slight chill in the air. Winter was over. It was spring!

Amita reached for a second piece of pie. Suddenly something touched her nose. She wiped it away. It was wet! Then it came again—and again! "Snowflakes!" she cried. She looked at the clouds. Their color had **altered** from gray to black. She shivered. It was suddenly much colder. ◀

With a sigh, Mom packed up the picnic. Amita tried not to show it, but her happy **state** had vanished. Dad saw her disappointment. ◀

"Quick changes in weather often **occur** in spring," he said gently. "Moisture in the air gets **trapped** in the clouds. When the **temperature** drops, the moisture turns to snow." He smiled and wiped a sticky **substance** off Amita's chin.

"Another snowflake?" she asked.

"Pie juice," Dad answered.

They both laughed.

Sample Connection

"<u>This is about</u> a picnic.

<u>I think of</u> picnics with my family. They are always lots of fun.

<u>Now I understand</u> why Amita feels happy."

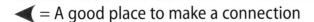 = A good place to make a connection

Read a Play

Genre

A **play** is a story that is acted out on stage. In a play, actors pretend to be the characters. A written **script** tells the actors what to say and do.

Elements of Drama

The script for a play shows the **dialogue**, or the words the characters say. The **stage directions** tell the actors how to speak, look, and act.

stage directions

HORMIGUITA [*shaking with fear*]:

How scary! But don't worry, Mami. dialogue
I'll be very careful.

[HORMIGUITA *bundles up and steps* stage directions
outside.]

Melt the Snow!

BY MARISA MONTES · ILLUSTRATED BY BRIAN AJHAR

Characters:
HORMIGUITA,
    a little ant
MAMI,
    Hormiguita's mother

Outdoor Characters:
SNOW
SUN
CLOUD
WIND
WALL
MOUSE

CHORUS

▶ **Set a Purpose**
Find out why Hormiguita's
mother does not want her to
play outside.

SCENE ONE

[HORMIGUITA **peers** *out the tiny
window of her underground home.
She sees* SUN *shining.*]

HORMIGUITA [*pointing*]:
¡*Mami,* **mira***!* Look, the sun
is shining. It's **melting** the
snow. It's been such a long
winter, and I'm tired of
staying indoors. May I go out
and play?

[MAMI *looks out the window.
Outside,* WIND *begins to blow.*
CLOUD **appears in** *the sky.*]

In Other Words
peers looks
mira look (in Spanish)
appears in comes into

284

MAMI: But the wind is starting to blow, and dark clouds are forming. The air is chilly. It may snow again.

HORMIGUITA [*begging*]: Please, Mami? *¿Por favor?* I won't stay long.

MAMI [*sighing*]: **Muy bien, m'ija.** But don't go far, and be very careful. If snow falls, you may get trapped . Then what would you do?

HORMIGUITA [*shaking with fear*]: How scary! But don't worry, Mami. I'll be very careful.

[HORMIGUITA **bundles up** *and steps outside.*]

In Other Words

begging asking
¿Por favor? Please? (in Spanish)
Muy bien, m'ija. Very well, my daughter. (in Spanish)
bundles up puts on warm clothes

▶ **Before You Move On**

1. **Drama** Find the dialogue that tells why Mami does not want Hormiguita to play outside.

2. **Make Connections** Tell about a time when you asked a parent to do something. How does this help you understand how Hormiguita and Mami act?

▶ **Predict**
What will happen to Hormiguita
when she plays outside?

SCENE TWO

[SUN *shines*. HORMIGUITA *skips happily in the forest. Suddenly,* WIND *blows*. CLOUD **drifts** *in front of* SUN. SNOW *falls*. HORMIGUITA **shivers** *and stops. A big snowflake lands on her leg and* traps *her. She* **tugs** *at her leg*.]

HORMIGUITA: *¡Ay, ay, ay!* Snow, I'm stuck!
Give me back my leg so I can go home!

CHORUS: Snow holds Hormiguita's leg,
And she wants to go home!

In Other Words
drifts moves slowly
shivers shakes from the cold
tugs pulls
¡Ay, ay, ay! Oh, oh, oh! (in Spanish)

SNOW: *Lo siento.* I cannot. But there is someone stronger than me.

HORMIGUITA [*tugging at leg again*]: Who is stronger than you, heavy Snow?

SNOW: The sun is stronger. It melts me into water.

HORMIGUITA [*reaching toward* SUN]: Sun, melt the snow, *por favor!*

CHORUS: Sun, please melt Snow.
Snow holds Hormiguita's leg,
And she wants to go home!

In Other Words
Lo siento. I'm sorry. (in Spanish)

SUN: I cannot. But there is someone stronger than me.

HORMIGUITA [*looking **puzzled***]: Who is stronger than you, bright Sun?

SUN: It is the cloud. It covers my **warm rays**.

HORMIGUITA [*looking up at* CLOUD, *who is partly covering* SUN]: Cloud, please **uncover** the sun!

CHORUS: Cloud, please uncover Sun.
Sun must melt Snow.
Snow holds Hormiguita's leg,
And she wants to go home!

In Other Words
puzzled confused
warm rays bright, warm light
uncover move away from

CLOUD: I am sorry. I cannot. But there is someone stronger than me.

HORMIGUITA [*shivering*]: Who is stronger than you, **thick** Cloud?

CLOUD: The wind is more powerful. It pushes me.

HORMIGUITA [*flinging arms up and begging*]: Wind, push the cloud away, *por favor*!

CHORUS: Wind, please push Cloud,
So Cloud can uncover Sun,
So Sun can melt Snow.
Snow holds Hormiguita's leg,
And she wants to go home!

In Other Words
thick big
flinging throwing

WIND: I'm sorry, Hormiguita. I cannot help you. But there is someone stronger than me.

HORMIGUITA [*rubbing arms to warm up*]: Who could be stronger than you, **mighty** Wind?

WIND: It is the wall. **It holds me back.**

HORMIGUITA [***hanging head sadly*** *and shaking it slowly*]: ¡Ay, ay, ay! [*turning to* WALL] Wall, do not hold back the wind, please!

In Other Words

mighty big, strong

It holds me back. I cannot blow through it.

hanging head sadly holding her head down in a sad way

290

CHORUS: Wall, please don't **block** Wind,
For Wind must push Cloud,
So Cloud can uncover Sun,
So Sun can melt Snow.
Snow holds Hormiguita's leg,
And she wants to go home!

WALL: I cannot, Hormiguita. But there is
someone stronger than me.

HORMIGUITA [*looking **amazed***]: Who
could be stronger than you, hard Wall?

In Other Words
block hold back; stop
amazed surprised

▶ **Before You Move On**

1. **Confirm Prediction** Was your prediction
about Hormiguita correct? Explain.
2. **Cause/Effect** What effect does the wall
have on Hormiguita's situation?

▶ **Predict**
Who will be strong enough to save Hormiguita from her **trap**?

WALL: The mouse is stronger. He **gnaws** holes in me.

HORMIGUITA [*looking around quickly and seeing* MOUSE *near* WALL]: Mouse, please gnaw at Wall so I can go home!

In Other Words
gnaws chews

292

CHORUS: Mouse, please gnaw at Wall,
So Wall will not block Wind,
For Wind must push Cloud,
So Cloud can uncover Sun,
So Sun can melt Snow.
Snow holds Hormiguita's leg,
And she wants to go home!

[MOUSE *scampers to* HORMIGUITA]

MOUSE: I will help you—of course! We tiny
creatures must **stick together** against those
stronger than us. It will be a tasty treat!
¡Muy sabrosa! [*showing teeth*]

In Other Words

scampers runs
creatures animals
stick together help each other
¡Muy sabrosa! Very tasty! (in Spanish)

CHORUS: Mouse, gnaw at Wall!
Wall, stop blocking Wind!
Wind, push Cloud!
Cloud, uncover Sun!
Sun, melt the snow!
Snow is holding Hormiguita's leg,
And she wants to go home!

[MOUSE *gnaws at* WALL. WALL **crumbles** *and stops blocking* WIND. WIND *blows over* WALL *and pushes* CLOUD. CLOUD **glides** *away from* SUN. SUN *melts* SNOW.]

[HORMIGUITA *shakes her leg loose.*]

HORMIGUITA; I'm free! I can go home! [**hooks elbows** *with* MOUSE *and dances*] **¡Gracias, Amigo!** Thank you, my friend, for saving me! You are the strongest one of all!

In Other Words

crumbles breaks into pieces
glides moves smoothly
hooks elbows joins arms
¡Gracias, Amigo! Thank you, friend! (in Spanish)

SCENE THREE

[HORMIGUITA *bursts through the kitchen door of her home.*]

HORMIGUITA: Mami, Mami! I'm back!

MAMI [*running toward the door and* **scooping** *up HORMIGUITA in her arms*]: You're just in time, m'ija.

HORMIGUITA [*jumping excitedly*]: In time for what, Mami?

MAMI: I made a pot of hot chocolate, **rich** and sweet! Are you cold? ❖

In Other Words
scooping picking
rich strong

▶ **Before You Move On**

1. **Confirm Prediction** Who is the strongest one? Are you surprised?
2. **Drama** How do the characters work together to free Hormiguita? Read the stage directions on page 295.

Meet the Author

Marisa Montes

Marisa Montes was born in Puerto Rico, but today she lives in California. Like Hormiguita, Montes speaks more than one language. Growing up, she spoke Spanish at home and English at school. As a young girl, she lived in France and spoke French with her neighborhood friends. Because of her experiences, Montes has created many bilingual characters in her children's books.

Montes is like Hormiguita in another way, too. Both love to be outdoors. "I can't stand the feeling that there is something out there that I might be missing out on."

▲ Montes loves animals, so she often includes them in her stories.

Writer's Craft ✏

Marisa Montes uses vivid words to describe the power of each character in the play. Write a sentence to describe your favorite character. Use vivid words in your description.

Think and Respond

Talk About It

1. Suppose you are going to perform in the **play**. How will the **dialogue** and **stage directions** help you?

   The dialogue tells me _____ . The stage directions tell me _____ .

2. Think of the beginning of the play. **Describe** the **actions** of Hormiguita and Mami.

   Hormiguita _____ . Mami _____ .

3. Think about the character of Mouse. Why does he help Hormiguita? What does this show about him?

   Mouse helps Hormiguita because _____ .
   This shows that he _____ .

Learn test-taking strategies.
NGReach.com

Write About It

At the end of the play, Mami says, "Are you cold?" What do you think Hormiguita will say? Write a line or two of dialogue for Hormiguita to answer Mami's question. Use at least one **Key Word**.

HORMIGUITA: Yes/No, _____ .

Character and Plot

Create a character-plot chart for "**Melt** the Snow!" Write dialogue that you think is important.

Character-Plot Chart

Character	What the Character Says	What This Shows About the Character	What This Shows About the Plot
Mami	"Don't go far, and be very careful."	Mami wants Hormiguita to be safe.	Mami lets Hormiguita go out to play.
Hormiguita			

Discuss your chart with a partner. Take turns reading what the characters say. Explain how the dialogue helps you understand the characters and the plot. Use the sentence frame and **Key Words**.

> This dialogue shows that _____ .

Fluency 🅞 Comprehension Coach

Use the Comprehension Coach to practice reading with expression. Rate your reading.

Talk Together

What caused the snow to melt? Draw a picture to show how Hormiguita got free. Share your picture with the class. Use **Key Words** as you tell about the picture.

Antonyms

Antonyms are words that have opposite meanings. Look at each pair of antonyms below. Compare the two words.

freeze

melt

trap

free

freeze : to turn a liquid substance into a solid one

melt : to turn a solid substance into a liquid one

trap : to hold a person or animal against its will

free : to let a person or animal go

Try It Together

Read the sentences. Then answer the questions.

Think of water you drink. That's <u>liquid</u> water. Think of a glacier. That's solid water. If a glacier starts to melt, is the temperature hot or <u>cold</u>?

1. What is an antonym for liquid?

   A cold

   B melt

   C solid

   D water

2. What is an antonym for cold?

   A hot

   B liquid

   C freeze

   D temperature

Connect Across Texts Read about another animal who got **trapped** when water changed to ice.

Genre An **e-mail** is an electronic message. A **Web-based news article** is a story on the Internet about something in the news.

SAVED IN ICE

Frozen Baby Mammoth Found

▶ **Before You Move On**

1. **Predict** Based on the title, what do you think this selection is about?

2. **Make Connections** Look at the photo. Does the baby mammoth look familiar to you? Explain.

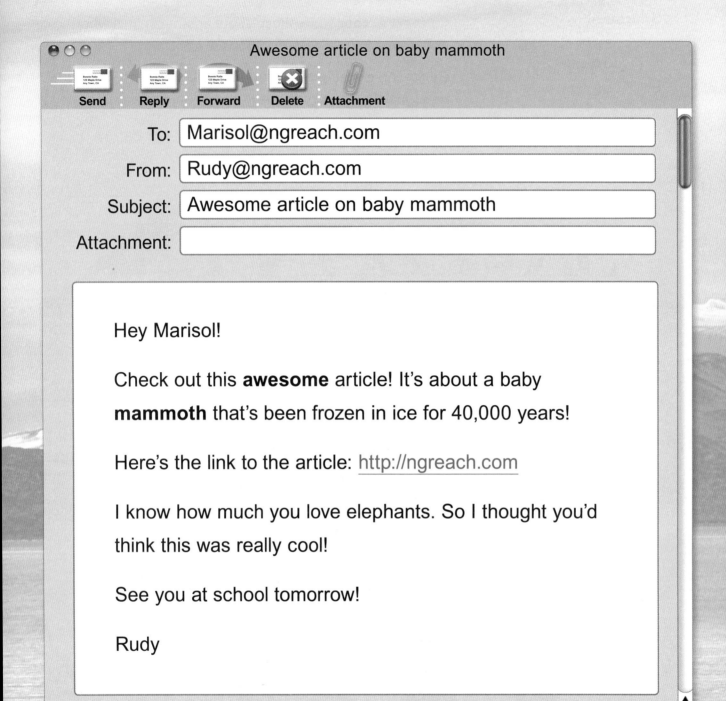

Send   **Reply**   **Forward**   **Delete**   **Attachment**

To: Marisol@ngreach.com

From: Rudy@ngreach.com

Subject: Awesome article on baby mammoth

Attachment:

Hey Marisol!

Check out this **awesome** article! It's about a baby **mammoth** that's been frozen in ice for 40,000 years!

Here's the link to the article: http://ngreach.com

I know how much you love elephants. So I thought you'd think this was really cool!

See you at school tomorrow!

Rudy

In Other Words

awesome amazing

mammoth elephant-like animal

NEWS ARTICLE | Photo Gallery | Related Articles | Maps | Search ▶

Photo in the News:
Baby Mammoth Found Frozen in Russia

by **Christine Dell'Amore**

July 11, 2007— Talk about a **mammoth** surprise.

In May 2007, a hunter was walking in the Yamalo-Nenetsk region, in the far north of Russia. Suddenly, he saw something sticking out of the damp snow. He thought it was a frozen **reindeer**. When the hunter looked closer, he realized that it was something else. The "reindeer" was really a 40,000-year-old baby mammoth. It was **perfectly preserved** in ice.

ARCTIC OCEAN

RUSSIA

Yamalo-Nenetsk Region

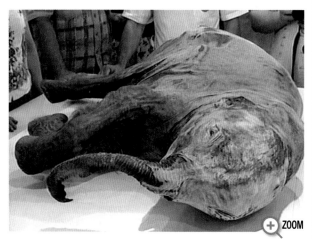

ZOOM

▲ **The last mammoths died long ago, but they are related to the elephants that live today in Africa and Asia.**

NEXT ››

In Other Words
mammoth big
reindeer kind of deer that lives in very cold places
perfectly preserved completely saved

▶ **Before You Move On**
1. **Media** Where does Rudy find the article about the mammoth? How does he send it?
2. **Draw Conclusions** Where did some mammoths live 40,000 years ago?

HOME • FEATURES • FOLLOW UP • KIDS • BLOG • RESOURCES

NEWS ARTICLE | Photo Gallery | Related Articles | Maps   Search ▶

Lovely Lyuba

The mammoth is a one-month-old female. She is the most well-preserved mammoth ever found. Mammoths have not lived on Earth since the last **Ice Age**. That was 11,500 to 1.8 million years ago.

"It's a lovely little baby mammoth," says a Russian scientist. "She **was found in perfect condition**."

The baby mammoth weighs 110 pounds and **measures 51 inches**. She is the size of a large dog, reporters say.

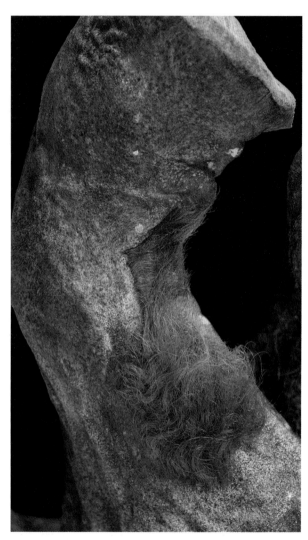

▲ **Hair is still attached to the mammoth's leg.**

In Other Words

Ice Age time when ice covered much of Earth

was found in perfect condition looks like she did when she was alive

measures 51 inches is 51 inches long

▲ A boy touches Lyuba in a museum in Russia.

The female mammoth was named "Lyuba" after the Russian hunter's wife. Scientists believe Lyuba will help them discover some of the secrets of these animals from long ago.

Lyuba **has recently gone on display**. Now people can share in the discovery by seeing her for themselves. ❖

▲ Lyuba on display in Tokyo

≪ PREVIOUS

In Other Words

has recently gone on display can now be seen in a museum

▶ **Before You Move On**

1. **Details** How old was the mammoth when she was trapped in ice?

2. **Make Connections** The mammoth is the size of a large dog. How does this help you understand more about her?

Respond and Extend

Key Words

alter	solid
form	state
freeze	substance
liquid	temperature
melt	thermometer
occur	trap

Compare Media

Rudy's e-mail and the online article, "Saved in Ice," are both electronic forms of communication. In what other ways are the forms the same? How are they different?

Work with a partner to complete the comparison chart. Write *yes* or *no* for each feature.

Comparison Chart

	Rudy's E-mail	"Saved in Ice"
electronic form of communication	yes	yes
formal language		
informal language		
personal information		
factual information		

Talk Together

In the e-mail and the article, you read about a 40,000-year-old baby mammoth. Why was the mammoth's body **trapped**? Think about what causes water to change its **form**. Use **Key Words** to talk about your ideas.

306

Adjectives and Articles

An **adjective** tells about a noun. An **article** points to a noun.

Grammar Rules **Adjectives and Articles**

• Use **adjectives** to tell what something is like.	The **bright** sun shines. The sky is **blue**.
• For most adjectives, add -**er** to compare two things. Add -**est** to compare three or more things.	My horn is small**er** than your horn. His horn is the small**est** one of all.
• Use **this** or **that** to tell "which one."	**This** horn is old. Is **that** horn new?
• Use **articles** to identify a **noun**.	**An ant** looks at **the sun** through **a window**.

Read Adjectives and Articles

Read these sentences about "Melt the Snow!" Find two articles and three different kinds of adjectives. Show them to a partner.

Heavy snow falls in the forest. A snowflake falls on Hormiguita's leg! Sun is stronger than Snow. Can Sun melt that snowflake?

Write Adjectives and Articles

Write two sentences about the weather. Use at least one adjective and one article. Read your sentences to a partner.

Language Frames

- Here is _____ .
- The _____ is
  _____ .
- It feels _____ .

Describe Places

Listen to Marita's chant. Then use **Language Frames** to describe a place you know.

At the Beach

Chant ((MP3))

Here is a beach, a sunny beach.
I cannot wait for a swim.
The sand is hot and dry from the sun.
It feels gritty on my skin.

Here is the water, the chilly water.
The gentle waves are a treat.
The sand is wet and soft from the waves.
It feels squishy under my feet.

wave

sand

Key Words

ground

mixture

sand

water

wetland

Key Words

Look at this picture. Use **Key Words** and other words to talk about how a **wetland** can form.

How a Wetland Forms

sand

water

This **ground** contains a **mixture** of sand and water.

Talk Together

What causes water and sand to change into a wetland? Use **Key Words** to explain. Then use **Language Frames** from page 308 to describe a wetland.

Cause and Effect

Most events have a **cause** and an **effect**.

- To figure out an effect, ask, "What happened?"
- To figure out a cause, ask, "Why did it happen?"

Cause   **Effect**

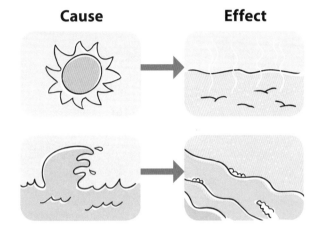

Map and Talk

You can use a chart to show causes and effects. To make one, write an event in column 1. In column 2, write what happened because of the event.

Cause-and-Effect Chart

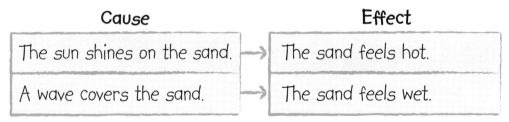

Cause	Effect
The sun shines on the sand.	The sand feels hot.
A wave covers the sand.	The sand feels wet.

Talk Together

Tell a partner about something that happened. Then work together to make a cause-and-effect chart for the event.

More Key Words

Use these words to talk about "Quicksand: When Earth Turns to Liquid" and "Meet Maycira Costa."

area
(**air**-ē-u) *noun*

An **area** is a part of a place. A classroom can have an **area** for reading.

combine
(kum-**bīn**) *verb*

When you **combine** things, you mix them together. What foods does she **combine**?

composition
(kom-pu-**zi**-shun) *noun*

Composition is what things are made of. The **composition** of mud is dirt and water.

firm
(**furm**) *adjective*

ice

Something that is **firm** is hard. You can skate on ice because it is **firm**.

surface
(**sur**-fus) *noun*

The **surface** is the outside part of something. The **surface** of this object is uneven.

Talk Together

Make a Word Map for each **Key Word**. Then compare your maps with a partner's.

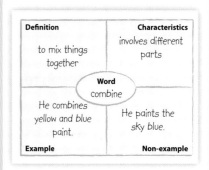

Definition	Characteristics
to mix things together	involves different parts
Word — combine	
He combines yellow and blue paint.	He paints the sky blue.
Example	Non-example

Add words to My Vocabulary Notebook.
NGReach.com

Learn to Make Connections

Look at the photograph. Does it make you think of something you have read in a text or know about the world? This is called **making connections**.

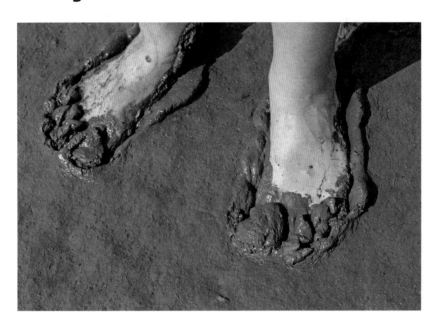

When you read, you can understand more if you **make connections**.

How to Make Connections

💭	**1.** Think about what the text is about.	The topic is _____ .
❓	**2.** As you read, think about other things you have read or an issue in the world. Does the text relate to these?	This makes me think of _____ .
💭	**3.** Decide how the connection helps you understand the text.	Now I understand _____ .

Talk Together

Read Marita's e-mail. Read the sample connection.
Then use **Language Frames** to make connections.
Tell a partner about them.

E-Mail

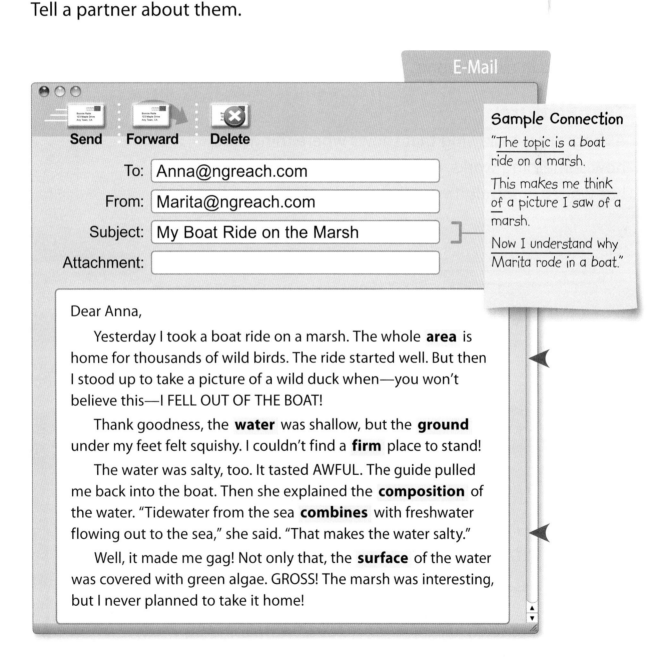

Send   Forward   Delete

To: Anna@ngreach.com

From: Marita@ngreach.com

Subject: My Boat Ride on the Marsh

Attachment:

Sample Connection

"The topic is a boat
ride on a marsh.

This makes me think
of a picture I saw of a
marsh.

Now I understand why
Marita rode in a boat."

Dear Anna,

Yesterday I took a boat ride on a marsh. The whole **area** is
home for thousands of wild birds. The ride started well. But then
I stood up to take a picture of a wild duck when—you won't
believe this—I FELL OUT OF THE BOAT!

Thank goodness, the **water** was shallow, but the **ground**
under my feet felt squishy. I couldn't find a **firm** place to stand!

The water was salty, too. It tasted AWFUL. The guide pulled
me back into the boat. Then she explained the **composition** of
the water. "Tidewater from the sea **combines** with freshwater
flowing out to the sea," she said. "That makes the water salty."

Well, it made me gag! Not only that, the **surface** of the water
was covered with green algae. GROSS! The marsh was interesting,
but I never planned to take it home!

◀ = A good place to make a connection

313

Read a Science Article

Genre
A **science article** is nonfiction. It can tell how something in nature works.

Text Feature
A **diagram** is a drawing that shows where things are, how something works, or when something happens. It has words, or **labels**, that tell more about the drawing.

diagram

underground water flow

Quicksand:
When Earth Turns to Liquid

by Kris Hirschmann

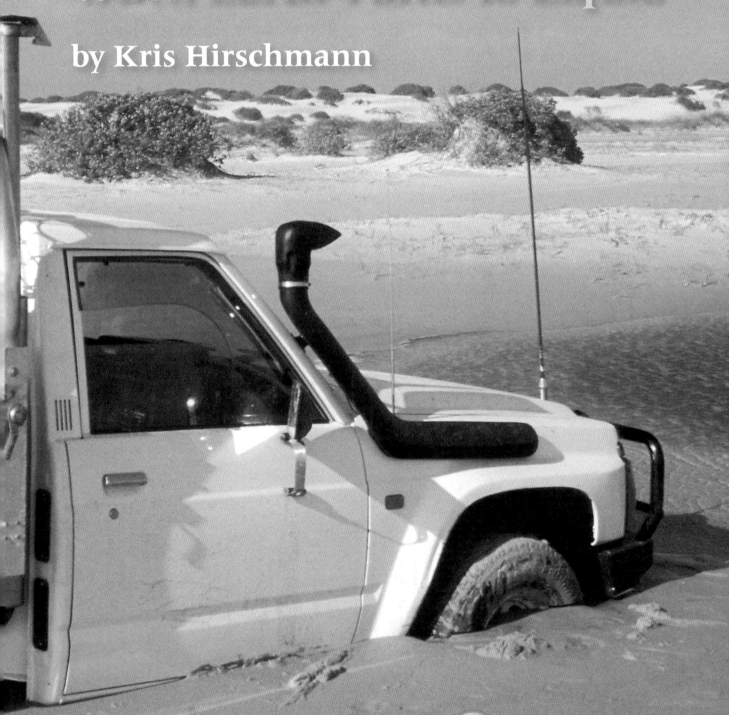

Comprehension Coach

▶ **Set a Purpose**
Find out if quicksand is really
as dangerous as it seems.

What Is Quicksand?

The word *quicksand* makes some people **shiver with fear**. This is probably because of the way many movies show quicksand. In films, quicksand is often **a mysterious substance** that sucks people and animals to their deaths!

◀ **Movies do not always show the truth about quicksand.**

In Other Words

shiver with fear feel very afraid

a mysterious substance something that cannot be explained

316

Actual quicksand is very different from movie quicksand. It **rarely harms** people or animals. Real quicksand is not mysterious. It is a simple substance that forms naturally.

Quicksand is often just **sand** with a lot of **water** between its **particles**. This makes the sand soupy, or runny. When the **waterlogged** sand can no longer **support** weight, it is called "quick."

Quicksand is not very hard to find. It is often just a **mixture** of water and sand. ▶

▶ **Before You Move On**

1. **Make Connections** Have you ever walked in sand or on sandy **ground**? Compare it with the way quicksand is described on this page.
2. **Cause/Effect** What happens when a lot of **water** mixes with **sand**?

▲ Quicksand can form at the beach.

Sand and Other Materials

A beach is a good place to see how water **affects** sand. In the **area** where waves roll onto the land, the sand changes. Here, water sinks into the sand. The water makes the sand loose and soft. For a few seconds, the **surface** acts like **shallow quicksand**.

In Other Words
Materials Things in Nature
affects can make a change in
shallow quicksand quicksand that is not deep

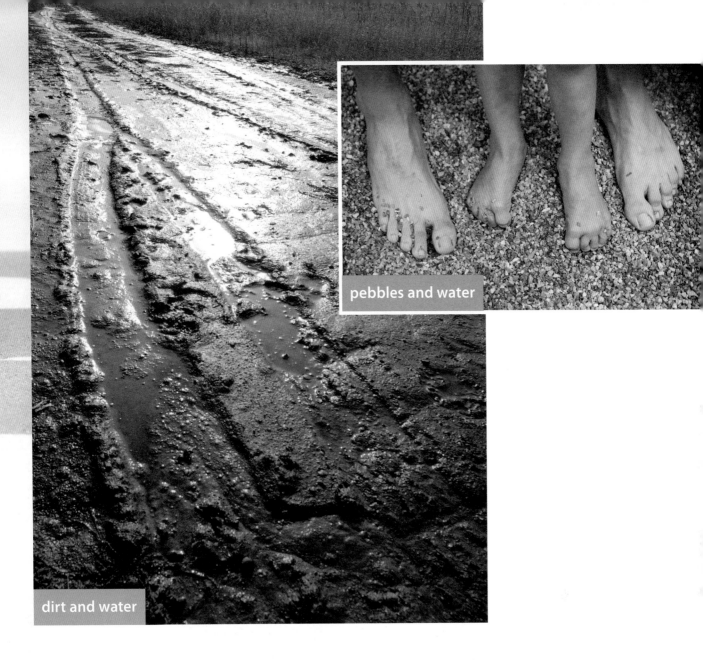

pebbles and water

dirt and water

Sand is not the only substance that can become quick. Dirt, pebbles, and gravel can also **quicken** under the right conditions. This means that sometimes water mixes with one of these materials in just the right way. Then quicksand forms.

In Other Words
quicken become quicksand

▶ **Before You Move On**

1. **Cause/Effect** How do waves affect the **sand** on a beach?
2. **Details** What other materials can combine with **water** to quicken?

How Does Quicksand Form?

Most of the time, particles of sand, dirt, and pebbles are packed close together to form a solid, **stable** `ground`. **Firm** ground can support the weight of a person, a car, or even a building.

Solid ground is firm enough to hold up this car. ▶

In Other Words
stable strong, unmoving
Firm Strong, solidly packed

How Quicksand Forms

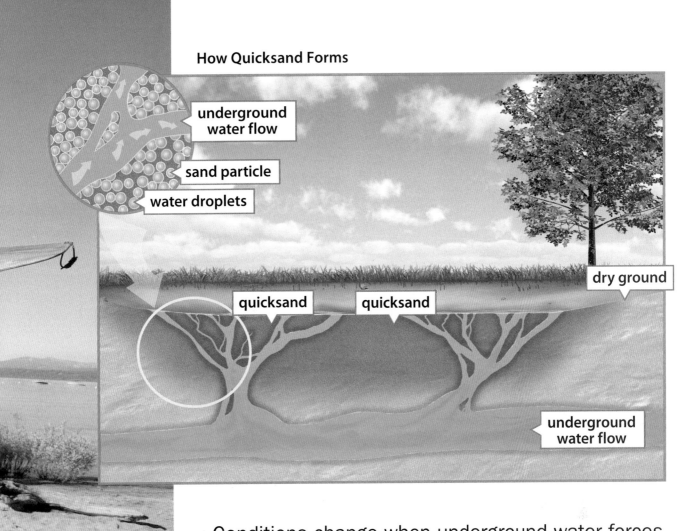

underground water flow

sand particle

water droplets

quicksand

quicksand

dry ground

underground water flow

Conditions change when underground water forces its way between particles. The water pushes the particles farther apart. The solid ground **starts to act like a liquid**. It is now quicksand. As long as the water **flows**, the particles will stay in their liquid state.

In Other Words

starts to act like a liquid becomes thin and watery

flows keeps moving

▶ **Before You Move On**

1. **Cause/Effect** Why does solid ground support heavy weights?

2. **Use Text Features** Use the diagram to tell a partner how quicksand forms.

Where Is Quicksand Found?

Water is the **key ingredient in** quicksand. This means that quicksand is usually found in **wetlands**, or watery places. Marshes, rivers, creeks, and swamps often hide pools of quicksand.

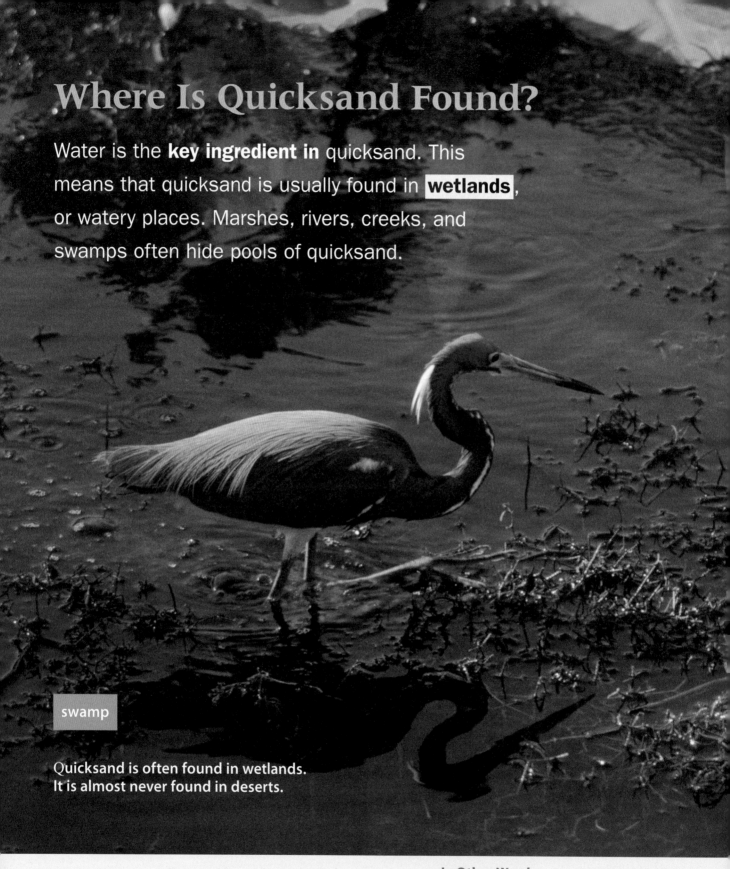

swamp

Quicksand is often found in wetlands.
It is almost never found in deserts.

In Other Words

key ingredient in most important part of

Deserts have a lot of sand, but they almost never **contain** quicksand. Deserts are dry places. Quicksand usually will not form without water. It does not matter how much sand there is in a place!

desert

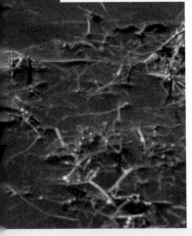

Think about movie quicksand again. Is quicksand really a mysterious substance? Does it really suck people and animals to their deaths? Now that you know the truth, you might not be so scared the next time you see quicksand in a movie! ❖

In Other Words
contain have

▶ **Before You Move On**

1. **Cause/Effect** Why do deserts rarely have quicksand?

2. **Make Connections** Where could quicksand form in your neighborhood? Why? Use details from the text to explain your answer.

Quicksand Myths

Fiction	*Fact*
Quicksand sucks you down.	Quicksand is thicker than water. It is easier for things to float in quicksand than in water. It is almost impossible to sink under completely.

Fiction	*Fact*
Quicksand is alive.	Quicksand is not alive. When a person steps into quicksand, it moves **with the person's motion**. Quicksand only looks like it is alive.

In Other Words

Quicksand Myths False Things People Believe About Quicksand

Fiction Things That Are Not True

Fact Things That Are True

with the person's motion when the person moves

More Quicksand Myths

Fiction	Fact
Leeches and worms live in quicksand.	There is rarely anything alive in quicksand. So don't worry about leeches or worms.

Fiction	Fact
Quicksand **is bottomless**.	There are places with very deep quicksand. However, quicksand is not bottomless. Most quicksand is a few inches deep to less than waist-deep.

In Other Words

Leeches Worms that suck blood

is bottomless goes down forever

▶ **Before You Move On**

1. **Draw Conclusions** Should you be afraid to walk in quicksand? Explain.
2. **Explain** Choose a myth about quicksand from the article. What is fiction about it? What is fact?

Talk About It

1. Tell one fact you learned in the **science article** about quicksand.

   I learned _____ .

2. Quicksand usually forms in **areas** with a lot of **water**. Use the photos in the article to **describe** a **place** like this.

   A place with quicksand often looks _____ .

3. In your own words, tell how quicksand forms.

   Quicksand forms when _____ .

Learn test-taking strategies.
NGReach.com

Write About It

There are a lot of myths about quicksand. What did you believe about quicksand before you read the article? Write a paragraph. Tell what you believed and whether or not it is true. Use **Key Words** if you can.

Before I read the article, I thought _____ .
As I read, I learned _____ .

Cause and Effect

Complete a cause-and-effect chart for "Quicksand: When Earth Turns to Liquid."

Cause-and-Effect Chart

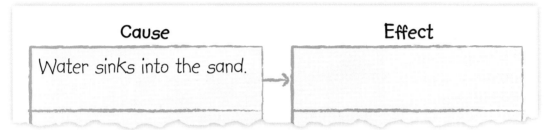

Cause	Effect
Water sinks into the sand.	

With a partner, use your chart to summarize the causes and effects of quicksand. Ask the questions in the speech balloon and use **Key Words**. Record your summary.

> What happened?
> Why did it happen?

Fluency ■● Comprehension Coach

Use the Comprehension Coach to practice reading with intonation. Rate your reading.

Talk Together

What causes matter to change? Make two pictures to show how **water** can cause quicksand. Use **Key Words** as labels. Share your pictures with the class.

Synonyms

Synonyms are words that have almost the same meaning.

Mixture and **blend** are synonyms. Read the caption for the picture. How are the meanings of the two words alike?

Concrete is a blend of many materials. It is a mixture of lime, cement, water, sand, and tiny pieces of rock.

concrete

Try It Together

Read the passage. Then answer the questions.

At the beach, quicksand is usually in an <u>area</u> close to the water. If you stand in this place for a few seconds, your feet might sink into the soft sand. If you want to stand on a <u>firm</u>, or hard, surface, you need to climb on some rocks!

1. What is a synonym for <u>area</u>?

  A sand

  B place

  C water

  D stand

2. What is a synonym for <u>firm</u>?

  A soft

  B hard

  C rocks

  D surface

Connect Across Texts Read an interview with a scientist to find out more about **wetlands**.

Genre During an **interview**, one person asks another person questions to get information. The results of the interview are often shared in a question-and-answer format.

Meet Maycira Costa

by Nora Brook

Dr. Maycira Costa

Squish, splash, slosh!
That's the sound of feet
walking through a wetland.
To Dr. Maycira Costa,
that sound is like music.
Dr. Costa studies wetlands.
Find out why she loves
these **soggy** spaces.

In Other Words
soggy wet and soft

▶ **Before You Move On**

1. **Visualize** Describe what it feels and sounds like to walk over wet, soggy land.
2. **Make Inferences** Why does the author say sounds of the wetlands are like music to Dr. Costa?

329

Q: What are **wetlands**?

A: Wetlands are places where the soil is always, or almost always, wet. They are often found where land meets **water**, such as near ocean shores and the banks of rivers and lakes. Low **areas** on land and **watersheds** might also have wetlands. Marshes, bogs, wet meadows, potholes, and swamps are all wetlands.

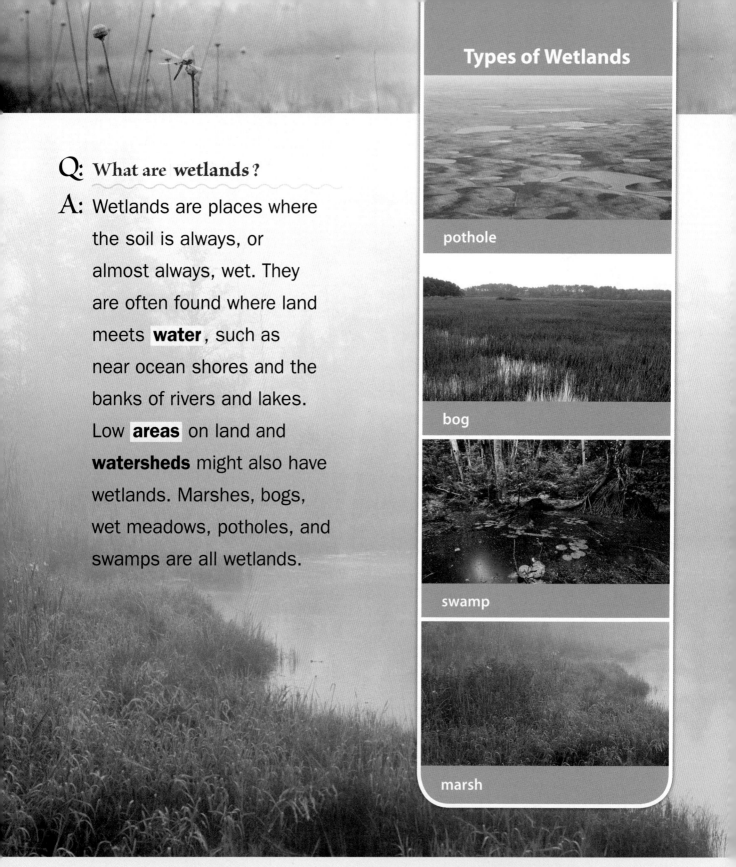

Types of Wetlands

pothole

bog

swamp

marsh

In Other Words
watersheds places that hold water

Q: What makes wetlands special? Why do you study them?

A: Wetland ecosystems are very important. They are a **habitat** for many kinds of plants and animals. They help control floods. They can even filter, or clean, water. I want to learn how **climate changes** and human activities, like farming, affect wetlands. I hope my work helps people understand wetlands and **value** them.

Animals In the Wetlands

tapir

caiman

egret

jaguar

In Other Words

habitat home

climate changes changes in weather over the years

value take care of

▶ **Before You Move On**

1. **Cause/Effect** What kinds of things could affect wetlands? Name them. Use details from the text.
2. **Make Connections** Think of a time you saw a wetland, in images or in real life. How do your ideas about them compare with Dr. Costa's ideas? Explain.

Q: Where are the wetlands you study?

A: I study the Pantanal and Amazon wetlands in South America. They are the largest **tropical** wetlands in the world. The Pantanal alone is almost as big as the state of New York!

Q: How are you able to study such large areas?

A: I look at images taken from satellites orbiting high above Earth. They show where the water is, and how much **sand**, dirt, and other **sediment** is in it. I also **go into the field** and take samples.

▲ satellite image of Brazil

◀ This is Dr. Costa with her son. They are at a lake in Brazil.

In Other Words
tropical hot and steamy
sediment pieces of things like sand and dirt
go into the field walk into a wetland

332

Q: When you are in the field, do you ever worry about things like quicksand?

A: No! Humans are not as **dense** as quicksand, so we easily float in it. If you step in quicksand, do not panic. You will not sink!

Q: What advice do you have for young explorers?

A: Be curious about nature. Do not be afraid. No matter where you live, there is probably a wetland nearby. Gather your friends and family and go explore it! ❖

◀ Students explore a wetland.

In Other Words
dense heavy

▶ **Before You Move On**

1. **Make Connections** What does Dr. Costa say about quicksand? Does this remind you of another selection you've read? Explain.

2. **Cause/Effect** How does technology developed for space exploration affect Dr. Costa's research on wetlands?

Compare Text Features

Key Words

area	mixture
combine	sand
composition	surface
firm	water
ground	wetland

Study the Venn diagram with a partner. Then use the text features below to complete the diagram.

chart   diagram   photos   captions
    map   questions   answers

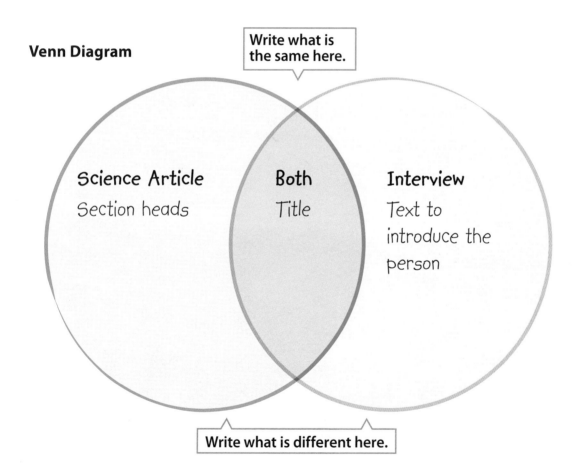

Venn Diagram

Write what is the same here.

Science Article
Section heads

Both
Title

Interview
Text to introduce the person

Write what is different here.

Talk Together

What can cause the **ground** to change? Think about the science article and the interview. Use **Key Words** to explain your ideas.

Possessive Nouns/Adjectives

A **possessive noun** is the name of an owner. A **possessive adjective** can take the place of an owner's name.

apostrophe

Example: **Linda's** family goes to the beach.

Her family goes to the beach.

Grammar Rules Possessive Nouns/Adjectives

	One Owner	More Than One Owner
• Always use an **apostrophe** (') with a possessive noun.	the truck's wheels Corey's shirt	the frogs' log the boys' pebbles
• Be sure to use the correct possessive adjective to tell about the number of owners.	my your his, her, its	our your their

Read Possessive Nouns and Adjectives

Read the sentences. Can you identify one possessive noun and one possessive adjective? Show them to a partner.

Anil's feet sink in the sand. His feet disappear!

Write Possessive Nouns and Adjectives

Write a caption for each photograph on page 316. Use a possessive noun and a possessive adjective. Read your captions to your partner.

335

Write as a Reader

Write a Literary Response

Describe how you felt about one of the selections you read in this unit. Share your opinions with your classmates during a Reader's Circle.

Study a Model

In a literary response, you give your opinions, or personal feelings, about a selection. You support your opinion with details.

Melt the Snow!

by Maria Montes

reviewed by Rachel Zimmerman

Melt the Snow! is a wonderful play about an ant trapped by a snowflake. I liked it because it was funny and full of surprises.

First, I laughed when Hormiguita's leg got caught by the snowflake. I would never have thought that a snowflake could trap someone!

I was also surprised that none of the strong characters could help the ant. For example, Sun couldn't help because it was covered by Cloud. Cloud couldn't move without Wind.

Finally, I liked how little Mouse was the hero. I was happy that he helped Hormiguita and saved the day!

The beginning gives a short summary of the play and the writer's opinion.

The writer develops her ideas with details from the play. She presents her ideas in an interesting way.

The ending makes the writing feel complete.

Prewrite

1. **Choose a Topic** With a partner, review the selections in this unit. Talk about how you reacted to each one.

> ### Language Frames
>
> **Tell Your Ideas**
>
> I thought the selection was _____ .
>
> When I read the selection, I felt _____ .
>
> My favorite part of the selection was _____ .
>
> **Respond to Ideas**
>
> I'm surprised you thought _____ . Can you explain why?
>
> I don't understand what you mean by _____ . Can you say it another way?
>
> What parts of _____ did you like the best?

2. **Gather Information** How will you explain your response? Find details in the selection that support your opinion and develop your ideas.

3. **Get Organized** A cause-and-effect chart is one way to organize your thoughts.

Cause-and-Effect Chart

Draft

Use your chart to help you write your draft. State your opinion clearly. Use details from the selection to develop your ideas.

Revise

1. **Read, Retell, Respond** Read your draft aloud to a partner. Your partner listens and then retells your response. Next, talk about ways to improve your writing.

Language Frames	
Retell	**Make Suggestions**
You thought the selection was _____ .	I'm not sure what your response to _____ was. Can you say it more clearly?
Your reasons were _____ .	I don't think _____ is a strong reason.
Some details you used to support your opinion were _____ .	You didn't include many details. Maybe you could add _____ .

2. **Make Changes** Think about your draft and your partner's suggestions. Then use the Revising Marks on page 573 to mark your changes.

   - Is your opinion or response clear? If not, try rewording it.

   > because it was funny and full of surprises.
   > I liked it ~~a lot.~~

   - Use details from the selection to support your reasons.

   > I was also surprised that none of the strong characters could help the ant. For example, Sun couldn't help because it was covered by Cloud.

Edit and Proofread

Work with a partner to edit and proofread your literary response. Check that you used possessive nouns and adjectives correctly. Use the marks on page 574 to show your changes.

page 574

Punctuation Tip

✓ Always use an apostrophe (') with a possessive noun.

• Hormiguita's leg

• the students' play

Publish

1. **On Your Own** Make a final copy of your literary response. Read it to a partner who wrote about the same selection. Compare your ideas.

Presentation Tips	
If you are the speaker…	**If you are the listener…**
Read slowly and clearly.	Compare the speaker's ideas to your own.
Look up once in a while to make sure your reader understands what you are saying.	Tell whether you agree or disagree, and why.

2. **With a Group** Form a Reader's Circle to discuss the selections you read. Ask one another questions about your responses and make comments. You could also start a Reader's Blog and share your ideas that way.

What causes matter to change?

Talk Together

In this unit, you found lots of answers to the **Big Question**. Now, use your concept map to discuss the **Big Question** with the class.

Concept Map

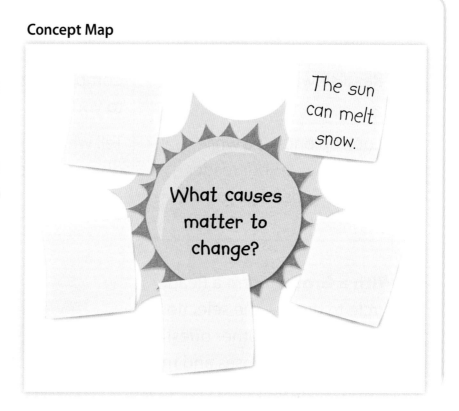

The sun can melt snow.

What causes matter to change?

Write an Explanation

Choose one example on your concept map. Explain how matter changes and what makes it change.

Share Your Ideas

Choose one of these ways to share your ideas about the **Big Question**.

Write It!

Write a Blog

Think of a time when you went on a camping trip or somewhere else outdoors. Tell how changes in matter affected you. Did it snow? Did the ground become muddy? Share your personal experience in a blog.

Talk About It!

Give a Weather Broadcast

Work with a classmate. Pretend you are a weather team. Report on the hottest or coldest day of the year. Tell what is happening outside.

Do It!

Perform a Dance

Get together with a group of classmates. Make up a dance to represent a solid, a liquid, or a gas. Perform your dance for the class.

Write It!

Classify Matter

Work with a partner. Look at objects in the classroom and out a window. List some of the objects. Write the name of each object under the word *Liquid*, *Solid*, or *Gas*.

From Past to Present

BIG Question

How can we preserve our traditions?

Unit at a Glance
▶ **Language**: Ask for and Give Information, Give and Follow Instructions, Social Studies Words
▶ **Literacy**: Visualize
▶ **Content**: Culture and Traditions

Unit
6

Share What You Know

Do It!

❶ **Talk** about traditions in your home.

❷ **Share** a song, story, or recipe that you learned from someone in your family.

❸ **Draw** a picture that shows something about your traditions and culture.

> We sing old songs together.

Build Background: Watch a video about culture and traditions.
🔵 **NGReach.com**

Ask for and Give Information

Language Frames

- How do _____ ?
- Why do _____ ?
- It's _____ .
- We hear/see/do different _____ .

Listen to the dialogue between Jesse and Inez.
Then use **Language Frames** with a partner. Ask for and give information about something that you do.

Dialogue ((MP3))

1.

Why do you go to Cinco de Mayo every year?

It's a family tradition.

2.

What do you do at the fair?

We do different things. We eat Mexican foods. We listen to the bands and watch the shows.

3.

Is the music good? How do you like it?

The music is really good. There are lots of guitars and loud horns. People love to dance.

4.

It sounds like fun! Are there a lot of people?

Yes! It's really crowded.

Key Words

heritage

music

region

rhythm

vary

Key Words

Use **Key Words** and other words to talk about **music** in different **regions**.

Mariachi bands perform in a plaza in Mexico.

A blues singer in the United States plays a guitar.

A band plays Cuban **rhythms** in Havana.

How does the music **vary**? What music do you like from your **heritage**?

Talk Together

How can you help preserve music you like? Talk with a partner. Use **Key Words** to ask for and give information about the music. Use Language Frames from page 344 if you can.

Classify Details

When you **classify details**, you group together details that are alike in some way.

Look at the pictures of the celebration that Inez went to.

hat

singer

horn

violin

taco

guacamole and chips

Map and Talk

You can use a web to classify details about something, such as the fair. Here's how you make one.

The topic of the web goes in the center. The name of each category, or group, goes in a small oval. The details go at the ends of the lines.

Details Web

band people food   horn guitar singer

I see   I hear

At the Fair

I smell and taste

taco   guacamole   chips

Talk Together

Tell a partner what you see, hear, smell, and taste at a fair or other celebration. Your partner makes a details web.

More Key Words

Use these words to talk about "Oye, Celia! A Song for Celia Cruz" and "Blues Legend: Blind Lemon Jefferson."

express
(ik-**spres**) *verb*

To **express** a thought or an emotion is to show it. She **expresses** her love for her dog.

feelings
(**fē**-lingz) *noun*

Feelings are how you experience something. Happiness and surprise are kinds of **feelings**.

perform
(pur-**form**) *verb*

When you **perform**, you put on a show for a group of people. The girls **perform** on stage.

popular
(**pah**-pyu-lur) *adjective*

When many people like a place or a thing, it is **popular**.

style
(**stīul**) *noun*

Style is a way of doing something. He paints in a colorful **style**.

Talk Together

Make a chart to tell how you feel about each **Key Word**. Compare your chart with a partner's.

Word	Positive (+) Negative (-) Neither (=)	Reason
feelings	=	I think feelings can be both good and bad.

Add words to My Vocabulary Notebook.
NGReach.com

347

Learn to Visualize

Look at the picture. Find details that show how things look, sound, smell, taste, and feel. Close your eyes and **visualize** the scene. How does this make you feel about the picture?

When you read, you can **visualize** details, too.

How to Visualize

👁	**1.** Look for details. Find words that tell how things look, sound, smell, taste, and feel.
☁	**2.** Picture a detail in your mind.
🙂	**3.** Tell how the picture makes you feel. How does it help you make sense of the text?

I read _____ .

I picture _____ .

I feel _____ .

Talk Together

Read Inez's chat. Read the sample visualization. Then use **Language Frames** to visualize details. Tell a partner what you pictured.

Online Chat

Inez: I went to the Cinco de Mayo fair this weekend.

Alice: Really? Did you have fun?

Inez: Oh, yeah! Bands played. Dancers **performed**. I rode on the roller coaster! Woo-whee!

Alice: Did you buy any souvenirs?

Inez: I bought a silver bracelet.

Alice: O-o-o-o! Is it real silver?

Inez: Yes. I had to grab it fast. Lots of people were in the booth pushing and shoving, and the **style** I wanted was really **popular**. I also got a turquoise ring.

Alice: How was the food?

Inez: Super! I almost ordered a burger with fries, but I changed my mind. I had a burrito instead. For dessert I had flan, which is a kind of custard. ◄

Alice: Sounds yummy! What was your favorite event?

Inez: The fireworks! Boom! Boom! They were brilliant! ◄

Alice: Sounds like a day to remember, Inez.

Inez: It was! I can hardly **express** my **feelings** about Cinco de Mayo. It's one of my favorite holidays!

Sample Visualization

"I read the description.

I picture bands playing Mexican music, dancers in bright costumes, and people screaming on a roller coaster ride.

I feel the excitement of the fair."

◄ = A good place to visualize

Read Song Lyrics

Genre

Song lyrics are the words of a song. The lyrics of this song express a young girl's thoughts and feelings about a famous singer named Celia Cruz.

Sensory Language

Sensory language helps create pictures in the reader's mind. It tells how things look, sound, smell, taste, and feel.

Your voice pulsates with
The *doong–doong–doong* of the *tambor*,
The *chaka–chaka chaka–chaka* of
    the maracas,
And the *stroom stroom stroom* of
    the guitar.

Sensory language can describe sounds.

Oye, Celia!
A Song for Celia Cruz

by **Katie Sciurba** ◆ illustrated by **Edel Rodriguez**

Comprehension Coach

▶ **Set a Purpose**
A girl listens to Celia Cruz's
music. Read to find out how it affects her.

*O*ye, Celia!

When I hear you, I hear Cuba—
Your Cuba, my Cuba,
Our Cuba.

Your voice pulsates with
The *doong–doong–doong* of the *tambor*,
The *chaka–chaka chaka–chaka* of
    the maracas,
And the *stroom stroom stroom* of
    the guitar.

My heart beats along.

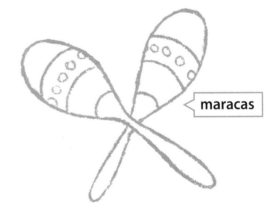

maracas

In Other Words
Oye Listen
pulsates with makes sounds just like
tambor drum (in Spanish)
maracas rattles

353

Celia Cruz,
When I hear you, I hear *la gente*—
Your people, my people,

Our people.

You sing to us, for us, in Spanish—
The language of Cuba, Puerto Rico,
    Mexico, Ecuador . . .
But even people who don't understand
    the words
Understand the passion.

I understand the words and the passion.

guitar

In Other Words
la gente the people (in Spanish)
passion strong **feelings**

flute

▶ **Before You Move On**

1. **Classify** Name at least three instruments that Cruz's band uses.

2. **Visualize** How do you picture Celia Cruz? What words from the text help you see and hear her?

▶ **Predict**
How will Cruz's **music**
make the girl feel?

*N*uestra Celia,

When I hear you, I hear *la tristeza*—
Your sadness, my sadness,
Our sadness.

You tell about your home—
The land you left behind,
The people you will always love,
The country you will never forget.

Sometimes I cry, too.

Cuba

In Other Words
Nuestra Our (in Spanish)
la tristeza the sadness (in Spanish)
never forget always remember

357

Unforgettable Celia,
When I hear you, I hear *la historia*—
Your history, my history,
Our history.

Your lyrics breathe life into our ancestors—
Slaves who gathered in stolen moments
To create a rhythm
That was passed down to us.

I thank them.

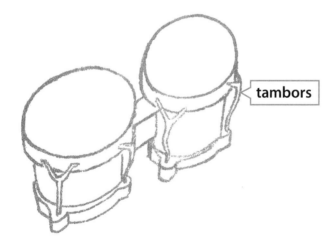

tambors

In Other Words

Unforgettable Wonderful

la historia the stories about the past in Cuba (in Spanish)

breathe life into our ancestors make people from long
   ago seem alive again

gathered in stolen moments met in secret

▶ **Before You Move On**

1. **Confirm Prediction** Was your prediction about the girl's feelings correct? Explain.
2. **Sensory Language** Reread lines 5–8 on page 358. What do you see and hear? How do the words make you feel?

▶ **Predict**
Cruz's **music** has strong **rhythms**.
What do people do when they
hear the music?

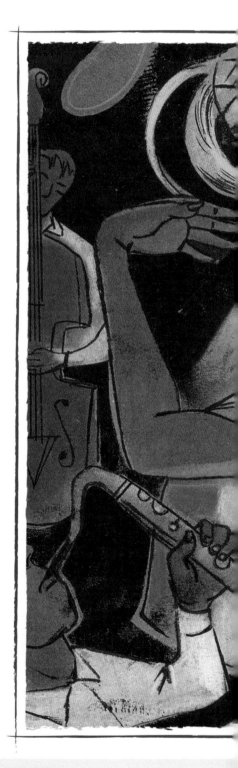

*L*a *Reina*, Celia,
When I hear you, I hear *la salsa*—
Your salsa, my salsa,
Our salsa.

Your music becomes a blend, a *salsa*,
   just like us—
African, Caribbean, and European.

I am *la salsa*.

Smiling Celia,
When I hear you, I hear *la alegría*—
Your happiness, my happiness,
Our happiness.

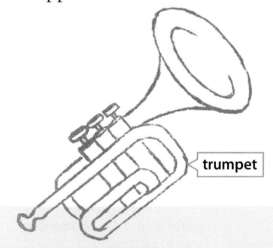

trumpet

In Other Words

La Reina Queen (in Spanish)

la salsa a type of dance **music**
    (in Spanish)

la alegría the happiness (in Spanish)

360

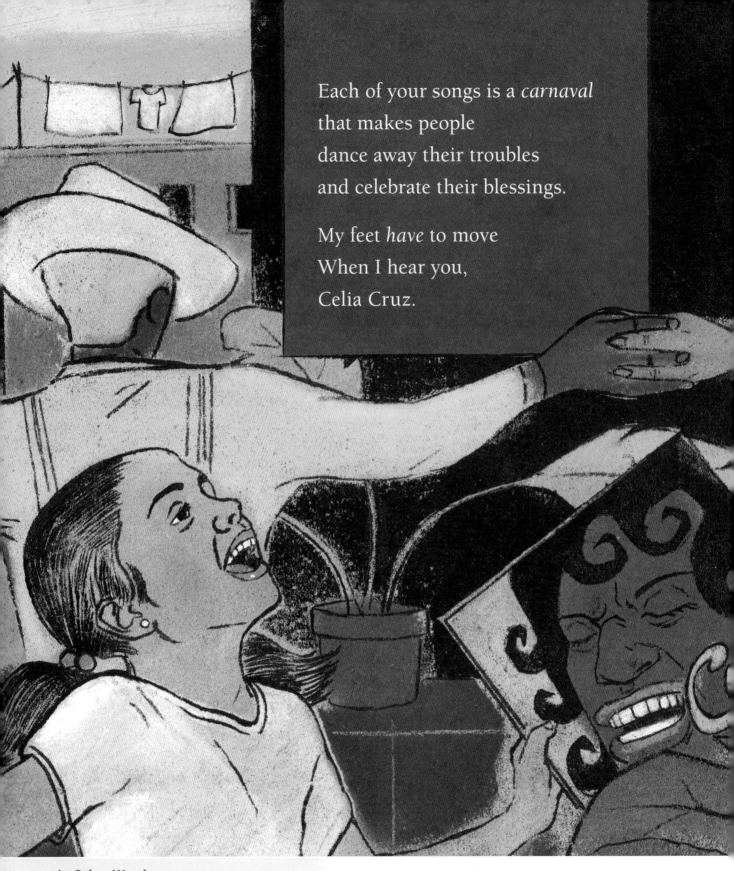

Each of your songs is a *carnaval*
that makes people
dance away their troubles
and celebrate their blessings.

My feet *have* to move
When I hear you,
Celia Cruz.

In Other Words

carnaval party (in Spanish)

dance away their troubles feel happy

celebrate their blessings show thanks
for the good things in their lives

▶ **Before You Move On**

1. **Confirm Prediction** How do the strong **rhythms** of Cruz's **music** affect people? Did you guess correctly?

2. **Classify** Cruz's **music** is a blend, or mix, of three cultures. What are they?

Meet the Author

Katie Sciurba

Katie Sciurba lives in New York City. Before Celia Cruz died in 2003, Ms. Sciurba saw her **perform** at a concert in Central Park. As thousands of fans danced, clapped, and sang along, hail began to fall. But even with the terrible weather, Cruz's loyal fans stayed until the very end of the memorable show.

Oye, Celia is one way Ms. Sciurba celebrates Celia Cruz's life and music. "It is my hope that this message, *Oye, Celia*, reaches her in *el cielo* (heaven)," she says.

► Author Katie Sciurba

◄ Singer Celia Cruz

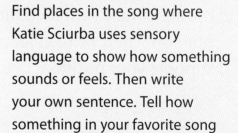

Writer's Craft

Find places in the song where Katie Sciurba uses sensory language to show how something sounds or feels. Then write your own sentence. Tell how something in your favorite song sounds or feels.

Key Words	
express	popular
feelings	region
heritage	rhythm
music	style
perform	vary

Talk About It

1. How does the girl feel about Celia Cruz? Find some lines in the **song lyrics** that show the girl's **feelings**.

   The writer _____ . Lines that show her feelings are: _____ .

2. Pretend that you play in Cruz's band. What might someone ask you about it? **Give information to explain.**

   What instruments _____ ? How do _____ ? I play _____ . They sound _____ .

3. Does the selection have a first-person narrator or a third-person narrator? How do you know?

   It has a _____ . I know because _____ .

Learn test-taking strategies.
⊘ NGReach.com

Write About It

Think of a band or a singer that you like. Write a short persuasive essay to tell why others should listen to this music. Write a sentence that **expresses** your opinion. Then write at least three sentences to support your position. Use **Key Words**.

I think everyone _____ . First of all, _____ .

Classify Details

Make a details web for "Oye, Celia! A Song for Celia Cruz." Classify information about the **music** of Cruz. Include words that describe the sounds and **feelings** of the music.

Details Web

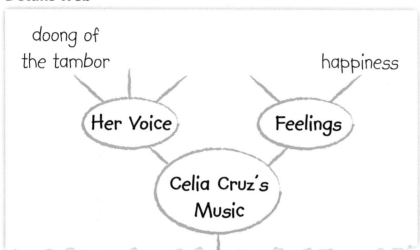

Now use your details web to tell a partner about Cruz's music. Use the sentence frames and **Key Words**. Record your description.

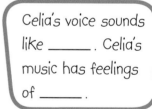

Celia's voice sounds like _____. Celia's music has feelings of _____.

Fluency · Comprehension Coach

Use the Comprehension Coach to practice reading with expression. Rate your reading.

Talk Together

How do both Cruz and the girl preserve traditions? Answer the question with a partner. Use **Key Words**.

Playful Language

A **tongue twister** is a phrase or sentence that has many of the same sounds. It's fun to try to say a tongue twister quickly.

Say this tongue twister aloud with a partner.

> Cindy says Celia is a singer with a salsa style.

What sounds do you hear that are the same? Now say the sentence aloud five times as fast as you can!

Try It Together

Read the tongue twister aloud and complete item 1. Then complete item 2.

> The rhythms of rap really rule!

1. **Most of the words begin with the sound of _____ .**

   A l

   B r

   C p

   D th

2. **Which phrase is an example of a tongue twister?**

   A listen to music

   B ten teen tunes

   C rhythm of drums

   D play with the band

Connect Across Texts Read about another musician who added to the musical **heritage** of the United States.

Genre In a **biography**, an author tells about the important events in another person's life.

Blues Legend:

Blind Lemon Jefferson

BY LIBBY LEWIS

Blind Lemon Jefferson was a singer and guitar player. He was born on a farm in Texas around 1893. Jefferson **was born blind**, but that didn't stop him from reaching his dreams. He became one of the most **famous** American musicians of all time.

▲ Blind Lemon Jefferson

In Other Words
was born blind could not see
famous loved

▷ **Before You Move On**

1. **Make Inferences** What might have made it harder for Jefferson to reach his dreams? Why?
2. **Classify Details** Find three words on this page that describe Blind Lemon Jefferson.

Music Man

Jefferson started to play guitar and sing when he was a boy. At first, he played **music** on street corners in small towns near his home. Then, as a teenager, he traveled all around the southern states. There, he **performed** his **unique** music for audiences in big cities such as Dallas, Texas.

In 1925, Jefferson went to Chicago, Illinois, to **record** his music. Before his death in 1929, he made more than 100 recordings. This kept his music alive for people to enjoy **decades** later.

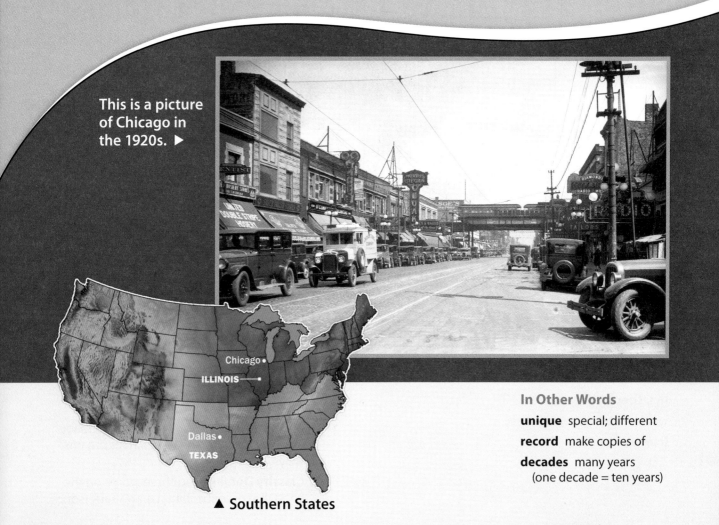

This is a picture of Chicago in the 1920s. ▶

Chicago •

ILLINOIS

Dallas •

TEXAS

▲ Southern States

In Other Words
unique special; different
record make copies of
decades many years
(one decade = ten years)

The Blues

Blind Lemon Jefferson played a **style** of music called "the blues." Blues songs are often about bad luck or trouble, but they can also be fun.

Blues music started from songs sung by enslaved people around the time of the Civil War. The hard work on the farms made them sad and **weary**. They sang the blues to **express** their **feelings**.

Over time, those songs mixed together with church **hymns** and newer types of music.

kazoo

Many early blues musicians played on street corners. ▶

▶ **Before You Move On**

1. **Classify Details** What kinds of **music** did the blues come from?
2. **Visualize** Who first sang the blues? How does this help you imagine how blues **music** sounded then?

▼ Record companies used ads to sell Jefferson's music.

▼ In the 1920s, artists recorded on records like this one.

Get Your
Paramount Book of Blues

Ask your dealer or write us for the new 44-page Paramount Book of Blues. Attractively bound and decorated. Includes big Blues hits by such famous artists as Blind Lemon Jefferson, "Ma" Rainey, Blind Blake, Ida Cox, and others, with separate sections for songs of each. Pictures and autobiographies of the well known stars. Retail price, 35 cents.

Keeping the Blues Alive

People all over the country listened to Blind Lemon Jefferson's recordings. He performed the blues in a way that no one had ever heard before.

Over time, Jefferson's style of blues became very **popular**. He was one of the first African American blues singers to have a big audience. Since then, his music has **influenced many musicians**.

In Other Words

influenced many musicians changed the way people play

▲ B.B. King

▲ Bob Dylan

▲ The White Stripes

Jefferson is gone now, but his blues lives on. He sang with a **high-pitched voice** and played his guitar with **irregular** **rhythm** . Others have tried to follow this style, too. Many modern musicians such as Bob Dylan, B.B. King, and The White Stripes have recorded his songs.

People still listen to Jefferson's music today. Blind Lemon Jefferson has **truly** helped keep the blues alive. ❖

In Other Words

high-pitched voice voice that was high and sharp, not deep or low

irregular uneven

truly really

▶ **Before You Move On**

1. **Visualize** Which words help you imagine what Jefferson sounded like when he sang?
2. **Classify Details** Name three musicians or bands who sang Jefferson's songs.

Compare Language

Key Words

express	popular
feelings	region
heritage	rhythm
music	style
perform	vary

The song lyrics are literary and the biography is informational, but both texts have similar ideas. Each one tells about a real singer.

With a partner, compare the language in the selections. Complete the T chart. Write four examples of sensory language from the lyrics. Write four facts from the biography.

T Chart

Sensory Language in the Lyrics	Facts in the Biography
1. Her voice is like the doong-doong-doong of the tambor.	1. Jefferson was born in Texas.
2.	2.
3.	3.
4.	4.

Talk Together

How can we preserve our musical traditions? Think about the song lyrics and the biography. Use **Key Words** to talk about your ideas.

Pronoun Agreement

Use the right **subject pronoun** or **object pronoun**.

Grammar Rules — Pronoun Agreement

	One 🧍	More Than One 🧍🧍
• Use for yourself:	**I**, **me**	
• Use for yourself and one or more people:		**we**, **us**
• Use when you speak to one or more people:	**you**, **you**	**you**, **you**
• Use for one other person or thing:	**he**, **she**, **it** **him**, **her**, **i t**	
• Use for more than one other person or thing:		**they**, **them**

Read Pronouns

Read these sentences. Find one subject pronoun and two object pronouns. Show them to a partner.

Celia Cruz died in 2003, but she is still a popular singer. Many people like her. Cruz is special to them.

Write Pronouns

Write two sentences about Cruz or Jefferson. Use a subject and an object pronoun. Check your work with your partner.

Give and Follow Instructions

Listen to Ben's song. Then use **Language Frames** to give and follow instructions. Tell a partner how to make something that helps preserve traditions, such as a family album.

Song

SPOON FISH

First, to make a spoon fish
I find a wooden spoon.
Then, I paint some symbols
Older than the moon.
Next, I add a fish eye bead
And feathers for a fin.
Finally, I hang it up
And watch the spoon
     fish spin.

Tune: "The Eensy-Weensy Spider"

374

Key Words

Key Words
artist
carve
storyteller
tale
tradition
wood

Look at the pictures. Use **Key Words** and other words to talk about **traditions**.

Long ago, **artists** **carved** figures in **wood**.

Some modern artists continue the tradition.

Long ago, people listened to **storytellers**.

People hear some of the same **tales** today.

Talk Together

How do the people in the photos preserve traditions? With a partner, give and follow instructions based on what the photos show. Use **Language Frames** and **Key Words**.

375

Steps in a Process

When you make something, you follow steps in a certain order. One step builds on the other. This is called **steps in a process**.

The pictures show how to make a mask. Look at the four steps.

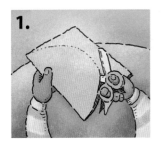  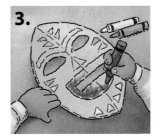 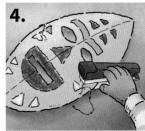

Map and Talk

You can write the steps in a process in a flow chart. Here's how you make one.

Each step goes in a box. The first step goes in the first box. The second step goes in the second box, and so on.

Flow Chart

1. Cut a mask shape out of heavy paper.	2. Cut holes for the eyes and the mouth.	3. Draw colorful designs on the mask.	4. Add pieces of yarn so that you can put the mask on.

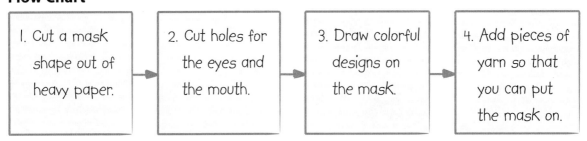

Think of something simple to make. Tell a partner the steps. Your partner restates each step and writes it in a flow chart. Then your partner pantomimes the steps as you read them aloud.

More Key Words

Use these words to talk about "Carving Stories in Cedar" and "Stories to Tell."

communicate
(ku-**myū**-nu-kāt) *verb*

When you **communicate**, you share words or feelings. She **communicates** with a friend.

generation
(je-nu-**rā**-shun) *noun*

A **generation** is made up of people born around the same time. They are in different **generations**.

preservation
(pre-zur-**vā**-shun) *noun*

Preservation is the act of keeping something safe for a long time. The **preservation** of old documents is important.

process
(**prah**-ses) *noun*

When you follow a **process**, you do something step by step.

represent
(re-pri-**zent**) *verb*

To **represent** means to stand for. A heart **represents** love.

Talk Together

Make a Study Card for each **Key Word**. Then compare your cards with a partner's.

> Preservation is the act of keeping something safe.
>
> **Example:** a museum
>
> **Not an example:** a city dump

Add words to My Vocabulary Notebook.
NGReach.com

Learn to Visualize

Look at the picture and read the caption. Then look away and **visualize** details of the people, place, and event. Make a quick sketch of what you visualized. How does this help you understand the picture?

Ben tells his classmates a traditional tale.

When you read, you can **visualize** to help you understand the text.

How to Visualize

👁	**1.** As you read, look for words that describe people, places, and events.	I read _____ .
☁	**2.** Use the words to create a picture in your mind.	I picture _____ .
✏	**3.** Draw the picture.	I draw _____ .
❓	**4.** Ask yourself, "How does this help me understand the text?"	Now I _____ .

378

Talk Together

Read Ben's instructions. Read the sample visualization.
Then use **Language Frames** to visualize as you read. Tell a
partner what you pictured.

Instructions

How to Prepare to Tell a Story

1. Find stories you know from your own culture. These are
   the stories that are passed down from **generation** to
   generation.

2. Choose the **tale** you want to tell. Stories that have
   action and humor are the best.

3. Find or draw pictures that **represent** parts of the
   story. Show the pictures while you tell the story. Pictures
   help the audience visualize the people, places, and events.

4. Practice reading with expression to **communicate**
   emotion.

5. Practice speaking clearly. If possible, record your story
   and play it back to hear how your voice sounds.

6. Use body movements to help tell the story. To get the
   movements right, practice in front of a mirror.

Finally, kids enjoy listening to stories.
So tell stories whenever you can.
Use this **process** to prepare. And
remember, the **preservation** of
traditional tales is serious, but it also
can be fun!

Sample Visualization

"I read that stories with
action and humor are best.

I picture myself telling a
funny story to the class.

I draw my classmates.

Now I understand why it's
good to choose stories
with humor."

◀ = A good place to visualize

Read a Descriptive Article

Genre
A **descriptive article** can describe the steps someone uses to do or make something.

Text Features
The **title** tells what the article is about. A **subtitle** gives more information about the title.

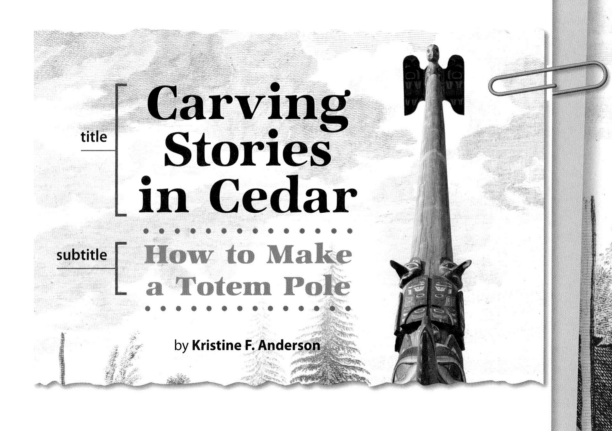

title [**Carving Stories in Cedar**

subtitle [**How to Make a Totem Pole**

by **Kristine F. Anderson**

Carving
Stories
in Cedar

How to Make
a Totem Pole

by **Kristine F. Anderson**

▶ **Set a Purpose**
Find out what totem poles are
and how they are made.

What Is a Totem Pole?

Everyone likes to hear family stories and **legends**.
Many **tales** are passed down from **generation** to
generation. Hundreds of years ago, **native people** lived
along the northwest coast of the United States and
Canada. They did not have a written language. These
"First People" created a special way to tell their tales
and family histories.

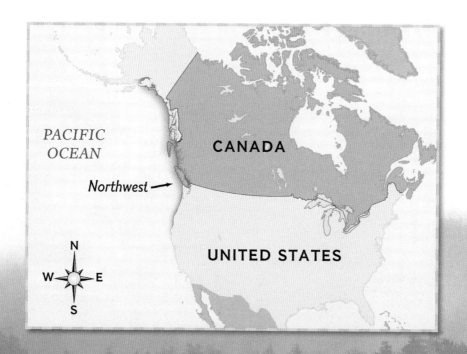

In Other Words
legends old **tales**
native people the first people in the area

382

Master carvers chose cedar trees from the forests. These trees were tall and straight, and some had red-colored bark. The carvers carved pictures into the soft **wood** to **record** family stories. They also carved poles to **honor their chiefs** and other important people who had died. These carvings are called totem poles. Sometimes they are called silent books.

This is a finished totem pole. It stands next to uncut cedar trees. ▶

In Other Words

Master carvers People who cut **wood** really well

record keep and remember

honor their chiefs show that they cared about their leaders

▶ **Before You Move On**

1. **Visualize** What words help you picture what a cedar tree is like?

2. **Use Text Features** Reread the subtitle for the article. What will you look for as you read on?

How Were the Totem Poles Different?

Each family or **clan** used an animal to **represent** them. The animal stood for something special about **their culture and identity**. So carvers used those animals and other family symbols to create the totem poles. The families placed the tall **sculptures** in front of their homes to show who lived there. They also used the poles like signs to welcome visitors to their villages.

"The poles helped us tell our stories," says Israel Shotridge, a Tlingit (KLINK-it) carver from Ketchikan (KETCH-ih-kan), Alaska. "They helped us preserve our culture and identity."

Shotridge in traditional Tlingit clothing ▶

In Other Words
clan group of families living together
their culture and identity who they were and their history
sculptures works of art; carvings

How Do You Carve A Totem Pole?

Shotridge has been carving for twenty years. He uses **methods** that were used in the past. " **Tradition** is an important part of what I do," he says.

Here is how Shotridge makes a totem pole.

▲ This is a reproduction of the Sun Raven totem pole. Shortridge finished it in 2003.

1. He chooses a design.

Before he begins carving, Shotridge talks with the person who wants him to carve the pole. They discuss the design. Some of the poles are **reproductions** of old poles. Others are new designs used for businesses, government buildings, and schools.

◄ Two earlier reproductions were made by different **artists** in 1902 and 1938.

In Other Words

methods the same steps

reproductions copies

▶ **Before You Move On**

1. **Make Inferences** Why is **tradition** important to Shotridge?

2. **Steps in a Process** What do you do first to carve a totem pole?

2. He prepares the tree.

Next, Shotridge finds and cuts down a tall, straight cedar tree. He sings special songs his mother, a **tribal elder,** taught him as he works. Then he **removes the bark**. He draws the design on the **wood** with a special pencil. Sometimes he adds extra pieces of wood to show a bird's wings or a fish's fins.

▲ Shotridge draws a design for a bird's beak.

In Other Words

prepares the tree gets the tree ready

tribal elder wise older person

removes the bark cuts off the outside layer of the tree

3. He carves the pole.

Then Shotridge uses tools, such as an adze and chisel, to carve the design into the wood. An **assistant** may work with him on the larger poles. But even with help, some poles take almost a year to complete.

adze

chisel

4. He paints the pole.

Shotridge paints his poles in the traditional colors of red, teal, blue, and black. Early carvers made their paints from **local minerals**, such as copper and iron, mixed with salmon eggs. But Shotridge, like most modern carvers, buys his paint.

▲ Sue Shotridge paints in traditional colors.

In Other Words
assistant helper
local minerals materials from nature

▶ **Before You Move On**

1. **Details** What tools does Shotridge need to make a totem pole?
2. **Steps in a Process** What must Shotridge do before he starts carving?

5. People raise the totem pole.

When the pole is almost finished, plans are made to raise it. **Cranes** lift big poles into place. The poles often weigh more than a thousand pounds! Smaller poles are raised by hand.

"We usually raise poles the **old-fashioned** way," says Shotridge. "We use **lots of manpower** and ropes."

▲ People use ropes to raise a totem pole.

In Other Words

Cranes Large machines used to lift heavy objects

old-fashioned old

lots of manpower the strength of many people

▲ These traditional costumes are worn to a potlatch.

6. Everyone celebrates!

When a pole is raised, the person who asked for it often has a big celebration. It is called a potlatch. Everyone **feasts**. Sometimes people give gifts to each other. The bigger the pole, the bigger the party. If the pole is **commissioned by** a clan member, guests sing songs from their family's clan.

Once the pole has been raised, another silent book stands to tell the story of the people of the Northwest.

In Other Words
feasts eats a lot
comissioned by made for

▶ **Before You Move On**

1. **Visualize** Picture yourself at a potlatch. What do you see, hear, smell, taste, and feel?
2. **Cause/Effect** What are two ways the size of the pole can affect what happens in the last two steps?

▶ **Set a Purpose**
Now read a legend that reminds
people to value the gifts of others.

◀ Shotridge's totem pole
shows Fog Woman's
gift of salmon.

The Legend of
Raven and Fog Woman

retold by **Susan Blackaby**
illustrated by **Amanda Hall**

One day long ago, Raven went fishing. He needed to get ready for winter. Again and again he **cast** his nets, but he didn't catch a single fish. As he **paddled** toward shore, Raven became lost in **a swirl of fog**. The fog was so thick that Raven didn't notice the beautiful woman sitting next to him. Then suddenly she spoke.

"**Lend** me your hat," she said.

In Other Words
cast threw
paddled rowed
a swirl of fog clouds close to the ground
  that are hard to see through
Lend Give

Raven took off his hat, and Fog Woman used it to gather up the fog. When the sky cleared, Raven returned home with the **mysterious** woman. Soon after, Raven and Fog Woman were married.

Winter arrived, and food was **scarce**. One rainy morning, Raven felt grumpy and hungry. He **scolded** Fog Woman, who was making a basket.

"You're wasting your time," snapped Raven. "What good is an empty basket?"

Fog Woman didn't answer.

In Other Words
mysterious unusual, interesting
scarce hard to find
scolded spoke angrily to

Fog Woman filled the new basket with water and washed her hands in it. When she dumped the water back into the creek, four silvery **salmon** slipped out.

Raven asked, "How did you do that?"

Fog Woman didn't answer.

Day after day she filled the basket with water, and soon the creek **ran bright with** salmon. No one in the village went hungry.

But Raven wasn't **satisfied**. He clawed the ground with his feet and flapped his wings angrily.

In Other Words
◀ **salmon** fish
ran bright with was full of
satisfied happy; pleased

"Tell me your secret," Raven **demanded**.
Fog Woman wouldn't answer.

Raven **lost his temper**. "If you won't tell me, then go!" he shouted.

As Fog Woman left, the salmon rushed after her. Raven rushed after her, too. He reached for her, but he couldn't hold on. Fog Woman had turned into **mist**.

Raven lost Fog Woman forever, but each year she sends a basket of salmon so that no one in the village goes hungry. ❖

In Other Words
demanded ordered
lost his temper became angry
mist small drops of water

▶ **Before You Move On**

1. **Clarify** Why did Fog Woman leave Raven?
2. **Visualize** What do you think the villagers did when they discovered all the salmon? Draw the scene.

Talk About It

1. As you read this **descriptive article**, what did you visualize? Give an example.

I pictured _____ .

2. With a partner, pretend to make a totem pole. **Give and follow instructions**. Use the article to help you.

First, _____ . Then, _____ . Next, _____ . Finally, _____ .

3. Look back at the picture of the totem pole on page 390. How does it **represent** the story of Raven and Fog Woman?

The totem pole has _____ . It shows _____ .

Learn test-taking strategies.
 NGReach.com

Write About It

It takes a lot of time and work to make a totem pole. What would you like to ask the **artist** about the **process**? Write one question for each step. Use **Key Words**.

1. What _____ ?
2. How _____ ?

Steps in a Process

"**Carving** Stories in Cedar" tells how people make and display a totem pole. Write the steps in a flow chart. To help you remember, look at the numbered heads and text on pages 385–389.

Flow Chart

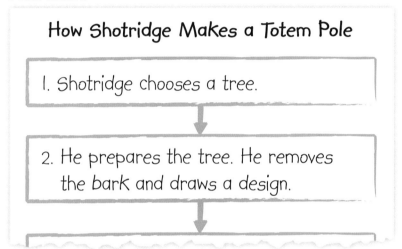

How Shotridge Makes a Totem Pole

1. Shotridge chooses a tree.

2. He prepares the tree. He removes the bark and draws a design.

Use your flow chart to explain the steps to a partner. Your partner restates each step and pantomimes it. Use the sentence frames and **Key Words**. Record your explanation.

First, _____ .
Then, _____ .
Next, _____ .

Fluency ▶ Comprehension Coach

Use the Comprehension Coach to practice reading with intonation. Rate your reading.

Talk Together

How do **artists** and **storytellers** preserve **traditions**? Use **Key Words** to help you write your ideas. Share your ideas with the class.

Homophones

Homophones are words that sound the same, but have different spellings and meanings.

This **tale** is about a clever fox.

Meaning: a story

The fox has a long, fluffy **tail**.

Meaning: an animal's body part

Try It Together

Read the sentences. Then answer the questions.

I think it <u>would</u> be fun to carve a whale out of wood. My friend carved <u>one</u> and won a prize.

1. What word is a homophone for <u>would</u>?
   A prize
   B carve
   C wood
   D whale

2. What word is a homophone for <u>one</u>?
   A fun
   B out
   C won
   D would

396

Connect Across Texts Read about another way to share **traditions**.

Genre A **profile** is nonfiction. It gives facts about a person and his or her life. A **folk tale** is an old story that tells why something is the way it is.

Stories to Tell

by **Janine Boylan**

When Elizabeth Lindsey was seven years old, the **elders** predicted that she would **keep the voices of her ancestors alive**. When her father asked her what she would do in her life, Elizabeth said she would tell stories.

Elizabeth Lindsey was born and raised in Hawaii. ▶

In Other Words

elders older people

keep the voices of her ancestors alive share her family's history and **traditions** with others

▶ **Before You Move On**

1. **Use Text Features** Read the title. How does Elizabeth keep her ancestors' voices alive?

2. **Make Inferences** How do you think the elders felt about what Elizabeth wanted to do?

▲ The moon over Kalalau Beach in Kauai, Hawaii.

Like other **native Hawaiian children**, Elizabeth was raised by a group of elders as well as her parents. The elders teach the children how the **cycles of the moon** can show them the best times to plant and fish. They teach the children to respect nature, too. The children learn to take only what they need and return the rest.

In Other Words

native Hawaiian children children born and raised in Hawaii

◄ **cycles of the moon** changes in the way the moon looks at night

◀ Elizabeth listens to a legend told by an elder.

During sharing time in the fourth grade, Elizabeth loved to tell stories about the people she cared about. As she grew, she realized she wanted to **preserve** the stories from native people around the world, like those who had raised her.

Now, Elizabeth travels to listen to stories from native **cultures** few people know about. She says, "The more I learn about other people, the more amazed I am at how much we are alike."

"The Rainbow Bridge" on the following pages is just one of the many stories Elizabeth tells to share her Hawaiian culture.

In Other Words

preserve save

cultures groups of people with the same history and way of life

▶ **Before You Move On**

1. **Visualize** If you traveled with Elizabeth, what do think you would see and do? Sketch your ideas. Then describe your picture.

2. **Draw Conclusions** Do you think Elizabeth likes her job as a **storyteller**? Explain.

▶ **Set a Purpose**
Read this folk **tale** to find out how a rainbow came to be.

THE RAINBOW BRIDGE

A NATIVE FOLK TALE FROM HAWAII • ILLUSTRATED BY BELLE YANG

A long time ago in Hawaii, the people **set out** in their **canoes**. They rowed a long way north of their home. They rowed for days and days. The air got colder. The days **grew shorter**. Finally, they reached a new, cold place.

Wonderful people came to greet them. These people took them into their homes. They fixed their **worn** canoes. They treated the Hawaiians like family.

In Other Words
set out left their home
canoes long, thin boats
grew shorter had less and less sunshine
worn broken

At first, the Hawaiians loved this new place. They were happy. They married. They had children.

But then they remembered the warm, tropical land where they had come from. The more they remembered this land, the more they wanted to return there with their new families.

But they loved their new home, too. They knew that if they rowed back to Hawaii, they might never be able to return to this land.

They hoped **silently** for a way to return to their old home. They also wanted a way to travel back to their new home.

In Other Words
silently without telling anyone

▶ **Before You Move On**

1. **Use Text Features** Read the title. What do you think a rainbow bridge is?
2. **Compare and Contrast** How was the Hawaiian people's new home different from their old home? How were they the same?

401

▶ **Predict**

Do you think the people will find a way to travel back to their old home?

Kind-hearted Weasel heard their wishes. He had an idea.

Weasel began to play his flute. As the notes filled the air, a **colorful arc** rose from the land and into the sky. Weasel played until the bridge grew high above the ocean. It ended beyond where they could see. Weasel explained that this bridge would take them between their new and old homes.

The people were so excited they ran toward the bridge. They grabbed their children's hands. They grabbed their wives' and husbands' hands. "When you climb this bridge, do not look down," Weasel warned them. But they did not listen.

In Other Words
Kind-hearted Nice
colorful arc rainbow

Some people got to the top of the bridge. They looked down. The ocean was far below them. They **got dizzy** and fell into the water. These people became dolphins who could travel the seas.

The people used the rainbow bridge to travel between their two homes. The dolphins swam from place to place.

Now people know that the rainbow **represents the colors of people** around the world. It also represents the bridge that brings them together.

Where I love there are rainbows.
*Where I live is a place of **harmony***
that follows whatever is.

— traditional Hawaiian saying

▶ **Before You Move On**

1. **Confirm Prediction** Did the people find a way to travel back to their old home? Explain.

2. **Visualize** What would it be like to walk across a rainbow bridge? Describe what you would see and feel.

Key Words

artist	represent
carve	storyteller
communicate	tale
generation	tradition
preservation	wood
process	

Compare Themes

What is the theme, or main message, of "The Legend of Raven and Fog Woman"? What is the theme of "The Rainbow Bridge"?

Make a theme web for each story. In your own words, write the theme and details that support the theme.

Theme Web

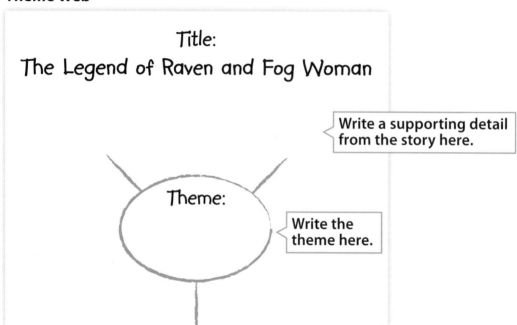

Title:
The Legend of Raven and Fog Woman

Write a supporting detail from the story here.

Theme:

Write the theme here.

Talk Together

Share your webs with a partner. Discuss how the themes of the two **tales** are alike and different. Use **Key Words** to talk about your ideas.

Pronoun Agreement

Possessive pronouns tell who or what owns something. Be sure to use the right possessive pronoun.

Grammar Rules **Pronoun Agreement**	
• For yourself, use **mine**.	The pencil is **mine**.
• For yourself and one or more people, use **ours**.	The tools are **ours**.
• When you speak to one or more people, use **yours**.	Is that design **yours**?
• For one other person or thing, use **his**, **hers**, or **its**.	The hat is **his**. She likes **hers**.
• For two or more other people or things, use **theirs**.	The costumes are **theirs**.

Read Possessive Pronouns

Read these sentences. Find two possessive pronouns.

> We made paper totem poles like theirs. This one is mine.

Write Possessive Pronouns

With a partner, talk about the photograph on page 389. Then write a sentence for the photo. Use a possessive pronoun.

Write Like a Reporter

Write an Interview ✏️

Interview someone who helps preserve a special tradition. Share your interviews with classmates and others in your school.

Study a Model

In an interview, you ask a person questions to get information. Read Kia's interview with her aunt, who makes Hmong story cloths.

Aunt Yi's Story Cloths

by Kia Lau

The Hmong people of Laos are known for their beautiful story cloths. My Aunt Yi makes these coths. I asked her about them.

Kia: What are story cloths?
Aunt Yi: They are a special type of needlework. The pictures that I sew into the cloths tell stories about our people.

Kia: When did you start making them?
Aunt Yi: Oh, it was years ago, when I was a young girl living in a Thai refugee camp.

Kia: Why do you still make them?
Aunt Yi: People around the world now admire Hmong story cloths. I am proud to be one of the artists who helps preserve this tradition.

The first paragraph tells who is interviewed and what the interview is about.

The **questions** are organized in a natural order. One question flows into the next one.

Each **answer** gives the person's exact words.

Prewrite

1. **Choose a Topic** What traditions would you like to learn about? Who could you interview? Discuss your ideas with a partner.

Language Frames	
Tell Your Ideas	**Respond to Ideas**
We have lots of family traditions. One tradition _____. I could ask _____.	I think/do not think it's a good idea to write about _____ because _____.
I've always wondered why people still _____. Maybe _____ could tell me.	Who else could you interview about _____?
I know someone who _____. I could find out about that.	Are you really interested in _____? What would you like to find out?

2. **Gather Ideas** Now think about your first paragraph and questions you want to ask.

3. **Get Organized** Use a details web to organize your ideas.

Details Web

Draft

Use your details web to help you plan your opening paragraph and questions. After the interview, prepare a draft. Remember to write the person's own words for the answers.

Revise

1. **Read, Retell, Respond** Read your draft aloud to a partner. Your partner listens and then retells what the interview is about. Next, talk about ways to improve your writing.

Language Frames	
Retell	**Make Suggestions**
You interviewed _____ .	The questions didn't seem to be in a natural order. Could you organize them differently?
The tradition you asked about was _____ .	
The questions _____ .	I didn't understand _____ . Did you write down the answer correctly?

2. **Make Changes** Think about your draft and your partner's suggestions. Then use the Revising Marks on page 573 to mark your changes.

   • Are your questions in a natural order that flows? If not, try changing the order.

   > **Kia: When did you start making them?**
   > **Aunt Yi:** Oh, it was years ago in a Thai refugee camp.
   > **Kia: What are story cloths?**
   > **Aunt Yi:** They are a special type of needlework.

   • Did you write the person's exact words? Check your notes and make corrections.

   > ∧when I was a young girl living
   > **Aunt Yi:** Oh, it was years ago in a Thai refugee camp.
   >   ∧

Edit and Proofread

Work with a partner to edit and proofread your interview. Pay special attention to pronouns. Use the marks on page 574 to show your changes.

Grammar Tip

 Make sure you use the right pronoun. Look back at pages 373 and 405 if you need help.

Publish

1. **On Your Own** Make a final copy of your interview. Then choose a way to share it with your classmates. You may want to read the interview aloud with a partner and record it.

Presentation Tips	
If you are the speaker…	**If you are the listener…**
Pause after you finish reading a question or the answer to a question.	Think about whether the interviewer asked good questions. What might you have asked instead?
Change your pitch and tone to match reading a question or reading an answer.	What else would you like to know about this tradition? Ask the speaker for more details.

2. **With a Group** Collect all the interviews in a book called "Let's Preserve Traditions." Display the book in a classroom reading station or in your school library along with any recordings.

BIG Question

How can we preserve our traditions?

Talk Together

In this unit, you found lots of answers to the **Big Question**. Now, use your concept map to discuss the **Big Question** with the class.

Concept Map

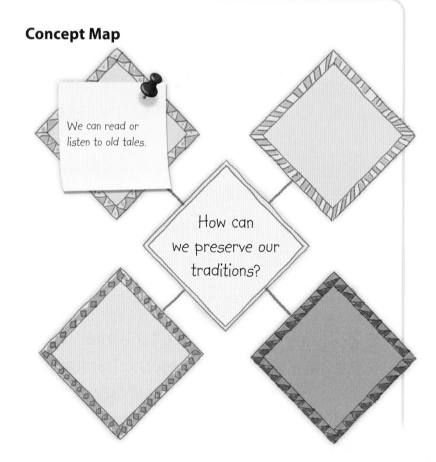

We can read or listen to old tales.

How can we preserve our traditions?

Write a Personal Narrative ✏️

Use your concept map to help you think of a time when you preserved a tradition. Write a personal narrative about it.

Share Your Ideas

Choose one of these ways to share your ideas about the **Big Question**.

Write It!

Write Song Lyrics

Think of a favorite singer or musician. What is this person's style of music? Write song lyrics about the person. Share your lyrics with the class.

Talk About It!

Interview a Musician

Work in a group of four. Two group members pretend to be Cruz and Jefferson. The other two interview them. One question could be, "Why would you like to pass your music on to future generations?"

Do It!

Make Instructions

Think of something traditional that a family member taught you to do. Write or draw a short set of steps. Read the instructions to a partner. Your partner restates each step and pantomimes it. Switch roles.

Write It!

Write a Letter

Pretend you are making a time capsule. Think of a tradition that you want to save. Write a letter to future children. Tell why it is important to preserve this tradition.

Dear Kids of the Future,

We need to preserve blues music. It tells stories of how people have survived.

Blast! Crash! Splash!

? BIG Question

What forces can change Earth?

Unit at a Glance

▶ **Language**: Tell an Original Story, Express Opinions and Ideas, Science Words
▶ **Literacy**: Synthesize
▶ **Content**: Forces of Nature

Unit
7

Share What You Know

Do It!

❶ **Think** of a force of nature, such as an earthquake or a storm, that you have read about or seen on TV.

❷ **Draw** a picture of it.

❸ **Share** your picture with the class. Explain your drawing.

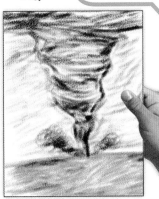

I saw a tornado on TV.

Build Background: Watch a video about forces of nature.
NGReach.com

Tell an Original Story

Listen to Jenny's poem. Then use **Language Frames** to tell a story of your own.

A Scary Ride

Poem

This story is about a boy
With truly unruly hair.
It happens in a hot volcano.
You wouldn't think he'd dare!

First, he rides his tiny red cart
Down tunnels long and deep.
Soon, bubbling magma, thick as mud,
Begins to warm his feet.

Then, suddenly the place erupts!
Upward shoots his cart.
Bump! He lands—back on track,
In an amusement park.

Science Vocabulary

Key Words

erupt	magma
flow	ocean
island	rock
lava	volcano

Key Words

Look at this diagram. Use **Key Words** and other words to talk about what happens when a **volcano erupts**.

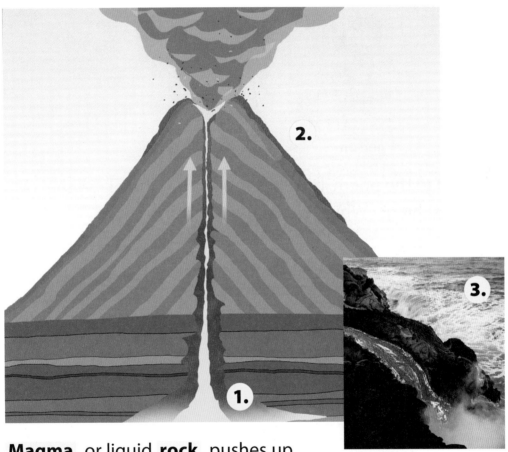

1. **Magma**, or liquid **rock**, pushes up.

2. **Lava flows** out.

3. Lava cools in the **ocean**. Over time, this can form **islands**.

Talk Together

With a partner, tell an original story about forces that change something on Earth. Who is the story about? Where does it happen? Use **Language Frames** from page 414 and **Key Words**.

415

Imagery

Words can create pictures in people's minds. Word pictures, or **imagery**, tell how things look, sound, smell, taste, and feel.

Look at these pictures from Jenny's poem. Read the labels.

| place | person | thing |

As you listened to the poem, how did you picture the place, the person, and the things? Which words helped you do that?

Map and Talk

You can use an imagery chart to record word pictures from a story. To make one, write categories at the top of the chart. Then find word pictures for each category.

Imagery Chart

Place	Person	Thing
hot volcano	boy with truly unruly hair	tiny red cart
tunnels long and deep	magma warms his feet	bubbling magma, thick as mud

Talk Together

Make up a story with a partner. Use word pictures to describe places, people, and things. Record the word pictures in an imagery chart.

More Key Words

Use these words to talk about "An Island Grows" and "Volcano Views."

core
(kor) *noun*

The **core** is the middle part of something. An apple **core** is the center part of an apple.

create
(krē-āt) *verb*

To **create** means to make something new. She **creates** a picture.

develop
(di-**vel**-up) *verb*

When something **develops**, it grows over time. The small plant will **develop** into a large tree.

force
(fors) *noun*

Force means power or strength. The **force** of the wind bends this tree.

pressure
(**pre**-shur) *noun*

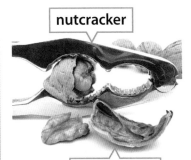

nutcracker

cracked nut

When one thing pushes against another, it makes **pressure**.

Talk Together

Write a sentence for each **Key Word**. Include clues. Copy each sentence with a blank for the **Key Word**. A partner fills in the word.

The center of Earth is the _____ .

Add words to My Vocabulary Notebook.
NGReach.com

417

Learn to Synthesize

Look at the picture. The land looks bad, but new plants are growing. Think about how those parts of the picture go with one another. Then **draw a conclusion**, or decide something about what the picture shows.

When you read, you **draw conclusions**, too.

How to Draw Conclusions

	1. Notice an important idea in the text.	I read _____ .
	2. Look for another idea that you think is important.	I also read _____ .
	3. How do the ideas go with one another? Put the ideas together to make a conclusion about the text.	I connect the ideas and conclude _____ .

Talk Together

Read Jenny's description of a volcanic explosion. Read
the sample conclusion. Then use **Language Frames** to
draw conclusions as you read. Tell a partner about them.

Description

Mount St. Helens

Mount St. Helens is a **volcano** in Washington
State. It used to be a pretty place. It had green
forests, clear rivers, and lakes. Lots of wildlife lived
in the region.

The volcano had **erupted** in 1800, followed by
many small eruptions. In 1857 it was quiet again.
Then on March 15, 1980, earthquakes began to
shake the mountain. Ash and steam came up
through the volcano's **core** with great **force**. Gas
eruptions **created** two more craters near the top.

Around this time, a huge bulge **developed** on the
side of the mountain. It grew larger and larger, like a
lopsided balloon.   ◀

Finally, on May 18, the **pressure** became too
strong. BLAM! WHAM! Two mighty eruptions blew
the top off the mountain.

Steam and ash rose thousands of feet into the sky.
Hot mudflows raced down the mountainsides. Mud
and **rocks** flattened the forests. They blocked the
rivers. They smothered most of the wildlife. Mount St.
Helens wasn't a pretty place anymore.   ◀

Sample Conclusion

"I <u>read</u> that Mount St.
Helens is a volcano.

I <u>also read</u> that it used
to be a pretty place.

I <u>connect the ideas and
conclude</u> that Mount
St. Helens erupted and
ruined the area."

◀ = A good place to draw a conclusion

Read a Narrative Poem

Genre

A **narrative poem** is a poem that tells a story.

Elements of Poetry

Rhythm is the beat of the words in a poem. **Rhyme** is the repetition of sounds at the ends of words.

The lines have a quick, sharp rhythm, or beat.

Deep, deep beneath the sea...
Stone breaks.
Water quakes.

Rhyming words have the same ending sound.

An Island Grows

by **Lola M. Schaefer** · illustrated by **Cathie Felstead**

Comprehension Coach

▶ **Set a Purpose**
Find out how an **island** forms in the **ocean**.

Deep, deep beneath the sea...
Stone breaks.
Water quakes.

Magma glows.
Volcano blows.
Lava flows and flows and flows.
An island grows.

422

Rocks appear,

black and sheer.

Weather batters.

Rock shatters.

In Other Words
beneath under
quakes shakes
sheer very tall and straight
Weather batters. Wind and rain hit the rocks.
shatters breaks into tiny pieces

Waves pound.
Sands mound.

Winds sow
seeds that blow.

In Other Words

pound hit hard

Sands mound. The sand piles up in hills.

Winds sow Winds help to plant

Roots grow.
Leaves show.
Trees tower.
Vines flower.
Insects thrive.
Birds arrive.

In Other Words
tower grow tall
Vines Plants ▶
thrive live

▶ **Before You Move On**

1. **Draw Conclusions** Look at the details about how an **island** forms. What can you conclude about how long it takes?

2. **Rhyme** Look for words that rhyme. Find two examples.

425

▸ **Predict**
What do you think will happen
next on the **island**?

Sailors spot.
Maps plot.

Ships dock.
Traders flock.

In Other Words
spot see something
Maps plot. People use maps.
dock stop and stay
flock come

Settlers stay.
Children play.

Workers build.
Soil is tilled.

In Other Words
Settlers People looking for a new home
Soil is tilled. People prepare the soil for planting.

Markets sell.
Merchants yell.

"Fresh fish!"
"Pepper dish!"

"Ripe fruit!"
"Spicy root!"

In Other Words
Merchants Sellers
root vegetable

Bells ring.
Voices sing.
Drums play.
Dancers sway.

In Other Words
sway move from side to side

▶ **Before You Move On**

1. **Confirm Prediction** Who comes to the **island**? Was your prediction right?
2. **Visualize** Reread this page. What pictures and sounds do the words make in your mind?

▶ **Predict**
What will happen if another
volcano erupts under the **ocean**?

Busy island in the sea where
only water used to be.

Then, one day, not far away,
deep beneath the sea,

a volcano blows,
and lava flows.

Another island grows.

▶ **Before You Move On**

1. **Confirm Prediction** Did you think the **volcano erupting** would make another **island**? Why or why not?

2. **Rhythm** Read the poem again. Clap out the rhythm.

Talk About It

Key Words

core	lava
create	magma
develop	ocean
erupt	pressure
flow	rock
force	volcano
island	

1. Think of the characteristics of a **narrative poem**. Why is the selection a narrative poem?

   The selection is a narrative poem because _____ .

2. Think about the new **island** that **developed**. Will it be the same as the first one? **Tell a story** about what happens.

   First, _____ . Then, _____ . Finally _____ .

3. When the first island formed, people came to live on it. What conclusion can you draw about these people?

   People who settle on a new island are probably _____ and _____ . They _____ .

Learn test-taking strategies.
⊘ NGReach.com

Write About It

The selection tells about different things settlers do, such as **create** farms, build houses, and sell food. If you lived on the island, what job would you like? Why would you like that job? Use **Key Words** in your answers.

If I lived on the island, I would _____ .
I would like that job because _____ .

Imagery

"An **Island** Grows" tells the story of an island. With a partner, discuss how word pictures help tell the story. Then make an imagery chart for the poem. Write words for each category that tell how things look, sound, smell, taste, or feel.

Imagery Chart

Volcano	Land	Plants	Animals	People
Stone breaks. Water quakes.				

With your partner, use your completed chart to tell how an island grows. Use the sentence frames and **Key Words**. Record your retelling.

> These lines tell about volcanoes: _____ .
> These lines tell about land: _____ .

Fluency ◼️ ⌖ Comprehension Coach

Use the Comprehension Coach to practice reading with intonation. Rate your reading.

Talk Together

How can a volcanic eruption change Earth? Draw a picture. Add a caption with **Key Words**. Explain your drawing to your classmates.

Greek and Latin Roots

Some English words contain **Greek and Latin roots**. A root is a word part that has meaning, but a root is not a word on its own.

If you know the meaning of a word's root, it can help you figure out the meaning of the word.

Greek and Latin Roots Chart

Origin	Root	Meaning	Example
Greek	*geo*	Earth	**geology**: the study of Earth's history and structure
Latin	*volcan*	a god of fire	**volcano**: a mountain that hot melted rock can come out of
	rupt	to break	**erupt**: to explode or shoot out

Try It Together

Read each item. Choose the best answer.

1. **Which word has something to do with Earth?**

   A germ

   B gallon

   C legend

   D geography

2. **Which word has something to do with an opening or a crack?**

   A rush

   B melt

   C erase

   D rupture

Connect Across Texts Read a photo-essay to see just how dangerous **volcanoes** can be.

Genre A **photo-essay** is nonfiction. It uses photographs and text to give information.

Volcano Views

with photographs by **Carsten Peter**
and text by **Chris Beem**

Carsten Peter is an award-winning photographer. He takes pictures in some of the most dangerous places on Earth. Look at these amazing photographs. To take the pictures, Peter had to get very close to **active volcanoes**!

Carsten Peter by an active volcano

In Other Words
Volcano Views Pictures of **Volcanoes**
active erupting

▶ **Before You Move On**
1. **Draw Conclusions** What kind of person is Carsten Peter? How do you know?
2. **Use Text Features** What can you learn about an active **volcano** from the photograph?

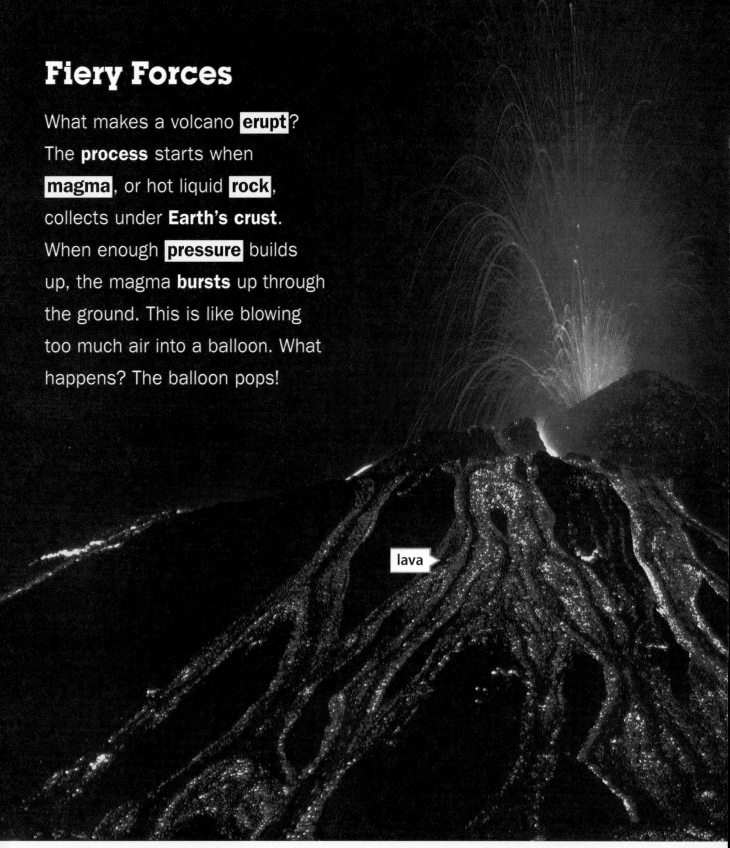

Fiery Forces

What makes a volcano erupt? The **process** starts when magma, or hot liquid rock, collects under **Earth's crust**. When enough pressure builds up, the magma **bursts** up through the ground. This is like blowing too much air into a balloon. What happens? The balloon pops!

lava

▲ When liquid rock streams out of a volcano, it is called **lava**.

In Other Words
process set of steps
Earth's crust the surface of earth
bursts pushes

Different things happen when volcanoes erupt. Some eruptions force gasses, rock, and smoke out of the **crater**. Other eruptions only **release** smoke. In some volcanoes, lava just **oozes** out of the volcano's top. Then the lava flows like a river down its sides.

▲ A Carsten Peter photo of rock exploding from a crater.

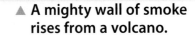

▲ A mighty wall of smoke rises from a volcano.

In Other Words
crater top of the **volcano**
release let out
oozes flows slowly

▶ **Before You Move On**

1. **Use Text Features** Read the caption on page 438. What is **lava**?
2. **Evaluate** Choose one type of eruption explained on this page. Describe the damage it might do.

Rivers of Heat

Lava is HOT. When it first **escapes from** a **volcano**, its temperature is between **1,300 and 2,200 degrees Fahrenheit**! As lava moves down a mountainside, it glows bright orange, like a fiery sunset. Thick lava may **inch along**, but thin lava can **flow** more quickly.

▲ Peter's photographs capture the heat of lava.

In Other Words

escapes from leaves

1,300 to 2,200 degrees Farenheit
about 700 to 1,200 degrees Celsius

inch along move very slowly

A Close-Up Look

Red-hot lava. Clouds of smoke and gas. Flying **rocks**. All of these things make active volcanoes **extremely** dangerous. Most people would run away from these **forces** of nature. Carsten Peter runs toward them. Thanks to his amazing photos, we can **get a close-up glimpse of** volcanoes in action. ❖

protective suit

▲ This photograph shows a special suit that can help keep out the heat.

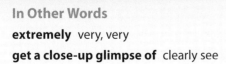

In Other Words
extremely very, very
get a close-up glimpse of clearly see

▶ **Before You Move On**

1. **Details** What did you learn about **lava**? Give at least two details from the text.
2. **Imagery** Which words on page 440 help you make a mental picture of **lava**?

Compare Texts

"An **Island** Grows" is a literary text, and "**Volcano** Views" is an informational text. The selections are different, but they have some similar ideas.

What does each selection tell about volcanoes? Complete a comparison chart with a partner. Find evidence in the selections that supports what you write on your chart.

Comparison Chart

"An Island Grows"	"Volcano Views"
Tells about volcanoes under the sea	Tells about a man who photographs volcanoes
Tells about magma and lava	Tells about magma and lava

Talk Together

What **forces** can change Earth? Think about both selections. What did you learn in one selection that you did not learn in the other? Use **Key Words** to discuss your ideas.

Adverbs

Adverbs usually tell more about a verb.

Grammar Rules Adverbs

• Use an **adverb** to tell how, where, or when something happens.	Islands grow **slowly**. (how) Rocks are **everywhere**. (where) Ships sail by **today**. (when)
• For some adverbs, add **-er** to compare two actions. Add **-est** to compare three or more actions.	Thin lava flows fast**er** than thick lava. This lava flows the fast**est** of all.
• If an adverb ends in **-ly**, use **more** or **less** to compare two actions. Use **the most** or **the least** to compare three or more actions.	Li swims **more** quick**ly** than Tom. Tom swims **less** quickly than Li. Uma swims **the most** quick**ly** of all. I swim **the least** quick**ly** of all.

Read Adverbs

Read these sentences with a partner. Find two adverbs.

> Waves pound the shore loudly. Winds blow the sand around.

Write Adverbs

Write three sentences about an island. Use at least two adverbs. Read your sentences to your partner.

Express Opinions and Ideas

Listen to Larry and Nia's song. Then use **Language Frames** to express your opinions and ideas about forces of nature.

Song

Here's What I Think

Larry:

I think it is important
That we understand—
Earthquakes will occur,
And they will shake the land.

Nia:

I believe most people
Needn't be too scared.
But, in my opinion,
We must be prepared.

Tune: "Au Clair de la Lune"

How to Prepare for an Earthquake

Make an Emergency Kit
• water
• food
• flashlight
• batteries
• radio
• money
• first-aid kit
• clothing

Key Words
earthquake
plate
shore
tsunami
wave

Key Words

Look at this diagram. Use **Key Words** and other words to talk about the picture. What happens because of an underwater **earthquake**?

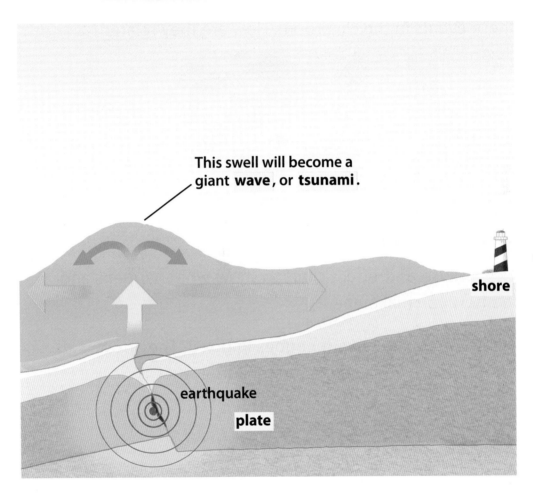

This swell will become a giant **wave**, or **tsunami**.

shore

earthquake

plate

Talk Together

What forces under the sea can change Earth? How should you prepare for a disaster near the ocean? Talk to a partner. Express your opinions and ideas. Use **Language Frames** from page 444 and **Key Words.**

Cause and Effect

The **cause** is why something happens. The **effect** is what happens. Causes and effects help you understand how events are related.

Look at these events in the classroom. How are they related?

Map and Talk

You can use a cause-and-effect chart to show what happens and why. Here's how you make one.

The cause goes in box 1. The effect goes in box 2. The arrow shows that the first event leads to the second event.

Cause-and-Effect Chart

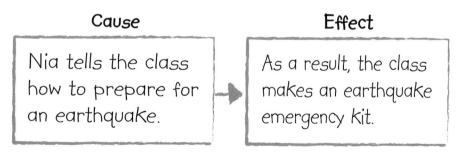

Talk Together

Look back at page 445. Make a cause-and-effect chart for something that happens in the diagram. Share your chart with a partner.

More Key Words

Use these words to talk about "Selvakumar Knew Better" and "Tsunami."

power
(**pow**-ur) *noun*

If something has **power**, it is strong. The waves have the **power** to destroy a building.

rescue
(**res**-kyū) *verb*

When you **rescue** someone, you save the person. A dog helps to **rescue** someone.

sense
(**sens**) *verb*

When you **sense** something, you know it without being told. A cat can **sense** danger.

signal
(**sig**-nul) *noun*

A **signal** is something that tells you what to do. The green light is a **signal** to walk.

warn
(**worn**) *verb*

To **warn** people is to tell them that something bad may happen. She **warns** people to leave.

Talk Together

With a partner, take turns telling a story with the **Key Words**.

> The storm has a lot of power!

> Mom warned us to stay inside.

Add words to My Vocabulary Notebook.
NGReach.com

Learn to Synthesize

Look at the photo. Notice the people. Would most people act like that if they saw huge **waves**? **Form a generalization**, or decide what most people would do.

A **generalization** is a statement that applies to many situations. When you read, you **form generalizations**, too.

How to Form Generalizations

👁	**1.** Pay attention to the important ideas in the text.	I read _____.
💭	**2.** Think about the ideas. How are they like things you know from your own life?	I know _____.
👄	**3.** Make a statement that seems true for both the text and what you know.	I think that most _____.

Read Nia's fact sheet. Read the sample generalization. Then use **Language Frames** to make generalizations as you read. Tell a partner about them.

Fact Sheet

Three Tsunamis

This fact sheet will give you an idea of a **tsunami's power**. People were not **warned** in time to escape these disasters. There were no warning **signals**. People did not **sense** the tsunamis coming. Many people were **rescued**, but many others lost their lives.

Sample Generalization

"I read that people did not sense the tsunamis.

I know about other tsunamis that people did not know were coming.

I think that most people cannot tell that a tsunami is coming."

Earthquake Energy Scale

4.0 Light   5.0 Strong   7.0 Major   8.0 Great   9.0 Greater   10.0 Greatest

Time, Place, Size	Cause	Effect
2004 Indian Ocean; Waves up to 50 feet	9.0 undersea earthquake	Flooded the coastlines of 12 countries; swept away islands and villages
1998 Papua, New Guinea; Waves up to 40 feet	Undersea landslide created by 7.1 undersea earthquake	Destroyed at least two villages
1964 Alaska and northwestern United States; Waves up to 220 feet	9.2 undersea earthquake	Caused hundreds of miles of coastal damage from Alaska to Northern California

◀ = A good place to form a generalization

Read Historical Fiction

Genre

Historical fiction is a made-up story based on real events and people from the past.

Dialogue

Dialogue is what characters say to one another in a story. Writers use quotation marks to show dialogue.

Selvakumar whined, and Mama said, "Hush." Selvakumar barked, and Dinakaran complained, "Quiet, I'm trying to concentrate."

Quotation marks show a character's exact words.

Selvakumar Knew Better

by Virginia Kroll

illustrated by Xiaojun Li

▶ **Set a Purpose**
Find out what a dog **senses** that
his human family does not.

The December day in south India **dawned** like any other, **kissed by the golden sun.** Papa came back with his boat full of fish. Mama made breakfast for seven-year-old Dinakaran and his two little brothers. That day seemed like any other day, but Selvakumar **knew better**.

Selvakumar felt a **rumbling** in his belly. His legs **were restless**, and his scruffy yellow fur stood on end. His ears perked up, listening for the sound that had already started.

In Other Words

dawned started

kissed by the golden sun with bright sunshine

knew better thought something else

rumbling shaking

were restless felt strange

His family didn't **notice**. Papa was busy unloading his **catch**, and Mama was hanging her laundry. Dinakaran was finishing his homework, while the younger boys ran around the yard.

Selvakumar **whined**, and Mama said, "Hush." Selvakumar barked, and Dinakaran complained, "Quiet, I'm trying to **concentrate**."

Suddenly, a strange roaring sound began. Mama thought that a thunderstorm was coming, but Dinakaran and his brothers thought it was an extra-loud train. Papa ran to a nearby building's roof to **investigate**.

In Other Words

notice see
catch fish
whined made a crying sound

concentrate think
investigate find out what was happening

But Selvakumar knew better. The **vibrations** traveled up his padded paws. His skin prickled with fearful goose bumps from his black nose to his tufted tail. He wanted to run, but he **dared not** leave his family. Sometimes humans didn't **realize**.

Why were they waiting? Didn't they know that a mighty **earthquake** had rumbled under the ocean and would soon bring raging **waves** onto the **shore**?

And then Papa shouted **desperately** from the rooftop, "**Tsunami**! Run!"

In Other Words

vibrations shaking of the ground

dared not did not want to

realize know what was happening

desperately with fear

Mama screamed, "Sons, come on!" She grabbed a little one under each arm. "Dinakaran, run! You're **swift** and strong. Follow me up the hill. Fast!"

But the roar had gotten louder, cutting off her words. All that Dinakaran had heard was, "Run!" And he ran back to his family's house close to the shore, where he thought he would be safe.

But Selvakumar knew better. He barked and howled, but the sound of **approaching waves drowned out** his voice, too.

In Other Words
swift fast
approaching waves drowned out
the **tsunami** made it hard to hear

▶ **Before You Move On**

1. **Form Generalizations** Based on the text and what you know, what can you say about Selvakumar? What kind of dog is he?

2. **Cause/Effect** Why does Dinakaran run home instead of up the hill?

▶ **Predict**
What will Selvakumar do to
help Dinakaran?

Selvakumar **nipped at Dinakaran's heels**, but the boy
wouldn't **budge**. "Go." Dinakaran **shooed** the dog away, but
Selvakumar knew better and would not give up. He grabbed
Dinakaran's shirt in his teeth. He pulled and tugged until
his teeth hurt. With all his strength, he dragged Dinakaran
back outside and bumped him from behind. Finally the boy
understood.

In Other Words
nipped at Dinakaran's heels bit
    the boy's feet
budge move
shooed pushed

Selvakumar ran toward the hill, looking back to make sure Dinakaran was following. They raced uphill as the **enormous** wall of water chased them. The **tsunami** roared louder than five thunderstorms and ten trains put together.

Selvakumar and Dinakaran didn't stop running until they reached the upper road. Their sides **ached**, and their breaths felt like hot coals burning in their chests.

In Other Words
enormous huge
ached hurt

Dinakaran wanted to stop, but Selvakumar knew better. He **nudged** Dinakaran's hand, and together they **continued** higher up the hill.

Finally, they turned and looked down toward the **shore**. They both blinked their eyes **in disbelief**.

In Other Words
nudged gently pushed
continued kept walking
in disbelief because they could not believe what they saw

The **wave** had swallowed everything. It had **snapped** trees as if they were **brittle** little sticks. It had **collapsed** all the houses flat as if they'd been birds' nests.

▶ **Before You Move On**

1. **Confirm Prediction** Did you predict what Selvakumar would do? Explain.

2. **Make Inferences** Why do you think Dinakaran was in disbelief when he looked at his village down below?

459

▶ **Predict**
What will happen next to
Selvakumar and Dinakaran?

In the distance, Selvakumar and Dinakaran heard Mama's voice. "Dinakaran," she **wailed** over and over. "My **firstborn** son is lost!" They walked toward the sound and found her rocking back and forth as her younger sons **sobbed** beside her.

Selvakumar **yipped and bounded** toward her, and Mama's head **snapped up**. She swiped her tears and stared at Dinakaran. "My precious son, you're alive!" she whispered. Dinakaran rushed into her arms, and she covered him in grateful kisses.

In Other Words
wailed cried
firstborn oldest
sobbed cried loudly

yipped and bounded
barked and ran
snapped up looked up
quickly

"I-I went to th-the house, Mama. I-I thought I'd be sa-safe. B-but Sel-Selvakumar knew better," he **sputtered** as his tears mixed with Mama's. He told her about what the dog had done.

Mama let go of Dinakaran and hugged Selvakumar hard. Selvakumar greeted the smaller boys with face licks.

Papa joined them after the **tsunami** disappeared, and when he heard the story, he sobbed into Selvakumar's fur, too. Then they were all a mother-father-brothers-dog **thankful heap** of hugging.

In Other Words
sputtered said excitedly
thankful heap happy group

Later, the other **survivors** of the village gathered in a **temporary shelter**. They heard about many, many lives that had been lost.

As Dinakaran and Selvakumar rested, they heard the grownups talking.

"We'll never **recover**," moaned one man.

"We've lost absolutely everything," someone else said.

But Selvakumar felt the regular rhythm of Dinakaran's chest rising and falling under his chin. Then he heard Dinakaran's little brothers nearby. He smelled the familiar scents of Papa and Mama.

And Selvakumar knew better. ❖

In Other Words

survivors people who escaped the **tsunami**

temporary shelter safe place

recover fix everything; have the same things we used to

▶ **Before You Move On**

1. **Confirm Prediction** What happened to the characters? Was your prediction correct?

2. **Dialogue** How does the dialogue on page 461 show exactly how Dinakaran is feeling?

462

Meet the Illustrator

Xiaojun Li

"Like many people around the world, the tsunami disaster shocked me and my family," says Xiaojun Li. After reading the story of *Selvakumar Knew Better*, Mr. Li researched images of the tsunami. "When I felt confident that I could express the powerful emotions felt by the victims, I began the illustrations."

Mr. Li used photographs to create the sketches of Dinakaran, his mother, and the setting.

▲ Xiaojun Li at his home studio

▲ Dinakaran, his mother, and Selvakumar

Artist's Craft

Mr. Li uses details in his art to show people's emotions. Point to a picture of a character in the story. Tell what the person is feeling or thinking. How does Mr. Li's art show this?

463

Talk About It

1. How do you know that the story is **historical fiction**?

   I know that it is historical fiction because _____ .

2. Dinakaran's family lives near the **shore**. What would you tell them if they asked whether they should rebuild their home there? **Express opinions and ideas** about it.

   I think _____ . In my opinion, _____ . But _____ .

3. Does the story have a first-person or a third-person narrator? How would the story be different if Dinakaran were the narrator?

   The narrator is _____ . If Dinakaran were the narrator, _____ .

Learn test-taking strategies.
NGReach.com

Write About It

What do you think about Selvakumar's actions? What would you say to him if he could understand you? Write three sentences. Use **Key Words** to help explain your thoughts.

Selvakumar, I think you _____ . You _____ .

Cause and Effect

Make a cause-and-effect chart for "Selvakumar Knew Better."

Cause-and-Effect Chart

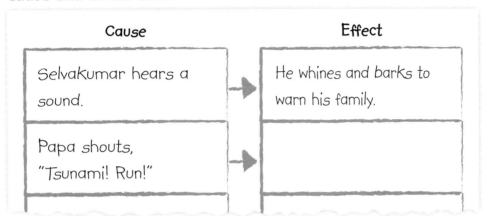

Cause	Effect
Selvakumar hears a sound.	He whines and barks to warn his family.
Papa shouts, "Tsunami! Run!"	

Look at the sequence of events in the chart. With a partner, discuss how each event influences a future event. Then use your chart to summarize the plot's main events. Use **Key Words**. Record your summary.

Selvakumar hears a sound, so he _____ .

Fluency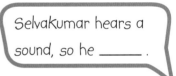

Use the Comprehension Coach to practice reading with expression. Rate your reading.

Talk Together

How can a **tsunami** change Earth? What might Dinakaran say to visitors? Write dialogue with **Key Words**. Read your dialogue with your partner.

Compound Words

A **compound word** is made up of two smaller words. To figure out what a compound word means, look at the smaller words.

earth: "land," "ground"
quake: "shake"
earth + quake = **earthquake**

Meaning: a sudden shaking of the ground

sea: "ocean"
shore: "land next to water"
sea + shore = **seashore**

Meaning: land next to the sea or ocean

Try It Together

Read the sentences. Then answer the questions.

As we hike up the volcano, we leave a trail of <u>footprints</u>. When we reach the <u>mountaintop</u>, we look down into a huge crater.

1. **What do you think <u>footprints</u> means?**

   A hiking shoes

   B written signs

   C food wrappings

   D marks left by shoes or feet

2. **What do you think <u>mountaintop</u> means?**

   A the end of a trail

   B a fence around a crater

   C a view from a mountain

   D the highest part of a mountain

Connect Across Texts Read this article to learn more about **tsunamis**.

Genre An **online article** is an article that is on the Internet.

Tsunami

http://ngreach.com

Tsunami

| Home | Recent Events | Warning Center | FAQs |
| Tsunami Basics | Terminology | Photos | Search » |

A **tsunami** (soo-NAHM-ee) is a **series** of huge **waves**. **A disturbance** under the sea, such as an **earthquake** or volcanic eruption, causes the waves.

In Other Words
series group
A disturbance An important event

▶ **Before You Move On**
1. **Main Idea** What is a **tsunami**?
2. **Cause/Effect** What causes a **tsunami**?

467

How a Tsunami Forms

During an event under the water, such as an **earthquake**, a lot of energy is produced. That strong force pushes upward and out. It makes **waves** move in all directions. When waves reach **shallow water** they grow higher. They can reach as high as 100 feet! These powerful waves then crash onto the **shore**. They can **cause heavy damage**.

A Tsunami Forms Under Water

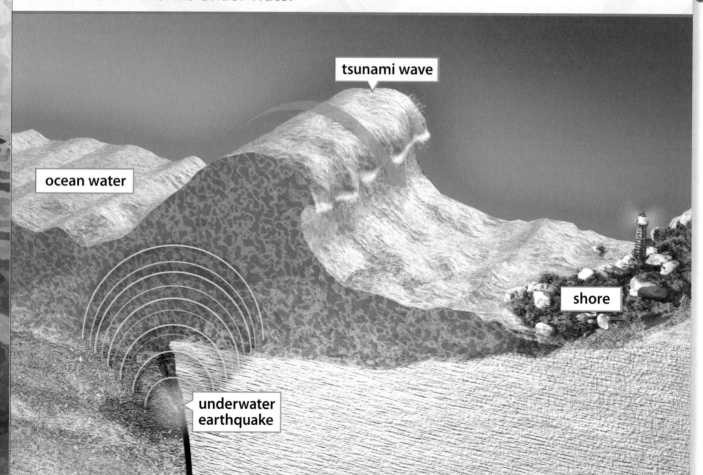

tsunami wave

ocean water

shore

underwater earthquake

In Other Words

shallow water places closer to land where the ocean is not as deep

cause heavy damage hurt many people and things

Areas at Risk

Hawaii is at the greatest risk for a tsunami. The state gets about one each year. It gets a damaging tsunami every seven years. Alaska is also at high risk. California, Oregon, and Washington **experience** a damaging tsunami about once every 18 years.

In 1946, a tsunami crashed into Hilo, Hawaii. The waves were as high as a three-story building.

In 1964, an earthquake shook the state of Alaska. It caused a tsunami along parts of the Washington, Oregon, and California shore. The waves were 10 to 20 feet high.

Learn about tsunami **warning** centers.

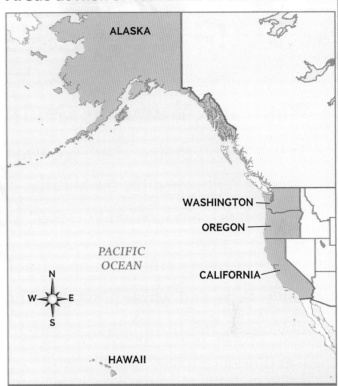

Areas at Risk of Tsunamis in the U.S.

ALASKA

WASHINGTON

OREGON

PACIFIC OCEAN

CALIFORNIA

N W E S

HAWAII

▲ Tsunami damage in Alaska, 1964

In Other Words

Areas at Risk Places in Danger from Tsunamis

experience have

▶ **Before You Move On**

1. **Form Generalizations** Think about the places that are at high risk of **tsunamis**. In what ways are they all alike?

2. **Cause/Effect** What can happen if a **tsunami** hits the **shore**?

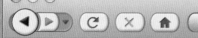

Tracking a Tsunami

Tsunami Warning Centers

In the United States, there are two **tsunami warning** centers. They **monitor** events that could cause a tsunami. The centers are located in Hawaii and Alaska.

In the warning centers, people **track** information about **wave sizes and water pressure**. The information comes from **devices** in the ocean. People use the information to predict if a tsunami is likely to happen.

▲ **The tsunami warning center in Hawaii**

In Other Words

monitor watch for

track look for changes in

wave sizes and water pressure changes in the water

devices machines

Early Warnings

Scientists place **recorders** on the ocean floor. They are placed in areas that have a history of disturbances that cause tsunamis. The recorders collect information and send it to **buoys**. The buoys then send all the information back to the warning centers **by satellite**.

Tsunamis can be deadly. So being able to warn people about a tsunami before it reaches **shore** can save a lot of lives.

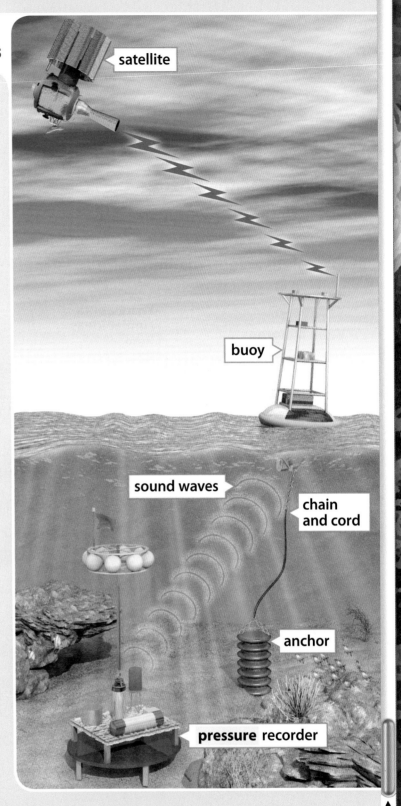

How a Buoy System Works

satellite

buoy

sound waves

chain and cord

anchor

pressure recorder

▶ **Before You Move On**

1. **Use Text Features** Use the diagram to explain how a buoy system works.
2. **Make Inferences** What information might the warning center include in its warning?

Respond and Extend

Key Words

earthquake	shore
plate	signal
power	tsunami
rescue	warn
sense	wave

Compare Texts

"Selvakumar Knew Better" is a literary text, and "**Tsunami**" is an informational text. How are the ideas in the selections similar, or the same? How are they different? Complete a Venn diagram with a partner.

Venn Diagram

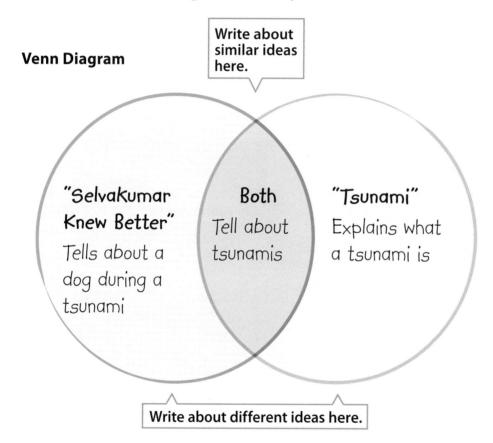

Write about similar ideas here.

"Selvakumar Knew Better"
Tells about a dog during a tsunami

Both
Tell about tsunamis

"Tsunami"
Explains what a tsunami is

Write about different ideas here.

Talk Together

What forces in the ocean can change Earth? Think about the story and the online article. Use **Key Words** in your discussion.

Prepositional Phrases

A preposition can tell where, show direction, show time, or add details. A **prepositional phrase** starts with a preposition and ends with a noun or pronoun. Use prepositional phrases to:

Grammar Rules Prepositional Phrases

	Prepositional Phrase in a Sentence
• show where something is	Our village is **by the ocean**.
• show direction	I climbed **up the mountain**.
• show time	**After the tsunami**, we went home.
• add details	Birds fly **around us**. Hot sand is **under our feet**.

Read Prepositional Phrases

Read this passage from "Selvakumar Knew Better." Can you find two prepositional phrases?

> She grabbed a little one under each arm. "Dinakaran, run! You're swift and strong. Follow me up the hill. Fast!"

Write Prepositional Phrases

Write a caption for the picture on page 457. Use a prepositional phrase. Share your caption with a partner.

473

Write Like a Researcher

Write a Research Report

Write a report about a force of nature that can change Earth. Combine your report with those of your classmates to create a science book or a multimedia show.

Study a Model

When you write a research report, you gather information from several sources. You organize the facts you find. Then you present the facts in a way that is all your own.

Earthquake!
by Zachary Wilkes

The ground shakes. Windows break. Roads crack. It's an earthquake!

There are between 2,000 and 3,000 earthquakes in the United States every year. Most of them are too small to feel. Bigger ones can destroy cities. Why can't we protect ourselves better from these disasters?

First, it's important to know what causes earthquakes. Earth is actually made up of layers. The top layer is called the crust. The crust is formed by large slabs of rock, called plates. These plates fit together like pieces of a puzzle.

The title and introduction tell what the report is about. The introduction gets the reader's attention.

The **focus** of the report is clear.

Each paragraph has a **topic sentence** that tells the main idea of the paragraph.

Facts and details support each topic sentence.

Sometimes the plates move and begin pushing against each other. This causes pressure along the edges of the plates. If the pressure builds up too much, then the plates suddenly bump past each other. The energy this releases makes the ground shake, and we feel an earthquake.

If we know what causes earthquakes, why can't we predict them? First of all, no one knows when the plates in Earth's crust will move. The closest we can come to guessing that is

The writing is well-organized and smooth. Each idea flows into the next idea.

Sources

"Earthquake." *World Book Encyclopedia*. 2009. 33–39. Print.

Earthquake Hazards Program. U.S. Geological Survey, 11 Feb. 2010. Web. 12 Feb. 2010. <http://earthquake.usgs.gov/learn/kids/>

Walker, Sally M. *Earthquakes*. Minneapolis, Minnesota: Carolrhoda Books, 2008. Print.

The sources that are used for the report are listed on a final page.

Prewrite

1. **Choose a Topic** What did you read about in the unit that interests you? What other forces of nature would you like to learn about?

   Share your ideas with a partner. Narrow your topic. Choose one that you can find sources for and cover well in a short report.

2. **List Your Research Questions** What do you already know about your topic? What do you need to find out? With your partner, think of questions to guide you as you do your research.

   > Research Questions
   >
   > • What causes earthquakes?
   > • Where do earthquakes happen?
   > • What is it like to be in an earthquake?
   > • Can earthquakes be predicted?

3. **Create a Research Plan** A research plan lists your questions. It also lists your ideas for how to answer them.

   Different sources can help you with different kinds of questions. Look at pages 567–570 to learn about different types of sources.

Gather Information

1. **Identify Sources** To find books that would be good sources for your topic, skim tables of contents, headings, and pictures. To see if Web sites are helpful, check menus on the home page.

   Make sure every source is up to date. Also make sure each one comes from a group or person who is an expert in the area.

2. **Create Source Cards** Keep track of your sources on cards.

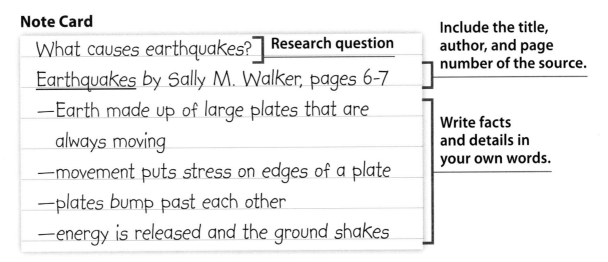

Source Card for a Book

Earthquakes — Title of book
Sally M. Walker — Author
Carolrhoda Books
Minneapolis, Minnesota, 2008 — Publication information
J551.22 — Library call number

Card number

3. **Make Note Cards** Create note cards to record important words, phrases, and ideas that you find as you research.

Note Card

What causes earthquakes? — Research question
Earthquakes by Sally M. Walker, pages 6-7 — Include the title, author, and page number of the source.
—Earth made up of large plates that are always moving
—movement puts stress on edges of a plate
—plates bump past each other
—energy is released and the ground shakes

Write facts and details in your own words.

Get Organized

1. **Arrange Your Cards** Put your cards in an order that makes sense. Use the research question on each card to help you. Put cards with similar research questions in the same group.

2. **Organize Your Information** Use a graphic organizer to help you organize main ideas and details. Each research question, or group of similar research questions, can become a main idea. Put the details for those questions under the main idea.

Main Idea and Details Diagram

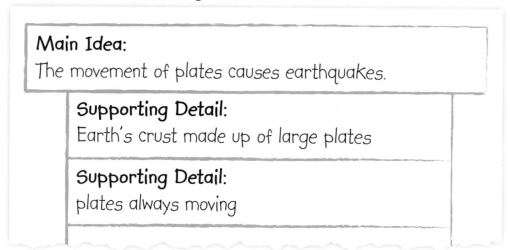

Draft

Use your graphic organizers to guide you as you write a draft. Put all the information in your own words. Never use words directly from the source. To use someone else's words is to plagiarize (**plā**-ju-rīz), which is a type of stealing.

Revise

1. **Read, Retell, Respond** Read your draft aloud to a partner. Your partner listens and summarizes the main points of the report. Next, talk about ways to improve your draft.

2. **Make Changes** Think about your partner's suggestions. Use the Revising Marks on page 573 to mark your changes.

   - Is the writing well-organized and smooth?

   > Earth is actually made up of layers. ∧The crust is formed by large slabs of rock, called plates. (The top layer is called the crust.)

   - Make sure all the information is in your own words.

   > ~~Plate movement puts stress, or pressure, on the edges of a plate.~~
   >
   > Sometimes the plates move and begin pushing against each other. This causes pressure along the edges of the plates.

Edit and Proofread

Work with a partner to edit and proofread your reports. Use the marks on page 574 to show your changes. Check all your facts.

Publish

1. **Make a Final Copy** Make a final copy of your research report. Add a list of sources at the end.

2. **Share with Others** Combine all the reports in a class book called "Forces of Nature." Or, you may want to turn your reports into a multimedia presentation.

Talk **Together**

In this unit, you found lots of answers to the **Big Question**. Now, make a concept map to discuss the **Big Question** with the class.

Concept Map

What forces can change Earth?

volcano

Write a Fact Sheet

Use your concept map. Write a fact sheet about one of the forces that can change Earth's surface.

Share Your Ideas

Choose one of these ways to share your ideas about the **Big Question**.

Write It!

Make a Storyboard

Make a storyboard to show what causes a tsunami or how an island forms. Show the power of Earth in your drawings. Share your storyboard with the class.

Talk About It!

Give a News Report

Work with a partner. Pretend that a natural disaster, such as an earthquake or a tsunami, has taken place. You and your partner are the news team on the scene. Tell your classmates what is happening.

Do It!

Perform a Dance

Work with two or three classmates. Create a dance that represents a force of nature. What movements can you use to show a volcano erupting or a wave crashing down? Perform your dance for the class.

Write It!

Write an E-Mail

Pretend that you and your family members have just experienced a natural disaster. Write an e-mail telling friends what happened.

To:	ann@ngreach.com; luis@ngreach.com
From:	kim@ngreach.com
Subject:	Tsunami!
Attachment:	

Hi, Ann and Luis,

Mom, Dad, and I are fine. We heard the tsunami warning siren and left!

481

Getting There

BIG Question

What tools can we use to achieve our goals?

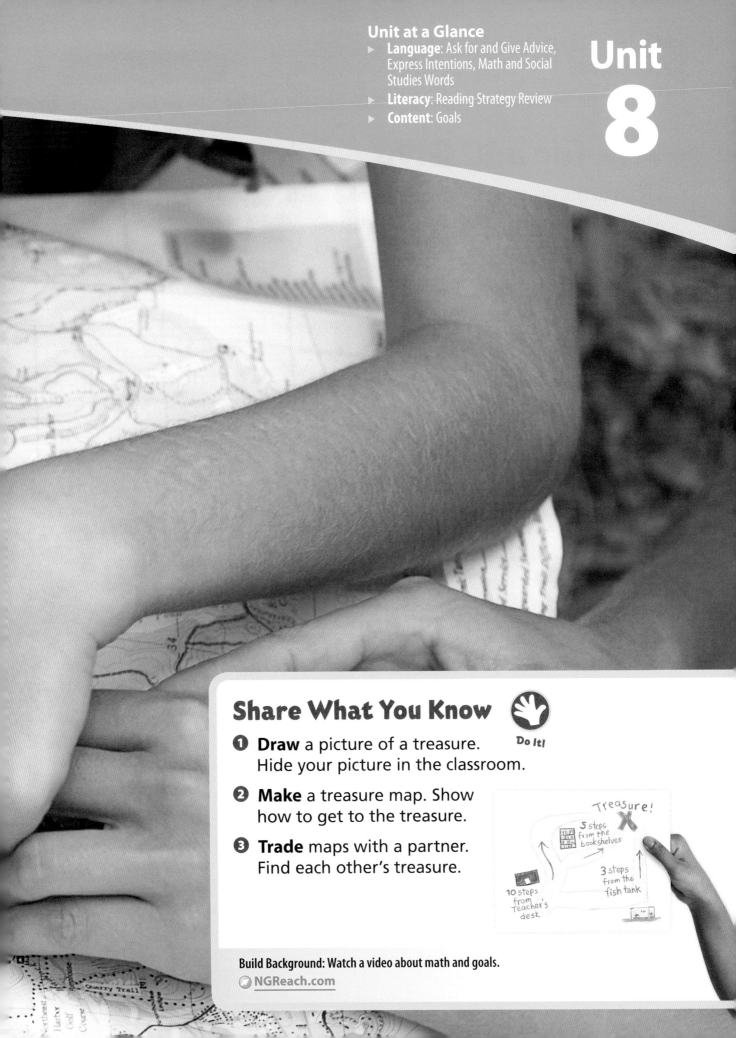

Unit at a Glance
▶ **Language**: Ask for and Give Advice, Express Intentions, Math and Social Studies Words
▶ **Literacy**: Reading Strategy Review
▶ **Content**: Goals

Unit
8

Share What You Know

Do It!

❶ **Draw** a picture of a treasure. Hide your picture in the classroom.

❷ **Make** a treasure map. Show how to get to the treasure.

❸ **Trade** maps with a partner. Find each other's treasure.

Build Background: Watch a video about math and goals.
🌐 NGReach.com

Ask for and Give Advice

Listen to the dialogue between José and Marta. Then use **Language Frames** with a partner. Ask for and give advice about a goal you have.

Dialogue

1.

I want to enter a Junior Olympics swim race. Do you know when I need to sign up?

You should sign up before April 10th at the Recreation Center.

2.

I'm wondering which race to enter. Should I sign up for the 400-meter race?

Have you competed in the 400-meter race before?

3.

No, but . . .

Then you should not try to swim such a long race. Swim the 100-meter race first. And good luck!

Key Words

Use **Key Words** and other words to talk about **units** of **measurement** in a race.

A 5K Race

The race is called a 5K because runners cover a **distance** of five **kilometers**.

Meter Stick

- A **meter** is about 3 **feet**.
- A kilometer is 1,000 meters.

Talk Together

Suppose you want to train for a race. What tools could you use to achieve your goal? Use **Language Frames** from page 484 and **Key Words** to ask for and give advice with a partner.

485

Goal and Outcome

A **goal** is something you want to do or achieve. The **outcome** is what happens. Connecting goal and outcome helps you understand what you read, see, or hear.

Look at these pictures about José's goal. Read the text.

José wants to be in a swim race.   **He signs up for the race.**   **He trains a lot.**   **He competes in the big race.**

Map and Talk

You can use a story map to show a goal and the outcome. To make one, write the goal in the square. Write the events in order in the circles. Put the outcome in the triangle.

Story Map

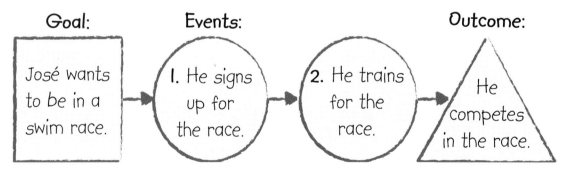

Goal: Events: Outcome:

José wants to be in a swim race.   1. He signs up for the race.   2. He trains for the race.   He competes in the race.

Talk Together

Tell a partner about a goal and outcome in your life. Your partner makes a story map.

More Key Words

Use these words to talk about "Running Shoes" and "Two Clever Plans."

achieve
(u-**chēv**) *verb*

To **achieve** means to get something that you work for. What did this girl **achieve**?

direction
(du-**rek**-shun) *noun*

When you move toward something, you move in that **direction**. The arrow shows the **direction** of the road.

estimate
(**es**-tu-māt) *verb*

When you make a guess about something, you **estimate**. Can you **estimate** how many coins are in the jar?

goal
(gōl) *noun*

A **goal** is something that you want to do. His **goal** is to catch the ball.

strategy
(**stra**-tu-jē) *noun*

A **strategy** is a plan for success. She has a **strategy** for winning.

Talk Together

Make a Vocabulary Example Chart for each **Key Word**. Then compare your charts with a partner's.

Word	Definition	My Example
strategy	a plan	my soccer team's plan to win

Add words to My Vocabulary Notebook.
NGReach.com

487

Choose Reading Strategies

Good readers know that they need different strategies to understand different texts. Often, you use more than one strategy. It is important to know which strategies to use and when to use them. As you read:

- Think about the different strategies. Each one is a tool that can help you understand the text.

- Know what you are reading. Some strategies are better than others for different texts.

- Switch or add strategies if you need to. The more you read, the easier it gets to change strategies. Even the best readers switch and add!

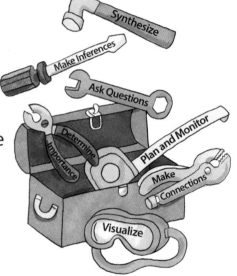

When you read, choose a reading strategy to help you understand.

How to Choose a Reading Strategy

💭	**1.** Think about what you are trying to understand.	I want to Know _____ .
💡	**2.** Decide which strategy you can use to help you understand.	I can _____ .
🧩	**3.** Think about how the strategy helped you.	That strategy helped me _____ .

Read José's letter. Tell a partner which reading strategies you used to help you understand the text.

Letter

May 27, 2010

Dear Manuela,

It was great to see you at the Junior Olympics. I'm sorry I was unable to talk to you before you left. But I'm glad you were there to cheer me on. I couldn't hear your shouts while I was in the water. I could barely tell if I was swimming in the right **direction**! But, your support really meant a lot. Thank you!

I plan to reenter the Junior Olympics next year. My **goal** is to win the 400-**meter** swim race. Four hundred meters is about a quarter mile. That's a long **distance** to swim at top speed. My trainer **estimates** I'll need to train six days a week to **achieve** the strength I'll need. That's a lot of work!

Mom tells me you plan to rejoin the city swim team. I was unaware that you had dropped out! Mom also told me that you spent the summer in Miami. I'll bet you had some great swims on those sunny beaches!

I'll see you at this year's family reunion. I can hardly wait. Maybe then you could teach me a good **strategy** for long-distance swimming. I'm going to need all the help I can get!

Your cousin,

José

489

Read a Story

Genre

Realistic fiction is a made-up story that sounds like real life. This story is circular. It begins and ends in the same way.

Character's Motive

A **motive** is the reason a character does something.

> Once a year, a man came from the city in a red jeep. The village people called him the number man. **He counted the number of people in the village for the government.**

This character comes to the village because he wants to do his job. That's his motive.

Running Shoes

by Frederick Lipp

illustrated by Jason Gaillard

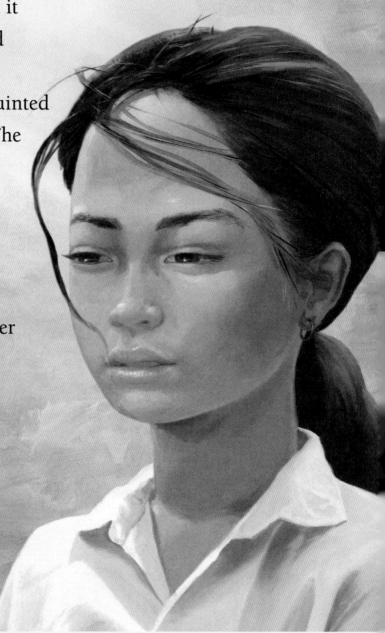

▶ **Set a Purpose**
Find out why Sophy wants a pair of running shoes.

Sophy lived in a land where it was nearly always hot and sunny. When it finally rained, it rained for days and nights without end.

One terribly hot day, Sophy squinted her eyes against the blinding sun. The air was still. Suddenly, a noise like bees **swarming** from a tree grew louder and louder. The pig began **snorting**. The chickens **cackled**.

Sophy sat up straight like a **bamboo shoot**. "Must be the number man's jeep," she thought as she rubbed her eyes.

In Other Words
swarming flying in a group
snorting breathing loudly
cackled made loud noises
◀ **bamboo shoot** tall plant

492

Once a year, a man came from the city in a red jeep. The village people called him the number man. He counted the number of people in the village for the government.

After **making the rounds**, the number man stopped at Sophy's house. "How many people live here?" he asked.

"Two," Sophy answered. "My mother and I."

"Let's see, that comes to one hundred fifty-four people in the village. Last year there were . . ." The number man stopped. He had heard that Sophy's father had died because there was no doctor or hospital near the village.

In Other Words

making the rounds counting all the other people

Sophy stared at the man's shoes.

"Ah, you have never seen running shoes before?" the man asked.

Sophy blushed. She thought about **her secret wish**. Her wish felt far, far away like a **hawk lazily soaring** in circles in the sky. Deep in her heart she knew her wish would come true if she had a pair of shoes like the number man's.

"Walk with me to the river," the number man said.

In Other Words
Sophy blushed. Sophy's face turned red.
her secret wish one thing that she really wanted
hawk lazily soaring bird flying slowly

"Stick your feet into the clay. Now step out." Sophy liked the warm feeling of mud **squishing** between her toes.

The number man took a stick with lots of numbers from his pocket. He **measured** Sophy's footprints.

Then the number man rubbed his chin as he **mumbled** numbers to himself. "Let's see. . . . In about a month, you will receive a surprise."

In Other Words
squishing moving
measured checked the length of
mumbled quietly said

Sophy counted the days until a **postal van** drove through the village and dropped off a **package** by her door. She held her breath as she tore open the package.

"Running shoes!" she yelled. She carefully put on each shoe. "Now my wish will come true."

"What wish?" her mother asked.

"I want to go to school."

"But the school is eight **kilometers** away over horrible roads."

"Yes, but now I have running shoes!" Sophy said as she bounced up and down.

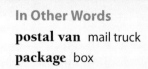

In Other Words
postal van mail truck
package box

A smile slowly came over her mother's face. She remembered how Sophy's father used to sit with Sophy in the shade of a coconut tree and write marks on a small blackboard. He called them words. "This word is your name, Sophy, and this is the name of our village," he explained.

"You may go to school," Sophy's mother said.

▶ **Before You Move On**

1. **Character's Motive** Why does Sophy want her own pair of running shoes? How are they part of her secret wish?

2. **Make Inferences** What do you know about Sophy's father? How would you describe him?

497

▶ **Predict**
What will happen when Sophy
goes to school?

The next day before the sun rose, Sophy ate a bowl of rice and a little salt fish. Then she **set off** through the rice fields, running.

The shoes protected her feet from the sharp, red rocks. She **sailed through the air** like a skipping stone over water.

Jumping over little streams, Sophy ran through the **jungle** on a **narrow, winding** road. She ran faster and faster until finally she saw the one-room schoolhouse.

In Other Words
set off went
sailed through the air moved quickly
jungle plants and trees
narrow, winding thin, twisting

Children's **sandals** were lined up outside the door.

Sophy **hurriedly** untied her running shoes, placed them by the door, and walked barefoot into the schoolroom.

"My name is Sophy. I want to learn how to read and write."

The class, all boys, **giggled**.

"Quiet," the teacher said. "Come, you are welcome here. Where did you come from?"

"Andong Kralong."

The teacher **gasped**. "That is eight kilometers away!"

"Yes, Miss, but I have running shoes!"

In Other Words

sandals open shoes worn in warm weather ▶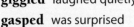
hurriedly quickly
giggled laughed quietly
gasped was surprised

The boys covered their teeth as they laughed. Tears rose in Sophy's eyes. "I want to learn how to read."

"But you're a girl," one boy whispered.

Sophy **pulled all her courage together** like a green snake ready to **strike**. She waited for the right time to speak.

After school, Sophy tied on her running shoes with three knots in each shoe. She looked over at the boys and said, "If you think you are so smart, try to catch me."

In Other Words

pulled all her courage together became brave enough to do something

strike bite

The boys pushed and shoved each other out of the way. They ran after Sophy. No one could catch her.

The next morning, Sophy woke **before the rooster's first call**. **Her head start** allowed her to arrive at school before there were any sandals lined up at the door. When the boys **paraded** into the classroom, they smiled shyly.

They remembered how Sophy had won the race.

From that day on, Sophy learned many subjects taught at the one-room schoolhouse.

In Other Words
before the rooster's first call very early
Her head start Leaving early
paraded came

▶ **Before You Move On**

1. **Confirm Prediction** Use your own words to tell what happens on Sophy's first day at school. Was your prediction right?
2. **Character's Motive** Why does Sophy challenge the boys to a race?

▶ **Predict**
The number man comes to the village again. What will Sophy do?

One morning a year later, Sophy was sitting with her mother when they saw a cloud of dust suddenly rise over the hill.

The pig began snorting. The chickens cackled.

It was the number man coming in his red jeep.

In that moment, the first **sprinkle** of rain made little circles in the river. The circles grew larger. **Monsoon** was beginning.

Sophy looked up at the gathering clouds and thought she would be cooler in her daily race to school.

In Other Words
sprinkle small drops
Monsoon The rainy season

The number man counted everyone in the village.
At the end of the day, he arrived at Sophy's house.
The number man looked down at Sophy's bare feet.
"Where are your running shoes?" he asked.

Sophy smiled and put her hands on her hips. "I only
wear my running shoes when I go to school," she said.

They both laughed.

"I have something for you this time," Sophy said.
"Follow me."

They walked to the side of the river. Sophy held a bamboo stick and scratched words into the clay:

Thank you for the running shoes. Now I can read and write.

Everything was so quiet that Sophy could hear the stream **bubbling** around the stones. She looked down and said shyly, "One day I want to help my people build a school and . . . "

"What?" the number man asked.

"I want to be the teacher," Sophy said, smiling and **wiggling her toes** in the mud. ❖

In Other Words

bubbling making soft sounds

wiggling her toes quickly moving her toes up and down

▶ **Before You Move On**

1. **Confirm Prediction** Was your prediction correct? What does Sophy do when the number man returns?

2. **Genre** Tell why you think "Running Shoes" is a circular story.

Meet the Author

Frederick Lipp

Sophy is a fictional character, but her story is real for many Cambodian girls. Frederick Lipp wrote "Running Shoes" to show how difficult it is for girls like Sophy to get an education.

To help educate girls in rural Cambodia, Mr. Lipp created an organization called the Cambodian Arts and Scholarship Foundation. The program gives girls in poor villages the money and support they need to go to school. Mr. Lipp visits Cambodia twice a year to check his organization's progress and visit with students.

◀ Frederick Lipp with students in Cambodia

Writer's Craft

The author uses vivid words such as *blushed, squishing,* and *giggled* to describe how things look, feel, or sound. Find two of your favorite vivid words from the story. Then write a sentence using the words.

Think and Respond

Talk About It

Key Words

achieve	kilometer
direction	measurement
distance	meter
estimate	strategy
feet	unit
goal	

1. How do you know that the story is **realistic fiction**?

I know that it is realistic fiction because _____ .

2. Suppose Sophy **asks for advice** on her first day of school. The teacher **gives her advice**. What might they each say?

Sophy: How _____ ? What should I _____ ?
Teacher: You should/should not _____ .

3. When Sophy goes to school, how do the boys treat her? What makes them change?

The boys _____ . They change when _____ .

Learn test-taking strategies.
⊘ NGReach.com

Write About It

Imagine you are Sophy. Write a journal entry to your father. Explain how the running shoes helped you **achieve** your **goal** of going to school. Use **Key Words**.

Hi, Dad,
    My running shoes _____ .

Goal and Outcome

Make a story map for "Running Shoes."

Story Map

Goal:

Events:

Sophy wants to go to school.

1. The number man comes to her village.

2. He orders running shoes for Sophy.

3.

Running Shoes

Use your story map to summarize the story for a partner. Use the sentence frames and **Key Words**. Then explain how the events influence a future event, or the outcome. Record your discussion.

Sophy wants to _____.
First, _____.
Then, _____.
In the end, she _____.

Fluency 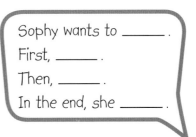 Comprehension Coach

Use the Comprehension Coach to practice reading with intonation. Rate your reading.

Talk Together

Find pictures in the story that show how the number man helps Sophy **achieve** her goal. Explain the pictures to a partner. Use **Key Words**.

Word Categories

When you make a **word category**, you put words that relate to the same topic in a group. This helps you learn more words about a topic.

In the example, **measurement** is the topic. Which words relate to the topic?

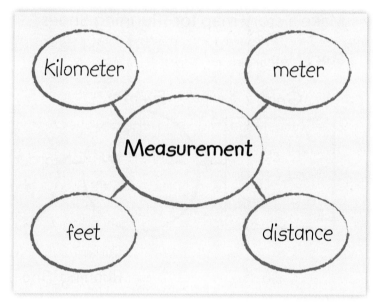

Try It Together

Read the passage. Then complete each item.

My brother's goal is to learn how to cook. His strategy is to cook two meals a week for our family. I think he will achieve his goal, but I am not looking forward to those meals!

1. **Goal and strategy could be placed in a category of words about _____ .**

   A time

   B meals

   C success

   D measurement

2. **Which word is in the same category as goal and strategy?**

   A cook

   B week

   C family

   D achieve

Connect Across Texts Now read a myth and a folk tale about some characters who use numbers to help them reach their goals.

Genre A **myth** is a very old story that often has gods and goddesses as characters. A **folk tale** is a story that people have told over and over. It often has animals as characters.

TWO CLEVER PLANS

In these stories, find out what two **clever** characters do to reach their goals.

In Other Words

clever smart

▶ **Before You Move On**

1. **Preview and Predict** Read the title and the text. Look at the picture. What do you think the stories will be about?

2. **Genre** Do you think the story about the turtle will be realistic? Explain.

THREE GOLDEN APPLES

a Greek myth retold by **Colleen Pellier**
Illustrated by **Raúl Colón**

Atalanta lived long ago in Greece. Her father, King Iasius, wanted her to marry, but Atalanta had her own ideas. "I'll only marry the man who can beat me in a race!" she said.

Of course, the beautiful young woman didn't **intend** to become any man's wife. She was the fastest runner in the land. No man would **outrun** her.

Day after day, **eager young men** tried, but each one failed. "I'll be free forever," Atalanta thought.

In Other Words
intend plan
outrun run faster than
eager young men young men who wanted to win

Melanion, one of **her suitors**, watched the races with sadness. He was in love with Atalanta, but how could he **outrun** her?

He begged Aphrodite, the goddess of love, for help. The kind goddess led him into her garden. Flowers bloomed on every bush. Their sweet **perfume** made Melanion think of Atalanta even more. Aphrodite **paused** under a tree in the center of the garden. She plucked three golden apples and handed them to the young man. "No one can **resist** these," she said.

In Other Words

her suitors the men who wanted to marry Atalanta

perfume smell

paused stopped

resist say no to

▶ **Before You Move On**

1. **Clarify** If Atalanta does not want to marry, why does she offer to marry any man who can outrun her? Explain her thinking.

2. **Character's Motive** Why does Melanion want to win the race?

Melanion chose the next day to race Atalanta. The two runners stood side by side, waiting to begin. Atalanta's golden hair streamed down her back. Her eyes sparkled like the jewels in her father's crown. **At the signal**, she shot ahead like an arrow.

Melanion rolled the first apple off the path and Atalanta **darted** after it. She scooped it up and flew past him again.

Melanion tossed the second apple farther. Atalanta **swerved** off the course to **grasp** it. Soon she was beside him again. She sailed ahead, her hair blowing behind her.

In Other Words
At the signal As soon as the race started
darted ran
swerved turned
grasp grab

Melanion **flung** the last apple as far as he could. It glittered in the grass, and Atalanta dashed after it. It took her only seconds to reach him again. Melanion's muscles burned with pain, but he pushed harder. With a final burst of energy, he shot over the finish line.

"That's unfair!" Atalanta cried. "I had to run three times as far to get these apples!"

But **a smile touched her lips**. Melanion was not as fast as she was, but he would make a handsome, **clever** husband.

In Other Words
flung threw
a smile touched her lips she smiled

▶ **Before You Move On**

1. **Visualize** What words help you picture Atalanta in your mind?

2. **Goal/Outcome** Explain the **strategy** Melanion used to reach his **goal**.

TURTLE AND HIS FOUR COUSINS

a Cuban folk tale retold by **Margaret Read MacDonald**
Illustrated by **Raúl Colón**

"Hey, Slow Poke Turtle! Move those little legs!" called Deer. Deer made fun of people. Turtle didn't care.

"Slow Poke yourself! I am faster than you," he **muttered**.

"Ha!" snorted Deer. "Look at my long legs! Want to RACE?"

Turtle stopped. "Hmm, I wonder . . ." he **mumbled**. Then he had an idea. "Meet me tomorrow at the beach. We will race all the way to the fourth hill."

Deer ran off laughing. "Tomorrow you LOSE!" he called.

In Other Words
muttered said quietly
mumbled said in a low voice

Turtle went to see his four cousins. "Cousin Number One, I want you to go to the first hill. Cousin Number Two, go to the second hill. You, Third Cousin, go to the third hill. Cousin Number Four, I want you to meet Deer at the beach to start the race."

Then Turtle slowly made his way to the fourth hill and waited.

Deer arrived on the beach, singing his proud song. "Deer Long Legs! Fast! Fast! Fast! Deer Long Legs! Fast! Fast! Fast!"

Cousin Number Four sang, too. "Turtle is here. Here. Here. Here."

▶ **Before You Move On**

1. **Character's Motive** Why does Deer challenge Turtle to a race?
2. **Ask Questions** Do you have any questions about Turtle's plan? What are they? What can you do to find the answers?

The race began. Deer ran off SO fast. The turtle moved slowly through the sand.

Deer reached the first hill! He sang his song to **prove** he was there. "Deer Long Legs! Fast! Fast! Fast!"

Then he heard a little voice in the grass. "Turtle is here. Here. Here. Here."

"What?" Deer cried. He ran faster to the second hill. "Deer Long Legs! Fast! Fast! Fast!"

But a tiny voice answered, "Turtle is here. Here. Here. Here."

"Not POSSIBLE!" thought Deer. He ran faster.

Deer reached the third hill. He was out of breath. "Deer Long Legs . . . Fast, fast, fast . . ."

Then he heard, "Turtle is here! Here. Here. Here."

"NO!" Deer cried, **stumbling along** to the last hill. He could hardly breathe. "Fourth hill! I win," he **gasped**. "Deer Long Legs . . ."

But someone was already singing. "Turtle is here. Here! Here! Here!" Then Turtle said in a **mocking** voice, "Sorry, Long Legs. Short Legs won the race."

After that, if Deer felt like making fun of somebody, he just **kept his comments to himself**. ❖

▶ **Before You Move On**

1. **Clarify** What happens to Deer on each hill?

2. **Goal/Outcome** What is Turtle's **goal**? Does he get what he wants? Explain.

Respond and Extend

Key Words

achieve	kilometer
direction	measurement
distance	meter
estimate	strategy
feet	unit
goal	

Compare Settings

"Three Golden Apples" and "Turtle and His Four Cousins" have different settings. Where does each story take place? When does each story happen? Complete the comparison chart with a partner.

Comparison Chart

	"Three Golden Apples"	"Turtle and His Four Cousins"
Where	Greece	
When		

With your partner, look back at the pictures in the stories. Use the pictures and your chart to compare and contrast the settings.

Talk Together

Now think about Melanion in the myth and Turtle in the folk tale. What tools help them **achieve** their **goals**? Use **Key Words** in your discussion.

Past Tense

Regular past-tense verbs end in *-ed*, but **irregular** past-tense verbs do not.

Grammar Rules Past Tense

	Now	In the Past ← Now
• For most verbs, add -**ed**.	**look**	We **looked** at the shoes.
• For some verbs, you have to change the base word before you add -**ed**.	**like** **drop** **study**	They **liked** the teacher. You **dropped** a book. We **studied** our lessons.
• Irregular verbs have special forms to show past tense. You have to remember the forms.	**come** **eat** **go**	The shoes **came** in a box. The boys **ate** the rice. I **went** to the village.

Read Past-Tense Verbs

Read this passage from "Running Shoes." Identify one regular past-tense verb and one irregular past-tense verb.

Once a year, a man came from the city in a red jeep. The village people called him the number man.

Write Past-Tense Verbs

What happened on page 499? Write three sentences for your partner. Use regular and irregular past-tense verbs.

Express Intentions

Listen to Emma's song. Then use **Language Frames** to express intentions about a goal you have.

Song

Getting Ready

I want to go to New York City.
I will pack my walking shoes.
I plan to see so many places
On the streets and avenues.

I will visit the museums.
I am going to see the zoo.
I'll take pictures to remember
All the things I see and do.

Tune: "Clementine"

Key Words

continent

destination

globe

journey

location

Key Words

Use **Key Words** and other words to talk about an exciting **journey**.

- Look at different **locations** on a **globe**.

- Which one would you like to visit?
  Which **continent** is it on?

- Point to your **destination**.

globe

Talk Together

Pretend that you really plan to go on a journey. Use **Language Frames** from page 520 and **Key Words** to express your intentions to a partner. Then tell how you will achieve your goal.

Main Idea and Details

When you talk about something, you start with the **main idea**. Then you give **details** about the main idea. Connecting the main idea and details helps you understand what you read, see, or hear.

Look at these pictures. They show how Emma and her aunt plan for a trip to New York City. Read the text.

They save money.

They make a budget.

They pick places to see.

Map and Talk

You can use a main idea diagram to show the most important idea and details that support it. To make one, write the main idea on the line on the left side. Write the details on the lines on the right side.

Main Idea Diagram

Main Idea	Details
	They save money.
Emma and her aunt plan for a trip.	They make a budget.
	They pick places to see.

Talk Together

Make a main idea diagram with this main idea: **There are many interesting places to visit**. Share your diagram with a partner.

More Key Words

Use these words to talk about "One Man's Goal" and "Climbing Toward Her Goal."

challenge

(**cha**-lunj) *noun*

A **challenge** is something that is hard to do. It is a **challenge** to climb up a rope.

discover

(dis-**ku**-vur) *verb*

When you **discover** something, you find it. She **discovers** an insect on this plant.

endurance

(in-**dur**-uns) *noun*

When you have **endurance**, you keep doing something. A long race takes **endurance**.

explore

(ik-**splor**) *verb*

To **explore** means to go somewhere to learn about people or things. He **explores** a new area.

prepare

(pri-**pair**) *verb*

To **prepare** means to get ready for something. She packs a suitcase to **prepare** for her trip.

Talk Together

Ask a question using a **Key Word**. A partner answers with a different **Key Word**.

Why do you want to explore the ocean?

I would like to discover new kinds of fish.

Add words to My Vocabulary Notebook.
NGReach.com

Use Reading Strategies

When do you use reading strategies? Good readers use strategies all the time! Get in the habit of using reading strategies before, during, and after you read. Here's how to read actively:

- Look through the text quickly. What is the text mostly about? Decide on your purpose, or reason, for reading.

- As you read, stop now and then to ask yourself: Does this make sense? Use a reading strategy to help you understand better.

- When you finish reading, stop and think. Decide what you gained from reading the text.

How to Use a Reading Strategy

 1. Before you open a text, stop and think: What strategies can help me get ready to read?

 2. During reading, think about what strategies can help you understand.

 3. After reading, ask yourself: What strategies can I use to help me think about what I read?

> Before I read, I will _____.
>
> As I read, I can _____.
>
> Now that I'm done, I think _____.

Read Emma's diary entries about her trip. Tell a partner which reading strategies you used to help you understand the text.

Diary

Thursday, July 15

Today we saw animals. First we **explored** the Children's Zoo on 64th Street. What an adventure! At the petting zoo I touched the tame pigs and a sheep. A woolly alpaca nibbled corn right out of my hand. It tickled!

Then we went to see the main zoo. All the animals there live in natural habitats—even the polar bears. I could see, but not touch. At the entrance we **discovered** a musical clock. Every hour and half-hour it plays nursery rhyme tunes.

Friday, July 16

Today we go home. This morning we took the ferry to see one last sight: the Statue of Liberty. I climbed all 354 steps up to Lady Liberty's crown. That really tested my **endurance**, but the view from the top was worth it.

To **prepare** for the long **journey** home, we stopped at a shop in the train station. Aunt Rita bought some magazines. I bought a book. Luckily, I had enough money. Trying to stay within the budget has been a real **challenge**, but I still have $12.35 left over!

Read a Human Interest Feature

Genre

A **human interest feature** tells about a person's interesting experiences or adventures.

Text Features

A **map** is a drawing that gives information about places. A **compass rose** shows the directions north, south, east, and west. A **legend** explains the pictures or symbols on a map.

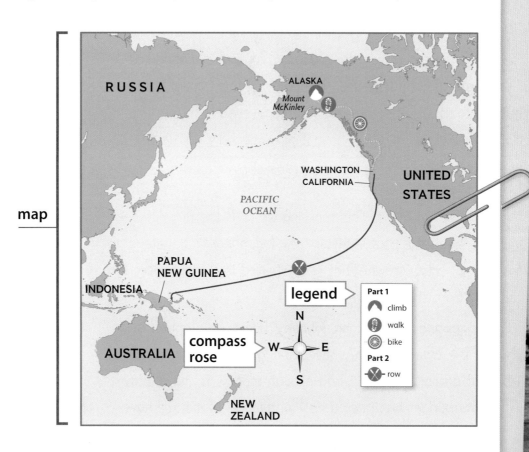

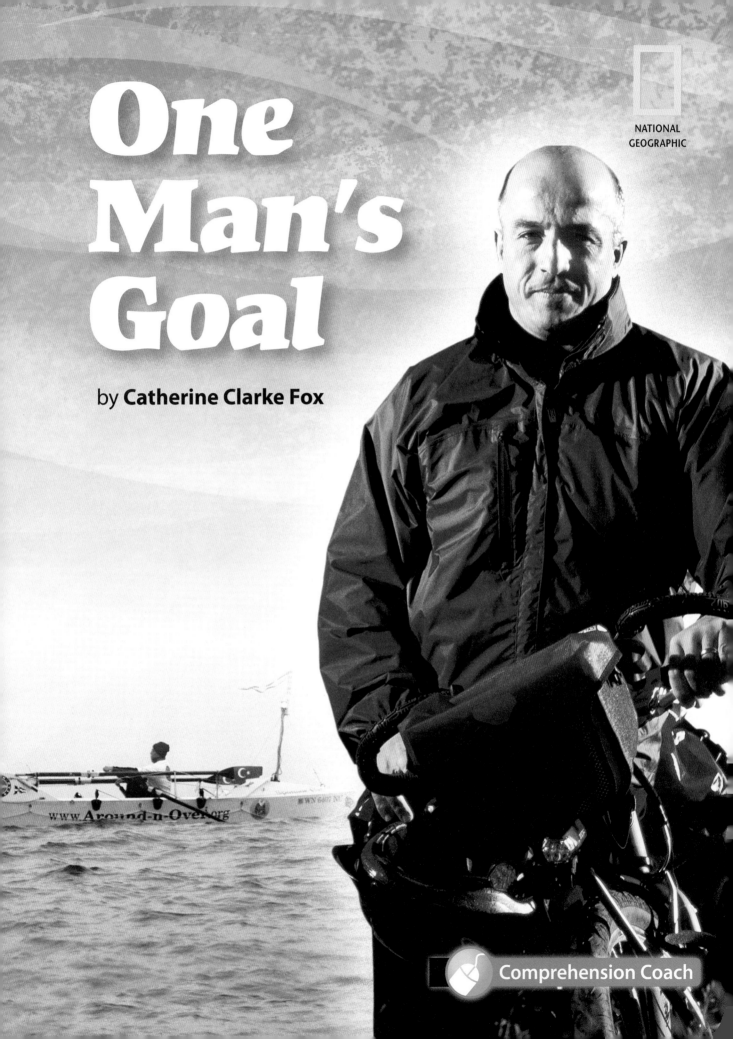

One Man's Goal

by **Catherine Clarke Fox**

www.Around-n-Over.org

Comprehension Coach

▶ **Set a Purpose**
Learn about the **challenges** a man
faced during his amazing **journey**.

Around the World

Erden Eruç (air-**den** e-r**ooch**) left California on July 10, 2007
in his 23-foot-long boat. He was rowing across the Pacific
Ocean toward Australia. Birds, fish, and sharks were his only
company.

Eruç rowed his boat across the
Pacific Ocean toward Australia.

In Other Words
company visitors

528

Crossing the Pacific was amazing, but that was only part of Eruç's **journey**. He was determined to go around the world—using his own **energy**!

During his journey, Eruç wanted to climb the tallest **peaks** on six **continents** to **honor the memory of** a fellow climber. Eruç planned to bike, walk, climb, and row the world—without any motors to help him.

bike

row

climb

In Other Words
energy power
peaks mountain tops
honor the memory of help others remember

▶ **Before You Move On**

1. **Classify** How did Eruç plan to travel around the world? Name the different ways.
2. **Make Inferences** What kind of person is Eruç? What makes you think so?

529

A Two-Part Adventure

For the first **leg** of his trip, Eruç bicycled 5,546 miles from Seattle, Washington, to Mount McKinley in Alaska and back. When he was in Alaska, he walked 67 miles to **base camp**. Then he climbed McKinley's peak, which is 20,320 feet high.

For the second part of his adventure, Eruç rowed toward Australia.

▲ Eruç tells kids about his **journey** to inspire them to dream and try to reach their own goals.

In Other Words

leg part

base camp the camp at the bottom of the mountain

Erden Eruç's Adventure

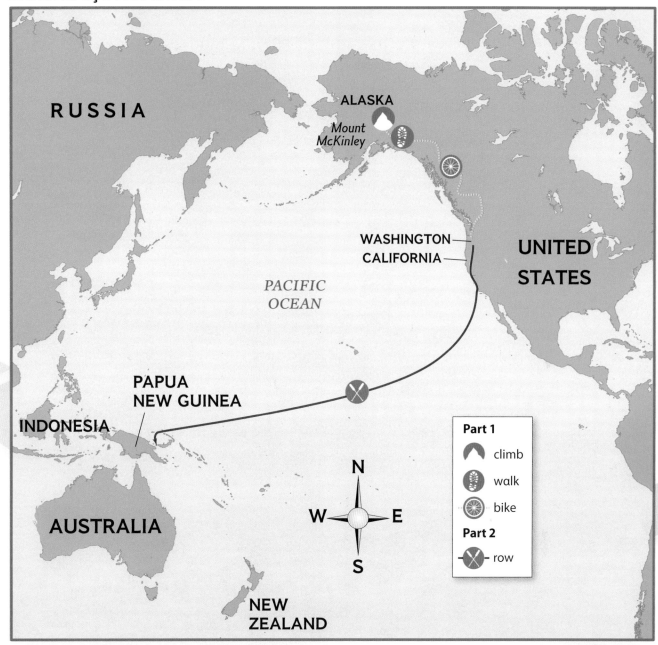

RUSSIA

ALASKA

Mount McKinley

WASHINGTON
CALIFORNIA

UNITED STATES

PACIFIC OCEAN

PAPUA NEW GUINEA

INDONESIA

N

W — E

S

AUSTRALIA

NEW ZEALAND

Part 1

- climb
- walk
- bike

Part 2

- row

▶ **Before You Move On**

1. **Sequence** According to the text, what did Eruç do after he bicycled to Alaska but before he left for Australia?

2. **Use Text Features** Look at the map legend. What do the most southern symbol on the map and the place name shown in blue tell you about Eruç's journey?

531

Alone on the Ocean

Traveling alone wasn't easy. Eruç **faced some disappointments** and challenges.

For example, he had to row at least 10 hours a day, so he brought along a music player. He hoped to listen to music and books and study Spanish to pass the time. Unfortunately, there was a lot of **tropical rain**. So Eruç had to pack his player away to keep it safe and dry.

Eruç rowed alone for many hours a day.

In Other Words
faced some disappointments had difficult times
tropical rain rain from hot, wet areas

On the Way to Australia

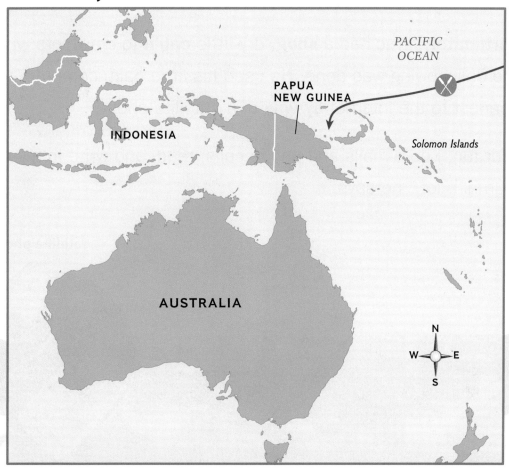

Not only that, but wind and waves kept pushing him **westward**. He wanted to go south toward the Solomon Islands. Big ships have powerful engines, but Eruç's rowboat and arm-power were **no match for** the winds.

If his luck didn't change, he would have to change his plan. He would try to land at Papua New Guinea. And, that's what happened! Eruç finally reached Papua New Guinea in February 2009.

▶ **Before You Move On**

1. **Visualize** What do you hear, feel, and see in your mind as you read about Eruç's **journey**?
2. **Use Text Features** Use the compass rose. What is south of Papua New Guinea?

A Home on the Waves

Fortunately, Eruç had a **snug**, dry little **cabin** to crawl into when the daily rowing was done. He used his little palm computer to connect to the Internet **by way of** a satellite phone.

"For fun, I do e-mails and phone calls, read, and write in my journal a lot," he says.

▼ **satellite phone**

cabin

▲ **Eruç measures the water temperature with a special tool.**

Protein bars gave him energy. He boiled water on a one-burner stove to prepare **freeze-dried** meals.

Using **solar panels**, he charged the batteries on his boat. Then he used an electric-powered machine to remove salt from the ocean water so he could drink it. But this only worked when the sun was shining. Because of the tropical rains, he often had to use a different machine with a handle he could pump by hand to remove salt from the water.

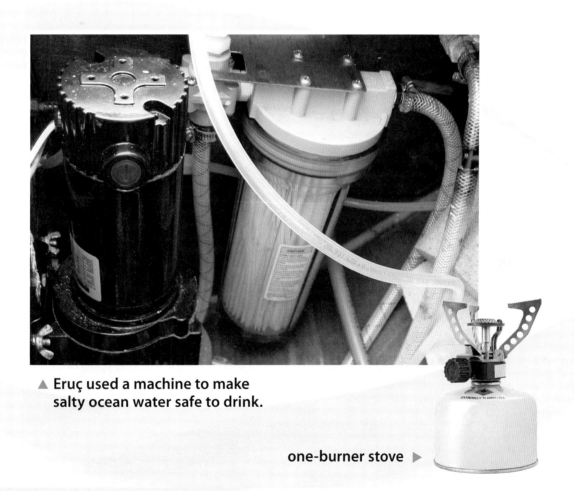

▲ Eruç used a machine to make salty ocean water safe to drink.

one-burner stove ▶

▶ **Before You Move On**

1. **Classify** Eruç has many pieces of equipment on his boat. What are they?
2. **Clarify** Why did Eruç need a different machine to remove salt from water when the sun wasn't shining?

A Lot to Learn

Eruç was not **bothered** by the hard work or even by being blown in the wrong direction. He sees the world as a **laboratory** where there is much to learn.

For example, he has learned from the birds that visit him on his boat at sea. If he sees **frigatebirds or noddy terns,** he knows that an island can't be far. These birds always return to the shore at the end of the day.

A friendly bird visits Eruç on his boat.

In Other Words
bothered upset
laboratory classroom
frigatebirds or noddy terns
certain kinds of sea birds

▲ Eruç talks to a group of girl scouts in the Philippines about making goals in life.

Sharing His Story

On his adventure, Eruç stopped from time to time to visit with people on land. He enjoyed meeting everyone—especially all the students. He shared his story with **dozens of** schools.

Even today, Eruç **encourages** all kids to **set their eyes on** a goal and not give up. Like his experience in the Pacific Ocean, it may be challenging.

"If you don't try, you don't (or won't) go anywhere," Eruç says. "With goals, we will **make progress**. We will be farther along than when we started, even if we don't reach some goals. That's called life!" ❖

In Other Words
dozens of many
encourages tells
set their eyes on make
make progress learn and grow

▶ **Before You Move On**
1. **Draw Conclusions** Eruç sees the world as a place to learn. What does this tell you about him?
2. **Main Idea** What does Eruç believe about goals?

Talk About It

Key Words

challenge	explore
continent	globe
destination	journey
discover	location
endurance	prepare

1. What part of this **human interest feature** did you enjoy the most?

   I enjoyed the part _____ .

2. Imagine that you are Eruç. Someone asks you why you want to row across the Pacific. **Express intentions** about your goal.

   I want to _____ . I am going to _____ .

3. Look at the map legend on page 531. How does it help you understand each part of the **journey**?

   The legend shows _____ .

Learn test-taking strategies.
NGReach.com

Write About It

Write a letter to Erden Eruç. Tell him what you think about his adventure. End your letter by telling him about a place you would like to **explore**. Use **Key Words**.

_____ , 20_____

Dear Erden,

    I just read an article about your trip around the world. I think _____ .

Main Idea and Details

Make a main idea diagram for different sections of "One Man's Goal." Base your main ideas on the section headings.

Main Idea Diagram

Main Idea	Details
Eruç decided to go around the world.	He left California in a boat in 2007.
	He rowed across the Pacific Ocean to Australia.

Work with a partner. Use your diagrams to summarize different sections of "One Man's Goal." Use the sentence frames and **Key Words**. Record your summaries.

> The main idea is _____.
> A detail that supports this is _____.

Fluency Comprehension Coach

Use the Comprehension Coach to practice reading with phrasing. Rate your reading.

Talk Together

Look at the maps on pages 531 and 533. Pretend to be Erden. Tell a partner how the maps helped you achieve your goal. Use **Key Words**.

Homographs

Homographs are words that have the same spelling, but different meanings. Some homographs have different pronunciations, too. You can use context to figure out the correct meanings.

Train is a homograph. Compare the examples.

They **train** (trān) for a race.
Meaning: to practice for something

The **train** (trān) travels fast.
Meaning: a line of railway cars on a track

Try It Together

Read the sentences. Then answer the questions.

A cold wind (wind) blows in my face as I sail my boat. I wind (wīnd) a scarf around my neck to keep me warm.

1. **What does wind mean in the first sentence?**

   A a machine

   B a kind of fish

   C air that moves

   D water that rises

2. **What does wind mean in the second sentence?**

   A to sail a boat

   B to stay warm

   C to put on a hat

   D to wrap around

Connect Across Texts Read about another adventurer who explores places around the world.

Genre A **profile** is nonfiction. It gives facts about a person and his or her life.

Climbing Toward Her Goal

by **Guadalupe López**

Constanza Ceruti

Constanza Ceruti loves mountains and learning about **ancient civilizations**. As **a high-altitude archaeologist**, she climbs to the tops of mountains to explore **worship sites**. So far, she has climbed more than 100 mountains over 16,500 feet high.

In Other Words

ancient civilizations people who lived very long ago

a high-altitude archaeologist someone who studies old objects found on mountains

worship sites places where people used to pray to gods

▶ **Before You Move On**

1. **Make Inferences** Why did Ceruti become a high-altitude archaeologist?

2. **Main Idea and Details** Which details in the text support the idea that Ceruti loves history?

541

The Children of Llullaillaco

In 1999, Ceruti and her team climbed Llullaillaco (yū-yī-**yaw**-kō), a mountain in Argentina. It was a harsh climb, with blowing snow, strong winds, and **low oxygen levels**.

When the explorers finally reached the top, they found three frozen **Incan mummies**. Two girls and a boy were buried 500 years ago. The mummies still have hair on their arms, which makes them the best-preserved mummies in the world. The explorers also found gold and silver statues, **textiles**, and pottery.

"This was not just an archaeological find," says Ceruti. "This was like meeting someone from the ancient past."

SOUTH AMERICA

ARGENTINA

◀ Ceruti found objects buried with the mummies.

In Other Words

low oxygen levels very little air to breathe

Incan mummies bodies from a group of people who lived long ago

textiles cloth

What the Explorers Found

▲ a dish shaped like a duck

▲ statues found buried with the mummies

statue of a llama (yɑh-muh) made of a shell ▶

▲ comb made of cactus thorns

▲ cloth food bags

▶ Before You Move On

1. **Ask Questions** What question did you ask yourself about the text? Tell a partner how you found the answer.

2. **Form Generalizations** What can you say about the objects the explorers found?

Paving the Path

Growing up in Argentina, Ceruti was always interested in ancient civilizations. Her dream was to live and work near the mountains. In school, Ceruti worked hard to reach her goal. Math was a subject she really had to **conquer**!

Now, Ceruti uses math all the time. "How many feet will we climb? How long will it take? What time do we start?" She knows that careful planning can mean the difference between **success and failure**.

Ceruti brushes dirt off a mummy.

In Other Words
Paving the Path Making a Plan
conquer work hard at to learn
success and failure a good trip or a bad trip

The **journey** to the top of Mount Llullaillaco was long and hard, but that did not stop Ceruti from climbing.

"Just think of the Incas who climbed these mountains hundreds of years ago," she says. "They **endured** the same conditions."

With **preparation** and **determination**, Ceruti proves one thing: no mountain—or goal—is too big to conquer! ❖

Ceruti climbed the same mountains the Incas did.

In Other Words

endured lived through
preparation good planning
determination courage

▶ **Before You Move On**

1. **Summarize** What are the most important ideas in the text under "Paving the Path" on page 544?
2. **Analyze** Describe Ceruti's goal, and whether or not she achieved it.

Respond and Extend

Key Words

challenge	explore
continent	globe
destination	journey
discover	location
endurance	prepare

Compare Causes

Both Erden Eruç and Constanza Ceruti like physical **challenges**. What else causes them to do adventurous things? How are their reasons alike? How are they different? Work with a partner to complete a Venn diagram.

Venn Diagram

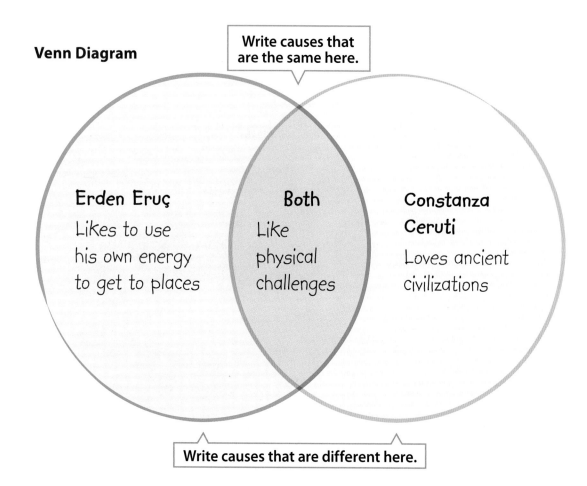

Write causes that are the same here.

Erden Eruç
Likes to use his own energy to get to places

Both
Like physical challenges

Constanza Ceruti
Loves ancient civilizations

Write causes that are different here.

Talk Together

What tools help people reach their goals? Think about the feature and the profile. Use **Key Words** to talk about your ideas.

546

Skills Trace: ▷ Future Tense with *will*
▷ Future Tense with *going to*
▶ **Future Tense**

Grammar

Future Tense

There are two ways to show the **future tense**.

Grammar Rules Future Tense

	Now	In the Future
• Use the helping verb **will** along with a **main verb**.	leave	We **will leave** on a trip tomorrow.
• Use **am going to**, **are going to**, or **is going to** before a **main verb**.	look	I **am going to look** at a map later.
	ride	My friends **are going to ride** their bikes to my house.
	hike	Randy **is going to hike** up the mountain on Saturday.

Read in the Future Tense

Read these sentences about a journey. Can you find two examples of the future tense? Show them to a partner.

> My cousins are going to travel around the world. They will row a boat much of the way.

Write in the Future Tense

What do you think will happen to the cousins on their trip? Write a paragraph for your partner. Use the future tense.

547

Write as a Storyteller

Write a Story ✏️

Write a story about someone who accomplishes an important goal. Add your story to a short story collection and share it with others.

Study a Model

When you write a story, you create characters, a setting, and a plot. The plot often has a problem that the main character solves.

Super Chicken!

by Devon Samuels

Marvin stood at the edge of the diving board. Every week, he climbed up the ladder of the high dive. Then, every week, he went right back down again. **The kids at the pool called him Super Chicken.**

Marvin looked down at the water. No way was he only three meters up! The pool people must have measured wrong.

"Jump!" some kids yelled.

Marvin counted to ten, which always made him calm, and sprang off the board. He hit the water with a big splash. When he came up, everyone cheered. He grinned. No more Super Chicken!

The beginning introduces the **main character**, the **setting**, and the **problem**.

The writing has a clear voice and style. The writer uses words that show who he is.

The ending shows how the character solves the problem.

Prewrite

1. **Choose a Topic** What will your story be about? Talk with a partner to come up with ideas.

2. **Gather Information** Who will your main character be? What is the person's goal? Write down your ideas.

3. **Get Organized** Use a story map to help you organize the events.

Story Map

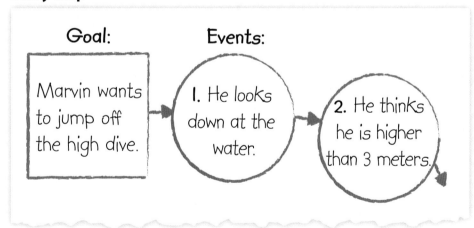

Draft

Write your first paragraph. Then use your story map to guide the rest of your draft. Use words that sound like you.

Revise

1. **Read, Retell, Respond** Read your draft aloud to a partner. Your partner listens and then retells the story. Next, talk about ways to improve your writing.

Language Frames

Retell	Make Suggestions
The story is about _____ . It takes place _____ . The first thing that happens is _____ .	I like the story, but I'm confused about where it happens. Is the setting _____ ? This story doesn't show who you are. You should use words that _____ .

---

2. **Make Changes** Think about your draft and your partner's suggestions. Then use the Revising Marks on page 573 to mark your changes.

  - Make sure your readers know where your story takes place.

    > at the pool
    > The kids called him Super Chicken.
    >   ∧

  - Do your words and sentences sound like you? If not, change some.

    > No way was he
    > ~~He couldn't believe he was~~ only three meters up!
    >   ∧

Edit and Proofread

Work with a partner to edit and proofread your story. Check verbs in the past tense. Use the marks on page 574 to show your changes.

Use the marks on page 574 to show your changes.

Spelling Tip

✔ For most regular verbs, add **-ed** to show past tense. For some regular verbs, change the base word before you add **-ed**.

Publish

1. **On Your Own** Make a final copy of your story. Read it aloud to a younger or older friend or to family members. Tell them how you got your ideas.

Presentation Tips	
If you are the speaker…	**If you are the listener…**
Use gestures to help your listeners imagine what is happening in the story.	Listen attentively and picture the events in the story.
If you tell your story to younger children, retell it with simpler words and sentences.	Think about what lesson you could learn from the story.

2. **With a Group** Make a short story collection. Put all your stories in a book or post them online. Think of a title that lets readers know that the stories are about goals.

BIG Question

What tools can we use to achieve our goals?

In this unit, you found lots of answers to the **Big Question**. Now, use your concept map to discuss the **Big Question** with the class.

Concept Map

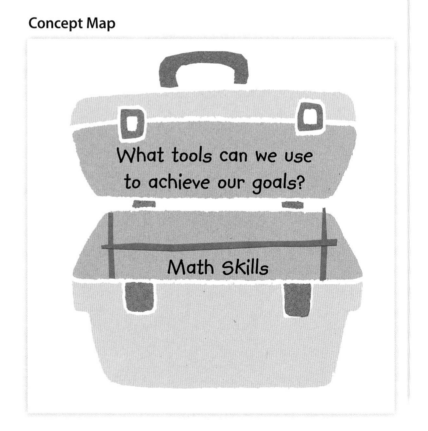

What tools can we use to achieve our goals?

Math Skills

Write a Story

Choose a tool for success from your concept map. Write a story about someone who used the tool to reach a goal.

552

Share Your Ideas

Choose one of these ways to share your ideas about the **Big Question**.

Talk About It!

Talk Show

Work with two classmates. Pretend you are on a TV talk show. One person is the host. The other two are the guests. Discuss tools you use to achieve goals at home and at school.

Write It!

Plan a Trip

Work with a partner. Pretend you are going on a camping trip. Make a list of information, such as how much food you will need, how far your destination is, and how far you will travel each day.

Do It!

Guessing Game

Work with a small group to play a guessing game. Take turns. Pantomime something you have to use numbers to do, such as make a recipe or keep score for a game. Other classmates guess your actions.

Write It!

Make a Map

Imagine a place you would like to visit. Draw a map. Show how to get there from your home. Put distances and other information on your map. Share it with a partner.

Strategies for Learning Language

These strategies can help you learn to use and understand the English language.

❶ Listen actively and try out language.

What to Do	Examples	
Repeat what you hear.	**You hear:** Way to go, Joe! Fantastic catch!	**You say:** Way to go, Joe! Fantastic catch!
Recite songs and poems.	My Family Tree Two grandmas, one brother, Two grandpas, one mother, One father, and then there's me. Eight of us together Make up my family tree.	Two grandmas, one brother,...
Listen to others and use their language.	**You hear:** "When did you know that something was missing?"	**You say:** "I knew that something was missing when I got to class."

❷ Ask for help.

What to Do	Examples	
Ask questions about how to use language.	Did I say that right? Did I use that word in the right way?	Which is correct, "bringed" or "brought"?
Use your native language or English to make sure that you understand.	**You say:** "Wait! Could you say that again more slowly, please?"	**Other options:** "Does 'violet' mean 'purple'?" "Is 'enormous' another way to say 'big'?"

3 Use gestures and body language, and watch for them.

What to Do	Examples
Use gestures and movements to help others understand your ideas.	I will hold up five fingers to show that I need five more minutes.
Watch people as they speak. The way they look or move can help you understand the meaning of their words.	Let's give him a hand. / Everyone is clapping. "Give him a hand" must mean to clap for him.

4 Think about what you are learning.

What to Do	Examples
Ask yourself: Are my language skills getting better? How can I improve?	Was it correct to use "they" when I talked about my grandparents? / Did I add 's to show ownership?
Keep notes about what you've learned. Use your notes to practice using English.	How to Ask Questions • I can start a question with "is," "can," or "do": Do you have my math book? • I can start a question with "who," "what," "where," "when," "how," or "why" to get more information: Where did you put my math book?

Vocabulary Strategies

When you read, you may find a word you don't know. But, don't worry! There are many things you can do to figure out the meaning of an unfamiliar word.

Use What You Know

Ask yourself "Does this new word look like a word I know?" If it does, use what you know about the familiar word to figure out the meaning of the new word. Think about:

- **word families**, or words that look similar and have related meanings. The words *locate*, *location*, and *relocate* are in the same word family.

- **cognates**, or pairs of words that look the same in English and in another language. The English word *problem* and the Spanish word *problema* are cognates.

On the Top of the World

Mount Everest is the highest mountain in the world. It is 29,028 feet (8,848 meters) high. This **magnificent** mountain is covered in permanently frozen snow and ice. But this doesn't stop **adventurous** climbers from trying to reach its peak.

> This English word looks like **magnifico**. That means "beautiful" in Spanish. I think that meaning makes sense here, too.

> I know that **adventure** means "an exciting event" and that an **adventurer** is "someone who takes risks." So, **adventurous** probably means "willing to be a part of risky activities."

Use Context Clues

Sometimes you can figure out a word's meaning by looking at other words and phrases near the word. Those words and phrases are called **context clues.**

There are different kinds of context clues. Look for signal words such as *means, like, but,* or *unlike* to help you find the clues.

Extremely cold temperatures are hazardous to mountain climbers.

Kind of Clue	Signal Words	Example
Definition Gives the word's meaning.	*is, are, was, refers to, means*	Hazardous *refers to* something that causes harm or injury.
Restatement Gives the word's meaning in a different way, usually after a comma.	*or*	Mountain climbing can be hazardous, *or* result in injuries to climbers.
Synonym Gives a word or phrase that means almost the same thing.	*like, also*	Sudden drops in temperature can be hazardous. *Also* dangerous are very high altitudes that make it hard to breathe.
Antonym Gives a word or phrase that means the opposite.	*but, unlike*	The subzero temperatures can be hazardous, *but* special gear keeps the climbers safe.
Examples Gives examples of what the word means.	*such as, for example, including*	Climbers prepare for hazardous situations. *For example*, they carry extra food, equipment for heavy snowfall, and first-aid kits.

Use Word Parts

Many English words are made up of parts. You can use these parts as clues to a word's meaning.

When you don't know a word, look to see if you know any of its parts. Put the meaning of the word parts together to figure out the meaning of the whole word.

Compound Words

laptop

A compound word is made up of two or more smaller words. To figure out the meaning of the whole word:

1. Break the long word into parts.

   keyboard = key + board

2. Put the meanings of the smaller words together to predict the meaning of the whole word.

   key = button
   +
   board = flat surface

   keyboard = flat part of computer with buttons

keyboard

3. If you can't predict the meaning from the parts, use what you know and the meaning of the other words to figure it out.

   lap + top = laptop

   laptop means "small portable computer," not "the top of your lap"

Prefixes

A prefix comes at the beginning of a word. It changes the word's meaning. To figure out the meaning of an unfamiliar word, look to see if it has a prefix.

1. Break the word into parts. Think about the meaning of each part.

   I need to **rearrange** the files on my computer.

   re- + arrange

   The prefix *re-* means "again." The word *arrange* means "to put in order."

2. Put the meanings of the word parts together.

   The word *rearrange* means "to put in order again."

Some Prefixes and Their Meanings

Prefix	Meaning
anti-	against
dis-	opposite of
In-	not
mis	wrongly
pre-	before
re-	again, back
un-	not

Suffixes

A suffix comes at the end of a word. It changes the word's meaning and part of speech. To figure out the meaning of new word, look to see if it has a suffix.

Some Suffixes and Their Meanings

Suffix	Meaning
-able	can be done
-al	having characteristics of
-ion	act, process
-er, -or	one who
-ful	full of
-less	without
-ly	in a certain way

1. Break the word into parts. Think about the meaning of each part.

My **teacher** helps me find online articles.

teach + -er

> verb

The word *teach* means "to give lessons." The suffix *-er* means "one who."

2. Put the meanings of the word parts together.

A *teacher* is "a person who gives lessons."

> noun

Greek and Latin Roots

Many words in English have Greek and Latin roots. A root is a word part that has meaning, but it cannot stand on its own.

1. Break the unfamiliar word into parts.

I won't be done in time if there's one more **interruption**!

inter + rupt + ion

> prefix   root   suffix

2. Focus on the root. Do you know other words with the same root?

"I've seen the root **rupt** in the words *erupt* and *rupture*.

'rupt' must have something to do with breaking or destroying something."

3. Put the meanings of all the word parts together.

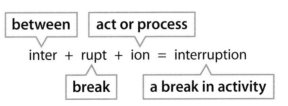

inter + rupt + ion = interruption

561

Look Beyond the Literal Meaning

Writers use colorful language to keep their readers interested. They use words and phrases that mean something different from their usual definitions. Figurative language and idioms are kinds of colorful language.

Figurative Language: Similes

A simile compares two things that are alike in some way. It uses the words *like* or *as* to make the comparison.

Simile	Things Compared	How They're Alike
Cory hiked across the desert **as sluggishly as a snail**.	Cory and a snail	They both move very slowly.
His skin was **like sheets of sandpaper.**	skin and sandpaper	They are both rough and very dry.

Figurative Language: Metaphors

A metaphor compares two things without using the words *like* or *as*.

Metaphor	Things Compared	Meaning
The **sun's rays were a thousand bee stings** on his face.	sun's rays and bee stings	The sun's rays blistered his face.
His only **companion was thirst.**	friend and thirst	His thirst was always there with him.

Figurative Language: Personification

When writers use personification they give human qualities to nonhuman things.

Personification	Object	Human Quality
The **angry sun** kept punishing him.	sun	has feelings
A **cactus reached out to** him.	cactus	is able to be friendly

Idioms

An idiom is a special kind of phrase that means something different from what the words mean by themselves.

What you say:	What you mean:
If the topic is Mars, **I'm all ears.**	If the topic is Mars, **I'll listen very carefully.**
Break a leg!	**Good luck!**
Rachel had **to eat her words.**	Rachel had **to say she was wrong.**
Give me a break!	**That's ridiculous!**
Hang on.	**Wait.**
I'm **in a jam.**	I'm **in trouble.**
The joke was so funny, Lisa **laughed her head off.**	The joke was so funny, Lisa **laughed very hard.**
Juan was **steamed** when I lost his video game.	Juan was **very angry** when I lost his video game.
Let's **surf the Net** for ideas for report ideas.	Let's **look around the contents of the Internet** for report ideas.
I'm so tired, I just want to **veg out**.	I'm so tired, I just want to **relax and not think about anything.**
Rob and Zak are together **24-seven**.	Rob and Zak are together **all the time.**
You can say that again.	**I totally agree with you.**
Zip your lips!	**Be quiet!**

Reading Strategies

Good readers use a set of strategies before, during, and after reading. Knowing which strategy to use and when will help you understand and enjoy all kinds of text.

Plan and Monitor

Good readers have clear plans for reading. Remember to:

- **Set a purpose** for reading. Ask yourself: Why am I reading this? What do I hope to get from it?

- **Preview** what you are about to read. Look at the title. Scan the text, pictures, and other visuals.

- **Make predictions**, or thoughtful guesses, about what comes next. Check your predictions as you read. Change them as you learn new information.

Monitor, or keep track of, your reading. Remember to:

- **Clarify ideas and vocabulary** to make sure you understand what the words and passages mean. Stop and ask yourself: Does that make sense?

- **Reread, read on,** or **change your reading speed** if you are confused.

Determine Importance

How can you keep track of all the facts and details as you read? Do what good readers do and focus on the most important ideas.

- Identify the **main idea**. Connect details to the main idea.

- **Summarize** as you read and after you read.

Ask Questions

Asking yourself questions as you read keeps your mind active. You'll ask different types of questions, so you'll need to find the answers in different ways.

- Some questions are connected to answers **right there** in the text.

- Others cover more than one part of the text. So, you'll have to **think and search** to find the answers.

Not all answers are found in the book.

- **On your own** questions can focus on your experiences or on the big ideas of the text.

- **Author and you** questions may be about the author's purpose or point of view.

Visualize

Good readers use the text and their own experiences to picture a writer's words. When you **visualize**, use all your senses to see, hear, smell, feel, and taste what the writer describes.

Make Connections

When you make connections, you put together information from the text with what you know from outside the text. As you read, think about:

- **your own ideas and experiences**
- what you know about the **world** from TV, songs, school, and so on
- **other texts** you've read by the same author, about the same topic, or in the same genre.

Make Inferences

Sometimes an author doesn't tell a reader everything. To figure out what is left unsaid:

- Look for what the author emphasizes.
- Think about what you already know.
- Combine what you read with what you know to figure out what the author means.

Synthesize

When you **synthesize**, you put together information from different places and come up with new understandings. You might:

- **Draw conclusions**, or combine what you know with what you read to decide what to think about a topic.
- **Form generalizations**, or combine ideas from the text with what you know to form an idea that is true in many situations.

Writing and Research

Writing is one of the best ways to express yourself. Sometimes you'll write to share a personal experience. Other times, you'll write to give information about a research topic. Whenever you write, use the following steps to help you say want you want clearly, correctly, and in your own special way.

Prewrite

When you prewrite, you choose a topic and collect all the details and information you need for writing.

1 **Choose a Topic and Make a Plan** Think about your writing prompt assignment or what you want to write about.

- Make a list. Then choose the best idea to use for your topic.

- Think about your writing role, audience, and form. Add those to a RAFT chart.

- Jot down any research questions, too. Those will help you look for the information you need.

> **RAFT Chart**
>
> **R**ole: scientist
> **A**udience: my teacher and classmates
> **F**orm: report
> **T**opic: honeybees

2 **Gather Information** Think about your topic and your plan. Jot down ideas. Or, use resources like those on pages 579–582 to find information that answers your questions. Take notes.

Use Information Resources

Books

A book is a good source of information.

Notecard

Where do honeybees live? < **research question**

The Honey Makers, by Gail Gibbons, page 6 < **name of source**

—Many honeybees live in dark places like hollow trees. < **notes in your own words**

—"Honeybees cared for by today's beekeepers live in box-shaped wooden hives." < **author's exact words in quotation marks**

Read the pages to find information you need. Take notes.

WILD HONEYBEE HIVE

Many honeybees like to make their homes in dark, enclosed places. Often a colony of wild honeybees builds its hive in a hollow tree. Honeybees cared for by today's beekeepers live in box-shaped wooden hives.

WOODEN BEEHIVE

Encyclopedias

Each encyclopedia volume has facts about different topics.

guide words

● Rain forest

Rain forest

Rain forests are thick forests of tall trees. They are found where the weather is warm the year around, and there is plenty of rain. Most rain forests grow near the equator, a make-believe line around Earth's middle. Africa, Asia, and Central and South America have large rain forests. Smaller rain forests are found in Australia and islands in the Pacific.

Tropical rain forests have more kinds of trees than anywhere else in the world. More than half of all the kinds of plants and animals on Earth live in tropical rain forests.

The tallest rain forest trees are as tall as 165 feet (50 meters). The treetops form a leafy covering called the canopy

Tropical rain forests have more kinds of trees than anywhere else in the world.

article

1. Look up your topic in the correct encyclopedia **volume** or on the **CD-ROM**.

2. Read the **guide words**. Keep turning the pages until you find the article you want. Use alphabetical order.

3. Read the **article** and take notes.

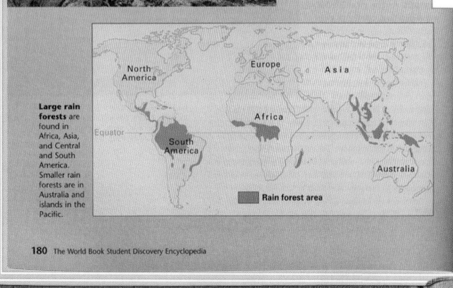

Large rain forests are found in Africa, Asia, and Central and South America. Smaller rain forests are in Australia and islands in the Pacific.

North America · Europe · Asia · Equator · Africa · South America · Australia

▇ Rain forest area

180 The World Book Student Discovery Encyclopedia

Magazines

The **date** tells when the **issue** was published.

This is the **title** of the magazine.

This is the **main topic** of the issue.

These are some of the **topics** in the issue.

... and Experts

Arrange a time to talk to an **expert,** or someone who knows a lot about your topic.

- Prepare questions you want to ask about the topic.

- Conduct the interview. Write down the person's answers.

- Choose the notes you'll use for your writing

Internet

The Internet is a connection of computers that share information through the World Wide Web. It is like a giant library. Check with your teacher for how to access the Internet from your school.

1. **Go to a search page.** Type in your key words. Click Search.

2. **Read the list of Web sites, or pages, that have your key words.** The underlined words are links to the Web sites.

3. **Click on a link to go directly to the site, or Web page.** Read the article online. Or print it if it is helpful for your research. Later on, you can use the article to take notes.

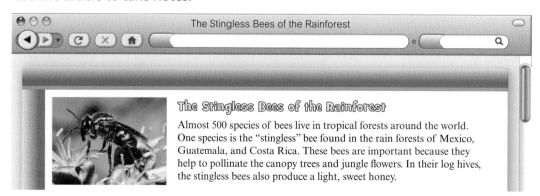

4. **Get Organized** Think about all the details you've gathered about your topic. Use a list, a chart, or other graphic organizer to show what you'll include in your writing. Use the organizer to show the order of your ideas, too.

Cluster

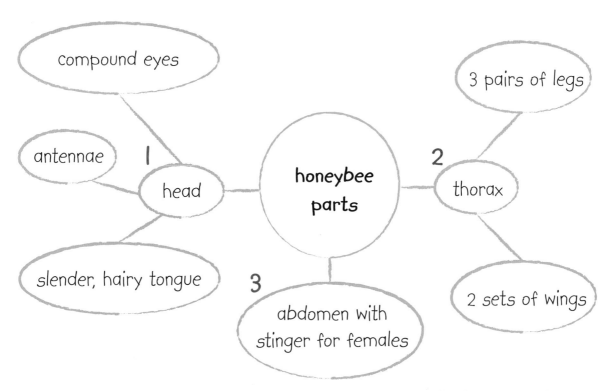

compound eyes

3 pairs of legs

antennae

1

head

honeybee parts

2

thorax

slender, hairy tongue

3

2 sets of wings

abdomen with stinger for females

Outline

The Helpful, Sweet Honeybee

I. Important insects

  A. help pollinate plants

    1. flowers and trees

    2. fruits

  B. turn nectar into honey

II. Honeybee homes

  A. around the world

  B. hives

Draft

When you write your first draft, you turn all your ideas into sentences. You write quickly just to get all your ideas down. You can correct mistakes later.

Cluster

Turn your main idea into a topic sentence. Then add the details.

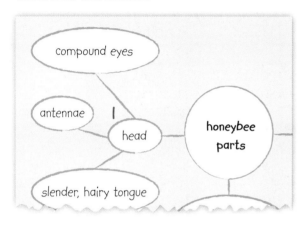

Beginning of a Description

One main part of a honeybee is the head. The bee's head seems to be mostly eyes! They are called compound eyes and have a lot of tiny lenses in them.

Outline

Turn the main idea after each Roman numeral into a topic sentence. Then turn the words next to the letters and numbers into detail sentences that tell more about the main idea.

The Helpful, Sweet Honeybee
I. Important insects
   A. help pollinate plants
      1. flowers and trees
      2. fruits

Beginning of a Report

The Helpful, Sweet Honeybee

You may think that all the honeybee does is make honey. But, believe it or not, this insect is always busy with another important job.

A honeybee helps keep plants growing. It helps to spread the pollen flowers and trees need to start new plants.

Revise

When you revise, you make changes to your writing to make it better and clearer.

1 Read, Retell, Respond Read your draft aloud to a partner. Your partner listens and then retells your main points.

You are describing a honeybee's hive. Isn't a bee's nest the same as a hive?

Yes, it is. I don't need the word "nest," so I'll take it out.

Your partner can help you discover what is unclear or what you need to add. Use your partner's suggestions to decide what you can to do to make your writing better.

2 Make Changes Think about your draft and what you and your partner discussed. What changes will you make? Use Revising Marks to mark your changes.

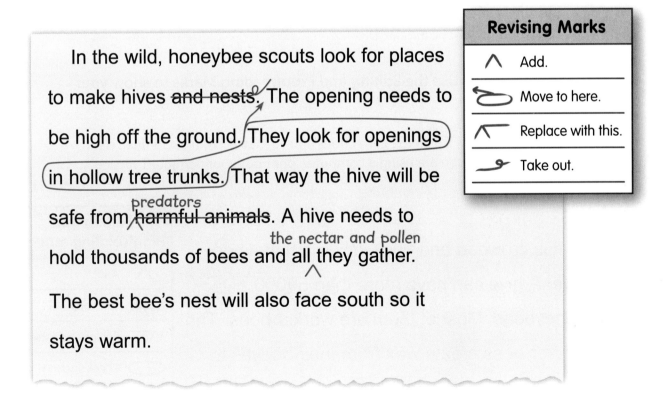

In the wild, honeybee scouts look for places to make hives ~~and nests.~~ The opening needs to be high off the ground. They look for openings in hollow tree trunks. That way the hive will be safe from predators ~~harmful animals~~. A hive needs to hold thousands of bees and all the nectar and pollen they gather. The best bee's nest will also face south so it stays warm.

Revising Marks	
∧	Add.
∽	Move to here.
⋏	Replace with this.
⌐	Take out.

Edit and Proofread

When you edit and proofread, you look for mistakes in capitalization, grammar, and punctuation.

1 Check Your Sentences Check that your sentences are clear, complete, and correct. Add any missing subjects or predicates

2 Check Your Spelling Look for any misspelled words. Check their spelling in a dictionary or a glossary.

3 Check for Capital Letters, Punctuation, and Grammar Look especially for correct use of

- capital letters in proper nouns
- apostrophes and quotation marks
- subject-verb agreement
- pronouns
- verb tenses

4 Mark Your Changes Use the Editing and Proofreading Marks to show your changes.

5 Make a Final Copy Make all the corrections you've marked to make a final, clean copy of your writing. If you are using a computer, print out your corrected version.

It is crowded and busy inside a honeybee hive. A hive can have more than 50,000 honeybees. Most of them are worker bees. The worker bees create wax from their bodies to build combs. The combs are layers of cells, or holes. The cells hold nectar, pollen, or larvae.

Editing and Proofreading Marks	
∧	Add.
✎	Take out.
∧	Replace with this.
◯	Check spelling.
≡	Capitalize.
/	Make lowercase.
¶	Make new paragraph.

Publish

When you publish your writing, you share it with others.

1 **Add Visuals** Visuals can make your writing more interesting and easier to understand. Maybe you will

- import photographs or illustrations
- insert computer clip art
- add graphs, charts, or diagrams

2 **Present Your Writing** There are a lot of ways to share your finished work. Here are just a few ideas.

- E-mail it to a friend or family member.
- Send it to your favorite magazine or publication.
- Turn it into a chapter for a group book about the topic.
- Make a video clip of you reading it to add to a group presentation.

A Home for the Honeybee

In the wild, honeybee scouts look for places to make hives. They look for openings in hollow tree trunks. The opening needs to be high off the ground. That way the hive will be safe from predators. A hive also needs to be big enough for thousands of bees and all the nectar and pollen they gather. The best hive will also face south so it stays warm.

Writing Traits

Good writing is clear, interesting, and easy to follow. To make your writing as good as it can be, check your writing to be sure it has the characteristics, or traits, of good writing.

Ideas

Writing is well-developed when the message is clear and interesting to the reader. It is supported by details that show the writer knows the topic well.

	Is the message clear and interesting?	Do the details show the writer knows the topic?
4	❑ All of the writing is clear and focused. ❑ The writing is very interesting.	❑ All the details tell about the topic. The writer knows the topic well.
3	❑ Most of the writing is clear and focused. ❑ Most of the writing is interesting.	❑ Most of the details are about the topic. The writer knows the topic fairly well.
2	❑ Some of the writing is not clear. The writing lacks some focus. ❑ Some of the writing is confusing.	❑ Some details are about the topic. The writer doesn't know the topic well.
1	❑ The writing is not clear or focused. ❑ The writing is confusing.	❑ Many details are not about the topic. The writer does not know the topic.

Organization

Writing is organized when it is easy to follow. All the ideas make sense together and flow from one idea to the next in an order that fits the writer's audience and purpose.

	Is the writing organized? Does it fit the audience and purpose?	Does the writing flow?
4	❑ The writing is very well-organized. ❑ It clearly fits both the writer's audience and purpose.	❑ The writing is smooth and logical. Each sentence flows into the next one.
3	❑ Most of the writing is organized. ❑ It mostly fits the writer's audience and purpose.	❑ Most of the writing is smooth. There are only a few sentences that do not flow logically.
2	❑ The writing is not well-organized. ❑ It fits the writer's audience or the writer's purpose, but not both.	❑ Some of the writing is smooth. Many sentences do not flow smoothly.
1	❑ The writing is not organized at all. ❑ It does not fit the writer's audience or purpose.	❑ The sentences do not flow smoothly or logically.

Organized

Not organized

Voice

Every writer has a special way of saying things, or a voice. The voice should sound genuine, or real, and be unique to that writer.

	Does the writing sound genuine and unique ?	Does the tone fit the audience and purpose?
4	❏ The writing is genuine and unique. It shows who the writer is.	❏ The writer's tone, formal or informal, fits the audience and purpose.
3	❏ Most of the writing sounds genuine and unique.	❏ The writer's tone mostly fits the audience and purpose.
2	❏ Some of the writing sounds genuine and unique.	❏ Some of the writing fits the audience and purpose.
1	❏ The writing does not sound genuine or unique.	❏ The writer's tone does not fit the audience or purpose.

Word Choice

Readers can always tell who the writer is by the words the writer uses.

	Do the writer's words fit the message?	Does the language fit the audience? Is it interesting?
4	❏ The writer chose words that really fit the message.	❏ The words and sentences fit the audience and are interesting.
3	❏ Most of the words really fit the writer's message.	❏ Most of the words and sentences fit the audience and are interesting.
2	❏ Some of the words fit the writer's message.	❏ Some of the words and sentences fit the audience and are interesting.
1	❏ Few or no words fit the writer's message.	❏ The language does not fit the audience and lose the readers' attention.

Fluency

Good writers use a variety of sentence types. They also use transitions, or signal words.

	Is there sentence variety? Are there transitions?	Does the writing sound natural and rhythmic?
4	❏ The writer uses lots of different types of sentences. ❏ The writer uses useful transitions.	❏ When I read the writing aloud, it sounds natural and rhythmic.
3	❏ The writer uses many different types of sentences. ❏ Most transition words are useful.	❏ When I read the writing aloud, most of it sounds natural and rhythmic.
2	❏ The writer uses some different kinds of sentences. ❏ Some transition words are useful.	❏ When I read the writing aloud, some of it sounds natural and rhythmic.
1	❏ The writer does not vary sentences. ❏ The writer does not use transitions.	❏ When I read the writing aloud, it sounds unnatural.

Conventions

Good writers always follow the rules of grammar, punctuation, and spelling.

	Is the writing correct?	Are the sentences complete?
4	❏ All the punctuation, capitalization, and spelling is correct.	❏ Every sentence has a subject and a predicate.
3	❏ Most of the punctuation, spelling, and capitalization is correct.	❏ Most of the sentences have a subject and a predicate.
2	❏ Some of the punctuation, spelling, and capitalization is correct.	❏ Some of the sentences are missing subjects or predicates.
1	❏ There are many punctuation, spelling, and capitalization errors.	❏ Several sentences are missing subjects or predicates.

Grammar, Usage, Mechanics, and Spelling

Sentences

A sentence expresses a complete thought.

Kinds of Sentences

There are four kinds of sentences.

A **statement** tells something. It ends with a **period**.	Ned is at the mall now**.** He needs a new shirt**.**
A **question** asks for information. It ends with a **question mark**.	Where can I find the shirts **?**

Kinds of Questions

Some questions ask for "Yes" or "No" answers. They start with words such as **Is**, **Do**, **Can**, **Are**, and **Will**.	**Do** you have a size 10?
	   Answer: Yes.
	Are these shirts on sale?
	   Answer: No.

Other questions ask for more information. They start with words such as **Who**, **What**, **Where**, **When**, and **Why**.	**What** colors do you have?
	   Answer: We have red and blue.
	Where can I try this on?
	   Answer: You can use this room.

An **exclamation** shows strong feeling. It ends with an **exclamation mark**.	This is such a cool shirt**!** I love it **!**
A **command** tells you what to do or what not to do. It usually begins with a **verb** and ends with a period. If a command shows strong emotion, it ends with an exclamation mark.	**Please** bring me a size 10. **Don't open** the door yet. Wait until I come out!

Negative Sentences

A negative sentence means "no."

A **negative sentence** uses a **negative word** to say "no."	That is **not** a good color for me. I **can't** find the right size.

Complete Sentences

A complete sentence has two parts.

The **subject** tells whom or what the sentence is about.	<u>My friends</u> buy clothes here. <u>The other store</u> has nicer shirts.
The **predicate** tells what the subject is, has, or does.	My friends <u>buy clothes here</u>. The other store <u>has nicer shirts</u>.

Subjects

All the words that tell about a subject is the **complete subject**.	<u>My younger sister</u> loves the toy store.
The **simple subject** is the most important word in the complete subject.	My younger <u>sister</u> loves the toy store.
A **compound subject** has two nouns joined together by the words **and** or **or**.	<u>Terry **and** Brittany</u> never shop at this store. <u>My mom **or** my dad</u> always comes with me.

Predicates

All the words in the predicate is the **complete predicate**.	The stores <u>open today at nine</u>.
The **simple predicate** is the **verb**. It is the most important word in the predicate.	The stores <u>open</u> today at nine.
A **compound predicate** has two or more verbs that tell about the same subject. The verbs are joined by **and** or **or**.	We <u>eat **and** shop</u> at the mall. Sometimes we <u>see a movie **or** just talk with our friends</u>.

Sentences *(continued)*

Compound Sentences

When you join two sentences together, you can make a compound sentence.

Use a comma and the conjunction **and** to combine two similar ideas.	My friends walk to the mall. I go with them. My friends walk to the mall**, and** I go with them.
Use a comma and the conjunction **but** to combine two different ideas.	My friends walk to the mall. I ride my bike. My friends walk to the mall**, but** I ride my bike.
Use a comma and the conjunction **or** to show a choice of ideas.	You can walk to the mall with me. You can ride with Dad. You can walk to the mall with me**, or** you can ride with Dad.

Complex Sentences

When you join independent and dependent clauses, you can make a complex sentence.

An **independent clause** expresses a complete thought. It can stand alone as a sentence.	Mom and her friends walk around the mall for exercise. They walk around the mall.
A **dependent clause** does not express a complete thought. It is not a sentence.	before it gets busy because they want to exercise
To make a **complex sentence**, join an **independent clause** with one or more **dependent clauses**. If the dependent clause comes first, put a **comma** after it.	**Before it gets busy , Mom and her friends walk around the mall for exercise.** **They walk around the mall because they want to exercise.**

Condensing Clauses

Condense clauses to create precise and detailed sentences.

Condense clauses by combining ideas and using complex sentences.	It's a plant. It's green and red. It's found in the tropical rainforest. ➡ It's a green and red plant that is found in the tropical rainforest.

Nouns

Nouns name people, animals, places, or things.

Common Nouns and Proper Nouns

There are two kinds of nouns.

A **common noun** names any person, animal, place, or thing of a certain type.	I know that **girl**. She rides a **horse**. I sometimes see her at the **park**. She walks her **dog** there.
A **proper noun** names a particular person, animal, place, or thing. • Start all the important words with a capital letter. • Start the names of streets, cities, and states with a capital letter. • Also use capital letters when you abbreviate state names.	I know **Marissa**. I sometimes see her at **Hilltop Park**. She walks her dog **Chase** there. Her family is from **Dallas, Texas**. They live on **Crockett Lane**.

Abbreviations for State Names in Mailing Addresses

Alabama	AL	Hawaii	HI	Massachusetts	MA	New Mexico	NM	South Dakota	SD
Alaska	AK	Idaho	ID	Michigan	MI	New York	NY	Tennessee	TN
Arizona	AZ	Illinois	IL	Minnesota	MN	North Carolina	NC	Texas	TX
Arkansas	AR	Indiana	IN	Mississippi	MS	North Dakota	ND	Utah	UT
California	CA	Iowa	IA	Missouri	MO	Ohio	OH	Vermont	VT
Colorado	CO	Kansas	KS	Montana	MT	Oklahoma	OK	Virginia	VA
Connecticut	CT	Kentucky	KY	Nebraska	NE	Oregon	OR	Washington	WA
Delaware	DE	Louisiana	LA	Nevada	NV	Pennsylvania	PA	West Virginia	WV
Florida	FL	Maine	ME	New Hampshire	NH	Rhode Island	RI	Wisconsin	WI
Georgea	GA	Maryland	MD	New Jersey	NJ	South Carolina	SC	Wyoming	WY

583

Nouns *(continued)*

Singular and Plural Count Nouns

Count nouns name things that you can count. A singular count noun shows "one." A plural count noun shows "more than one."

Add **-s** to most singular count nouns to form the plural count noun.	bicycle → bicycle**s** club → club**s**
Add **-es** to count nouns that end in **x**, **ch**, **sh**, **ss**, **z**, and sometimes **o**.	tax → tax**es** bench → bench**es** wish → wish**es** loss → loss**es** potato → potato**es**
For count nouns that end in a consonant plus **y**, change the **y** to **i** and then add **-es**. For nouns that end in a vowel plus **y**, just add **-s**.	berr~~y~~**i** → berri**es** famil~~y~~**i** → famili**es** boy → boy**s** day → day**s**
For a few count nouns, use special forms to show the plural.	man → men woman → women foot → feet tooth → teeth child → children

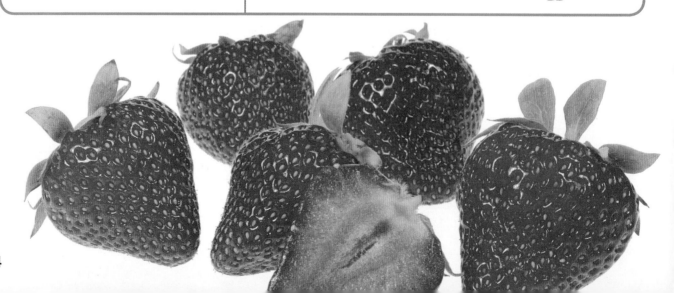

Noncount Nouns

Noncount nouns name things that you cannot count.
Noncount nouns have one form for "one" and "more than one."

Weather Words	fog heat lightning thunder rain **YES:** **Thunder** and **lightning** scare my dog. **NO:** Thunders and lightnings scare my dog.
Food Words Some food items can be counted by using a measurement word such as **cup, slice, glass,** or **head** plus the word **of**. To show the plural form, make the measurement word plural.	bread corn milk rice soup **YES:** I'm thirsty for **milk.** I want **two glasses of milk.** **NO:** I'm thirsty for milks. I want milks.
Ideas and Feelings	fun help honesty luck work **YES:** I need **help** to finish my homework. **NO:** I need helps to finish my homework.
Category Nouns	clothing equipment mail money time **YES:** My football **equipment** is in the car. **NO:** My football equipments is in the car.
Materials	air gold paper water wood **YES:** Is the **water** in this river clean? **NO:** Is the waters in this river clean?
Activities and Sports	baseball dancing golf singing soccer **YES:** I played **soccer** three times this week. **NO:** I played soccers three times this week.

Nouns *(continued)*

Words That Signal Nouns

The articles *a*, *an*, *some*, and *the* help identify a noun. They often appear before count nouns.

Use **a, an,** or **some** before a noun to talk about something in general. Use **an** instead of **a** before a word that begins with a vowel sound. Do <u>not</u> use **a** or **an** before a noncount noun.	**Some jokes** are funny. Do you have **a favorite joke**? I have **an uncle** who knows a lot of jokes. It is **an event** when my uncle comes to visit. He lives about **an hour** away from us. He drives in ~~a~~ snow, ~~a~~ fog, or ~~an~~ ice to get here.
Use **the** to talk about something specific. Do <u>not</u> use **the** before the name of: • a city or state • most countries • a language • a day, month, or most holidays • a sport or activity • most businesses • a person's name	Uncle Raul is **the** uncle I told you about. **The** jokes he tells make me laugh! Uncle Raul lives in **Dallas**. That's a city in **Texas**. He used to live in **Brazil**. He speaks **English** and **Spanish**. Uncle Raul often visits on **Saturday**. In **February**, he comes up for **President's Day**. Sometimes he'll play **soccer** with me. Then we go to **Sal's Café** to eat. He likes to talk to **Sal**, too.

The words *this*, *that*, *these*, and *those* point out nouns. Like other adjectives, they answer the question "Which one?"

Use **this** or **these** to talk about things that are near you. Use **that** or **those** to talk about things that are far from you.	**This** book has a lot of photographs. **Those** books on the shelf are all fiction.

	Near	Far
One thing	this	that
More than one thing	these	those

Possessive Nouns

A possessive noun is the name of an owner. An apostrophe (') is used to show ownership.

For one owner, add **'s** to the **singular noun**.	This is Raul**'s** cap. The cap**'s** color is a bright red.
For more than one owner, add just the apostrophe (') to the **plural noun**.	The boys**'** T-shirts are the same. The players**'** equipment is ready.
For plural nouns that have special forms, add **'s** to the **plural noun**.	Do you like the **children's** uniforms? The **men's** scores are the highest.

Pronouns

A pronoun takes the place of a noun or refers to a noun.

Pronoun Agreement

When you use a pronoun, be sure you are talking about the right person.

Use a capital **I** to talk about yourself.	
Use **you** to speak to another person.	
Use **she** for a girl or a woman.	Julia thinks Mars is a good topic. **She** will help write a report about the planet.
Use **he** for a boy or a man.	Jack downloaded some photos. **He** added the pictures to the report.
Use **it** for a thing.	The report is almost done. **It** will be interesting to read.

Pronouns *(continued)*

Pronoun Agreement

Be sure you are talking about the right number of people or things.

Use **you** to talk to two or more people.	
Use **we** for yourself and one or more other people.	*Are you prepared for tomorrow?* *Yes. Sam and I are ready. We give a report tomorrow.*
Use **they** for other people or things.	Scott and Tyrone set up the video camera. **They** will record each presentation.

Subject Pronouns

Subject pronouns take the place of the subject in the sentence.

Subject pronouns tell who or what does the action.	**Julia** is a good speaker. **She** tells the class about Mars. **The photos** show the surface of Mars. **They** are images from NASA.

Subject Pronouns	
Singular	**Plural**
I	we
you	you
he, she, it	they

Object Pronouns

Object pronouns replace a noun that comes after a verb or a preposition.

An **object pronoun** answers the question "What" or "Whom."	The class asked **Jack and Julia** about Mars.
	The class asked **them** about Mars.
Object pronouns come after a verb or a preposition such as **to**, **for**, **at**, **of**, or **with**.	Jack put **the report** online.
	Jack put **it** online.

Object Pronouns

Singular	Plural
me	us
you	you
him, her, it	them

Reciprocal Pronouns

Reciprocal pronouns replace objects that refer back to the subject.

The subject must be plural. It can be a compound subject.	**Jack and Julia** helped **each other** on the report.
The subject can also be a plural noun.	**The students** followed **one another** outside.

Reciprocal Pronouns

Plural
each other
one another

Possessive Pronouns

Like a possessive noun, a possessive pronoun tells who or what owns something.

To show that you own something, use **mine**.	**I** wrote a report about the sun.
	The report about the sun is **mine**.
Use **ours** to show that you and one or more people own something.	**Meg, Bob, and I** drew diagrams.
	The diagrams are **ours**.
Use **yours** to show that something belongs to one or more people you are talking to.	Have you seen my report, Matt?
	Yes, that report is **yours**.

Possessive Pronouns

Singular	Plural
mine	ours
yours	yours
his, hers	theirs

Use **his** for one boy or man. Use **hers** for one girl or woman.	Here is **Carole's** desk.
	The desk is **hers**.
For two or more people, places, or things, use **theirs**.	**Ross and Clare** made posters.
	The posters are **theirs**.

Grammar, Usage, Mechanics, and Spelling *continued*

Adjectives

An adjective describes, or tells about, a noun.

How Adjectives Work

Usually, an **adjective** comes before the noun it tells about.	You can buy **delicious** fruits at the market.
But, an **adjective** can also appear after verbs such as *is, are, look, feel, smell,* and *taste*.	All the fruit looks **fresh**. The shoppers are **happy**.
Adjectives describe • what something is like • the size, color, and shape of something • what something looks, feels, sounds, or smells like	The market is a **busy** place. The **round, brown** baskets are filled with fruits and vegetables. The **shiny** peppers are in one basket. Another basket has **crunchy** cucumbers. The pineapples are **sweet** and **juicy**.
Some **adjectives** tell "how many" or "in what order."	The sellers have **two** baskets of beans. The **first** basket is near the limes.

If you can count what you see, use:		If you can't count what you see, use:	
many	several	much	not much
a lot of	only a few	a lot of	only a little
few	not any	a little	not any
some	no	some	no

When you don't know the exact number of things, use the adjectives in the chart.	When there's **a lot of** sun, the sellers sit in the shade.
Possessive adjectives tell who owns something.	I pick out **some** oranges. **My** oranges are in the bag. That basket is **Ryan's**. **His** basket is full of apples. **The sellers'** chairs are in the shade. **Their** chairs are under umbrellas.

590

Adjectives That Compare

Adjectives can help you make a comparison, or show how things are alike or different.

To compare two things, add **-er** to the adjective. You will often use the word **than** in your sentence, too.	This is a **small** pineapple. The guava is **smaller than** the pineapple.
To compare three or more things, add **-est** to the adjective. Always use **the** before the adjective.	The lime is **the smallest** fruit of them all.
For some adjectives, change the spelling before you add **-er** or **-est**. • If the adjective ends in silent **e**, drop the final **e** and add **-er** or **-est**.	larg~~e~~ nic~~e~~ larg**er** nic**er** larg**est** nic**est**
• If the adjective ends in **y**, change the **y** to **i** and add **-er** or **-est**.	prett~~y~~**i** craz~~y~~**i** pretti**er** crazi**er** pretti**est** crazi**est**
• If the adjective has one syllable and ends in one vowel plus one consonant, double the final consonant and add **-er** or **-est**.	big **g** sad **d** bigg**er** sadd**er** bigg**est** sadd**est**
A few adjectives have special forms for comparing things.	good bad little better worse less best worst least
For adjectives with three or more syllables, do not use **-er** or **-est** to compare. Use **more**, **most**, **less**, or **least**.	**YES:** Of all the fruit, the guavas are the **most colorful**. **NO:** Of all the fruit, the guavas are the colorfulest. **YES:** The oranges are **more delicious** than the pears. **NO:** The oranges are deliciouser than the pears.
When you make a comparison, use either **-er** or **more**; or **-est** or **most**. Do not use both.	The oranges are the ~~most~~ juiciest of all the fruits.

Verbs

Verbs tell what the subject of a sentence is, has, or does. They show if something happened in the past, is happening now, or will happen in the future.

Action Verbs

| An **action verb** tells what someone or something does. | The children **ride** bikes.

 They **wear** helmets for safety.

 They **pedal** as fast as they can. | |

The Verbs *Have* and *Be*

| The verb **to have** tells what the subject of a sentence has. | I **have** a bicycle.

 It **has** twelve gears.

 My friend Pedro **has** a bicycle, too.

 Sometimes we **have** races. | **Forms of the Verb *have***

 have <br> has <br> had |
| The verb **to be** does not show action. It tells what the subject of a sentence is (a noun) or what it is like (an adjective). | I **am** a fan of bicycle races.

 Pedro **is** excited about our next race. | **Forms of the Verb *be***

 am   was <br> are   were <br> is |

Linking Verbs

| A few other verbs work like the verb **to be**. They do not show action. They just connect, or link, the subject to a word in the predicate. Some of these verbs are **look**, **seem**, **feel**, **smell**, and **taste**. | My bicycle **looks** fantastic!

 Pedro and I **feel** ready for the race. |

Helping Verbs

A **helping verb** works together with an action verb. A helping verb comes before a **main verb**. Some helping verbs have special meanings.

- Use **can** to tell that someone is able to do something.
- Use **could**, **may,** or **might** to tell that something is possible.
- Use **must** to tell that somebody has to do something.
- Use **should** to give an opinion or advice.

Pedro and I **are racing** today.
We **will do** our best.

We **can work** as a team.

We **may reach** the finish line first.

We **must pedal** hard to win!

You **should practice** more.

Contractions with Verbs

You can put a subject and verb together to make a **contraction**. In a contraction, an apostrophe (') shows where one or more letters have been left out.

They are riding fast.
They are riding fast.
They're riding fast.

You can make a contraction with the verbs **am**, **are**, and **is**.

Contractions with *Be*			
I + am = **I'm**	she + is = **she's**
you + are = **you're**	where + is = **where's**
we + are = **we're**	what + is = **what's**

You can make a contraction with the helping verbs **have**, **has**, and **will**.

Contractions with *Have* and *Will*			
I + have = **I've**	he + has = **he's**
you + have = **you've**	I + will = **I'll**
they + have = **they've**	it + will = **it'll**

In contractions with a verb and **not**, the word **not** is shortened to **n't**.

Contractions with *Not*			
do + not = **don't**	have + not = **haven't**
did + not = **didn't**	has + not = **hasn't**
are + not = **aren't**	could + not = **couldn't**
was + not = **wasn't**	should + not = **shouldn't**

The contraction of the verb **can** plus **not** has a special spelling.

can + not = **can't**

Verbs, *(continued)*

Actions in the Present	
All action verbs show when the action happens. Verbs in the **present tense** show • that the action happens now. • that the action happens often.	 Pedro **eats** his breakfast. Then he **takes** his bike out of the garage. Pedro and I **love** to ride our bikes on weekends.
To show the present tense for the subjects **he, she,** or **it**, add -**s** to the end of most action verbs. • For verbs that end in **x, ch, sh, ss,** or **z**, add -**es.** • For verbs that end in a consonant plus **y**, change the **y** to **i** and then add -**es**. For verbs that end in a vowel plus **y**, just add -**s**. • For the subjects **I, you, we,** or **they**, do not add -**s** or -**es**.	Pedro **checks** the tires on his bike. He **finds** a flat tire! Pedro **fixes** the tire. A pump **pushes** air into it. "That should do it," he **says** to himself. He **carries** the pump back into the garage. I **arrive** at Pedro's house. We **coast** down the driveway on our bikes.
The **present progressive** form of a verb tells about an action as it is happening. It uses **am, is,** or **are** and a main verb. The main verb ends in -**ing**.	We **are pedaling** faster. I **am passing** Pedro! He **is following** right behind me.

Actions in the Past

Verbs in the **past tense** show that the action happened in the past.	Yesterday, I **looked** for sports on TV.
The past tense form of a **regular verb** ends with -**ed**.	
• For most verbs, just add -**ed**.	I **watched** the race on TV.
• For verbs that end in silent **e**, drop the final **e** before you add -**ed**.	The bikers **arrived** from all different countries. They **raced** for several hours.
• For one-syllable verbs that end in one vowel plus one consonant, double the final consonant before you add -**ed**.	People **grabbed** their cameras. They **snapped** pictures of their favorite racer.
• For verbs that end in **y**, change the **y** to **i** before you add -**ed**. For verbs that end in a vowel plus **y**, just add -**ed**.	I **studied** the racer from Italy. I **stayed** close to the TV.
Irregular verbs do not add -**ed** to show the past tense. They have special forms.	The Italian racer **was** fast. He **broke** the speed record!

Some Irregular Verbs

Present Tense	Past Tense
begin	began
do	did
have	had
make	made
take	took
ride	rode
win	won

Grammar, Usage, Mechanics, and Spelling *continued*

Verbs, *(continued)*

Actions in the Future

Verbs in the **future tense** tell what will happen later, or in the future.	Tomorrow, Shelley **will clean** her bike.
To show the future tense, you can • add the helping verb **will** before the **main verb**. • use **am going to**, **are going to**, or **is going to** before the **main verb**.	She **will remove** all the dirt. She **is going to remove** all the dirt. I **am going to help** her.
If the **main verb** is a form of the verb **to be**, use **be** to form the future tense.	The bike **will be** spotless. Shelley **is going to be** pleased!
To make negative sentences in the future tense, put the word **not** just after **will**, **am**, **is**, or **are**.	We are **not** going to stop until the bike shines. Pedro is **not** going to believe it. Her bike will **not** be a mess any longer.

Adverbs

An adverb tells more about a verb, an adjective, or another adverb.

How Adverbs Work

An **adverb** can come before or after a **verb** to tell "how," "where," "when," or "how often."	Josh **walks quickly** to the bus stop. (how) He **will travel downtown** on the bus. (where) He **will arrive** at school **soon**. (when) Josh **never misses** a day of school. (how often)
An **adverb** can make an **adjective** or another adverb stronger.	Josh is **really good** at baseball. He plays **very well**.
Some **adverbs** compare actions. Add -**er** to compare two actions. Add -**est** to compare three or more actions.	Josh **runs fast**. Josh runs **faster** than his best friend. Josh runs the **fastest** of all the players.
A few adverbs have special forms for comparing things.	well ⟶ better ⟶ best badly ⟶ worse ⟶ worst
If the adverb ends in -**ly**, use **more**, **most**, **less**, or **least** to compare the actions.	 Josh drops a ball <u>less</u> frequently than the other players. ⋀
When you use **adverbs** to make a comparison with -**er**, -**est**, or with a special form, do not also use **more** or **most**.	Josh jumps ~~more~~ higher than I do. He is ~~more~~ better than I am at catching the ball.
Make sure to use an **adverb** (not an adjective) to tell about a verb.	 I do not catch ~~good~~ *well* at all.

Prepositions

A preposition links a noun or pronoun to other words in a sentence. A preposition is the first word in a prepositional phrase.

Prepositions

Some prepositions tell **where** something is.	above over / under below beneath / beside next to by near / in front of / in back of behind / between in / out / inside / outside / on / off
Some prepositions show **direction**.	up / down / through / across / around / into
Some prepositions tell **when something happens**.	**before** lunch **in** 2003 **on** September 16 **during** lunch **in** September **at** four o'clock **after** lunch **in** the afternoon **from** noon **to** 3:30
Other prepositions have many uses.	about among for to against at from with along except of without

Prepositional Phrases

A **prepositional phrase** starts with a **preposition** and ends with a **noun** or a **pronoun**. Use prepositional phrases to add information or details to your writing.	**At our** school, we did many activities **for** Earth Day. We picked up the trash **along the** fence. Then we planted some flowers **next to** it.

Capital Letters

A word that begins with a capital letter is special in some way.

How to Use Capital Letters

A word that begins with a capital letter is special in some way.

Use a **capital letter** at the beginning of a sentence.	**O**ur class is taking an exciting field trip. **W**e are going to an airplane museum.
Always use a capital letter for the pronoun **I**.	My friends and **I** can't wait!
Use a capital letter for a person's • first and last name • initials • title	**Matt J**. **K**elly and **M**att **R**oss will ride with **D**r. **B**ye. **M**agdalena and I are going with **M**rs. **L**iu.
Use a capital letter for the names of • the days of the week and their abbreviations • the twelve months of the year and their abbreviations	We're going the first **S**aturday in **J**anuary. **Days of the Week** **S**unday **S**un. **M**onday **M**on. **T**uesday **T**ue. **W**ednesday **W**ed. **T**hursday **T**hurs. **F**riday **F**ri. **S**aturday **S**at. **Months of the Year** **J**anuary **J**an. **F**ebruary **F**eb. **M**arch **M**ar. **A**pril **A**pr. **M**ay **J**une These months are not abbreviated. **J**uly **A**ugust **A**ug. **S**eptember **S**ep. **O**ctober **O**ct. **N**ovember **N**ov. **D**ecember **D**ec.
Use a capital letter for each important word in the names of special days and holidays.	That will be after **C**hristmas, **K**wanzaa, and **N**ew **Y**ear's **D**ay. **E**arth **D**ay **F**ourth of **J**uly **H**anukkah **T**hanksgiving

Capital Letters, *(continued)*

More Ways to Use Capital Letters

Use a capital letter for each important word in the names of	
• public places, buildings, and organizations	The **W**ilson **A**irplane **M**useum is in the **V**eterans **M**emorial **H**all. It's in the middle of **V**eterans **P**ark, right next to the **P**iney **W**oods **Z**oo.
• streets, cities, and states	The museum is on **F**light **A**venue. It is the biggest airplane museum in **F**lorida. It's the biggest in the whole **U**nited **S**tates!
• landforms and bodies of water, continents, and planets and stars	**Landforms and Bodies of Water** / **Continents** / **Planets and Stars**

Landforms and Bodies of Water	Continents	Planets and Stars
Rocky **M**ountains	**A**frica	**E**arth
Sahara **D**esert	**A**ntarctica	**M**ars
Grand **C**anyon	**A**sia	the **B**ig **D**ipper
Pacific **O**cean	**A**ustralia	the **M**ilky **W**ay
Colorado **R**iver	**E**urope	
Lake **E**rie	**S**outh **A**merica	
	North **A**merica	

Use a capital letter for the names of countries and adjectives formed from the names of countries.	My friend Magdalena is **C**hilean. She says they don't have a museum like that in **C**hile.
Use a capital letter for each important word in the title of a book, a story, a poem, or a movie.	We are reading ***F**irst **F**light* about the Wright brothers. Magdalena wrote a poem about Amelia Earhart. She called it "**V**anished from the **S**ky." What a great title!

Punctuation Marks

Punctuation marks make words and sentences easier to understand.

period

question mark

exclamation point

comma

quotation marks

apostrophe

Period .

Use a **period** at the end of a statement or a command.	I don't know if I should get a dog or a cat**.** Please help me decide**.**
Also use a **period** when you write a decimal, or to separate dollars from cents.	I saw a cute little dog last week**.** It only weighed 1**.**3 pounds. But it costs $349**.**99!
Use a **period** after an initial in somebody's name, and after most abbreviations. But, don't use a period after state abbreviations.	The salesperson gave me this business card: Kitty B**.** Perry Downtown Pet Sales 2456 N**.** Yale Ave**.** Houston, TX 77074 **TX is the abbreviation for the state of Texas.**

Question Mark ?

Use a **question mark** • at the end of a question • after a question that comes at the end of a statement.	Do you want to go to the pet store with me**?** You can go right now, can't you**?**

Exclamation Point !

Use an **exclamation point** at the end of a sentence to show strong feelings.	I'm glad you decided to come**!** This is going to be fun**!**

Punctuation, *(continued)*

Commas 9

Use a **comma**	
• when you write large numbers	There are more than 1,300 pets at this store.
• to separate three or more things in the same sentence	Should I get a dog, a cat, or a parrot?
• before the words **and**, **but**, or **or** in a compound sentence.	I came to the store last week, and the salesperson showed me some dogs.
	She was very helpful, but I couldn't make a decision.

Use a **comma** to set off	
• short words like **Oh**, **Yes**, and **Well** that begin a sentence	Oh, what a hard decision!
• someone's exact words	Well, I'd better choose something.
	The salesperson said, "This little dog wants to go with you."
	I said, "I like it, but I like those cats, too!"

Use a **comma** between two or more adjectives that tell about the same noun.	Do I get a big, furry puppy?
	Or do I get a cute, tiny kitten?

Use a **comma** in letters	
• between the city and state	177 North Avenue
• between the date and the year	New York, NY 10033
• after the greeting in a friendly letter	October 3, 2010
• after the closing	Dear Aunt Mia,
	Can you help me? I want a pet, but don't know which is easier to care for, a cat or a dog? I need your advice.
	Your niece,
	Becca

Quotation Marks " "

Use quotation marks	
• to show a speaker's exact words	"Ms. Perry, this is the dog for me!" Becca said.
• to show the exact words from a book or other printed material	The ad said "friendly puppies" for sale.
• the title of a magazine or newspaper article	I saw the idea in the article "Keeping Your Pet Happy."
• the title of a chapter from a book.	Now I'm on the chapter "Working Dogs" in my book.
Use periods and commas inside quotation marks.	"Many dogs are good with people," Ms. Perry said. "You just have to decide if you want to big dog or a little one."

> Ms. Perry, this is the dog for me!

Apostrophes '

Use an **apostrophe** when you write a **possessive noun**.	My **neighbor's** dog is huge. The **Smiths'** yard is just big enough for him.
Use an **apostrophe** to replace the letter or letters left out in a **contraction.**	**Let's** go back to the pet store. **I'll** look some more for the best pet for me.

Picture Dictionary

The definitions are for the words as they are introduced in the selections of this book.

Pronunciation Key

Say the sample word out loud to hear how to say, or pronounce, the symbol.

Symbols for Consonant Sounds

b	box		p	pan
ch	chick		r	ring
d	dog		s	bus
f	fish		sh	fish
g	girl		t	hat
h	hat		th	Earth
j	jar		th	father
k	cake		v	vase
ks	box		w	window
kw	queen		hw	whale
l	bell		y	yarn
m	mouse		z	zipper
n	pan		zh	treasure
ng	ring			

Symbols for Short Vowel Sounds

a	hat
e	bell
i	chick
o	box
u	bus

Symbols for Long Vowel Sounds

ā	cake
ē	key
ī	bike
ō	goat
yū	mule

Symbols for R-controlled Sounds

ar	barn
air	chair
ear	ear
īr	fire
or	corn
ur	girl

Symbols for Variant Vowel Sounds

ah	father
aw	ball
oi	boy
oo	book
ow	cow
ü	fruit

Miscellaneous Symbols

shun	fraction	$\frac{1}{2}$
chun	question	?
zhun	division	$2\overline{)100}^{50}$

Parts of an Entry

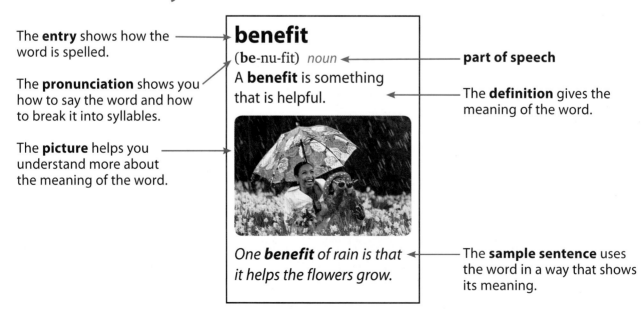

The **entry** shows how the word is spelled.

The **pronunciation** shows you how to say the word and how to break it into syllables.

The **picture** helps you understand more about the meaning of the word.

benefit
(**be**-nu-fit) *noun*
A **benefit** is something that is helpful.

One **benefit** of rain is that it helps the flowers grow.

part of speech

The **definition** gives the meaning of the word.

The **sample sentence** uses the word in a way that shows its meaning.

A

accomplish

(u-**kom**-plish) *verb*

To **accomplish** means to finish something that you want to do.

What did she accomplish?

achieve

(u-**chēv**) *verb*

To **achieve** means to get something that you work for.

She worked hard to achieve her wish of winning first place.

action

(**ak**-shun) *noun*

An **action** is something that you do.

Their actions made the park a clean place to play.

advertisement

(ad-vur-**tīz**-munt) *noun*

Advertisements can be photos, pictures, or even short movies that give information and try to make people buy things.

The advertisement made my dad want to buy that new car.

agriculture

(**a**-gri-kul-chur) *noun*

The work of growing crops and raising animals for people to eat is called **agriculture**.

Many people who live outside of cities and towns work in agriculture.

alter

(**awl**-tur) *verb*

When you **alter** something, you change it.

She alters the dress to make it shorter.

alternative

(awl-**tur**-nu-tiv) *noun*

An **alternative** is another choice.

An apple is a healthy alternative to candy.

amount

(u-**mownt**) *noun*

The **amount** of something is how much of it there is.

Three hundred jelly beans is a large amount of candy.

b
c
d
e
f
g
h
i
j
k
l
m
n
o
p
q
r
s
t
u
v
w
x
y
z

a
b
c
d
e
f
g
h
i
j
k
l
m
n
o
p
q
r
s
t
u
v
w
x
y
z

area

(air-ē-u) *noun*

An **area** is a part of a place.

*A classroom can have an **area** for reading.*

artist

(ar-tist) *noun*

An **artist** is someone who is skilled at drawing, painting, making things, or performing.

*This **artist** paints what she sees outdoors.*

Ⓑ

balance

(ba-luns) *noun*

When things are in **balance**, they are even.

*The two sides of the scale are in **balance**.*

behavior

(bi-hā-vyur) *noun*

Behavior is what a person or animal does.

*Squirrels store nuts for the winter. It's part of their **behavior**.*

benefit

(be-nu-fit) *noun*

A **benefit** is something that is helpful.

*One **benefit** of rain is that it helps the flowers grow.*

blossom

(blah-sum) *noun*

A **blossom** is the flower of a seed plant.

*This **blossom** comes from an apple tree.*

buyer

(bī-ur) *noun*

A **buyer** is someone who gets something by paying money for it.

*He wants a **buyer** for his flowers.*

carve

(**karv**) *verb*

To **carve** is to make something by cutting.

*Dad **carves** the pumpkin while I watch.*

challenge

(**cha**-lunj) *noun*

A **challenge** is something that is hard to do.

*It is a **challenge** to climb up a rope.*

characteristic

(kair-ik-tu-**ris**-tik) *noun*

A **characteristic** is how something looks or what something does.

*A **characteristic** of this plant is white flowers.*

city

(**si**-tē) *noun*

A **city** is a very large town.

*San Francisco is a large **city** in California.*

combine

(kum-**bīn**) *verb*

When you **combine** things, you mix them together.

*What foods does she **combine**?*

communicate

(ku-**myū**-ni-kāt) *verb*

When you **communicate**, you share words or feelings.

*She **communicates** with a friend.*

competition

(kom-pu-ti-shun) *noun*

A **competition** is a contest or struggle between two or more people or animals.

*These pelicans are in **competition** for food.*

composition

(kom-pu-**zi**-shun) *noun*

Composition is what things are made of.

*The **composition** of mud is dirt and water.*

a b **c** d e f g h i j k l m n o p q r s t u v w x y z

conditions

(kun-**di**-shunz) *noun*

When **conditions** are right, good things happen.

Clear skies and wind are good conditions for sailing.

conservation

(kon-sur-**vā**-shun) *noun*

Conservation means the opposite of waste.

Conservation of water is important.

continent

(**kon**-tu-nunt) *noun*

A **continent** is one of the major divisions of land on Earth.

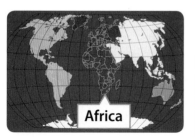

Africa is one of seven continents.

control

(kun-**trōl**) *verb*

To **control** means to make a person or thing do what you want.

The boys control where the car goes.

cooperation

(kō-ah-pu-**rā**-shun) *noun*

Cooperation is when people work together.

It takes cooperation to row the boat quickly.

core

(**kor**) *noun*

The **core** is the middle of something.

An apple core is the center part of an apple.

create

(krē-**āt**) *verb*

To **create** means to make something new.

She creates a picture.

crop

(**krop**) *noun*

A **crop** is a large amount of plants a farmer grows, usually for food.

This farm had a very large orange crop this year.

cycle

(**sī**-kul) *noun*

A **cycle** is a set of events that happen over and over again in a pattern.

This diagram shows the life cycle of a frog.

This diagram shows the life cycle of a butterfly.

decrease

(di-**krēs**) *verb*

When something **decreases**, it becomes smaller in number, amount or in size.

*The amount **decreases** after each slice is taken away.*

depend

(di-**pend**) *verb*

To **depend** means to need something or someone for support.

*A baby **depends** on its mother.*

desert

(**de**-zurt) *noun*

A **desert** is a hot, dry area where few plants grow.

*The **desert** gets very little rain.*

destination

(des-tu-**nā**-shun) *noun*

A **destination** is the place you are traveling to.

*They look for their **destination** on a map.*

develop

(di-**vel**-up) *verb*

When something **develops**, it grows over time.

*The small plant will **develop** into a large tree.*

difference

(**di**-fu-runts) *noun*

To make a **difference** is to make something better.

*They are making a **difference**. They are cleaning oil off the bird's body.*

a
b
c
d
e
f
g
h
i
j
k
l
m
n
o
p
q
r
s
t
u
v
w
x
y
z

direction

(du-**rek**-shun) *noun*

When you move toward something, you move in that **direction**.

The arrow shows the direction of the road.

discover

(dis-**ku**-vur) *verb*

When you **discover** something, you find it.

She discovers an insect on this plant.

distance

(**dis**-tunts) *noun*

The **distance** is the amount of space between two places.

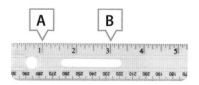

The distance between A and B is two inches.

diversity

(du-**vur**-su-tē) *noun*

Diversity means a lot of different people or things.

Our school has a great diversity of people.

drought

(**drowt**) *noun*

A **drought** is a long time of very dry weather.

The river is dry because of a drought.

duty

(**dü**-tē) *noun*

When you do your **duty**, you do what you are supposed to do.

The boy is doing his duty by throwing away his trash.

E

earthquake

(**urth**-kwāk) *noun*

An **earthquake** is a sudden violent shaking of Earth that may cause damage.

An earthquake damaged this building.

ecosystem

(ē-kō-sis-tum) *noun*

An **ecosystem** is a group of animals and plants, the place they live in, and how they act together.

This alligator is part of this wetland's ecosystem.

This gila monster is part of this desert's ecosystem.

endurance
(in-**dur**-uns) *noun*
When you have **endurance**, you keep doing something.

*A long race takes **endurance**.*

environment
(in-**vī**-run-munt) *noun*
Your **environment** is the kind of place where you live.

*This is a hot, dry **environment**.*

erupt
(i-**rupt**) *verb*
When a volcano **erupts,** it throws out smoke, rocks, hot ashes, and lava.

*It is dangerous to be nearby when a volcano **erupts**!*

estimate
(**es**-tu-māt) *verb*
When you make a guess about something, you **estimate**.

*Can you **estimate** how many coins are in the jar?*

explore
(ik-**splor**) *verb*
To **explore** means to go somewhere to learn about people or things.

*He **explores** a new area.*

express
(ik-**spres**) *verb*
To **express** a thought or an emotion is to say or show it.

*She **expresses** her love for her dog.*

farmer
(**far**-mur) *noun*
A **farmer** is someone who grows crops or raises animals.

*The **farmer** picks carrots from the field.*

feelings
(**fē**-lingz) *noun*
Feelings are how you experience something.

*Happiness and surprise are kinds of **feelings**.*

feet
(**fēt**) *noun*
Feet are units of length. One foot is twelve inches long.

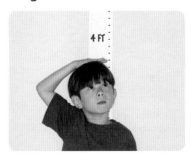

*He is almost four **feet** tall.*

a
b
c
d
e
f
g
h
i
j
k
l
m
n
o
p
q
r
s
t
u
v
w
x
y
z

a
b
c
d
e
f
g
h
i
j
k
l
m
n
o
p
q
r
s
t
u
v
w
x
y
z

field

(**fēld**) *noun*

A **field** is an open space of land, which is sometimes used to plant crops.

*This is a **field** of lettuce.*

*In some **fields**, farm animals eat grass.*

firm

(**furm**) *adjective*

Something that is **firm** is hard.

*You can skate on ice because it is **firm**.*

flow

(**flō**) *verb*

To **flow** means to move along smoothly.

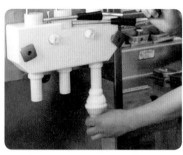

*The ice cream **flows** from the machine into the cone.*

food chain

(**füd chān**) *noun*

A **food chain** is a series of animals and plants in which each one feeds on the one below it.

*Which fish in the cartoon stands for the "shark" in an ocean food **chain**?*

force

(**fors**) *noun*

Force means power or strength.

*The **force** of the wind bends this tree.*

form

(**form**) *noun*

A **form** is a distinct state of matter.

steam

*Steam is one **form** of water.*

freeze

(**frēz**) *verb*

To **freeze** is to become solid or icy at a very low temperature.

*We **freeze** water to make ice cubes for iced tea.*

future

(**fyū**-chur) *noun*

The **future** is what will happen tomorrow or sometime after that.

*My twelfth birthday is in the **future**.*

G

generation

(je-nu-**rā**-shun) *noun*

A **generation** is made up of people born around the same year.

*They are part of different **generations**.*

gift

(**gift**) *noun*

A **gift** is something you give to someone.

*An act of kindness can be a **gift**.*

globe

(**glōb**) *noun*

A **globe** is a sphere with a map of the world on it.

*We can locate different places on the **globe**.*

goal

(**gōl**) *noun*

A **goal** is something that you want to do.

*His **goal** is to catch the ball.*

ground

(**grownd**) *noun*

Ground, or land, is the solid part of Earth's surface.

*He plants flowers in the **ground**.*

growth

(**grōth**) *noun*

The **growth** of something is how much bigger it gets.

*The ruler shows the **growth** of the plant.*

H

harvest

(**har**-vust) *verb*

When you **harvest**, you are gathering the crops that are ripe or ready to be picked.

*She **harvests** the ripe strawberries.*

heritage

(**hair**-u-tij) *noun*

Your **heritage** is the traditions, ideas, and language of your ancestors.

*People of our **heritage** celebrate Cinco de Mayo.*

a
b
c
d
e
f
g
h
i
j
k
l
m
n
o
p
q
r
s
t
u
v
w
x
y
z

a
b
c
d
e
f
g
h
i
j
k
l
m
n
o
p
q
r
s
t
u
v
w
x
y
z

I

identify
(ī-**den**-tu-fī) *verb*
When you **identify** something, you tell what it is.

*She wants to **identify** a type of bird.*

impact
(**im**-pɑkt) *noun*
What you do has an **impact** on things.

*The children have a positive **impact** on the park.*

improve
(im-**prüv**) *verb*
To **improve** something means to make it better.

*They **improve** the beach when they clean it.*

increase
(in-**krēs**) *verb*
To **increase** means to grow in size or in number.

*When our dog eats too much food, its weight **increases**.*

individual
(in-du-**vi**-ju-wul) *noun*
An **individual** is one person.

*This **individual** is reading on her own.*

interact
(in-tur-**ɑkt**) *verb*
To **interact** means to act together.

*The students **interact** with each other to do a science project.*

island
(**ī**-lund) *noun*
An **island** is a piece of land completely surrounded by water.

*This **island** is in the Caribbean Sea.*

J

journey
(**jur**-nē) *noun*
A **journey** is a long trip.

*Horses pulled covered wagons in the long, hard **journey** west.*

kilometer
(ku-**lah**-mu-tur) *noun*
A **kilometer** is a unit of measurement. Its length equals 1,000 meters.

*The Golden Gate Bridge is about 1 **kilometer** long.*

kindness
(**kīnd**-nus) *noun*
You show **kindness** when you are nice to someone.

*Teddy shows **kindness** when he helps his mom.*

lava
(**lah**-vu) *noun*
Lava is the hot, liquid rock that comes out of a volcano when it erupts.

*The **lava** flows from the volcano's crater.*

learn
(**lurn**) *verb*
To **learn** means to find out how to do something.

*You can **learn** to play music.*

level
(**le**-vul) *noun*
The **level** of something is how high or low it is.

1/2 cup level

*The **level** of milk is one half cup .*

liquid
(**li**-kwud) *adjective*
Something that is **liquid** can be poured.

*Milk is a **liquid** substance.*

location
(lō-**kā**-shun) *noun*
A **location** is a place or a position.

*This is a good **location** for looking at the clouds.*

magma
(**mag**-mu) *noun*
Magma is melted rock found beneath Earth's surface.

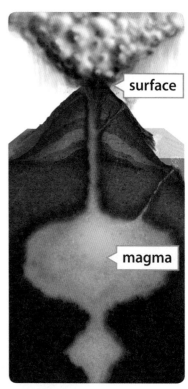

surface

magma

***Magma** becomes lava when it flows out of a volcano.*

a
b
c
d
e
f
g
h
i
j
k
l
m
n
o
p
q
r
s
t
u
v
w
x
y
z

market
(**mar**-kut) *noun*
A **market** is a place where people go to buy and sell food and other things.

*You can buy fruits and vegetables at this **market**.*

measurement
(**me**-zhur-munt) *noun*
Measurement is the process of finding out the size, weight, or amount of something.

*This scale is for the **measurement** of body weight.*

melt
(**melt**) *verb*
When something **melts**, it changes from a solid to a liquid.

*Ice cream **melts** quickly.*

meter
(**mē**-tur) *noun*
A **meter** is the basic unit of measurement in the metric system. It is equal to about three feet.

baseball bat

*A baseball bat is about one **meter** long.*

method
(**me**-thud) *noun*
A **method** is a way of doing something.

*Is using your fingers to count a good **method**?*

mixture
(**miks**-chur) *noun*
A **mixture** is something made by combining different things together.

*Add flour to this cake **mixture**.*

money
(**mu**-nē) *noun*
Money is the coins and paper bills people use for buying things.

*This is enough **money** to buy a t-shirt.*

music
(**myū**-zik) *noun*
Music is a pleasing group of sounds.

*She make **music** with this instrument.*

N

nature
(**nā**-chur) *noun*
Nature means things like rivers, trees, and animals.

*She likes to study **nature**.*

need
(**nēd**) *verb*
When you **need** something, you cannot live without it.

*People **need** to drink water.*

negative
(**ne**-gu-tiv) *adjective*
Something that is **negative** is bad.

*Screaming at someone is a **negative** action.*

neighborhood
(**nā**-bur-hood) *noun*
A neighborhood is the small area in a town around where a person lives.

*Children like to play in the **neighborhood**.*

o

occur
(u-**kur**) *verb*
When something **occurs**, it happens.

*A sunrise **occurs** every morning.*

ocean
(**ō**-shun) *noun*
The **ocean** is the large amount of salt water that covers most of Earth's surface.

ocean

*The blue area on the globe shows the different **oceans**.*

offer
(**aw**-fur) *verb*
An **offer** is saying you would like to help someone or give someone something.

*She **offers** food to her friends.*

organism
(**or**-gu-ni-zum) *noun*
An **organism** is a living thing.

insect

leaf

*This leaf and insect are both **organisms**.*

P

pay
(**pā**) *verb*
To **pay** is to give money for something.

*He will **pay** her for the sandwich.*

perform
(pur-**form**) *verb*
When you **perform**, you put on a show for a group of people.

*The girls **perform** on stage.*

a b c d e f g h i j k l m **n** **o** **p** q r s t u v w x y z

a
b
c
d
e
f
g
h
i
j
k
l
m
n
o
p
q
r
s
t
u
v
w
x
y
z

plate

(**plāt**) *noun*

A **plate** is one of many sheets of rock that make up Earth's outer crust.

*Moving **plates** can cause an earthquake.*

plenty

(**plen**-tē) *noun*

When you have **plenty** of something, you have a lot of it.

*The picture shows **plenty** of fruit.*

plow

(**plow**) *verb*

To **plow** is to break up and turn over the soil in a field.

*Mules help farmers **plow** the fields.*

popular

(**pah**-pyu-lur) *adjective*

When many people like a place or a thing, it is **popular**.

*This restaurant is **popular**.*

positive

(**pah**-zu-tiv) *adjective*

Something that is **positive** is good for you.

*Exercise is a **positive** activity.*

power

(**pow**-ur) *noun*

If something has **power**, it is strong.

*Strong waves have the **power** to destroy a building.*

prepare

(pri-**pair**) *verb*

To **prepare** means to get ready for something.

*She **prepares** for her trip.*

preservation
(pre-zur-**vā**-shun) *noun*
Preservation is the act of keeping something safe for a long time.

*The **preservation** of old documents is important.*

pressure
(**pre**-shur) *noun*
When one thing pushes against another, it makes **pressure**.

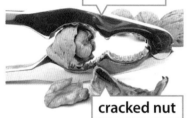

nutcracker

cracked nut

***Pressure** from the nutcracker causes the nuts to crack open.*

problem
(**prah**-blum) *noun*
A **problem** is a difficult situation that needs to be figured out.

*A broken toy is a **problem**.*

process
(**prah**-ses) *noun*
When you follow a **process**, you do something step by step.

*He follows a **process** to put the model together.*

produce
(pru-**düs**) *verb*
To **produce** means to make something.

*This factory **produces** cars.*

protect
(pru-**tekt**) *verb*
You **protect** something when you keep it safe.

spine

*Sharp spines **protect** the plant from animals.*

purpose
(**pur**-pus) *noun*
A **purpose** is the reason for doing something.

*What is the **purpose** of studying for a test?*

a
b
c
d
e
f
g
h
i
j
k
l
m
n
o
p
q
r
s
t
u
v
w
x
y
z

a
b
c
d
e
f
g
h
i
j
k
l
m
n
o
p
q
r
s
t
u
v
w
x
y
z

rainforest

(**rān**-for-ust) *noun*

A **rainforest** is a thick, tropical forest where a lot of rain falls.

Rainforests are home to lots of interesting wildlife.

react

(rē-**akt**) *verb*

When things happen, you usually **react** to them.

*The child **reacts** to the snowball.*

receive

(ri-**sēv**) *verb*

To **receive** is to get something from someone.

*She **received** my package in the mail today.*

region

(**rē**-jun) *noun*

A **region** is an area.

*There are many **regions** in the United States.*

represent

(re-pri-**zent**) *verb*

To **represent** means to stand for.

*A heart **represents** love.*

rescue

(**res**-kyū) *verb*

When you **rescue** someone, you save the person.

*A dog helps to **rescue** a skier.*

*A fireman **rescues** a girl from a burning building.*

resources

(**rē**-sors-uz) *noun*

Resources are things that you can use.

*A library has many **resources**.*

reward

(ri-**word**) *noun*

A **reward** is a gift or prize for doing something well.

*He gives the dog a **reward**.*

rhythm

(**ri**-<u>th</u>um) *noun*

Rhythm is a regular, repeated beat in music, poetry, or dance.

*This drummer keeps the **rhythm** of the song.*

river

(**ri**-vur) *noun*

A **river** is a large, natural stream of water.

*This **river** runs through the land.*

rock

(rok) *noun*

A **rock** is a piece of stone.

*She is holding a **rock**.*

root

(**rüt**) *noun*

A **root** is the part of a plant that grows under the soil.

*People eat the **root** of the carrot plant.*

S

sand

(sand) *noun*

Sand is very tiny pieces of rock that make up beaches and deserts.

*It is fun to play in the **sand**.*

scarce

(skairs) *adjective*

When something is **scarce**, it is hard to find or get.

*Food is **scarce** in this store.*

a b c d e f g h i j k l m n o p q **r** **s** t u v w x y z

a b c d e f g h i j k l m n o p q r **s** t u v w x y z

seed

(sēd) *noun*

A **seed** is the small part of a plant from which a new plant can grow.

*This **seed** is beginning to grow.*

seller

(se-lur) *noun*

A **seller** is someone who has things people can buy.

*This **seller** has many hats that you can buy.*

sense

(sens) *verb*

When you **sense** something, you know it without being told.

*A cat can **sense** danger.*

shore

(shor) *noun*

The **shore** is the land at the edge of an ocean, a river, or a lake.

*Seashells wash up on the **shore**.*

signal

(sig-nul) *noun*

A **signal** is something that tells you what to do.

*The green light is a **signal** to walk.*

*The red light is a **signal** to stop.*

soil

(soil) *noun*

Soil is the dirt in which plants grow.

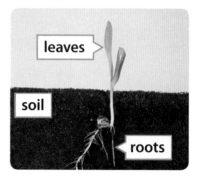

leaves

soil

roots

*The roots will grow in **soil**.*

solid

(sah-lud) *adjective*

Something that is **solid** is firm.

*The chair is **solid**. You can sit on it.*

*The sidewalk is **solid**. You can stand on it.*

solution
(su-lü-shun) *noun*
A **solution** is the answer to a problem.

problem

solution

*His **solution** is to change the tire.*

sprout
(sprowt) *noun*
A **sprout** is a young plant or the new growth on a plant.

*These **sprouts** are growing out of the soil.*

state
(stāt) *noun*
The **state** of a person or thing is the way it is at a certain time.

*He is in a happy **state**.*

*She is in a sad **state**.*

storyteller
(stor-ē-te-lur) *noun*
A **storyteller** tells tales to entertain people.

*The children listen to the **storyteller**.*

strategy
(stra-tu-jē) *noun*
A **strategy** is a plan for success.

*She has a **strategy** for winning.*

style
(stīul) *noun*
Style is a way of doing something.

*He paints in a colorful **style**.*

substance
(sub-stuns) *noun*
Substance is the material something is made of.

*Snow is a cold **substance**.*

a b c d e f g h i j k l m n o p q r **s** t u v w x y z

supply

(su-**plī**) *noun*

A **supply** is the amount you have of something.

*They have a large **supply** of canned peaches.*

surface

(**sur**-fus) *noun*

The **surface** is the outside part of something.

*The **surface** of this ball is bumpy.*

*The **surface** of this watermelon is smooth.*

sustain

(su-**stān**) *verb*

To **sustain** means to keep something or someone alive or in existence.

*A mother bird brings food to **sustain** her chicks.*

T

tale

(**tāl**) *noun*

A **tale** is a story about things that are made up.

*Children enjoy reading folk **tales**.*

temperature

(**tem**-pur-chur) *noun*

The **temperature** of something is how hot or cold it is.

hot

*The **temperature** is hot.*

*The **temperature** outside is very cold.*

thermometer

(thur-**mah**-mu-tur) *noun*

A **thermometer** is used to measure temperature.

*The doctor uses a **thermometer** to check for a fever.*

a b c d e f g h i j k l m n o p q r **s** **t** u v w x y z

tradition

(tru-**di**-shun) *noun*

A **tradition** is something that people have done for a long time and continue to do.

Traditions are important to many families.

trap

(**trap**) *verb*

To **trap** something means to catch it and not let it go.

*Spiders **trap** insects with webs.*

tsunami

(sü-**nah**-mē) *noun*

A **tsunami** is a huge, dangerous, ocean wave. Underwater earthquakes cause tsunamis.

*The **tsunami** crashes into buildings and floods the city.*

U

understand

(un-dur-**stand**) *verb*

When you **understand** something, you know what it means.

*Now he **understands** his homework.*

unique

(yū-**nēk**) *adjective*

Unique things are different from other things.

*The yellow flower is **unique**.*

*What is **unique** about this?*

unit

(**yū**-nut) *noun*

A **unit** is an amount used in measuring or counting.

one inch

*An inch is a **unit** of length.*

a b c d e f g h i j k l m n o p q r s t u v w x y z

value

(**val**-yū) *verb*

When you **value** something, you care about it.

*The girl loves and **values** her dog.*

vary

(**vair**-ē) *verb*

To **vary** something is to change it often.

*I like to **vary** my lunches.*

vine

(**vīn**) *noun*

A **vine** is a plant with a long stem that winds its way up trees or fences or runs along the ground.

vine

*The **vine** grows up the tree.*

volcano

(vol-**kā**-nō) *noun*

A **volcano** is a mountain that can erupt. It has a large hole at the top called a crater. When a volcano erupts it shoots out hot lava, burning rocks, ash, and hot gases.

gases

crater

lava

*This **volcano** is erupting.*

volunteer

(vah-lun-**tear**) *noun*

A **volunteer** is someone who wants to help or do a job without being paid for it.

*This **volunteer** is helping to put away books.*

want

(**wawnt**) *verb*

To **want** something is to hope or wish for it.

*He **wants** to get a guitar like this one.*

warn

(**worn**) *verb*

To **warn** people is to tell them that something bad may happen.

*The crossing guard **warns** people to stop.*

water

(wαw-tur) *noun*

Water is a clear liquid that you can drink or use to wash with.

lake

Water falls from the sky and fills oceans, lakes, and rivers.

wave

(wāv) *noun*

A **wave** is a vibration through the air or water.

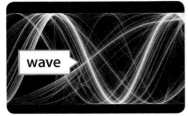
wave

ocean
beach
wave

*The **wave** is crashing on the beach.*

weed

(wēd) *noun*

A **weed** is a wild plant that grows where it is not wanted.

dandelion

*These dandelions are **weeds**.*

wetland

(wet-lαnd) *noun*

A **wetland** is a place where there is a lot of moisture or water in the soil.

*Many plants grow in a **wetland**.*

water lily

wood

(wood) *noun*

Wood is the hard material that tree trunks and branches are made of.

*He is cutting the tree so people can use its **wood**.*

*This man is making a table from **wood**.*

a b c d e f g h i j k l m n o p q r s t u v **w** x y z

Handwriting

It's important to use your best **penmanship**, or handwriting. That way your audience will be able to read what you write.

Handwriting Hints

You can **print** your words or write in **cursive**.

Cursive

Cursive is good to use for longer pieces, such as letters or stories, because you can write faster. You don't have to lift your pencil between letters. Also, cursive writing gives your finished pieces a polished look. When you write in cursive, hold the pencil and paper this way.

Left-handed   Right-handed

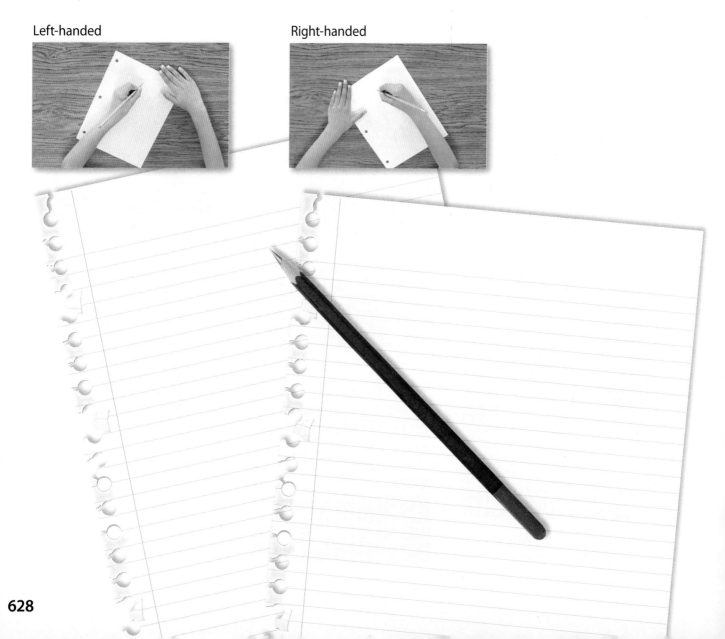

Cursive Alphabet

Capital Letters

Lowercase Letters

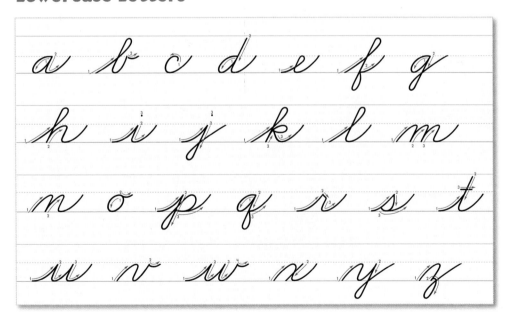

Writing Cursive Letters

Be careful not to make these common mistakes when you write in **cursive**.

MISTAKE	NOT OK	OK	IN A WORD
The **a** looks like a **u**.	*u*	*a*	*again*
The **d** looks like a **c** and an **l**.	*d*	*d*	*dad*
The **e** is too narrow.	*e*	*e*	*eagle*
The **h** looks like an **l** and an **i**.	*h*	*h*	*high*
The **i** has no dot.	*ı*	*i*	*inside*
The **n** looks like a **w**.	*w*	*n*	*none*
The **o** looks like an **a**.	*a*	*o*	*onion*
The **r** looks like an **i** with no dot.	*ı*	*r*	*roar*
The **t** is not crossed.	*l*	*t*	*title*
The **t** is crossed too high.	*T*	*t*	*that*

Writing Words and Sentences

- Slant your letters all the same way.

NOT OK

My Chinese-language class today was interesting.

OK

My Chinese-language class today was interesting.

- Put the right amount of space between words.

NOT OK

I learned how togreet   adults.

OK

I learned how to greet adults.

- Write smoothly. Do not press too hard or too lightly.

NOT OK

I practiced on my teacher. He was impressed.

OK

I practiced on my teacher. He was impressed.

Index

Index of Authors

Index of Illustrators

Acknowledgments, continued

Text Credits

Unit One

Candlewick Press: Excerpt from *Those Shoes* by Maribeth Boelts, illustrated by Noah Z. Jones. Text copyright © 2007 by Maribeth Boelts. Illustrations © 2007 by Noah Z. Jones. Reproduced by permission of the publisher, Candlewick Press, Sommerville, Mass.

Children's Book Press: "Guardian Angel," by Francisco X. Alarcon, from *Angels Ride Bikes*, Copyright © 1999 by Francisco X. Alarcon. Reprinted by permission of the publisher, Childrenis Book Press, San Francisco, Calif., www. childrensbookpress.org.

Highlights for Children: Excerpt from "The World's Greatest Underachiever" by Henry Winkler from *Highlights for Children*, March 2005. Copyright © 2005 by Highlights for Children. Reprinted by permission of Highlights for Children, Inc.

Unit Two

Penguin Group (USA) Inc.: Excerpt from *When the Pigs Took Over* by Arthur Dorros, illustrated by Diane Greenseid. Text copyright © 2002 by Arthur Dorros. Illustrations © 2002 by Diane Greenseid. Used by permission of Dutton Children's Books, a Division of Penguin Young Readers Group, a Member of Penguin Group (USA) Inc., 345 Hudson Street, New York, NY 10014. All rights reserved.

Walker & Company: Excerpt from *When the Wolves Returned* by Dorothy Hinshaw Patent. Text copyright © 2008 by Dorothy Hinshaw Patent. Photographs © 2008 by Dan Hartman and Cassie Hartman. Reprinted by permission of Walker & Company. All rights reserved.

Unit Three

Random House Children's Books: Excerpt from *Two Old Potatoes and Me* by John Coy, illustrated by Carolyn Fisher. Text copyright © 2009 by John Coy. Illustrations © 2009 by Carolyn Fisher. Reprinted by permission of Random House Children's Books.

Lee & Low Books: "Papaya", "Potato," and "Corn" from *Yum! ¡Mm Mm! ¡Qué rico! Americasí Sproutings* by Pat Mora. Text copyright © 2007 by Pat Mora. Illustrations © 2007 by Rafael López. Reprinted by permission of Lee & Low Books, Inc., New York, NY 10016.

Unit Four

Barefoot Books: Excerpt from *Mama Panya's Pancakes* by Mary and Rich Chamberlin. Text copyright © 2005 by Mary and Rich Chamberlin. Illustrations © 2005 by Julie Cairns. Reprinted by permission of Barefoot Books.

Unit Five

Cengage Learning, Inc.: Excerpt from *Quicksand* by Kris Hirschmann. Copyright © 2002 by Gale. Reprinted by permission of Cengage Learning, Inc., www.cengage.com/permissions.

Unit Six

Henry Holt and Company LLC: Excerpt from *Oye, Celia! A Song for Celia Cruz* by Katie Sciurba, illustrated by Edel Rodriguez. Text copyright © 2007 by Katherina Sciurba. Illustrations © 2007 by Edel Rodriguez. Reprinted by arrangement of Henry Holt and Company LLC.

Highlights for Children, Inc.: Excerpt from "Carving Stones in Cedar" by Kristine F. Anderson from *Highlights for Children*, November 2007. Copyright © 2007 by Highlights for Children. Reprinted by permission of Highlights for Children, Inc.

Unit Seven

HarperCollins Publishers: Excerpt from *An Island Grows* by Lola M. Schaefer, Illustrated by Cathie Felstead. Text copyright © 2006 by Lola M. Schaefer. Illustrations © 2006 by Cathie Felstead. Reprinted by permission of HarperCollins Children's Books.

Shen's Books: Excerpt from *Selvakumar Knew Better* by Virginia Kroll, illustrated by Xiaojun Li. Text copyright © 2009 by Virginia Kroll. Illustrations © 2009 by Xiaogun Li. Reprinted by permission of Shen's Books.

Unit Eight

Evans Brothers Ltd.: Excerpt from *Running Shoes* by Frederick Lipp, illustrated by Jason Gaillard. Text copyright © 2007 by Frederick Lipp. Illustrations © 2007 by Jason Gaillard. First published by Zero to Ten Limited (a member of the Evans Publishing Group). Text and illustrations reproduced with kind permission of Evans Brothers Ltd., 2A Portman Mansions, Chiltern Street, London, W1U 6NR.

▢ NATIONAL GEOGRAPHIC SCHOOL PUBLISHING

National Geographic School Publishing gratefully acknowledges the contributions of the following National Geographic Explorers to our program and to our planet:

Joseph Lekuton, 2006 National Geographic Emerging Explorer

Zeb Hogan, 2004 National Geographic Emerging Explorer

Cornielle Ewango, 2007 National Geographic Emerging Explorer

Cid Simoes and Paola Segura, 2008 National Geographic Emerging Explorers

Maycira Costa, National Geographic grantee

Elizabeth Kapu'uwailani Lindsey, National Geographic Fellow

Carsten Peter, National Geographic Contributing Photographer

Constanza Ceruti, 2005 National Geographic Emerging Explorer

Photographic Credits

iv (tl) Gideon Mendel/Corbis. v (tl) Mak Remissa/epa/Corbis. vi (tr) Eric Loddé/UNESCO - World Heritage Centre. vii (tr) Carlos Nascimento/Earth University. viii (tr) Emielke van Wyk/Gallo Images/Getty Images. ix (tl) Dinodia/Stock Connection. x (tl) Carsten Peter/National Geographic Image Collection. xi (tl) photo courtesy of Constanza Ceruti/copyright Constanza Ceruti. xv (br) Picture Contact/Alamy Images. 2-3 (UnitOp) Tim Pannell/Ivy/Corbis. 7 (bl) Don Mason/Blend Images/Getty Images. (br) James Woodson/Photodisc/Getty Images. (tc) Robert Brenner/PhotoEdit. (tl) Ariel Skelley/Blend Images/age fotostock. (tr) Hola Images/Corbis. 28 (b) DigitalStock/Corbis. (c) anna1311/Shutterstock. (t) RonTech2000/iStockphoto. 35 (b) Ted Foxx/Alamy Images. (tl, tr) Tim Pannell/Corbis. 37 (bl) Leland Bobbé/Corbis. (br) Stephen Simpson/Taxi/Getty Images. (tc) charlybutcher/iStockphoto. (tl) Ariel Skelley/Blend Images/Getty Images. (tr) Shaun Egan/Photodisc/Getty Images. 40-41 H. Armstrong Roberts/Getty Images. 42 (l, r) Henry Winkler. 43 ICM (International Creative Management). 46 Courtesy of Tom Mela. 50 Hampton-Brown/National Geographic School Publishing. 51 Paramount/Everett Collection. 52 (b) Stefan Rousseau/PA Wire/AP Images. (t) Lincoln Journal Star, Robert Becker/AP Images. 53 Fred Duval/FilmMagic/Getty Images. 57 (bg) Curt Wiler/Alamy Images. (inset) Suzannah Weiss. 58 (b) Carl & Ann Purcell/Corbis. (t) SV Photography/Alamy Images. 59 Courtesy of Joseph Lekuton. 60 Picture Contact/Alamy Images. 61 Gideon Mendel/Corbis. 62 (l) H. Armstrong Roberts/Getty Images. (r) Suzannah Weiss. 64 Myrleen Pearson/The Image Works, Inc. 68 Tim Pannell/Ivy/Corbis. 69 Ed Bock/Corbis. 70 (UnitOp) Michael Nichols/National Geographic Image Collection. 75 (bl) quavondo/iStockphoto. (br) Samuel Aranda/Stringer/Getty Images. (tc) Andersen Ross/Blend Images/Getty Images. (tl) Jozsef Szasz-Fabian/iStockphoto. (tr) Arthur Kwiatkowski/iStockphoto. 97 DigitalStock/Corbis. 98 PhotoDisc/Getty Images. 99 Jim Brandenburg/Minden Pictures/National Geographic Image Collection. 100 Digital Vision/Getty Images. (inset) PhotoDisc/Getty Images. 101 Jeff Schultes/Shutterstock. 105 (b) Tim Graham/Getty Images. (t) Alaska Stock. 106 (l) Dave Logan/iStockphoto. (r) bierchen/Shutterstock. 107 (bl) PhotoDisc/Getty Images. (br) Rob Marmion/Shutterstock. (tc) Judy Barranco/iStockphoto. (tl) ampower/Shutterstock. (tr) Tanya Constantine/Getty Images. 108 Justin Guariglia/National Geographic Image Collection. 109 Natalia Bratslavsky/iStockphoto. 110 (inset) Dan & Cassie Hartman. 110-111 (bg) Dan & Cassie Hartman. 112 (l, r) Dan & Cassie Hartman. 113 Dan & Cassie Hartman. 114 (b, bg, t) Dan & Cassie Hartman. 116 Dan & Cassie Hartman. 117 (b) Dan & Cassie Hartman. (inset) Dan & Cassie Hartman. 118 Dan & Cassie Hartman. 119 Dan & Cassie Hartman. 120 (inset) Dan & Cassie Hartman. 120-121 (bg) Dan & Cassie Hartman. 122 Dan & Cassie Hartman. 122-123 Dan & Cassie Hartman. 124 (l, r) Dan & Cassie Hartman. 125 Dan & Cassie Hartman. 126 Dan & Cassie Hartman. 129 (bg) Asia Images/Masterfile. (inset) Apichart Weerawong/AP Images. 130 (bc) Zeb Hogan/AP Images. (bl) Richard Vogel/AP Images. (br) Andy Eames/AP Images. 130-131 (t) Lou Oates/Shutterstock. 131 (l) Mak Remissa/epa/Corbis. 132 (l) Robert Nickelsberg/Time Life Pictures/Getty Images. (r) Bruno Morandi/age fotostock. 132-133 (t) Lou Oates/Shutterstock. 133 Apichart Weerawong/AP Images. 136 Dan & Cassie Hartman. 140 Michael Nichols/National Geographic Image Collection. 141 Hnin Khine/iStockphoto. 142-143 (UnitOp) Scott Sinklier/AgStock Images/Corbis. 145 (bl) Per Makitalo/Getty Images. (br) VikaValter/iStockphoto. (cl) Artville. (cr, t) Barry Runk/Grant Heilman Photography. 147 (bl) Walter B. McKenzie/Getty Images. (br) Sandro Tucci/Time & Life Pictures/Getty Images. (tc) Teodor Ostojic/Shutterstock. (tl) Geoff Kidd/Oxford Scientific (OSF)/Photolibrary. (tr) Theo Allofs/Corbis. 166 (l) Brandon Blinkenberg/Shutterstock. (r) Jiang Dao Hua/Shutterstock. 173 (bcl, bcr, bl) ranplett/iStockphoto. (tc, tl, tr) Dean Turner/iStockphoto. 174 (bl) PhotoDisc/Getty Images. (br) Tim Fitzharris/Minden Pictures/National Geographic Image Collection. (cl, cr, l, tl) Hampton-Brown/National Geographic School Publishing. (r) Michael and Patricia Fogden/Minden Pictures/

Illustrator Credits

California Common Core State Standards

California Common Core State Standards, continued

SE Pages	Lesson	Code	Standard
15	**Selection 1:** Before You Move On: Clarify	CA CC.3.Rlit.1	Ask and answer questions to demonstrate understanding of a text, referring explicitly to the text as the basis for the answers.
	Selection 1: Before You Move On: Character's Motive	CA CC.3.Rlit.3	Describe characters in a story (e.g., their traits, motivations, or feelings) and explain how their actions contribute to the sequence of events.
16	**Selection 1:** Predict	CA CC.3.Rlit.1	Ask and answer questions to demonstrate understanding of a text, referring explicitly to the text as the basis for the answers.
21	**Selection 1:** Before You Move On: Confirm Prediction	CA CC.3.Rlit.1	Ask and answer questions to demonstrate understanding of a text, referring explicitly to the text as the basis for the answers.
	Selection 1: Before You Move On: Character	CA CC.3.Rlit.3	Describe characters in a story (e.g., their traits, motivations, or feelings) and explain how their actions contribute to the sequence of events.
22	**Selection 1:** Predict	CA CC.3.Rlit.1	Ask and answer questions to demonstrate understanding of a text, referring explicitly to the text as the basis for the answers.
25	**Selection Character 1:** Before You Move On: Character	CA CC.3.Rlit.1	Ask and answer questions to demonstrate understanding of a text, referring explicitly to the text as the basis for the answers.
		CA CC.3.Rlit.3	Describe characters in a story (e.g., their traits, motivations, or feelings) and explain how their actions contribute to the sequence of events.
26	**Think and Respond:** Talk About It	CA CC.3.Rlit.5	Refer to parts of stories, dramas, and poems when writing or speaking about a text, using terms such as chapter, scene, and stanza; describe how each successive part builds on earlier sections.
		CA CC.3.SL.1	Engage effectively in a range of collaborative discussions (one-on-one, in groups, and teacher-led) with diverse partners on grade 3 topics and texts, building on others' ideas and expressing their own clearly.
		CA CC.3.SL.1.d	Explain their own ideas and understanding in light of the discussion.
		CA CC.3.SL.4	Report on a topic or text, tell a story, or recount an experience with appropriate facts and relevant, descriptive details, speaking clearly at an understandable pace.
	Think and Respond: Write About It	CA CC.3.W.10	Write routinely over extended time frames (time for research, reflection, and revision) and shorter time frames (a single sitting or a day or two) for a range of discipline-specific tasks, purposes, and audiences.
27	**Reread and Summarize:** Plot	CA CC.3.Rlit.2	Recount stories, including fables, folktales, and myths from diverse cultures; determine the central message, lesson, or moral and explain how it is conveyed through key details in the text.
		CA CC.3.Rlit.5	Refer to parts of stories, dramas, and poems when writing or speaking about a text, using terms such as chapter, scene, and stanza; describe how each successive part builds on earlier sections.

SE Pages	Lesson	Code	Standard
	Reread and Summarize Fluency		Read with sufficient accuracy and fluency to support comprehension.
		CA CC.3.Rfou.4.b	Read on-level prose and poetry orally with accuracy, appropriate rate, and expression on successive readings
	Reread and Summarize Talk Together	CA CC.3.SL.1	Engage effectively in a range of collaborative discussions (one-on-one, in groups, and teacher-led) with diverse partners on *grade 3 topics and texts*, building on others' ideas and expressing their own clearly.
28	**Word Work:** Alphabetical Order		Demonstrate command of the conventions of standard English capitalization, punctuation, and spelling when writing.
		CA CC.3.L.2.g	Consult reference materials, including beginning dictionaries, as needed to check and correct spellings.
			Determine or clarify the meaning of unknown and multiple-meaning word and phrases based on *grade 3 reading and content*, choosing flexibly from a range of strategies.
		CA CC.3.L.4.d	Use glossaries or beginning dictionaries, both print and digital, to determine or clarify the precise meaning of key words and phrases **in all content areas. CA**
29	**Selection 2 Opener:** Before You Move On: Ask Questions	CA CC.3.Rlit.1	Ask and answer questions to demonstrate understanding of a text, referring explicitly to the text as the basis for the answers.
	Selection 2 Opener: Before You Move On: Predict	CA CC.3.Rlit.3	Describe characters in a story (e.g., their traits, motivations, or feelings) and explain how their actions contribute to a sequence of events.
31	**Selection 2: Before You Move On: Confirm Prediction**	CA CC.3.Rlit.1	Ask and answer questions to demonstrate understanding of a text, referring explicitly to the text as the basis for the answers.
	Selection 2: Before You Move On: Character	CA CC.3.Rlit.3	Describe characters in a story (e.g., their traits, motivations, or feelings) and explain how their actions contribute to the sequence of events.
32	**Respond and Extend:** Compare Genres	CA CC.3.Rlit.10	By the end of the year, read and comprehend literature, including stories, dramas, and poetry, at the high end of the grades 2–3 text complexity band independently and proficiently.
33	**Grammar** Complete Sentences	CA CC.3.L.1.a	Explain the function of nouns, pronouns, verbs, adjectives, and adverbs in general and their functions in particular sentences.
		CA CC.3.L.1.i	Produce simple, compound, and complex sentences.
34	**Part 2:** Language: Make Comparisons	CA CC.3.SL.6	Speak in complete sentences when appropriate to task and situation in order to provide requested detail or clarification. (See grade 3 Language standards 1 and 3 for specific expectations.)

California Common Core State Standards, continued

SE Pages	Lesson	Code	Standard
35	**Social Studies Vocabulary:** Key Words	CA CC.3.Rinf.4	Determine the meaning of general academic and domain-specific words and phrases in a text relevant to a *grade 3 topic or subject area*. **(See grade 3 Language standards 4–6 for additional expectations.) CA** Determine or clarify the meaning of unknown and multiple-meaning word and phrases based on *grade 3 reading and content*, choosing flexibly from a range of strategies.
		CA CC.3.L.4.a	Use sentence-level context as a clue to the meaning of a word or phrase.
		CA CC.3.L.6	Acquire and use accurately grade-appropriate conversational, general academic, and domain-specific words and phrases, including those that signal spatial and temporal relationships (e.g., *After dinner that night we went looking for them*).
36	**Thinking Map:** Make Comparisons	CA CC.3.Rinf.10	By the end of the year, read and comprehend informational texts, including history/social studies, science, and technical texts, at the high end of the grades 2–3 text complexity band independently and proficiently.
37	**Academic Vocabulary:** More Key Words		Determine or clarify the meaning of unknown and multiple-meaning word and phrases based on *grade 3 reading and content*, choosing flexibly from a range of strategies.
		CA CC.3.L.4.a	Use sentence-level context as a clue to the meaning of a word or phrase.
		CA CC.3.L.4.d	Use glossaries or beginning dictionaries, both print and digital, to determine or clarify the precise meaning of key words and phrases in all content areas. CA
38	**Strategic Reading:** Learn to Plan and Monitor	CA CC.3.Rinf.10	By the end of the year, read and comprehend informational texts, including history/social studies, science, and technical texts, at the high end of the grades 2–3 text complexity band independently and proficiently.
43	**Selection 1:** Set a Purpose	CA CC.3.Rfou.4	Read with sufficient accuracy and fluency to support comprehension.
		CA CC.3.Rfou.4.a	Read on-level text with purpose and understanding.
45	**Selection 1:** Before You Move On	CA CC.3.Rinf.1	Ask and answer questions to demonstrate understanding of a text, referring explicitly to the text as the basis for the answers.
	Selection 1: Before You Move On: Point of View	CA CC.3.Rinf.6	Distinguish their own point of view from that of the author of a text.
46	**Selection 1:** Predict	CA CC.3.Rinf.1	Ask and answer questions to demonstrate understanding of a text, referring explicitly to the text as the basis for the answers.
49	**Selection 1:** Before You Move On	CA CC.3.Rinf.1	Ask and answer questions to demonstrate understanding of a text, referring explicitly to the text as the basis for the answers.
		CA CC.3.Rinf.2	Determine the main idea of a text; recount the key details and explain how they support the main idea.
50	**Selection 1:** Predict	CA CC.3.Rinf.1	Ask and answer questions to demonstrate understanding of a text, referring explicitly to the text as the basis for the answers.

SE Pages	Lesson	Code	Standard
52	**Selection 1:** Before You Move On	CA CC.3.Rinf.1	Ask and answer questions to demonstrate understanding of a text, referring explicitly to the text as the basis for the answers.
	Selection 1: Before You Move On: Make Connections	CA CC.3.Rinf.2	Determine the main idea of a text; recount the key details and explain how they support the main idea.
53	**Meet the Author:** Writer's Craft	CA CC.3.W.10	Write routinely over extended time frames (time for research, reflection, and revision) and shorter time frames (a single sitting or a day or two) for a range of discipline-specific tasks, purposes, and audiences.
			Demonstrate command of the conventions of standard English grammar and usage when writing or speaking.
		CA CC.3.L.1.i	Produce simple, compound, and complex sentences.
54	**Think and Respond:** Talk About It	CA CC.3.Rinf.1	Ask and answer questions to demonstrate understanding of a text, referring explicitly to the text as the basis for the answers.
		CA CC.3.Rinf.10	By the end of the year, read and comprehend informational texts, including history/social studies, science, and technical texts, at the high end of the grades 2–3 text complexity band independently and proficiently.
	Think and Respond: Write About It	CA CC.3.W.10	Write routinely over extended time frames (time for research, reflection, and revision) and shorter time frames (a single sitting or a day or two) for a range of discipline-specific tasks, purposes, and audiences.
55	**Reread and Compare:** Make Comparisons	CA CC.3.Rinf.8	Describe the logical connection between particular sentences and paragraphs in a text (e.g., comparison, cause/effect, first/second/third in a sequence).
		CA CC.3.Rinf.10	By the end of the year, read and comprehend informational texts, including history/social studies, science, and technical texts, at the high end of the grades 2–3 text complexity band independently and proficiently.
			Read with sufficient accuracy and fluency to support comprehension.
	Reread and Compare: Fluency	CA CC.3.Rfou.4.b	Read on-level prose and poetry orally with accuracy, appropriate rate, and expression on successive readings
	Reread and Compare: Talk Together		Engage effectively in a range of collaborative discussions (one-on-one, in groups, and teacher-led) with diverse partners on *grade 3 topics and texts*, building on others' ideas and expressing their own clearly.
		CA CC.3.SL.1.a	Come to discussions prepared, having read or studied required material; explicitly draw on that preparation and other information known about the topic to explore ideas under discussion.
56	**Word Work:** Determine Meanings	CA CC.3.L.4.d	Use glossaries or beginning dictionaries, both print and digital, to determine or clarify the precise meaning of key words and phrases in all content areas. CA
57	**Selection 2:** Before You Move On	CA CC.3.Rinf.1	Ask and answer questions to demonstrate understanding of a text, referring explicitly to the text as the basis for the answers.
		CA CC.3.Rinf.2	Determine the main idea of a text; recount the key details and explain how they support the main idea.

California Common Core State Standards, continued

SE Pages	Lesson	Code	Standard
59	**Selection 2:** Before You Move On	CA CC.3.Rinf.1	Ask and answer questions to demonstrate understanding of a text, referring explicitly to the text as the basis for the answers.
	Selection 2: Before You Move On: Point of View	CA CC.3.Rinf.6	Distinguish their own point of view from that of the author of a text.
61	**Selection 2:** Before You Move On	CA CC.3.Rinf.1	Ask and answer questions to demonstrate understanding of a text, referring explicitly to the text as the basis for the answers.
		CA CC.3.Rinf.2	Determine the main idea of a text; recount the key details and explain how they support the main idea.
62	**Respond and Extend:** Compare Points of View	CA CC.3.Rinf.9	Compare and contrast the most important points and key details presented in two texts on the same topic.
		CA CC.3.Rinf.10	By the end of the year, read and comprehend informational texts, including history/social studies, science, and technical texts, at the high end of the grades 2–3 text complexity band independently and proficiently.
	Respond and Extend: Talk Together	CA CC.3.SL.6	Engage effectively in a range of collaborative discussions (one-on-one, in groups, and teacher-led) with diverse partners on *grade 3 topics and texts*, building on others' ideas and expressing their own clearly.
		CA CC.3.L.6	Acquire and use accurately grade-appropriate conversational, general academic, and domain-specific words and phrases, including those that signal spatial and temporal relationships (e.g., *After dinner that night we went looking for them*).
63	**Grammar and Spelling:** More Subjects and Predicates		Demonstrate command of the conventions of standard English grammar and usage when writing or speaking.
		CA CC.3.L.1.f	Ensure subject-verb and pronoun-antecedent agreement.
65	**Writing Project:** Personal Narrative Study a Model Prewrite Draft	CA CC.3.W.3	Write narratives to develop real or imagined experiences or events using effective technique, descriptive details, and clear event sequences.
		CA CC.3.W.3.a	Establish a situation and introduce a narrator and/or characters; organize an event sequence that unfolds naturally.
		CA CC.3.W.3.b	Use dialogue and descriptions of actions, thoughts, and feelings to develop experiences and events or show the response of characters to situations.
		CA CC.3.W.3.c	Use temporal words and phrases to signal event order.
		CA CC.3.W.3.d	Provide a sense of closure.
66	**Writing Project:** Revise	CA CC.3.W.5	With guidance and support from peers and adults, develop and strengthen writing as needed by planning, revising, and editing. (Editing for conventions should demonstrate command of Language standards 1–3 up to and including grade 3.)
		CA CC.3.SL.1.d	Explain their own ideas and understanding in light of the discussion.

SE Pages	Lesson	Code	Standard
67	**Writing Project:** Edit and Proofread	CA CC.3.W.5	With guidance and support from peers and adults, develop and strengthen writing as needed by planning, revising, and editing. (Editing for conventions should demonstrate command of Language standards 1–3 up to and including grade 3.)
			Demonstrate command of the conventions of standard English grammar and usage when writing or speaking.
		CA CC.3.L.1.f	Ensure subject-verb and pronoun-antecedent agreement.
	Writing Project: Publish	CA CC.3.W.6	With guidance and support from adults, use technology to produce and publish writing (using keyboarding skills) as well as to interact and collaborate with others.
68	**Talk Together:** Write a Plan	CA CC.3.W.10	Write routinely over extended time frames (time for research, reflection, and revision) and shorter time frames (a single sitting or a day or two) for a range of discipline-specific tasks, purposes, and audiences.
			Engage effectively in a range of collaborative discussions (one-on-one, in groups, and teacher- led) with diverse partners on grade 3 topics and texts, building on others' ideas and expressing their own clearly.
		CA CC.3.SL.1.a	Come to discussions prepared, having read or studied required material; explicitly draw on that preparation and other information known about the topic to explore ideas under discussion
69	**Unit Wrap-Up:** Share Your Ideas	CA CC.3.W.10	Write routinely over extended time frames (time for research, reflection, and revision) and shorter time frames (a single sitting or a day or two) for a range of discipline-specific tasks, purposes, and audiences.
			Engage effectively in a range of collaborative discussions (one-on-one, in groups, and teacher-led) with diverse partners on *grade 3 topics and texts*, building on others' ideas and expressing their own clearly.
		CA CC.3.SL.1.b	Follow agreed-upon rules for discussions (e.g., gaining the floor in respectful ways, listening to others with care, speaking one at a time about the topics and texts under discussion).
		CA CC.3.SL.1.c	Ask questions to check understanding of information presented, stay on topic, and link their comments to the remarks of others.

Unit 2: Nature's Balance

SE Pages	Lesson	Code	Standard
71	**Unit Launch:** Share What You Know		Engage effectively in a range of collaborative discussions (one-on-one, in groups, and teacher-led) with diverse partners on *grade 3 topics and texts*, building on others' ideas and expressing their own clearly.
		CA CC.3.SL.1.a	Come to discussions prepared, having read or studied required material; explicitly draw on that preparation and other information known about the topic to explore ideas under discussion.

California Common Core State Standards, continued

SE Pages	Lesson	Code	Standard
72	**Part 1:** Language: Ask and Answer Questions		Engage effectively in a range of collaborative discussions (one-on-one, in groups, and teacher-led) with diverse partners on *grade 3 topics and texts*, building on others' ideas and expressing their own clearly.
		CA CC.3.SL.1.c	Ask questions to check understanding of information presented, stay on topic, and link their comments to the remarks of others.
		CA CC.3.SL.3	Ask and answer questions about information from a speaker, offering appropriate elaboration and detail.
73	**Science Vocabulary:** Key Words	CA CC.3.Rlit.4	Determine the meaning of words and phrases as they are used in a text, distinguishing literal from nonliteral language. **(See grade 3 Language standards 4–6 for additional expectations.)** CA
		CA CC.3.L.6	Acquire and use accurately grade-appropriate conversational, general academic, and domain-specific words and phrases, including those that signal spatial and temporal relationships (e.g., *After dinner that night we went looking for them*).
74	**Thinking Map:** Compare and Contrast	CA CC.3.Rlit.1	Ask and answer questions to demonstrate understanding of a text, referring explicitly to the text as the basis for the answers.
75	**Academic Vocabulary:** More Key Words	CA CC.3.L.6	Acquire and use accurately grade-appropriate conversational, general academic, and domain-specific words and phrases, including those that signal spatial and temporal relationships (e.g., *After dinner that night we went looking for them*).
		CA CC.3.Rlit.4	Determine the meaning of words and phrases as they are used in a text, distinguishing literal from nonliteral language. **(See grade 3 Language standards 4–6 for additional expectations.)** CA
76	**Strategic Reading:** Learn to Ask Questions	CA CC.3.Rlit.1	Ask and answer questions to demonstrate understanding of a text, referring explicitly to the text as the basis for the answers.
80	**Selection 1:** Set a Purpose		Read with sufficient accuracy and fluency to support comprehension.
		CA CC.3.Rfou.4.a	Read on-level text with purpose and understanding.
83	**Selection 1:** Before You Move On	CA CC.3.Rlit.1	Ask and answer questions to demonstrate understanding of a text, referring explicitly to the text as the basis for the answers.
	Selection 1: Before You Move On: Cause/Effect	CA CC.3.Rlit.2	Recount stories, including fables, folktales, and myths from diverse cultures; determine the central message, lesson, or moral and explain how it is conveyed through key details in the text.
	Selection 1: Before You Move On: Ask Questions	CA CC.3.Rlit.3	Describe characters in a story (e.g., their traits, motivations, or feelings) and explain how their actions contribute to the sequence of events.
84	**Selection 1:** Predict	CA CC.3.Rlit.1	Ask and answer questions to demonstrate understanding of a text, referring explicitly to the text as the basis for the answers.
		CA CC.3.Rlit.7	Explain how specific aspects of a text's illustrations contribute to what is conveyed by the words in a story (e.g., create mood, emphasize aspects of a character or setting).

SE Pages	Lesson	Code	Standard
87	**Selection 1:** Before You Move On	CA CC.3.Rlit.1	Ask and answer questions to demonstrate understanding of a text, referring explicitly to the text as the basis for the answers.
88	**Selection 1:** Predict	CA CC.3.Rlit.1	Ask and answer questions to demonstrate understanding of a text, referring explicitly to the text as the basis for the answers.
89	**Selection 1:** Before You Move On	CA CC.3.Rlit.1	Ask and answer questions to demonstrate understanding of a text, referring explicitly to the text as the basis for the answers.
	Selection 1: Before You Move On: Setting	CA CC.3.Rlit.2	Recount stories, including fables, folktales, and myths from diverse cultures; determine the central message, lesson, or moral and explain how it is conveyed through key details in the text.
90	**Selection 1:** Predict	CA CC.3.Rlit.1	Ask and answer questions to demonstrate understanding of a text, referring explicitly to the text as the basis for the answers.
93	**Selection 1:** Before You Move On	CA CC.3.Rlit.1	Ask and answer questions to demonstrate understanding of a text, referring explicitly to the text as the basis for the answers.
		CA CC.3.Rlit.3	Describe characters in a story (e.g., their traits, motivations, or feelings) and explain how their actions contribute to the sequence of events.
94	**Think and Respond:** Talk About It	CA CC.3.Rlit.1	Ask and answer questions to demonstrate understanding of a text, referring explicitly to the text as the basis for the answers.
		CA CC.3.Rlit.10	By the end of the year, read and comprehend literature, including stories, dramas, and poetry, at the high end of the grades 2–3 text complexity band independently and proficiently.
	Think and Respond: Write About It	CA CC.3.W.10	Write routinely over extended time frames (time for research, reflection, and revision) and shorter time frames (a single sitting or a day or two) for a range of discipline-specific tasks, purposes, and audiences.
		CA CC.3.L.6	Acquire and use accurately grade-appropriate conversational, general academic, and domain-specific words and phrases, including those that signal spatial and temporal relationships (e.g., *After dinner that night we went looking for them*).
95	**Reread and Compare and Contrast** Compare and Contrast	CA CC.3.Rlit.4	Determine the meaning of words and phrases as they are used in a text, distinguishing literal from nonliteral language. **(See grade 3 Language standards 4–6 for additional expectations.) CA**
		CA CC.3.Rlit.10	By the end of the year, read and comprehend literature, including stories, dramas, and poetry, at the high end of the grades 2–3 text complexity band independently and proficiently.
	Reread and Compare and Contrast: Fluency		Read with sufficient accuracy and fluency to support comprehension.
		CA CC.3.Rfou.4.b	Read on-level prose and poetry orally with accuracy, appropriate rate, and expression on successive readings.
	Reread and Compare and Contrast: Talk Together	CA CC.3.SL.1.a	Engage effectively in a range of collaborative discussions (one-on-one, in groups, and teacher-led) with diverse partners on *grade 3 topics and texts*, building on others' ideas and expressing their own clearly.
96	**Word Work:** Syllables	CA CC.3.Rfou.3	Know and apply grade-level phonics and word analysis skills in decoding words **both in isolation and in text. CA**

California Common Core State Standards, continued

SE Pages	Lesson	Code	Standard
97	**Selection 2: Before You Move On:** Identify	CA CC.3.Rlit.1	Ask and answer questions to demonstrate understanding of a text, referring explicitly to the text as the basis for the answers.
	Selection 2: Before You Move On: Apply	CA CC.3.SL.6	Speak in complete sentences when appropriate to task and situation in order to provide requested detail or clarification. (See grade 3 Language standards 1 and 3 for specific expectations.)
99	**Selection 2: Before You Move On**	CA CC.3.Rlit.1	Ask and answer questions to demonstrate understanding of a text, referring explicitly to the text as the basis for the answers.
		CA CC.3.Rlit.4	Determine the meaning of words and phrases as they are used in a text, distinguishing literal from nonliteral language. **(See grade 3 Language standards 4–6 for additional expectations.) CA**
101	**Selection 2: Before You Move On**	CA CC.3.Rlit.1	Ask and answer questions to demonstrate understanding of a text, referring explicitly to the text as the basis for the answers.
		CA CC.3.Rlit.4	Determine the meaning of words and phrases as they are used in a text, distinguishing literal from nonliteral language. **(See grade 3 Language standards 4–6 for additional expectations.) CA**
102	**Respond and Extend:** Compare Genres	CA CC.3.Rlit.10	By the end of the year, read and comprehend literature, including stories, dramas, and poetry, at the high end of the grades 2–3 text complexity band independently and proficiently.
103	**Grammar:** Kinds of Sentences	CA CC.3.W.10	**Write routinely over extended time frames (time for research, reflection, and revision) and shorter time frames (a single sitting or a day or two) for a range of discipline-specific tasks, purposes, and audiences.**
		CA CC.3.SL.6	Demonstrate command of the conventions of standard English grammar and usage when writing or speaking.
104	**Part 2:** Language: Give and Carry Out Commands	CA CC.3.SL.6	Speak in complete sentences when appropriate to task and situation in order to provide requested detail or clarification. (See grade 3 Language standards 1 and 3 for specific expectations.)
			Demonstrate command of the conventions of standard English grammar and usage when writing or speaking.
105	**Science Vocabulary:** Key Words	CA CC.3.Rinf.4	Determine the meaning of general academic and domain-specific words and phrases in a text relevant to a *grade 3 topic or subject area.* **(See grade 3 Language standards 4–6 for additional expectations.) CA**
		CA CC.3.L.6	Acquire and use accurately grade-appropriate conversational, general academic, and domain-specific words and phrases, including those that signal spatial and temporal relationships (e.g., *After dinner that night we went looking for them*).
106	**Thinking Map:** Cause and Effect	CA CC.3.Rinf.3	Describe the relationship between a series of historical events, scientific ideas or concepts, or steps in technical procedures in a text, using language that pertains to time, sequence, or cause/effect.
107	**Academic Vocabulary:** More Key Words	CA CC.3.Rinf.4	Determine the meaning of general academic and domain-specific words and phrases in a text relevant to a *grade 3 topic or subject area.* **(See grade 3 Language standards 4–6 for additional expectations.) CA**

SE Pages	Lesson	Code	Standard
			Determine or clarify the meaning of unknown and multiple-meaning word and phrases based on grade 3 reading and content, choosing flexibly from a range of strategies.
		CA CC.3.L.4.a	Use sentence-level context as a clue to the meaning of a word or phrase.
		CA CC.3.L.6	Acquire and use accurately grade-appropriate conversational, general academic, and domain-specific words and phrases, including those that signal spatial and temporal relationships (e.g., *After dinner that night we went looking for them*).
108	**Strategic Reading:** Learn to Ask Questions	CA CC.3.Rinf.1	Ask and answer questions to demonstrate understanding of a text, referring explicitly to the text as the basis for the answers.
112	**Selection 1:** Set a Purpose		Read with sufficient accuracy and fluency to support comprehension.
		CA CC.3.Rfou.4.a	Read on-level text with purpose and understanding.
113	**Selection 1:** Before You Move On	CA CC.3.Rinf.1	Ask and answer questions to demonstrate understanding of a text, referring explicitly to the text as the basis for the answers.
	Selection 1: Before You Move On: Cause/Effect	CA CC.3.Rinf.3	Describe the relationship between a series of historical events, scientific ideas or concepts, or steps in technical procedures in a text, using language that pertains to time, sequence, and cause/effect.
	Selection 1: Before You Move On: Cause/Effect	CA CC.3.Rinf.8	Describe the logical connection between particular sentences and paragraphs in a text (e.g., comparison, cause/effect, first/second/ third in a sequence).
	Selection 1: Before You Move On: Explain	CA CC.3.Rinf.2	Determine the main idea of a text; recount the key details and explain how they support the main idea.
		CA CC.3.SL.2	Determine the main ideas and supporting details of a text read aloud or information presented in diverse media and formats, including visually, quantitatively, and orally.
115	**Selection 1:** Before You Move On: Cause/Effect	CA CC.3.Rinf.1	Ask and answer questions to demonstrate understanding of a text, referring explicitly to the text as the basis for the answers.
	Selection 1: Before You Move On: Cause/Effect	CA CC.3.Rinf.3	Describe the relationship between a series of historical events, scientific ideas or concepts, or steps in technical procedures in a text, using language that pertains to time, sequence, and cause/effect.
		CA CC.3.Rinf.8	Describe the logical connection between particular sentences and paragraphs in a text (e.g., comparison, cause/effect, first/second/third in a sequence).
	Selection 1: Before You Move On:Ask Questions	CA CC.3.Rinf.1	Ask and answer questions to demonstrate understanding of a text, referring explicitly to the text as the basis for the answers.
117	**Selection 1:** Before You Move On: Ask Questions	CA CC.3.Rinf.1	Ask and answer questions to demonstrate understanding of a text, referring explicitly to the text as the basis for the answers.
		CA CC.3.Rinf.8	Describe the logical connection between particular sentences and paragraphs in a text (e.g., comparison, cause/effect, first/second third in a sequence).

California Common Core State Standards, continued

Unit 2	Nature's Balance, continued		
SE Pages	Lesson	Code	Standard
	Selection 1: Before You Move On Sequence	CA CC.3.Rinf.3	Describe the relationship between a series of historical events, scientific ideas or concepts, or steps in technical procedures in a text, using language that pertains to time, sequence, and cause/effect.
119	**Selection 1:** Before You Move On	CA CC.3.Rinf.1	Ask and answer questions to demonstrate understanding of a text, referring explicitly to the text as the basis for the answers.
	Selection 1: Before You Move On: Cause/Effect	CA CC.3.Rinf.3	Describe the relationship between a series of historical events, scientific ideas or concepts, or steps in technical procedures in a text, using language that pertains to time, sequence, and cause/effect.
		CA CC.3.Rinf.8	Describe the logical connection between particular sentences and paragraphs in a text (e.g., comparison, cause/effect, first/second/third in a sequence).
	Selection 1: Before You Move On: Summarize	CA CC.3.Rinf.2	Determine the main idea of a text; recount the key details and explain how they support the main idea.
121	**Selection 1:** Before You Move On	CA CC.3.Rinf.1	Ask and answer questions to demonstrate understanding of a text, referring explicitly to the text as the basis for the answers.
		CA CC.3.Rinf.1	Ask and answer questions to demonstrate understanding of a text, referring explicitly to the text as the basis for the answers.
	Selection 1: Before You Move On Evaluate	CA CC.3.Rinf.6	Distinguish their own point of view from that of the author of a text.
123	**Selection 1:** Before You Move On	CA CC.3.Rinf.1	Ask and answer questions to demonstrate understanding of a text, referring explicitly to the text as the basis for the answers.
	Selection 1: Before You Move On Cause/Effect	CA CC.3.Rinf.3	Describe the relationship between a series of historical events, scientific ideas or concepts, or steps in technical procedures in a text, using language that pertains to time, sequence, and cause/effect.
		CA CC.3.Rinf.8	Describe the logical connection between particular sentences and paragraphs in a text (e.g., comparison, cause/effect, first/second/third in a sequence).
	Selection 1: Before You Move On: Details	CA CC.3.Rinf.2	Determine the main idea of a text; recount the key details and explain how they support the main idea.
125	**Selection 1:** Before You Move On	CA CC.3.Rinf.1	Ask and answer questions to demonstrate understanding of a text, referring explicitly to the text as the basis for the answers.
	Selection 1: Before You Move On: Author's Purpose	CA CC.3.Rinf.6	Distinguish their own point of view from that of the author of a text.
126	**Think and Respond:** Talk About It	CA CC.3.Rinf.1	Ask and answer questions to demonstrate understanding of a text, referring explicitly to the text as the basis for the answers.
		CA CC.3.Rinf.2	Determine the main idea of a text; recount the key details and explain how they support the main idea.

SE Pages	Lesson	Code	Standard
		CA CC.3.Rinf.3	Describe the relationship between a series of historical events, scientific ideas or concepts, or steps in technical procedures in a text, using language that pertains to time, sequence, and cause/effect.
		CA CC.3.Rinf.5	Use text features and search tools (e.g., key words, sidebars, hyperlinks) to locate information relevant to a given topic efficiently.
		CA CC.3.Rinf.10	By the end of the year, read and comprehend informational texts, including history/social studies, science, and technical texts, at the high end of the grades 2–3 text complexity band independently and proficiently.
			Engage effectively in a range of collaborative discussions (one-on-one, in groups, and teacher-led) with diverse partners on *grade 3 topics and texts*, building on others' ideas and expressing their own clearly.
		CA CC.3.SL.1.a	Come to discussions prepared, having read or studied required material; explicitly draw on that preparation and other information known about the topic to explore ideas under discussion.
	Think and Respond: Write About It		Write opinion pieces on topics or texts, supporting a point of view with reasons.
		CA CC.3.W.1.a	Introduce the topic or text they are writing about, state an opinion, and create an organizational structure that lists reasons.
		CA CC.3.W.10	Write routinely over extended time frames (time for research, reflection, and revision) and shorter time frames (a single sitting or a day or two) for a range of discipline-specific tasks, purposes, and audiences.
127	**Reread and Retell** Compare	CA CC.3.Rinf.3	Describe the relationship between a series of historical events, scientific ideas or concepts, or steps in technical procedures in a text, using language that pertains to time, sequence, and cause/effect.
		CA CC.3.Rinf.8	Describe the logical connection between particular sentences and paragraphs in a text (e.g., comparison, cause/effect, first/second/third in a sequence).
		CA CC.3.Rinf.10	By the end of the year, read and comprehend informational texts, including history/social studies, science, and technical texts, at the high end of the grades 2–3 text complexity band independently and proficiently.
	Reread and Retell Fluency	CA CC.3.W.10	Write routinely over extended time frames (time for research, reflection, and revision) and shorter time frames (a single sitting or a day or two) for a range of discipline-specific tasks, purposes, and audiences.
			Read with sufficient accuracy and fluency to support comprehension.
		CA CC.3.Rfou.4.b	Read on-level prose and poetry orally with accuracy, appropriate rate, and expression on successive readings.

665

California Common Core State Standards, continued

SE Pages	Lesson	Code	Standard
	Reread and Retell Talk Together		Engage effectively in a range of collaborative discussions (one-on-one, in groups, and teacher-led) with diverse partners on *grade 3 topics and texts*, building on others' ideas and expressing their own clearly.
		CA CC.3.SL.4	Report on a topic or text, tell a story, or recount an experience with appropriate facts and relevant, descriptive details, speaking clearly at an understandable pace.
128	**Word Work:** Pronunciation	CA CC.3.Rfou.3.c	Know and apply grade-level phonics and word analysis skills in decoding words **both in isolation and in text. CA** Decode multisyllable words
129	**Selection 2 Opener:** Before You Move On	CA CC.3.Rinf.1	Ask and answer questions to demonstrate understanding of a text, referring explicitly to the text as the basis for the answers.
	Selection 2 Opener: Before You Move On: Use Text Features	CA CC.3.Rinf.5	Use text features and search tools (e.g., key words, sidebars, hyperlinks) to locate information relevant to a given topic efficiently.
131	**Selection 2:** Before You Move On	CA CC.3.Rinf.1	Ask and answer questions to demonstrate understanding of a text, referring explicitly to the text as the basis for the answers.
	Selection 2: Before You Move On: Make Inferences	CA CC.3.Rinf.2	Determine the main idea of a text; recount the key details and explain how they support the main idea.
	Selection 2: Before You Move On: Clarify	CA CC.3.Rinf.4	Determine the meaning of general academic and domain-specific words and phrases in a text relevant to a *grade 3 topic or subject area.* **(See grade 3 Language standards 4–6 for additional expectations.) CA**
133	**Selection 2:** Before You Move On	CA CC.3.Rinf.1	Ask and answer questions to demonstrate understanding of a text, referring explicitly to the text as the basis for the answers.
	Selection 2: Before You Move On: Cause/Effect	CA CC.3.Rinf.3	Describe the relationship between a series of historical events, scientific ideas or concepts, or steps in technical procedures in a text, using language that pertains to time, sequence, and cause/effect.
	Respond and Extend: Compare Genres	CA CC.3.Rinf.2	Determine the main idea of a text; recount the key details and explain how they support the main idea.
134	**Respond and Extend:** Compare Ecosystems	CA CC.3.Rinf.10	By the end of the year, read and comprehend informational texts, including history/social studies, science, and technical texts, at the high end of the grades 2–3 text complexity band independently and proficiently. Engage effectively in a range of collaborative discussions (one-on-one, in groups, and teacher-led) with diverse partners on *grade 3 topics and texts*, building on others' ideas and expressing their own clearly.
135	**Grammar:** Compound Sentences	CA CC.3.W.10	Demonstrate command of the conventions of standard English grammar and usage when writing or speaking.
		CA CC.3.L.1.h	Use coordinating and subordinating conjunctions.
		CA CC.3.L.1.i	Produce simple, compound, and complex sentences.

SE Pages	Lesson	Code	Standard
137	**Writing Project:** Summary Study a Model Prewrite Draft		Write informative/explanatory texts to examine a topic and convey ideas and information clearly.
		CA CC.3.W.2.a	Introduce a topic and group related information together; include illustrations when useful to aiding comprehension.
		CA CC.3.W.2.b	Develop the topic with facts, definitions, and details.
		CA CC.3.W.8	Recall information from experiences or gather information from print and digital sources; take brief notes on sources and sort evidence into provided categories.
138	**Writing Project:** Revise	CA CC.3.W.5	With guidance and support from peers and adults, develop and strengthen writing as needed by planning, revising, and editing. (Editing for conventions should demonstrate command of Language standards 1–3 up to and including grade 3.)
139	**Writing Project:** Edit and Proofread	CA CC.3.W.5	With guidance and support from peers and adults, develop and strengthen writing as needed by planning, revising, and editing. (Editing for conventions should demonstrate command of Language standards 1–3 up to and including grade 3.)
		CA CC.3.L.1.h	Use coordinating and subordinating conjunctions.
		CA CC.3.L.1.i	Produce simple, compound, and complex sentences.
		CA CC.3.L.2	Demonstrate command of the conventions of standard English capitalization, punctuation, and spelling when writing.
	Writing Project: Publish	CA CC.3.W.6	With guidance and support from adults, use technology to produce and publish writing (using keyboarding skills) as well as to interact and collaborate with others.
140	**Talk Together**	CA CC.3.W.10	Write routinely over extended time frames (time for research, reflection, and revision) and shorter time frames (a single sitting or a day or two) for a range of discipline-specific tasks, purposes, and audiences.
			Engage effectively in a range of collaborative discussions (one-on-one, in groups, and teacher-led) with diverse partners on *grade 3 topics and texts*, building on others' ideas and expressing their own clearly.
	Write a Description	CA CC.3.SL.1.a	Come to discussions prepared, having read or studied required material; explicitly draw on that preparation and other information known about the topic to explore ideas under discussion.
141	**Unit Wrap-Up:** Share Your Ideas	CA CC.3.W.10	Write routinely over extended time frames (time for research, reflection, and revision) and shorter time frames (a single sitting or a day or two) for a range of discipline-specific tasks, purposes, and audiences.
			Engage effectively in a range of collaborative discussions (one-on-one, in groups, and teacher-led) with diverse partners on *grade 3 topics and texts*, building on others' ideas and expressing their own clearly.
		CA CC.3.SL.1.a	Come to discussions prepared, having read or studied required material; explicitly draw on that preparation and other information known about the topic to explore ideas under discussion.
		CA CC.3.SL.1.d	Explain their own ideas and understanding in light of the discussion.

California Common Core State Standards, continued

SE Pages	Lesson	Code	Standard
143	**Unit Launch:** Share What You Know	CA CC.3.SL.2	Determine the main ideas and supporting details of a text read aloud or information presented in diverse media and formats, including visually, quantitatively, and orally.
144	**Part 1: Language:** Give Information	CA CC.3.SL.3	Ask and answer questions about information from a speaker, offering appropriate elaboration and detail.
		CA CC.3.SL.6	Speak in complete sentences when appropriate to task and situation in order to provide requested detail or clarification. (See grade 3 Language standards 1 and 3 for specific expectations.)
145	**Science Vocabulary:** Key Words	CA CC.3.Rinf.4	Determine the meaning of general academic and domain-specific words and phrases in a text relevant to a *grade 3 topic or subject area*. **(See grade 3 Language standards 4–6 for additional expectations.) CA**
		CA CC.3.L.6	Acquire and use accurately grade-appropriate conversational, general academic, and domain-specific words and phrases, including those that signal spatial and temporal relationships (e.g., *After dinner that night we went looking for them*).
146	**Thinking Map:** Sequence	CA CC.3.Rlit.10	By the end of the year, read and comprehend literature, including stories, dramas, and poetry, at the high end of the grades 2–3 text complexity band independently and proficiently. Ask and answer questions to demonstrate understanding of a text, referring explicitly to the text as the basis for the answers.
147	**Academic Vocabulary:** More Key Words	CA CC.3.Rlit.4	Determine the meaning of words and phrases as they are used in a text, distinguishing literal from nonliteral language. **(See grade 3 Language standards 4–6 for additional expectations.) CA** Determine or clarify the meaning of unknown and multiple-meaning word and phrases based on *grade 3 reading and content*, choosing flexibly from a range of strategies.
		CA CC.3.L.6	Acquire and use accurately grade-appropriate conversational, general academic, and domain-specific words and phrases, including those that signal spatial and temporal relationships (e.g., *After dinner that night we went looking for them*). Engage effectively in a range of collaborative discussions (one-on-one, in groups, and teacher-led) with diverse partners on *grade 3 topics and texts*, building on others' ideas and expressing their own clearly.
148	**Strategic Reading:** Learn to Make Inferences	CA CC.3.Rlit.1	Ask and answer questions to demonstrate understanding of a text, referring explicitly to the text as the basis for the answers.
152	**Selection 1:** Set a Purpose	CA CC.3.Rfou.4.a	Read with sufficient accuracy and fluency to support comprehension. Read on-level text with purpose and understanding.

SE Pages	Lesson	Code	Standard
153	**Selection 1:** Before You Move On	CA CC.3.Rlit.1	Ask and answer questions to demonstrate understanding of a text, referring explicitly to the text as the basis for the answers.
	Selection 1: Before You Move On: Sequence	CA CC.3.Rlit.2	Recount stories, including fables, folktales, and myths from diverse cultures; determine the central message, lesson, or moral and explain how it is conveyed through key details in the text.
	Selection 1: Before You Move On: Make Inferences	CA CC.3.Rlit.3	Describe characters in a story (e.g., their traits, motivations, or feelings) and explain how their actions contribute to the sequence of events.
154	**Selection 1:** Predict	CA CC.3.Rlit.1	Ask and answer questions to demonstrate understanding of a text, referring explicitly to the text as the basis for the answers.
157	**Selection 1:** Before You Move On	CA CC.3.Rlit.1	Ask and answer questions to demonstrate understanding of a text, referring explicitly to the text as the basis for the answers.
	Selection 1: Before You Move On: Character	CA CC.3.Rlit.3	Describe characters in a story (e.g., their traits, motivations, or feelings) and explain how their actions contribute to the sequence of events.
158	**Selection 1:** Predict	CA CC.3.Rlit.1	Ask and answer questions to demonstrate understanding of a text, referring explicitly to the text as the basis for the answers.
162	**Selection 1:** Before You Move On	CA CC.3.Rlit.1	Ask and answer questions to demonstrate understanding of a text, referring explicitly to the text as the basis for the answers.
	Selection 1: Before You Move On: Point of View	CA CC.3.Rlit.6	Distinguish their own point of view from that of the narrator or those of the characters.
163	**Meet the Author:** Writer's Craft	CA CC.3.Rlit.7	Explain how specific aspects of a text's illustrations contribute to what is conveyed by the words in a story (e.g., create mood, emphasize aspects of a character or setting).
		CA CC.3.W.10	Write routinely over extended time frames (time for research, reflection, and revision) and shorter time frames (a single sitting or a day or two) for a range of discipline-specific tasks, purposes, and audiences.
164	**Think and Respond:** Talk About It	CA CC.3.Rlit.1	Ask and answer questions to demonstrate understanding of a text, referring explicitly to the text as the basis for the answers.
		CA CC.3.Rlit.3	Describe characters in a story (e.g., their traits, motivations, or feelings) and explain how their actions contribute to the sequence of events.
		CA CC.3.Rlit.10	By the end of the year, read and comprehend literature, including stories, dramas, and poetry, at the high end of the grades 2–3 text complexity band independently and proficiently.
			Engage effectively in a range of collaborative discussions (one-on-one, in groups, and teacher-led) with diverse partners on *grade 3 topics and texts,* building on others' ideas and expressing their own clearly.
		CA CC.3.SL.1.a	Come to discussions prepared, having read or studied required material; explicitly draw on that preparation and other information known about the topic to explore ideas under discussion.

California Common Core State Standards, continued

SE Pages	Lesson	Code	Standard
	Think and Respond: Write About It	CA CC.3.W.10	Write routinely over extended time frames (time for research, reflection, and revision) and shorter time frames (a single sitting or a day or two) for a range of discipline-specific tasks, purposes, and audiences.
		CA CC.3.L.6	Acquire and use accurately grade-appropriate conversational, general academic, and domain-specific words and phrases, including those that signal spatial and temporal relationships (e.g., *After dinner that night we went looking for them*).
165	**Reread and Retell** Sequence	CA CC.3.Rlit.10	By the end of the year, read and comprehend literature, including stories, dramas, and poetry, at the high end of the grades 2–3 text complexity band independently and proficiently.
	Reread and Retell Talk Together	CA CC.3.Rfou.4.b	Read on-level prose and poetry orally with accuracy, appropriate rate, and expression on successive readings.
			Engage effectively in a range of collaborative discussions (one-on-one, in groups, and teacher-led) with diverse partners on *grade 3 topics and texts,* building on others' ideas and expressing their own clearly.
		CA CC.3.SL.1.a	Come to discussions prepared, having read or studied required material; explicitly draw on that preparation and other information known about the topic to explore ideas under discussion.
		CA CC.3.L.6	Acquire and use accurately grade-appropriate conversational, general academic, and domain-specific words and phrases, including those that signal spatial and temporal relationships (e.g., *After dinner that night we went looking for them*).
166	**Word Work:** Multiple-Meaning Words	CA CC.3.L.4	Determine or clarify the meaning of unknown and multiple-meaning word and phrases based on *grade 3 reading and content,* choosing flexibly from a range of strategies.
		CA CC.3.L.4.a	Use sentence-level context as a clue to the meaning of a word or phrase.
167	**Selection 2:** Before You Move On	CA CC.3.Rlit.1	Ask and answer questions to demonstrate understanding of a text, referring explicitly to the text as the basis for the answers.
	Selection 2: Before You Move On: Describe	CA CC.3.Rlit.4	Determine the meaning of words and phrases as they are used in a text, distinguishing literal from nonliteral language. **(See grade 3 Language standards 4–6 for additional expectations.) CA**
169	**Selection 2:** Before You Move On	CA CC.3.Rlit.1	Ask and answer questions to demonstrate understanding of a text, referring explicitly to the text as the basis for the answers.
	Selection 2: Before You Move On: Details	CA CC.3.Rlit.4	Determine the meaning of words and phrases as they are used in a text, distinguishing literal from nonliteral language. **(See grade 3 Language standards 4–6 for additional expectations.) CA**
		CA CC.3.Rlit.5	Refer to parts of stories, dramas, and poems when writing or speaking about a text, using terms such as chapter, scene, and stanza; describe how each successive part builds on earlier sections.
171	**Selection 2:** Before You Move On	CA CC.3.Rlit.1	Ask and answer questions to demonstrate understanding of a text, referring explicitly to the text as the basis for the answers.
	Selection 2: Before You Move On: Imagery	CA CC.3.Rlit.4	Determine the meaning of words and phrases as they are used in a text, distinguishing literal from nonliteral language. **(See grade 3 Language standards 4–6 for additional expectations.) CA**

SE Pages	Lesson	Code	Standard
	Selection 2: Before You Move On: Details	CA CC.3.Rlit.2	Recount stories, including fables, folktales, and myths from diverse cultures; determine the central message, lesson, or moral and explain how it is conveyed through key details in the text.
172	**Respond and Extend:** Compare Genres	CA CC.3.Rlit.10	By the end of the year, read and comprehend literature, including stories, dramas, and poetry, at the high end of the grades 2–3 text complexity band independently and proficiently.
		CA CC.3.L.6	Acquire and use accurately grade-appropriate conversational, general academic, and domain-specific words and phrases, including those that signal spatial and temporal relationships (e.g., *After dinner that night we went looking for them*).
173	**Grammar and Spelling:** Plural Nouns		Demonstrate command of the conventions of standard English grammar and usage when writing or speaking.
		CA CC.3.L.1.a	Explain the function of nouns, pronouns, verbs, adjectives, and adverbs in general and their functions in particular sentences.
		CA CC.3.L.1.b	Form and use regular and irregular plural nouns.
174	**Part 2:** Language: Define and Explain		Engage effectively in a range of collaborative discussions (one-on-one, in groups, and teacher-led) with diverse partners on *grade 3 topics and texts,* building on others' ideas and expressing their own clearly.
		CA CC.3.SL.1.a	Come to discussions prepared, having read or studied required material; explicitly draw on that preparation and other information known about the topic to explore ideas under discussion.
		CA CC.3.SL.1.d	Explain their own ideas and understanding in light of the discussion.
175	**Science Vocabulary:** Key Words	CA CC.3.Rinf.4	Determine the meaning of general academic and domain-specific words and phrases in a text relevant to a *grade 3 topic or subject area.* **(See grade 3 Language standards 4–6 for additional expectations.) CA**
		CA CC.3.L.6	Acquire and use accurately grade-appropriate conversational, general academic, and domain-specific words and phrases, including those that signal spatial and temporal relationships (e.g., *After dinner that night we went looking for them*).
		CA CC.3.L.4.a	Use sentence-level context as a clue to the meaning of a word or phrase.
176	**Thinking Map:** Main Idea and Details	CA CC.3.Rinf.2	Determine the main idea of a text; recount the key details and explain how they support the main idea.
177	**Academic Vocabulary:** More Key Words	CA CC.3.Rinf.4	Determine the meaning of general academic and domain-specific words and phrases in a text relevant to a *grade 3 topic or subject area.* **(See grade 3 Language standards 4–6 for additional expectations.) CA**
		CA CC.3.L.6	Acquire and use accurately grade-appropriate conversational, general academic, and domain-specific words and phrases, including those that signal spatial and temporal relationships (e.g., *After dinner that night we went looking for them*).
178	**Strategic Reading:** Learn to Make Inferences	CA CC.3.Rinf.7	Use information gained from illustrations (e.g., maps, photographs) and the words in a text to demonstrate understanding of the text (e.g., where, when, why, and how key events occur).

California Common Core State Standards, continued

SE Pages	Lesson	Code	Standard
182	**Selection 1:** Set a Purpose	CA CC.3.Rfou.4	Read with sufficient accuracy and fluency to support comprehension.
		CA CC.3.Rfou.4.a	Read on-level text with purpose and understanding.
183	**Selection 1:** Before You Move On	CA CC.3.Rinf.1	Ask and answer questions to demonstrate understanding of a text, referring explicitly to the text as the basis for the answers.
	Selection 1: Before You Move On: Main Idea and Details	CA CC.3.Rinf.2	Determine the main idea of a text; recount the key details and explain how they support the main idea.
	Selection 1: Before You Move On: Make Inferences	CA CC.3.Rinf.4	Determine the meaning of general academic and domain-specific words and phrases in a text relevant to a *grade 3 topic or subject area.* **(See grade 3 Language standards 4–6 for additional expectations.) CA**
185	**Selection 1:** Before You Move On	CA CC.3.Rinf.1	Ask and answer questions to demonstrate understanding of a text, referring explicitly to the text as the basis for the answers.
	Selection 1: Before You Move On: Use Text Features	CA CC.3.Rinf.7	Use information gained from illustrations (e.g., maps, photographs) and the words in a text to demonstrate understanding of the text (e.g., where, when, why, and how key events occur).
	Selection 1: Before You Move On: Make Inferences	CA CC.3.Rinf.6	Distinguish their own point of view from that of the author of a text.
187	**Selection 1:** Before You Move On	CA CC.3.Rinf.1	Ask and answer questions to demonstrate understanding of a text, referring explicitly to the text as the basis for the answers.
	Selection 1: Before You Move On Details	CA CC.3.Rinf.2	Determine the main idea of a text; recount the key details and explain how they support the main idea.
189	**Selection 1:** Before You Move On	CA CC.3.Rinf.1	Ask and answer questions to demonstrate understanding of a text, referring explicitly to the text as the basis for the answers.
	Selection 1: Before You Move On: Make Inferences	CA CC.3.Rinf.4	Determine the meaning of general academic and domain-specific words and phrases in a text relevant to a *grade 3 topic or subject area.* **(See grade 3 Language standards 4–6 for additional expectations.) CA**
	Selection 1: Before You Move On: Make Inferences	CA CC.3.Rinf.6	Distinguish their own point of view from that of the author of a text.
	Selection 1: Before You Move On: Details	CA CC.3.Rinf.2	Determine the main idea of a text; recount the key details and explain how they support the main idea.
191	**Selection 1:** Before You Move On	CA CC.3.Rinf.1	Ask and answer questions to demonstrate understanding of a text, referring explicitly to the text as the basis for the answers.
	Selection 1: Before You Move On: Details	CA CC.3.Rinf.2	Determine the main idea of a text; recount the key details and explain how they support the main idea.
193	**Selection 1:** Before You Move On	CA CC.3.Rinf.1	Ask and answer questions to demonstrate understanding of a text, referring explicitly to the text as the basis for the answers.
	Selection 1: Before You Move On: Details	CA CC.3.Rinf.2	Determine the main idea of a text; recount the key details and explain how they support the main idea.

SE Pages	Lesson	Code	Standard
	Selection 1: Before You Move On: Paraphrase	CA CC.3.Rinf.3	Describe the relationship between a series of historical events, scientific ideas or concepts, or steps in technical procedures in a text, using language that pertains to time, sequence, and cause/effect.
194	**Think and Respond:** Talk About It	CA CC.3.Rinf.10	By the end of the year, read and comprehend informational texts, including history/social studies, science, and technical texts, at the high end of the grades 2–3 text complexity band independently and proficiently.
	Think and Respond: Write About It	CA CC.3.W.10	Write routinely over extended time frames (time for research, reflection, and revision) and shorter time frames (a single sitting or a day or two) for a range of discipline-specific tasks, purposes, and audiences.
195	**Reread and Summarize:** Main Idea and Details	CA CC.3.Rinf.2	Determine the main idea of a text; recount the key details and explain how they support the main idea.
		CA CC.3.L.6	Acquire and use accurately grade-appropriate conversational, general academic, and domain-specific words and phrases, including those that signal spatial and temporal relationships (e.g., *After dinner that night we went looking for them*).
	Reread and Summarize: Fluency		Read with sufficient accuracy and fluency to support comprehension.
		CA CC.3.Rfou.4.b	Read on-level prose and poetry orally with accuracy, appropriate rate, and expression on successive readings.
	Reread and Summarize: Talk Together	CA CC.3.Rinf.7	Use information gained from illustrations (e.g., maps, photographs) and the words in a text to demonstrate understanding of the text (e.g., where, when, why, and how key events occur).
			Engage effectively in a range of collaborative discussions (one-on-one, in groups, and teacher-led) with diverse partners on *grade 3 topics and texts,* building on others' ideas and expressing their own clearly.
		CA CC.3.SL.1.a	Come to discussions prepared, having read or studied required material; explicitly draw on that preparation and other information known about the topic to explore ideas under discussion.
196	**Word Work:** Suffixes		Determine or clarify the meaning of unknown and multiple-meaning word and phrases based on *grade 3 reading and content,* choosing flexibly from a range of strategies.
		CA CC.3.L.4.b	Determine the meaning of the new word formed when a known affix is added to a known word (e.g., *agreeable/disagreeable, comfortable/uncomfortable, care/careless, heat/preheat*).
197	**Selection 2 Opener:** Before You Move On	CA CC.3.Rinf.1	Ask and answer questions to demonstrate understanding of a text, referring explicitly to the text as the basis for the answers.
199	**Selection 2 Opener:** Before You Move On	CA CC.3.Rinf.1	Ask and answer questions to demonstrate understanding of a text, referring explicitly to the text as the basis for the answers.
	Selection 2 Opener: Before You Move On: Make Inferences	CA CC.3.Rinf.4	Determine the meaning of general academic and domain-specific words and phrases in a text relevant to a *grade 3 topic or subject area.* **(See grade 3 Language standards 4–6 for additional expectations.) CA**

California Common Core State Standards, continued

SE Pages	Lesson	Code	Standard
	Selection 2 Opener: Before You Move On: Steps in a Process	CA CC.3.Rinf.3	Describe the relationship between a series of historical events, scientific ideas or concepts, or steps in technical procedures in a text, using language that pertains to time, sequence, and cause/effect.
	Selection 2 Opener: Before You Move On: Steps in a Process	CA CC.3.Rinf.8	Describe the logical connection between particular sentences and paragraphs in a text (e.g., comparison, cause/effect, first/second/third in a sequence).
200	**Respond and Extend:** Compare Text Features	CA CC.3.Rinf.5	Use text features and search tools (e.g., key words, sidebars, hyperlinks) to locate information relevant to a given topic efficiently.
		CA CC.3.Rinf.9	Compare and contrast the most important points and key details presented in two texts on the same topic.
	Respond and Extend: Talk Together		Engage effectively in a range of collaborative discussions (one-on-one, in groups, and teacher-led) with diverse partners on *grade 3 topics and texts,* building on others' ideas and expressing their own clearly.
		CA CC.3.SL.1.a	Come to discussions prepared, having read or studied required material; explicitly draw on that preparation and other information known about the topic to explore ideas under discussion.
		CA CC.3.L.6	Acquire and use accurately grade-appropriate conversational, general academic, and domain-specific words and phrases, including those that signal spatial and temporal relationships (e.g., *After dinner that night we went looking for them*).
201	**Grammar and Spelling:** More Plural Nouns	CA CC.3.L.1	Demonstrate command of the conventions of standard English grammar and usage when writing or speaking.
		CA CC.3.L.1.a	Explain the function of nouns, pronouns, verbs, adjectives, and adverbs in general and their functions in particular sentences.
		CA CC.3.L.1.b	Form and use regular and irregular plural nouns.
203	**Writing Project:** Article Study a Model Prewrite Draft	CA CC.3.W.2	Write informative/explanatory texts to examine a topic and convey ideas and information clearly.
		CA CC.3.W.2.a	Introduce a topic and group related information together; include illustrations when useful to aiding comprehension.
		CA CC.3.W.2.b	Develop the topic with facts, definitions, and details.
204	**Writing Project:** Revise	CA CC.3.W.4	With guidance and support from adults, produce writing in which the development and organization are appropriate to task and purpose. (Grade-specific expectations for writing types are defined in standards 1–3 above.)
		CA CC.3.W.5	With guidance and support from peers and adults, develop and strengthen writing as needed by planning, revising, and editing. (Editing for conventions should demonstrate command of Language standards 1–3 up to and including grade 3.)

SE Pages	Lesson	Code	Standard
		CA CC.3.W.5	With guidance and support from peers and adults, develop and strengthen writing as needed by planning, revising, and editing. (Editing for conventions should demonstrate command of Language standards 1–3 up to and including grade 3.)
		CA CC.3.L.2	Demonstrate command of the conventions of standard English capitalization, punctuation, and spelling when writing.
		CA CC.3.L.2.f	Use spelling patterns and generalizations (e.g., word families, position-based spellings, syllable patterns, ending rules, meaningful word parts) in writing words.
	Writing Project: Publish	CA CC.3.W.6	With guidance and support from adults, use technology to produce and publish writing (using keyboarding skills) as well as to interact and collaborate with others.
206	**Talk Together** **Write a Journal Entry**	CA CC.3.W.10	Write routinely over extended time frames (time for research, reflection, and revision) and shorter time frames (a single sitting or a day or two) for a range of discipline-specific tasks, purposes, and audiences.
			Engage effectively in a range of collaborative discussions (one-on-one, in groups, and teacher-led) with diverse partners on *grade 3 topics and texts,* building on others' ideas and expressing their own clearly.
		CA CC.3.SL.1.a	Come to discussions prepared, having read or studied required material; explicitly draw on that preparation and other information known about the topic to explore ideas under discussion.
		CA CC.3.SL.1.d	Explain their own ideas and understanding in light of the discussion.
207	**Unit Wrap-Up:** Share Your Ideas	CA CC.3.W.10	Write routinely over extended time frames (time for research, reflection, and revision) and shorter time frames (a single sitting or a day or two) for a range of discipline-specific tasks, purposes, and audiences.
		CA CC.3.SL.1	Engage effectively in a range of collaborative discussions (one-on-one, in groups, and teacher-led) with diverse partners on *grade 3 topics and texts,* building on others' ideas and expressing their own clearly.
		CA CC.3.SL.1.a	Come to discussions prepared, having read or studied required material; explicitly draw on that preparation and other information known about the topic to explore ideas under discussion.
		CA CC.3.SL.1.b	Follow agreed-upon rules for discussions (e.g., gaining the floor in respectful ways, listening to others with care, speaking one at a time about the topics and texts under discussion).
		CA CC.3.SL.1.d	Explain their own ideas and understanding in light of the discussion.
		CA CC.3.SL.4	Report on a topic or text, tell a story, or recount an experience with appropriate facts and relevant, descriptive details, speaking clearly at an understandable pace.

California Common Core State Standards, continued

SE Pages	Lesson	Code	Standard
223	**Selection 1:** Before You Move On	CA CC.3.Rlit.1	Ask and answer questions to demonstrate understanding of a text, referring explicitly to the text as the basis for the answers.
	Selection 1: Before You Move On: Make Inferences	CA CC.3.Rlit.3	Describe characters in a story (e.g., their traits, motivations, or feelings) and explain how their actions contribute to the sequence of events.
	Selection 1: Before You Move On: Point of View	CA CC.3.Rlit.6	Distinguish their own point of view from that of the narrator or those of the characters.
224	**Selection 1:** Predict	CA CC.3.Rlit.1	Ask and answer questions to demonstrate understanding of a text, referring explicitly to the text as the basis for the answers.
		CA CC.3.Rlit.3	Describe characters in a story (e.g., their traits, motivations, or feelings) and explain how their actions contribute to the sequence of events.
227	**Selection 1:** Before You Move On	CA CC.3.Rlit.1	Ask and answer questions to demonstrate understanding of a text, referring explicitly to the text as the basis for the answers.
228	**Selection 1:** Set a Purpose	CA CC.3.Rlit.1	Ask and answer questions to demonstrate understanding of a text, referring explicitly to the text as the basis for the answers.
		CA CC.3.Rlit.3	Describe characters in a story (e.g., their traits, motivations, or feelings) and explain how their actions contribute to the sequence of events.
230	**Selection 1:** Before You Move On	CA CC.3.Rlit.1	Ask and answer questions to demonstrate understanding of a text, referring explicitly to the text as the basis for the answers.
	Selection 1: Before You Move On: Theme	CA CC.3.Rlit.2	Recount stories, including fables, folktales, and myths from diverse cultures; determine the central message, lesson, or moral and explain how it is conveyed through key details in the text.
231	**Meet the Illustrator** **Writer's Craft**	CA CC.3.W.10	Write routinely over extended time frames (time for research, reflection, and revision) and shorter time frames (a single sitting or a day or two) for a range of discipline-specific tasks, purposes, and audiences.
232	**Think and Respond:** Talk About It	CA CC.3.Rlit.3	Describe characters in a story (e.g., their traits, motivations, or feelings) and explain how their actions contribute to the sequence of events.
		CA CC.3.Rlit.5	Refer to parts of stories, dramas, and poems when writing or speaking about a text, using terms such as chapter, scene, and stanza; describe how each successive part builds on earlier sections.
		CA CC.3.Rlit.10	By the end of the year, read and comprehend literature, including stories, dramas, and poetry, at the high end of the grades 2–3 text complexity band independently and proficiently.
		CA CC.3.L.6	Acquire and use accurately grade-appropriate conversational, general academic, and domain-specific words and phrases, including those that signal spatial and temporal relationships (e.g., *After dinner that night we went looking for them*).
	Think and Respond: Write About It	CA CC.3.W.10	Write routinely over extended time frames (time for research, reflection, and revision) and shorter time frames (a single sitting or a day or two) for a range of discipline-specific tasks, purposes, and audiences.

California Common Core State Standards, continued

SE Pages	Lesson	Code	Standard
233	**Reread and Paraphrase** Theme	CA CC.3.Rlit.2	Recount stories, including fables, folktales, and myths from diverse cultures; determine the central message, lesson, or moral and explain how it is conveyed through key details in the text.
	Reread and Paraphrase Fluency	CA CC.3.Rfou.4	Read with sufficient accuracy and fluency to support comprehension.
		CA CC.3.Rfou.4.b	Read on-level prose and poetry orally with accuracy, appropriate rate, and expression on successive readings.
	Reread and Paraphrase Talk Together		Engage effectively in a range of collaborative discussions (one-on-one, in groups, and teacher-led) with diverse partners on *grade 3 topics and texts,* building on others' ideas and expressing their own clearly.
		CA CC.3.SL.1.a	Come to discussions prepared, having read or studied required material; explicitly draw on that preparation and other information known about the topic to explore ideas under discussion.
		CA CC.3.L.6	Acquire and use accurately grade-appropriate conversational, general academic, and domain-specific words and phrases, including those that signal spatial and temporal relationships (e.g., *After dinner that night we went looking for them*).
234	**Word Work:** Prefixes	CA CC.3.L.4.b	Determine the meaning of the new word formed when a known affix is added to a known word (e.g., *agreeable/disagreeable, comfortable/uncomfortable, care/careless, heat/preheat*).
235	**Selection 2:** Before You Move On	CA CC.3.Rlit.1	Ask and answer questions to demonstrate understanding of a text, referring explicitly to the text as the basis for the answers.
	Selection 2: Before You Move On: Point of View	CA CC.3.Rlit.6	Distinguish their own point of view from that of the narrator or those of the characters.
	Selection 2: Before You Move On: Clarify	CA CC.3.Rlit.4	Determine the meaning of words and phrases as they are used in a text, distinguishing literal from nonliteral language. **(See grade 3 Language standards 4–6 for additional expectations.) CA**
237	**Selection 2:** Before You Move On	CA CC.3.Rlit.1	Ask and answer questions to demonstrate understanding of a text, referring explicitly to the text as the basis for the answers.
	Selection 2: Before You Move On: **Theme**	CA CC.3.Rlit.2	Recount stories, including fables, folktales, and myths from diverse cultures; determine the central message, lesson, or moral and explain how it is conveyed through key details in the text.
238	**Respond and Extend:** Compare Characters	CA CC.3.Rlit.3	Describe characters in a story (e.g., their traits, motivations, or feelings) and explain how their actions contribute to the sequence of events.
		CA CC.3.Rlit.10	By the end of the year, read and comprehend literature, including stories, dramas, and poetry, at the high end of the grades 2–3 text complexity band independently and proficiently.
		CA CC.3.SL.1	Engage effectively in a range of collaborative discussions (one-on-one, in groups, and teacher-led) with diverse partners on *grade 3 topics and texts,* building on others' ideas and expressing their own clearly.
		CA CC.3.SL.1.a	Come to discussions prepared, having read or studied required material; explicitly draw on that preparation and other information known about the topic to explore ideas under discussion.

SE Pages	Lesson	Code	Standard
		CA CC.3.L.6	Acquire and use accurately grade-appropriate conversational, general academic, and domain-specific words and phrases, including those that signal spatial and temporal relationships (e.g., *After dinner that night we went looking for them*).
239	**Grammar and Spelling:** Present-Tense Action Verbs	CA CC.3.W.10	Write routinely over extended time frames (time for research, reflection, and revision) and shorter time frames (a single sitting or a day or two) for a range of discipline-specific tasks, purposes, and audiences.
		CA CC.3.L.1	Demonstrate command of the conventions of standard English grammar and usage when writing or speaking.
		CA CC.3.L.1.a	Explain the function of nouns, pronouns, verbs, adjectives, and adverbs in general and their functions in particular sentences.
		CA CC.3.L.1.d	Form and use regular and irregular verbs.
		CA CC.3.L.1.e	Form and use the simple (e.g., *I walked; I walk; I will walk*) verb tenses.
240	**Part 2:** Language: Persuade		Engage effectively in a range of collaborative discussions (one-on-one, in groups, and teacher-led) with diverse partners on *grade 3 topics and texts*, building on others' ideas and expressing their own clearly.
		CA CC.3.SL.1.d	Explain their own ideas and understanding in light of the discussion.
		CA CC.3.SL.3	Ask and answer questions about information from a speaker, offering appropriate elaboration and detail.
241	**Social Studies Vocabulary:** Key Words	CA CC.3.Rinf.4	Determine the meaning of general academic and domain-specific words and phrases in a text relevant to a *grade 3 topic or subject area*. **(See grade 3 Language standards 4–6 for additional expectations.) CA**
			Demonstrate command of the conventions of standard English grammar and usage when writing or speaking.
		CA CC.3.L.6	Acquire and use accurately grade-appropriate conversational, general academic, and domain-specific words and phrases, including those that signal spatial and temporal relationships (e.g., *After dinner that night we went looking for them*).
			Engage effectively in a range of collaborative discussions (one-on-one, in groups, and teacher-led) with diverse partners on *grade 3 topics and texts*, building on others' ideas and expressing their own clearly.
242	**Thinking Map:** Opinion and Evidence	CA CC.3.Rinf.2	Determine the main idea of a text; recount the key details and explain how they support the main idea.
243	**Academic Vocabulary:** More Key Words	CA CC.3.Rinf.4	Determine the meaning of general academic and domain-specific words and phrases in a text relevant to a *grade 3 topic or subject area. (See grade 3 Language standards 4–6 for additional expectations.) CA*
			Demonstrate command of the conventions of standard English grammar and usage when writing or speaking.

California Common Core State Standards, continued

SE Pages	Lesson	Code	Standard
		CA CC.3.L.6	Acquire and use accurately grade-appropriate conversational, general academic, and domain-specific words and phrases, including those that signal spatial and temporal relationships (e.g., *After dinner that night we went looking for them*).
244	**Strategic Reading:** Learn to Determine Importance	CA CC.3.Rinf.1	Ask and answer questions to demonstrate understanding of a text, referring explicitly to the text as the basis for the answers.
		CA CC.3.Rinf.2	Determine the main idea of a text; recount the key details and explain how they support the main idea.
248	**Selection 1:** Set a Purpose	CA CC.3.Rfou.4	Read with sufficient accuracy and fluency to support comprehension.
		CA CC.3.Rfou.4.a	Read on-level text with purpose and understanding.
249	**Selection 1:** Before You Move On	CA CC.3.Rinf.1	Ask and answer questions to demonstrate understanding of a text, referring explicitly to the text as the basis for the answers.
	Selection 1: Before You Move On: Summarize	CA CC.3.Rinf.2	Determine the main idea of a text; recount the key details and explain how they support the main idea.
	Selection 1: Before You Move On: Steps in a Process	CA CC.3.Rinf.3	Describe the relationship between a series of historical events, scientific ideas or concepts, or steps in technical procedures in a text, using language that pertains to time, sequence, and cause/effect.
	Selection 1: Before You Move On: Steps in a Process	CA CC.3.Rinf.8	Describe the logical connection between particular sentences and paragraphs in a text (e.g., comparison, cause/effect, first/second/third in a sequence).
251	**Selection 1:** Before You Move On	CA CC.3.Rinf.1	Ask and answer questions to demonstrate understanding of a text, referring explicitly to the text as the basis for the answers.
	Selection 1: Before You Move On Use Text Features	CA CC.3.Rinf.5	Use text features and search tools (e.g., key words, sidebars, hyperlinks) to locate information relevant to a given topic efficiently.
	Selection 1: Before You Move On Summarize	CA CC.3.Rinf.2	Determine the main idea of a text; recount the key details and explain how they support the main idea.
253	**Selection 1:** Before You Move On	CA CC.3.Rinf.1	Ask and answer questions to demonstrate understanding of a text, referring explicitly to the text as the basis for the answers.
	Selection 1: Before You Move On: Summarize	CA CC.3.Rinf.2	Determine the main idea of a text; recount the key details and explain how they support the main idea.
255	**Selection 1: Before You Move On**	CA CC.3.Rinf.1	Ask and answer questions to demonstrate understanding of a text, referring explicitly to the text as the basis for the answers.
	Selection 1: Before You Move On: Opinion/Evidence	CA CC.3.Rinf.4	Determine the meaning of general academic and domain-specific words and phrases in a text relevant to a *grade 3 topic or subject area.* **(See grade 3 Language standards 4–6 for additional expectations.) CA**
	Selection 1: Before You Move On: Use Text Features	CA CC.3.Rinf.7	Use information gained from illustrations (e.g., maps, photographs) and the words in a text to demonstrate understanding of the text (e.g., where, when, why, and how key events occur).

SE Pages	Lesson	Code	Standard
257	**Selection 1:** Before You Move On	CA CC.3.Rinf.1	Ask and answer questions to demonstrate understanding of a text, referring explicitly to the text as the basis for the answers.
	Selection 1: Before You Move On: Author's Purpose	CA CC.3.Rinf.6	Distinguish their own point of view from that of the author of a text.
	Selection 1: Before You Move On: Cause and Effect	CA CC.3.Rinf.3	Describe the relationship between a series of historical events, scientific ideas or concepts, or steps in technical procedures in a text, using language that pertains to time, sequence, and cause/effect.
	Selection 1: Before You Move On: Cause and Effect	CA CC.3.Rinf.8	Describe the logical connection between particular sentences and paragraphs in a text (e.g., comparison, cause/effect, first/second third in a sequence).
258	**Think and Respond:** Talk About It	CA CC.3.Rinf.10	By the end of the year, read and comprehend informational texts, including history/social studies, science, and technical texts, at the high end of the grades 2–3 text complexity band independently and proficiently.
			Engage effectively in a range of collaborative discussions (one-on-one, in groups, and teacher-led) with diverse partners on *grade 3 topics and texts*, building on others' ideas and expressing their own clearly.
	Think and Respond: Write About It	CA CC.3.W.10	10. Write routinely over extended time frames (time for research, reflection, and revision) and shorter time frames (a single sitting or a day or two) for a range of discipline-specific tasks, purposes, and audiences.
259	**Reread and Explain** Opinion and Evidence	CA CC.3.Rinf.10	By the end of the year, read and comprehend informational texts, including history/social studies, science, and technical texts, at the high end of the grades 2–3 text complexity band independently and proficiently.
	Reread and Explain Fluency		Read with sufficient accuracy and fluency to support comprehension.
		CA CC.3.Rfou.4.b	Read on-level prose and poetry orally with accuracy, appropriate rate, and expression on successive readings
	Reread and Explain Talk Together	CA CC.3.SL.1	Engage effectively in a range of collaborative discussions (one-on-one, in groups, and teacher-led) with diverse partners on *grade 3 topics and texts*, building on others' ideas and expressing their own clearly.
		CA CC.3.SL.1.d	Explain their own ideas and understanding in light of the discussion.
		CA CC.3.SL.4.a	Plan and deliver an informative/explanatory presentation on a topic that: organizes ideas around major points of information, follows a logical sequence, includes supporting details, uses clear and specific vocabulary, and provides a strong conclusion. CA
		CA CC.3.L.6	Acquire and use accurately grade-appropriate conversational, general academic, and domain-specific words and phrases, including those that signal spatial and temporal relationships (e.g., *After dinner that night we went looking for them*).

681

California Common Core State Standards, continued

SE Pages	Lesson	Code	Standard
260	**Word Work:** Classify Words	CA CC.3.L.5	Demonstrate understanding of word relationships and nuances in word meanings.
		CA CC.3.L.6	Acquire and use accurately grade-appropriate conversational, general academic, and domain-specific words and phrases, including those that signal spatial and temporal relationships (e.g., *After dinner that night we went looking for them*).
261	**Selection 2 Opener:** Before You Move On	CA CC.3.Rlit.1	Ask and answer questions to demonstrate understanding of a text, referring explicitly to the text as the basis for the answers.
	Selection 2 Opener: Before You Move On: Set Purpose/Clarify		Read with sufficient accuracy and fluency to support comprehension.
		CA CC.3.Rfou.4.c	Use context to confirm or self-correct word recognition and understanding, rereading as necessary.
	Selection 2 Opener: Before You Move On: Character	CA CC.3.Rlit.3	Describe characters in a story (e.g., their traits, motivations, or feelings) and explain how their actions contribute to the sequence of events.
263	**Selection 2 Opener:** Before You Move On	CA CC.3.Rlit.1	Ask and answer questions to demonstrate understanding of a text, referring explicitly to the text as the basis for the answers.
	Selection 2 Opener: Before You Move On: Summarize	CA CC.3.Rlit.2	Recount stories, including fables, folktales, and myths from diverse cultures; determine the central message, lesson, or moral and explain how it is conveyed through key details in the text.
	Selection 2 Opener: Before You Move On: Character	CA CC.3.Rlit.3	Describe characters in a story (e.g., their traits, motivations, or feelings) and explain how their actions contribute to the sequence of events.
265	**Selection 2:** Before You Move On	CA CC.3.Rlit.1	Ask and answer questions to demonstrate understanding of a text, referring explicitly to the text as the basis for the answers.
	Selection 2: Before You Move On: Character	CA CC.3.Rlit.3	Describe characters in a story (e.g., their traits, motivations, or feelings) and explain how their actions contribute to the sequence of events.
	Selection 2: Before You Move On: Theme	CA CC.3.Rlit.2	Recount stories, including fables, folktales, and myths from diverse cultures; determine the central message, lesson, or moral and explain how it is conveyed through key details in the text.
266	**Respond and Extend:** Compare Purposes	CA CC.3.Rlit.10	By the end of the year, read and comprehend literature, including stories, dramas, and poetry, at the high end of the grades 2–3 text complexity band independently and proficiently.
	Respond and Extend: Talk Together	CA CC.3.SL.1	Engage effectively in a range of collaborative discussions (one-on-one, in groups, and teacher-led) with diverse partners on *grade 3 topics and texts*, building on others' ideas and expressing their own clearly.
		CA CC.3.SL.1.a	Come to discussions prepared, having read or studied required material; explicitly draw on that preparation and other information known about the topic to explore ideas under discussion.
		CA CC.3.SL.1.d	Explain their own ideas and understanding in light of the discussion.

SE Pages	Lesson	Code	Standard
		CA CC.3.L.6	Acquire and use accurately grade-appropriate conversational, general academic, and domain-specific words and phrases, including those that signal spatial and temporal relationships (e.g., *After dinner that night we went looking for them*).
267	**Grammar:** Forms of *be, have*	CA CC.3.L.1	Demonstrate command of the conventions of standard English grammar and usage when writing or speaking.
			Explain the function of nouns, pronouns, verbs, adjectives, and adverbs in general and their functions in particular sentences.
		CA CC.3.L.1.d	Form and use regular and irregular verbs.
		CA CC.3.L.1.e	Form and use the simple (e.g., *I walked; I walk; I will walk*) verb tenses.
268–269	**Writing Project:** Persuasive Essay Study a Model Prewrite Draft	CA CC.3.W.1	Write opinion pieces on topics or texts, supporting a point of view with reasons.
		CA CC.3.W.1.a	Introduce the topic or text they are writing about, state an opinion, and create an organizational structure that lists reasons.
		CA CC.3.W.1.b	Provide reasons that support the opinion.
		CA CC.3.W.1.d	Provide a concluding statement or section.
270	**Writing Project:** Revise	CA CC.3.W.4	With guidance and support from adults, produce writing in which the development and organization are appropriate to task and purpose. (Grade-specific expectations for writing types are defined in standards 1–3 above.)
		CA CC.3.W.5	With guidance and support from peers and adults, develop and strengthen writing as needed by planning, revising, and editing. (Editing for conventions should demonstrate command of Language standards 1–3 up to and including grade 3.)
271	**Writing Project:** Edit and Proofread	CA CC.3.W.4	With guidance and support from adults, produce writing in which the development and organization are appropriate to task and purpose. (Grade-specific expectations for writing types are defined in standards 1–3 above.)
		CA CC.3.W.5	With guidance and support from peers and adults, develop and strengthen writing as needed by planning, revising, and editing. (Editing for conventions should demonstrate command of Language standards 1–3 up to and including grade 3.)
271	**Writing Project:** Publish	CA CC.3.W.6	With guidance and support from adults, use technology to produce and publish writing (using keyboarding skills) as well as to interact and collaborate with others.
272	**Talk Together** **Write a Description**	CA CC.3.W.10	Write routinely over extended time frames (time for research, reflection, and revision) and shorter time frames (a single sitting or a day or two) for a range of discipline-specific tasks, purposes, and audiences.
			Engage effectively in a range of collaborative discussions (one-on-one, in groups, and teacher-led) with diverse partners on *grade 3 topics and texts*, building on others' ideas and expressing their own clearly.

California Common Core State Standards, continued

SE Pages	Lesson	Code	Standard
285	**Selection 1:** Before You Move On	CA CC.3.Rlit.1	Ask and answer questions to demonstrate understanding of a text, referring explicitly to the text as the basis for the answers.
	Selection 1: Before You Move On: Drama	CA CC.3.Rlit.5	Refer to parts of stories, dramas, and poems when writing or speaking about a text, using terms such as chapter, scene, and stanza; describe how each successive part builds on earlier sections.
	Selection 1: Before You Move On: Make Connections	CA CC.3.Rlit.3	Describe characters in a story (e.g., their traits, motivations, or feelings) and explain how their actions contribute to the sequence of events.
		CA CC.3.SL.4	Report on a topic or text, tell a story, or recount an experience with appropriate facts and relevant, descriptive details, speaking clearly at an understandable pace.
		CA CC.3.SL.4.a	Plan and deliver an informative/explanatory presentation on a topic that: organizes ideas around major points of information, follows a logical sequence, includes supporting details, uses clear and specific vocabulary, and provides a strong conclusion. CA
286	**Selection 1:** Predict	CA CC.3.Rlit.1	Ask and answer questions to demonstrate understanding of a text, referring explicitly to the text as the basis for the answers.
		CA CC.3.Rlit.3	Describe characters in a story (e.g., their traits, motivations, or feelings) and explain how their actions contribute to the sequence of events.
291	**Selection 1:** Before You Move On	CA CC.3.Rlit.1	Ask and answer questions to demonstrate understanding of a text, referring explicitly to the text as the basis for the answers.
		CA CC.3.Rlit.3	Describe characters in a story (e.g., their traits, motivations, or feelings) and explain how their actions contribute to the sequence of events.
	Selection 1: Before You Move On: Cause/Effect	CA CC.3.Rlit.5	Refer to parts of stories, dramas, and poems when writing or speaking about a text, using terms such as chapter, scene, and stanza; describe how each successive part builds on earlier sections.
292	**Selection 1:** Predict	CA CC.3.Rlit.1	Ask and answer questions to demonstrate understanding of a text, referring explicitly to the text as the basis for the answers.
		CA CC.3.Rlit.3	Describe characters in a story (e.g., their traits, motivations, or feelings) and explain how their actions contribute to the sequence of events.
		CA CC.3.Rlit.5	Refer to parts of stories, dramas, and poems when writing or speaking about a text, using terms such as chapter, scene, and stanza; describe how each successive part builds on earlier sections.
296	**Selection 1:** Before You Move On	CA CC.3.Rlit.1	Ask and answer questions to demonstrate understanding of a text, referring explicitly to the text as the basis for the answers.
	Selection 1: Before You Move On: Drama	CA CC.3.Rlit.3	Describe characters in a story (e.g., their traits, motivations, or feelings) and explain how their actions contribute to the sequence of events.
		CA CC.3.Rlit.5	Refer to parts of stories, dramas, and poems when writing or speaking about a text, using terms such as chapter, scene, and stanza; describe how each successive part builds on earlier sections.

California Common Core State Standards, continued

SE Pages	Lesson	Code	Standard
297	**Meet the Author:** Writer's Craft	CA CC.3.W.3.b	Use dialogue and descriptions of actions, thoughts, and feelings to develop experiences and events or show the response of characters to situations.
298	**Think and Respond:** Talk About It	CA CC.3.Rlit.3	Describe characters in a story (e.g., their traits, motivations, or feelings) and explain how their actions contribute to the sequence of events.
		CA CC.3.Rlit.5	Refer to parts of stories, dramas, and poems when writing or speaking about a text, using terms such as chapter, scene, and stanza; describe how each successive part builds on earlier sections.
		CA CC.3.Rlit.10	By the end of the year, read and comprehend literature, including stories, dramas, and poetry, at the high end of the grades 2–3 text complexity band independently and proficiently.
		CA CC.3.L.6	Acquire and use accurately grade-appropriate conversational, general academic, and domain-specific words and phrases, including those that signal spatial and temporal relationships (e.g., *After dinner that night we went looking for them*).
	Think and Respond: Write About It	CA CC.3.W.10	Write routinely over extended time frames (time for research, reflection, and revision) and shorter time frames (a single sitting or a day or two) for a range of discipline-specific tasks, purposes, and audiences.
299	**Reread and Explain** Character and Plot	CA CC.3.Rlit.3	Describe characters in a story (e.g., their traits, motivations, or feelings) and explain how their actions contribute to the sequence of events.
		CA CC.3.Rlit.10	By the end of the year, read and comprehend literature, including stories, dramas, and poetry, at the high end of the grades 2–3 text complexity band independently and proficiently.
		CA CC.3.L.6	Acquire and use accurately grade-appropriate conversational, general academic, and domain-specific words and phrases, including those that signal spatial and temporal relationships (e.g., *After dinner that night we went looking for them*).
	Reread and Explain Fluency	CA CC.3.Rfou.4	Read with sufficient accuracy and fluency to support comprehension.
		CA CC.3.Rfou.4.b	Read on-level prose and poetry orally with accuracy, appropriate rate, and expression on successive readings.
	Reread and Explain Talk Together	CA CC.3.SL.1	Engage effectively in a range of collaborative discussions (one-on-one, in groups, and teacher-led) with diverse partners on *grade 3 topics and texts*, building on others' ideas and expressing their own clearly.
		CA CC.3.SL.1.a	Come to discussions prepared, having read or studied required material; explicitly draw on that preparation and other information known about the topic to explore ideas under discussion.
300	**Word Work:** Antonyms	CA CC.3.L.5	Demonstrate understanding of word relationships and nuances in word meanings.
301	**Selection 2:** Before You Move On	CA CC.3.Rinf.1	Ask and answer questions to demonstrate understanding of a text, referring explicitly to the text as the basis for the answers.

SE Pages	Lesson	Code	Standard
	Selection 2: Before You Move On: Make Connections	CA CC.3.Rinf.5	Use text features and search tools (e.g., key words, sidebars, hyperlinks) to locate information relevant to a given topic efficiently.
		CA CC.3.Rinf.7	Use information gained from illustrations (e.g., maps, photographs) and the words in a text to demonstrate understanding of the text (e.g., where, when, why, and how key events occur).
303	**Selection 2:** Before You Move On	CA CC.3.Rinf.1	Ask and answer questions to demonstrate understanding of a text, referring explicitly to the text as the basis for the answers.
	Selection 2: Before You Move On: Media	CA CC.3.Rinf.2	Determine the main idea of a text; recount the key details and explain how they support the main idea.
305	**Selection 2:** Before You Move On	CA CC.3.Rinf.1	Ask and answer questions to demonstrate understanding of a text, referring explicitly to the text as the basis for the answers.
	Selection 2: Before You Move On: Details	CA CC.3.Rinf.2	Determine the main idea of a text; recount the key details and explain how they support the main idea.
306	**Respond and Extend:** Compare Media	CA CC.3.Rinf.9	Compare and contrast the most important points and key details presented in two texts on the same topic.
		CA CC.3.SL.1	Engage effectively in a range of collaborative discussions (one-on-one, in groups, and teacher-led) with diverse partners on *grade 3 topics and texts,* building on others' ideas and expressing their own clearly.
		CA CC.3.SL.1.d	Explain their own ideas and understanding in light of the discussion.
		CA CC.3.SL.4	Report on a topic or text, tell a story, or recount an experience with appropriate facts and relevant, descriptive details, speaking clearly at an understandable pace.
		CA CC.3.SL.4.a	Plan and deliver an informative/explanatory presentation on a topic that: organizes ideas around major points of information, follows a logical sequence, includes supporting details, uses clear and specific vocabulary, and provides a strong conclusion. CA
		CA CC.3.L.6	Acquire and use accurately grade-appropriate conversational, general academic, and domain-specific words and phrases, including those that signal spatial and temporal relationships (e.g., *After dinner that night we went looking for them*).
307	**Grammar and Spelling:** Adjectives and Articles		Demonstrate command of the conventions of standard English grammar and usage when writing or speaking.
		CA CC.3.L.1.a	Explain the function of nouns, pronouns, verbs, adjectives, and adverbs in general and their functions in particular sentences.
		CA CC.3.L.1.g	Form and use comparative and superlative adjectives and adverbs, and choose between them depending on what is to be modified.

California Common Core State Standards, continued

SE Pages	Lesson	Code	Standard
308	**Part 2: Language:** Describe Places	CA CC.3.SL.4	Report on a topic or text, tell a story, or recount an experience with appropriate facts and relevant, descriptive details, speaking clearly at an understandable pace.
309	**Science Vocabulary:** Key Words	CA CC.3.Rinf.4	Determine the meaning of general academic and domain-specific words and phrases in a text relevant to a *grade 3 topic or subject area.* **(See grade 3 Language standards 4–6 for additional expectations.) CA**
		CA CC.3.L.6	Acquire and use accurately grade-appropriate conversational, general academic, and domain-specific words and phrases, including those that signal spatial and temporal relationships (e.g., *After dinner that night we went looking for them*).
			Engage effectively in a range of collaborative discussions (one-on-one, in groups, and teacher-led) with diverse partners on *grade 3 topics and texts,* building on others' ideas and expressing their own clearly.
310	**Thinking Map:** Cause and Effect	CA CC.3.Rinf.3	Describe the relationship between a series of historical events, scientific ideas or concepts, or steps in technical procedures in a text, using language that pertains to time, sequence, and cause/effect.
311	**Academic Vocabulary:** More Key Words	CA CC.3.Rinf.4	Determine the meaning of general academic and domain-specific words and phrases in a text relevant to a *grade 3 topic or subject area.* **(See grade 3 Language standards 4–6 for additional expectations.) CA**
		CA CC.3.L.6	Acquire and use accurately grade-appropriate conversational, general academic, and domain-specific words and phrases, including those that signal spatial and temporal relationships (e.g., *After dinner that night we went looking for them*).
312	**Strategic Reading:** Learn to Make Connections	CA CC.3.Rinf.10	By the end of the year, read and comprehend informational texts, including history/social studies, science, and technical texts, at the high end of the grades 2–3 text complexity band independently and proficiently.
316	**Selection 1:** Set a Purpose	CA CC.3.Rfou.4	Read with sufficient accuracy and fluency to support comprehension.
		CA CC.3.Rfou.4.a	Read on-level text with purpose and understanding.
317	**Selection 1:** Before You Move On: Make Connections	CA CC.3.Rinf.1	Ask and answer questions to demonstrate understanding of a text, referring explicitly to the text as the basis for the answers.
	Selection 1: Before You Move On: Cause/Effect	CA CC.3.Rinf.3	Describe the relationship between a series of historical events, scientific ideas or concepts, or steps in technical procedures in a text, using language that pertains to time, sequence, and cause/effect.
		CA CC.3.Rinf.4	Determine the meaning of general academic and domain-specific words and phrases in a text relevant to a *grade 3 topic or subject area.* **(See grade 3 Language standards 4–6 for additional expectations.) CA**
		CA CC.3.Rinf.8	Describe the logical connection between particular sentences and paragraphs in a text (e.g., comparison, cause/effect, first/second/third in a sequence).

SE Pages	Lesson	Code	Standard
319	**Selection 1:** Before You Move On	CA CC.3.Rinf.1	Ask and answer questions to demonstrate understanding of a text, referring explicitly to the text as the basis for the answers.
	Selection 1: Before You Move On: Cause/Effect	CA CC.3.Rinf.3	Describe the relationship between a series of historical events, scientific ideas or concepts, or steps in technical procedures in a text, using language that pertains to time, sequence, and cause/effect.
		CA CC.3.Rinf.8	Describe the logical connection between particular sentences and paragraphs in a text (e.g., comparison, cause/effect, first/second/third in a sequence).
	Selection 1: Before You Move On: Details	CA CC.3.Rinf.2	Determine the main idea of a text; recount the key details and explain how they support the main idea.
321	**Selection 1:** Before You Move On: Cause/Effect	CA CC.3.Rinf.1	Ask and answer questions to demonstrate understanding of a text, referring explicitly to the text as the basis for the answers.
	Selection 1: Before You Move On: Cause/Effect	CA CC.3.Rinf.3	Describe the relationship between a series of historical events, scientific ideas or concepts, or steps in technical procedures in a text, using language that pertains to time, sequence, and cause/effect.
	Selection 1: Before You Move On: Use Text Features	CA CC.3.Rinf.5	Use text features and search tools (e.g., key words, sidebars, hyperlinks) to locate information relevant to a given topic efficiently.
323	**Selection 1:** Before You Move On	CA CC.3.Rinf.1	Ask and answer questions to demonstrate understanding of a text, referring explicitly to the text as the basis for the answers.
	Selection 1: Before You Move On: Cause/Effect	CA CC.3.Rinf.3	Describe the relationship between a series of historical events, scientific ideas or concepts, or steps in technical procedures in a text, using language that pertains to time, sequence, and cause/effect.
325	**Selection 1:** Before You Move On	CA CC.3.Rinf.1	Ask and answer questions to demonstrate understanding of a text, referring explicitly to the text as the basis for the answers.
	Selection 1: Before You Move On: Explain	CA CC.3.Rinf.9	Compare and contrast the most important points and key details presented in two texts on the same topic.
326	**Think and Respond:** Talk About It	CA CC.3.Rinf.3	Describe the relationship between a series of historical events, scientific ideas or concepts, or steps in technical procedures in a text, using language that pertains to time, sequence, and cause/effect.
		CA CC.3.Rinf.7	Use information gained from illustrations (e.g., maps, photographs) and the words in a text to demonstrate understanding of the text (e.g., where, when, why, and how key events occur).
		CA CC.3.Rinf.10	By the end of the year, read and comprehend informational texts, including history/social studies, science, and technical texts, at the high end of the grades 2–3 text complexity band independently and proficiently.
	Think and Respond: Write About It	CA CC.3.W.10	Write routinely over extended time frames (time for research, reflection, and revision) and shorter time frames (a single sitting or a day or two) for a range of discipline-specific tasks, purposes, and audiences.

California Common Core State Standards, continued

SE Pages	Lesson	Code	Standard
		CA CC.3.L.6	Acquire and use accurately grade-appropriate conversational, general academic, and domain-specific words and phrases, including those that signal spatial and temporal relationships (e.g., *After dinner that night we went looking for them*).
327	**Reread and Summarize** Cause and Effect	CA CC.3.Rinf.3	Describe the relationship between a series of historical events, scientific ideas or concepts, or steps in technical procedures in a text, using language that pertains to time, sequence, and cause/effect.
		CA CC.3.W.10	
	Reread and Summarize Fluency	CA CC.3.Rfou.4	Read with sufficient accuracy and fluency to support comprehension.
		CA CC.3.Rfou.4.b	Read on-level prose and poetry orally with accuracy, appropriate rate, and expression on successive readings.
	Reread and Summarize Talk Together	CA CC.3.SL.1	Engage effectively in a range of collaborative discussions (one-on-one, in groups, and teacher- led) with diverse partners on *grade 3 topics and texts,* building on others' ideas and expressing their own clearly.
		CA CC.3.SL.1.a	Come to discussions prepared, having read or studied required material; explicitly draw on that preparation and other information known about the topic to explore ideas under discussion.
		CA CC.3.L.6	Acquire and use accurately grade-appropriate conversational, general academic, and domain-specific words and phrases, including those that signal spatial and temporal relationships (e.g., *After dinner that night we went looking for them*).
328	**Word Work:** Synonyms	CA CC.3.L4	Determine or clarify the meaning of unknown and multiple-meaning word and phrases based on *grade 3 reading and content*, choosing flexibly from a range of strategies.
		CA CC.3.L.4.a	Use sentence-level context as a clue to the meaning of a word or phrase.
		CA CC.3.L.5	Demonstrate understanding of word relationships and nuances in word meanings.
		CA CC.3.L.5.c	Distinguish shades of meaning among related words that describe states of mind or degrees of certainty (e.g., *knew, believed, suspected, heard, wondered*).
329	**Selection 2 Opener:** Before You Move On	CA CC.3.Rinf.1	Ask and answer questions to demonstrate understanding of a text, referring explicitly to the text as the basis for the answers.
	Selection 2 Opener: Before You Move On: Visualize	CA CC.3.Rinf.4	Determine the meaning of general academic and domain-specific words and phrases in a text relevant to a *grade 3 topic or subject area*. **(See grade 3 Language standards 4–6 for additional expectations.) CA**
	Selection 2 Opener: Before You Move On: Make Inferences	CA CC.3.Rinf.6	Distinguish their own point of view from that of the author of a text.
331	**Selection 2 Opener:** Before You Move On	CA CC.3.Rinf.1	Ask and answer questions to demonstrate understanding of a text, referring explicitly to the text as the basis for the answers.

SE Pages	Lesson	Code	Standard
	Selection 2 Opener: Before You Move On: Cause/Effect	CA CC.3.Rinf.3	Describe the relationship between a series of historical events, scientific ideas or concepts, or steps in technical procedures in a text, using language that pertains to time, sequence, and cause/effect.
		CA CC.3.Rinf.4	Determine the meaning of general academic and domain-specific words and phrases in a text relevant to a *grade 3 topic or subject area.* **(See grade 3 Language standards 4–6 for additional expectations.) CA**
	Selection 2: Before You Move On: Make Comparisons	CA CC.3.Rinf.6	Distinguish their own point of view from that of the author of a text.
		CA CC.3.Rinf.9	Compare and contrast the most important points and key details presented in two texts on the same topic.
333	**Selection 2:** Before You Move On	CA CC.3.Rinf.1	Ask and answer questions to demonstrate understanding of a text, referring explicitly to the text as the basis for the answers.
	Selection 2: Before You Move On: Make Connections	CA CC.3.Rinf.6	Distinguish their own point of view from that of the author of a text.
		CA CC.3.Rinf.9	Compare and contrast the most important points and key details presented in two texts on the same topic.
	Selection 2: Before You Move On: Cause/Effect	CA CC.3.Rinf.3	Describe the relationship between a series of historical events, scientific ideas or concepts, or steps in technical procedures in a text, using language that pertains to time, sequence, and cause/effect.
		CA CC.3.Rinf.8	Describe the logical connection between particular sentences and paragraphs in a text (e.g., comparison, cause/effect, first/second/ third in a sequence).
334	**Respond and Extend:** Compare Text Features	CA CC.3.Rinf.5	Use text features and search tools (e.g., key words, sidebars, hyperlinks) to locate information relevant to a given topic efficiently.
		CA CC.3.Rinf.9	Compare and contrast the most important points and key details presented in two texts on the same topic.
	Respond and Extend: Talk Together	CA CC.3.L.6	Acquire and use accurately grade-appropriate conversational, general academic, and domain-specific words and phrases, including those that signal spatial and temporal relationships (e.g., *After dinner that night we went looking for them*).
335	**Grammar and Spelling:** Possessive Nouns/ Adjectives	CA CC.3.L.1	Demonstrate command of the conventions of standard English grammar and usage when writing or speaking.
		CA CC.3.L.1.a	Explain the function of nouns, pronouns, verbs, adjectives, and adverbs in general and their functions in particular sentences.
336–337	**Writing Project:** Literary Response Study a Model	CA CC.3.W.1	Write opinion pieces on topics or texts, supporting a point of view with reasons.
	Prewrite Draft	CA CC.3.W.1.a	Introduce the topic or text they are writing about, state an opinion, and create an organizational structure that lists reasons.

California Common Core State Standards, continued

SE Pages	Lesson	Code	Standard
		CA CC.3.W.1.b	Provide reasons that support the opinion.
		CA CC.3.W.1.d	Provide a concluding statement or section.
338	**Writing Project:** Revise	CA CC.3.W.4	With guidance and support from adults, produce writing in which the development and organization are appropriate to task and purpose. (Grade-specific expectations for writing types are defined in standards 1–3 above.)
		CA CC.3.W.5	With guidance and support from peers and adults, develop and strengthen writing as needed by planning, revising, and editing. (Editing for conventions should demonstrate command of Language standards 1–3 up to and including grade 3.)
339	**Writing Project:** Edit and Proofread	CA CC.3.W.4	With guidance and support from adults, produce writing in which the development and organization are appropriate to task and purpose. (Grade-specific expectations for writing types are defined in standards 1–3 above.)
		CA CC.3.W.5	With guidance and support from peers and adults, develop and strengthen writing as needed by planning, revising, and editing. (Editing for conventions should demonstrate command of Language standards 1–3 up to and including grade 3.)
	Writing Project: Publish	CA CC.3.W.6	With guidance and support from adults, use technology to produce and publish writing (using keyboarding skills) as well as to interact and collaborate with others.
340	**Talk Together** **Write an Explanation**	CA CC.3.W.10	Write routinely over extended time frames (time for research, reflection, and revision) and shorter time frames (a single sitting or a day or two) for a range of discipline-specific tasks, purposes, and audiences.
		CA CC.3.SL.1.a	Engage effectively in a range of collaborative discussions (one-on-one, in groups, and teacher-led) with diverse partners on *grade 3 topics and texts*, building on others' ideas and expressing their own clearly.
			Come to discussions prepared, having read or studied required material; explicitly draw on that preparation and other information known about the topic to explore ideas under discussion.
341	**Unit Wrap-Up:** Share Your Ideas	CA CC.3.W.10	Write routinely over extended time frames (time for research, reflection, and revision) and shorter time frames (a single sitting or a day or two) for a range of discipline-specific tasks, purposes, and audiences.
			Engage effectively in a range of collaborative discussions (one-on-one, in groups, and teacher-led) with diverse partners on *grade 3 topics and texts,* building on others' ideas and expressing their own clearly.
		CA CC.3.SL.1.a	Come to discussions prepared, having read or studied required material; explicitly draw on that preparation and other information known about the topic to explore ideas under discussion.
		CA CC.3.SL.1.d	Explain their own ideas and understanding in light of the discussion.
		CA CC.3.SL.4	Report on a topic or text, tell a story, or recount an experience with appropriate facts and relevant, descriptive details, speaking clearly at an understandable pace.

SE Pages	Lesson	Code	Standard
343	**Unit Launch:** Share What You Know	CA CC.3.SL.1	Engage effectively in a range of collaborative discussions (one-on-one, in groups, and teacher-led) with diverse partners on *grade 3 topics and texts,* building on others' ideas and expressing their own clearly.
344	**Part 1:** **Language:** Ask for and Give Information	CA CC.3.SL.3	Ask and answer questions about information from a speaker, offering appropriate elaboration and detail.
345	**Social Studies Vocabulary:** Key Words	CA CC.3.Rinf.4	Determine the meaning of general academic and domain-specific words and phrases in a text relevant to a *grade 3 topic or subject area.* **(See grade 3 Language standards 4–6 for additional expectations.) CA**
		CA CC.3.Rlit.4	Determine the meaning of words and phrases as they are used in a text, distinguishing literal from nonliteral language. **(See grade 3 Language standards 4–6 for additional expectations.) CA**
		CA CC.3.L.6	Acquire and use accurately grade-appropriate conversational, general academic, and domain-specific words and phrases, including those that signal spatial and temporal relationships (e.g., *After dinner that night we went looking for them*).
346	**Thinking Map:** Classify Details	CA CC.3.L.3	Use knowledge of language and its conventions when writing, speaking, reading, or listening.
347	**Academic Vocabulary:** More Key Words	CA CC.3.Rlit.4	Determine the meaning of words and phrases as they are used in a text, distinguishing literal from nonliteral language. **(See grade 3 Language standards 4–6 for additional expectations.) CA**
		CA CC.3.L.6	Acquire and use accurately grade-appropriate conversational, general academic, and domain-specific words and phrases, including those that signal spatial and temporal relationships (e.g., *After dinner that night we went looking for them*).
348	**Strategic Reading:** Learn to Visualize	CA CC.3.Rlit.10	By the end of the year, read and comprehend literature, including stories, dramas, and poetry, at the high end of the grades 2–3 text complexity band independently and proficiently.
352	**Selection 1:** Set a Purpose	CA CC.3.Rlit.1	Ask and answer questions to demonstrate understanding of a text, referring explicitly to the text as the basis for the answers.
			Read with sufficient accuracy and fluency to support comprehension.
		CA CC.3.Rfou.4.a	Read on-level text with purpose and understanding.
355	**Selection 1:** Before You Move On	CA CC.3.Rlit.1	Ask and answer questions to demonstrate understanding of a text, referring explicitly to the text as the basis for the answers.
	Selection 1: Before You Move On: Visualize	CA CC.3.Rlit.7	Explain how specific aspects of a text's illustrations contribute to what is conveyed by the words in a story (e.g., create mood, emphasize aspects of a character or setting).
356	**Selection 1:** Predict	CA CC.3.Rlit.1	Ask and answer questions to demonstrate understanding of a text, referring explicitly to the text as the basis for the answers.
	Selection 1: Predict	CA CC.3.Rlit.3	Describe characters in a story (e.g., their traits, motivations, or feelings) and explain how their actions contribute to the sequence of events.

California Common Core State Standards, continued

SE Pages	Lesson	Code	Standard
359	**Selection 1:** Before You Move On	CA CC.3.Rlit.1	Ask and answer questions to demonstrate understanding of a text, referring explicitly to the text as the basis for the answers.
	Selection 1: Before You Move On: Confirm Prediction	CA CC.3.Rlit.3	Describe characters in a story (e.g., their traits, motivations, or feelings) and explain how their actions contribute to the sequence of events.
	Selection 1: Before You Move On: Sensory Language	CA CC.3.Rlit.4	Determine the meaning of words and phrases as they are used in a text, distinguishing literal from nonliteral language. **(See grade 3 Language standards 4–6 for additional expectations.) CA**
360	**Selection 1:** Predict	CA CC.3.Rlit.1	Ask and answer questions to demonstrate understanding of a text, referring explicitly to the text as the basis for the answers.
	Selection 1: Predict	CA CC.3.Rlit.3	Describe characters in a story (e.g., their traits, motivations, or feelings) and explain how their actions contribute to the sequence of events.
362	**Selection 1:** Before You Move On	CA CC.3.Rlit.1	Ask and answer questions to demonstrate understanding of a text, referring explicitly to the text as the basis for the answers.
	Selection 1: Before You Move On: Classify	CA CC.3.Rlit.2	Recount stories, including fables, folktales, and myths from diverse cultures; determine the central message, lesson, or moral and explain how it is conveyed through key details in the text.
363	**Meet the Author:** Writer's Craft	CA CC.3.W.10	Write routinely over extended time frames (time for research, reflection, and revision) and shorter time frames (a single sitting or a day or two) for a range of discipline-specific tasks, purposes, and audiences.
364	**Think and Respond:** Talk About It	CA CC.3.Rlit.3	Describe characters in a story (e.g., their traits, motivations, or feelings) and explain how their actions contribute to the sequence of events.
		CC CA.3.Rlit.5	Refer to parts of stories, dramas, and poems when writing or speaking about a text, using terms such as chapter, scene, and stanza; describe how each successive part builds on earlier sections.
		CA CC.3.Rlit.6	Distinguish their own point of view from that of the narrator or those of the characters.
		CC CA.3.SL.3	Ask and answer questions about information from a speaker, offering appropriate elaboration and detail.
		CA CC.3.L.6	Acquire and use accurately grade-appropriate conversational, general academic, and domain-specific words and phrases, including those that signal spatial and temporal relationships (e.g., *After dinner that night we went looking for them*).
	Think and Respond: Write About It	CA CC.3.W.10	Write routinely over extended time frames (time for research, reflection, and revision) and shorter time frames (a single sitting or a day or two) for a range of discipline-specific tasks, purposes, and audiences.
365	**Reread and Classify** Classify Details	CA CC.3.L.5	Demonstrate understanding of word relationships and nuances in word meanings.
	Reread and Classify Fluency	CA CC.3.Rfou.4	Read with sufficient accuracy and fluency to support comprehension.
		CA CC.3.Rfou.4.b	Read on-level prose and poetry orally with accuracy, appropriate rate, and expression on successive readings.

SE Pages	Lesson	Code	Standard
	Reread and Classify Talk Together	CA CC.3.SL.3	Ask and answer questions about information from a speaker, offering appropriate elaboration and detail.
366	**Word Work:** Playful Language		Demonstrate understanding of word relationships and nuances in word meanings.
		CA CC.3.L.5.a	Distinguish the literal and non-literal meanings of words and phrases in context (e.g., *take steps*).
367	**Selection 2:** Before You Move On	CA CC.3.Rinf.1	Ask and answer questions to demonstrate understanding of a text, referring explicitly to the text as the basis for the answers.
	Selection 2: Before You Move On: Classify Details	CA CC.3.Rinf.4	Determine the meaning of general academic and domain-specific words and phrases in a text relevant to a *grade 3 topic or subject area.* **(See grade 3 Language standards 4–6 for additional expectations.) CA**
		CA CC.3.L.4	Determine or clarify the meaning of unknown and multiple-meaning word and phrases based on *grade 3 reading and content,* choosing flexibly from a range of strategies.
		CA CC.3.L.4.a	Use sentence-level context as a clue to the meaning of a word or phrase.
		CA CC.3.L.6	Acquire and use accurately grade-appropriate conversational, general academic, and domain-specific words and phrases, including those that signal spatial and temporal relationships (e.g., *After dinner that night we went looking for them*).
369	**Selection 2:** Before You Move On	CA CC.3.Rinf.1	Ask and answer questions to demonstrate understanding of a text, referring explicitly to the text as the basis for the answers.
	Selection 2: Before You Move On: Visualize	CA CC.3.Rinf.2	Determine the main idea of a text; recount the key details and explain how they support the main idea.
		CA CC.3.Rinf.3	Describe the relationship between a series of historical events, scientific ideas or concepts, or steps in technical procedures in a text, using language that pertains to time, sequence, and cause/effect.
371	**Selection 2:** Before You Move On	CA CC.3.Rinf.1	Ask and answer questions to demonstrate understanding of a text, referring explicitly to the text as the basis for the answers.
	Selection 2: Before You Move On: Visualize	CA CC.3.Rinf.2	Determine the main idea of a text; recount the key details and explain how they support the main idea.
	Selection 2: Before You Move On: Classify Details	CA CC.3.Rinf.3	Describe the relationship between a series of historical events, scientific ideas or concepts, or steps in technical procedures in a text, using language that pertains to time, sequence, and cause/effect.
372	**Respond and Extend:** Compare Language	CA CC.3.Rinf.7	Use information gained from illustrations (e.g., maps, photographs) and the words in a text to demonstrate understanding of the text (e.g., where, when, why, and how key events occur).

California Common Core State Standards, continued

SE Pages	Lesson	Code	Standard
		CA CC.3.Rinf.9	Compare and contrast the most important points and key details presented in two texts on the same topic.
		CA CC.3.SL.1	Engage effectively in a range of collaborative discussions (one-on-one, in groups, and teacher-led) with diverse partners on *grade 3 topics and texts,* building on others' ideas and expressing their own clearly.
		CA CC.3.L.6	Acquire and use accurately grade-appropriate conversational, general academic, and domain-specific words and phrases, including those that signal spatial and temporal relationships (e.g., *After dinner that night we went looking for them*).
373	**Grammar** Pronoun Agreement	CA CC.3.L.1	Demonstrate command of the conventions of standard English grammar and usage when writing or speaking.
374	**Part 2: Language:** Give and Follow Instructions	CA CC.3.SL.1	Engage effectively in a range of collaborative discussions (one-on-one, in groups, and teacher-led) with diverse partners on *grade 3 topics and texts,* building on others' ideas and expressing their own clearly.
			Come to discussions prepared, having read or studied required material; explicitly draw on that preparation and other information known about the topic to explore ideas under discussion.
		CA CC.3.SL.3	Ask and answer questions about information from a speaker, offering appropriate elaboration and detail.
			Report on a topic or text, tell a story, or recount an experience with appropriate facts and relevant, descriptive details, speaking clearly at an understandable pace.
		CA CC.3.SL.4.a	Plan and deliver an informative/explanatory presentation on a topic that: organizes ideas around major points of information, follows a logical sequence, includes supporting details, uses clear and specific vocabulary, and provides a strong conclusion. CA
		CA CC.3.SL.6	Speak in complete sentences when appropriate to task and situation in order to provide requested detail or clarification. (See grade 3 Language standards 1 and 3 for specific expectations.)
375	**Social Studies Vocabulary:** Key Words	CA CC.3.Rinf.4	Determine the meaning of general academic and domain-specific words and phrases in a text relevant to a *grade 3 topic or subject area.* **(See grade 3 Language standards 4–6 for additional expectations.) CA**
		CA CC.3.Rlit.4	Determine the meaning of words and phrases as they are used in a text, distinguishing literal from nonliteral language. **(See grade 3 Language standards 4–6 for additional expectations.) CA**
		CA CC.3.L.6	Acquire and use accurately grade-appropriate conversational, general academic, and domain-specific words and phrases, including those that signal spatial and temporal relationships (e.g., *After dinner that night we went looking for them*).
376	**Thinking Map:** Steps in a Process	CA CC.3.Rinf.3	Describe the relationship between a series of historical events, scientific ideas or concepts, or steps in technical procedures in a text, using language that pertains to time, sequence, and cause/effect.

SE Pages	Lesson	Code	Standard
377	**Academic Vocabulary:** More Key Words	CA CC.3.Rinf.4	Determine the meaning of general academic and domain-specific words and phrases in a text relevant to a *grade 3 topic or subject area.* **(See grade 3 Language standards 4–6 for additional expectations.) CA**
		CA CC.3.Rlit.4	Determine the meaning of words and phrases as they are used in a text, distinguishing literal from nonliteral language. **(See grade 3 Language standards 4–6 for additional expectations.) CA**
		CA CC.3.L.6	Acquire and use accurately grade-appropriate conversational, general academic, and domain-specific words and phrases, including those that signal spatial and temporal relationships (e.g., *After dinner that night we went looking for them*).
378	**Strategic Reading:** Learn to Visualize	CA CC.3.Rinf.10	By the end of the year, read and comprehend informational texts, including history/social studies, science, and technical texts, at the high end of the grades 2–3 text complexity band independently and proficiently.
382	**Selection 1:** Set a Purpose		Read with sufficient accuracy and fluency to support comprehension.
		CA CC.3.Rfou.4.a	Read on-level text with purpose and understanding.
383	**Selection 1:** Before You Move On	CA CC.3.Rinf.1	Ask and answer questions to demonstrate understanding of a text, referring explicitly to the text as the basis for the answers.
	Selection 1: Before You Move On: Use Text Features	CA CC.3.Rinf.5	Use text features and search tools (e.g., key words, sidebars, hyperlinks) to locate information relevant to a given topic efficiently.
385	**Selection 1:** Before You Move On: Make Inferences	CA CC.3.Rinf.1	Ask and answer questions to demonstrate understanding of a text, referring explicitly to the text as the basis for the answers.
	Selection 1: Before You Move On: Steps in a Process	CA CC.3.Rinf.3	Describe the relationship between a series of historical events, scientific ideas or concepts, or steps in technical procedures in a text, using language that pertains to time, sequence, and cause/effect.
		CA CC.3.Rinf.8	Describe the logical connection between particular sentences and paragraphs in a text (e.g., comparison, cause/effect, first/second/third in a sequence).
		CA CC.3.L.6	Acquire and use accurately grade-appropriate conversational, general academic, and domain-specific words and phrases, including those that signal spatial and temporal relationships (e.g., *After dinner that night we went looking for them*).
387	**Selection 1:** Before You Move On: Classify	CA CC.3.Rinf.1	Ask and answer questions to demonstrate understanding of a text, referring explicitly to the text as the basis for the answers.
	Selection 1: Before You Move On: Steps in a Process	CA CC.3.Rinf.8	Describe the logical connection between particular sentences and paragraphs in a text (e.g., comparison, cause/effect, first/second/third in a sequence).
389	**Selection 1:** Before You Move On: Visualize	CA CC.3.Rinf.1	Ask and answer questions to demonstrate understanding of a text, referring explicitly to the text as the basis for the answers.

California Common Core State Standards, continued

SE Pages	Lesson	Code	Standard
	Selection 1: Before You Move On: Use Text Features	CA CC.3.Rinf.2	Determine the main idea of a text; recount the key details and explain how they support the main idea.
		CA CC.3.Rinf.8	Describe the logical connection between particular sentences and paragraphs in a text (e.g., comparison, cause/effect, first/second/third in a sequence).
		CA CC.3.Rinf.3	Describe the relationship between a series of historical events, scientific ideas or concepts, or steps in technical procedures in a text, using language that pertains to time, sequence, and cause/effect.
390	**Selection 1:** Set a Purpose		Read with sufficient accuracy and fluency to support comprehension.
		CA CC.3.Rfou.4.a	Read on-level text with purpose and understanding.
393	**Selection 1:** Before You Move On	CA CC.3.Rlit.1	Ask and answer questions to demonstrate understanding of a text, referring explicitly to the text as the basis for the answers.
	Selection 1: Before You Move On: Clarify	CA CC.3.Rlit.3	Describe characters in a story (e.g., their traits, motivations, or feelings) and explain how their actions contribute to the sequence of events.
	Selection 1: Before You Move On: Visualize	CA CC.3.Rlit.3	Describe characters in a story (e.g., their traits, motivations, or feelings) and explain how their actions contribute to the sequence of events.
394	**Think and Respond:** Talk About It	CA CC.3.Rlit.10	By the end of the year, read and comprehend literature, including stories, dramas, and poetry, at the high end of the grades 2–3 text complexity band independently and proficiently.
	Think and Respond: Write About It	CA CC.3.W.10	Write routinely over extended time frames (time for research, reflection, and revision) and shorter time frames (a single sitting or a day or two) for a range of discipline-specific tasks, purposes, and audiences.
395	**Reread and Explain** Steps in a Process	CA CC.3.Rinf.3	Describe the relationship between a series of historical events, scientific ideas or concepts, or steps in technical procedures in a text, using language that pertains to time, sequence, and cause/effect.
		CA CC.3.SL.6	
		CA CC.3.L.6	Acquire and use accurately grade-appropriate conversational, general academic, and domain-specific words and phrases, including those that signal spatial and temporal relationships (e.g., *After dinner that night we went looking for them*).
	Reread and Explain Fluency	CA CC.3.Rfou.4	Read with sufficient accuracy and fluency to support comprehension.
		CA CC.3.Rfou.4.b	Read on-level prose and poetry orally with accuracy, appropriate rate, and expression on successive readings.
	Reread and Explain Talk Together	CA CC.3.SL.1	Engage effectively in a range of collaborative discussions (one-on-one, in groups, and teacher-led) with diverse partners on *grade 3 topics and texts,* building on others' ideas and expressing their own clearly.

SE Pages	Lesson	Code	Standard
396	**Word Work:** Homophones	CA CC.3.L.5	Demonstrate understanding of word relationships and nuances in word meanings.
397	**Selection 2 Opener:** Before You Move On	CA CC.3.Rinf.5	Use text features and search tools (e.g., key words, sidebars, hyperlinks) to locate information relevant to a given topic efficiently.
	Selection 2 Opener: Before You Move On: Make Inferences	CA CC.3.Rinf.1	Ask and answer questions to demonstrate understanding of a text, referring explicitly to the text as the basis for the answers.
399	**Selection 2:** Before You Move On	CA CC.3.Rinf.1	Ask and answer questions to demonstrate understanding of a text, referring explicitly to the text as the basis for the answers.
	Selection 2: Before You Move On: Visualize	CA CC.3.Rinf.2	Determine the main idea of a text; recount the key details and explain how they support the main idea.
		CA CC.3.W.10	Write routinely over extended time frames (time for research, reflection, and revision) and shorter time frames (a single sitting or a day or two) for a range of discipline-specific tasks, purposes, and audiences.
	Selection 2: Before You Move On: Draw Conclusions	CA CC.3.Rinf.6	Distinguish their own point of view from that of the author of a text.
400	**Selection 2:** Set a Purpose		Read with sufficient accuracy and fluency to support comprehension.
		CA CC.3.Rfou.4.a	Read on-level text with purpose and understanding.
401	**Selection 2:** Before You Move On	CA CC.3.Rlit.1	Ask and answer questions to demonstrate understanding of a text, referring explicitly to the text as the basis for the answers.
	Selection 2: Before You Move On: Use Text Features	CA CC.3.Rlit.4	Determine the meaning of words and phrases as they are used in a text, distinguishing literal from nonliteral language. **(See grade 3 Language standards 4–6 for additional expectations.) CA**
	Selection 2: Before You Move On: Make Connections	CA CC.3.Rlit.3	Describe characters in a story (e.g., their traits, motivations, or feelings) and explain how their actions contribute to the sequence of events.
402	**Selection 2:** Predict	CA CC.3.Rlit.1	Ask and answer questions to demonstrate understanding of a text, referring explicitly to the text as the basis for the answers.
403	**Selection 2:** Before You Move On	CA CC.3.Rlit.1	Ask and answer questions to demonstrate understanding of a text, referring explicitly to the text as the basis for the answers.
	Selection 2: Before You Move On: Visualize	CA CC.3.Rlit.3	Describe characters in a story (e.g., their traits, motivations, or feelings) and explain how their actions contribute to the sequence of events.
404	**Respond and Extend:** Compare Themes	CA CC.3.Rlit.9	Compare and contrast the themes, settings, and plots of stories written by the same author about the same or similar characters (e.g., in books from a series).
	Respond and Extend: Talk Together		Engage effectively in a range of collaborative discussions (one-on-one, in groups, and teacher-led) with diverse partners on *grade 3 topics and texts,* building on others' ideas and expressing their own clearly.

California Common Core State Standards, continued

SE Pages	Lesson	Code	Standard
		CA CC.3.SL.1.a	Come to discussions prepared, having read or studied required material; explicitly draw on that preparation and other information known about the topic to explore ideas under discussion.
		CA CC.3.L.6	Acquire and use accurately grade-appropriate conversational, general academic, and domain-specific words and phrases, including those that signal spatial and temporal relationships (e.g., *After dinner that night we went looking for them*).
405	**Grammar:** Pronoun Agreement	C CC.3.L.1	Demonstrate command of the conventions of standard English grammar and usage when writing or speaking.
		CA CC.3.L.1.a	Explain the function of nouns, pronouns, verbs, adjectives, and adverbs in general and their functions in particular sentences.
406–407	**Writing Project:** Interview Study a Model Prewrite Draft		Write informative/explanatory texts to examine a topic and convey ideas and information clearly.
		CA CC.3.W.2.a	Introduce a topic and group related information together; include illustrations when useful to aiding comprehension.
		CA CC.3.W.2.b	Develop the topic with facts, definitions, and details.
		CA CC.3.W.2.c	Use linking words and phrases (e.g., *also, another, and, more, but*) to connect ideas within categories of information.
			Demonstrate command of the conventions of standard English grammar and usage when writing or speaking.
		CA CC.3.L.1.i	Produce simple, compound, and complex sentences.
408	**Writing Project:** Revise	CA CC.3.W.4	With guidance and support from adults, produce writing in which the development and organization are appropriate to task and purpose. (Grade-specific expectations for writing types are defined in standards 1–3 above.)
		CA CC.3.W.5	With guidance and support from peers and adults, develop and strengthen writing as needed by planning, revising, and editing. (Editing for conventions should demonstrate command of Language standards 1–3 up to and including grade 3.)
409	**Writing Project:** Edit and Proofread	CA CC.3.W.5	With guidance and support from peers and adults, develop and strengthen writing as needed by planning, revising, and editing. (Editing for conventions should demonstrate command of Language standards 1–3 up to and including grade 3.)
409	**Writing Project:** Publish	CA CC.3.W.6	With guidance and support from adults, use technology to produce and publish writing (using keyboarding skills) as well as to interact and collaborate with others.
		CA CC.3.SL.5	Create engaging audio recordings of stories or poems that demonstrate fluid reading at an understandable pace; add visual displays when appropriate to emphasize or enhance certain facts or details.
410	**Talk Together** **Write a Personal Narrative**	CA CC.3.W.3	Write narratives to develop real or imagined experiences or events using effective technique, descriptive details, and clear event sequences.

SE Pages	Lesson	Code	Standard
		CA CC.3.W.3.a	Establish a situation and introduce a narrator and/or characters; organize an event sequence that unfolds naturally.
		CA CC.3.W.10	Write routinely over extended time frames (time for research, reflection, and revision) and shorter time frames (a single sitting or a day or two) for a range of discipline-specific tasks, purposes, and audiences.
			Engage effectively in a range of collaborative discussions (one-on-one, in groups, and teacher-led) with diverse partners on *grade 3 topics and texts,* building on others' ideas and expressing their own clearly.
		CA CC.3.SL.2	Determine the main ideas and supporting details of a text read aloud or information presented in diverse media and formats, including visually, quantitatively, and orally.
411	**Unit Wrap-Up:** Share Your Ideas	CA CC.3.W.10	Write routinely over extended time frames (time for research, reflection, and revision) and shorter time frames (a single sitting or a day or two) for a range of discipline-specific tasks, purposes, and audiences.
			Engage effectively in a range of collaborative discussions (one-on-one, in groups, and teacher-led) with diverse partners on *grade 3 topics and texts,* building on others' ideas and expressing their own clearly.
		CA CC.3.SL.1.b	Follow agreed-upon rules for discussions (e.g., gaining the floor in respectful ways, listening to others with care, speaking one at a time about the topics and texts under discussion).

Unit 7: Blast! Crash! Splash!

SE Pages	Lesson	Code	Standard
413	**Unit Launch:** Share What You Know	CA CC.3.SL.1	Engage effectively in a range of collaborative discussions (one-on-one, in groups, and teacher-led) with diverse partners on *grade 3 topics and texts,* building on others' ideas and expressing their own clearly.
		CA CC.3.SL.1.a	Come to discussions prepared, having read or studied required material; explicitly draw on that preparation and other information known about the topic to explore ideas under discussion.
414	**Part 1: Language:** Tell an Original Story	CA CC.3.SL.3	
		CA CC.3.SL.4	Report on a topic or text, tell a story, or recount an experience with appropriate facts and relevant, descriptive details, speaking clearly at an understandable pace.
415	**Science Vocabulary:** Key Words	CA CC.3.Rlit.4	Determine the meaning of words and phrases as they are used in a text, distinguishing literal from nonliteral language. **(See grade 3 Language standards 4–6 for additional expectations.) CA**
		CA CC.3.Rinf.4	Determine the meaning of general academic and domain-specific words and phrases in a text relevant to a *grade 3 topic or subject area.* **(See grade 3 Language standards 4–6 for additional expectations.) CA**

California Common Core State Standards, continued

SE Pages	Lesson	Code	Standard
		CA CC.3.L.6	Acquire and use accurately grade-appropriate conversational, general academic, and domain-specific words and phrases, including those that signal spatial and temporal relationships (e.g., *After dinner that night we went looking for them*).
416	**Thinking Map:** Imagery	CA CC.3.Rlit.4	Determine the meaning of words and phrases as they are used in a text, distinguishing literal from nonliteral language. **(See grade 3 Language standards 4–6 for additional expectations.) CA**
417	**Academic Vocabulary:** More Key Words	CA CC.3.Rlit.4	Determine the meaning of words and phrases as they are used in a text, distinguishing literal from nonliteral language. **(See grade 3 Language standards 4–6 for additional expectations.) CA**
		CA CC.3.Rinf.4	Determine the meaning of general academic and domain-specific words and phrases in a text relevant to a *grade 3 topic or subject area*. **(See grade 3 Language standards 4–6 for additional expectations.) CA**
		CA CC.3.L.6	Acquire and use accurately grade-appropriate conversational, general academic, and domain-specific words and phrases, including those that signal spatial and temporal relationships (e.g., *After dinner that night we went looking for them*).
418	**Strategic Reading:** Learn to Synthesize	CA CC.3.Rinf.1	Describe the logical connection between particular sentences and paragraphs in a text (e.g., comparison, cause/effect, first/second/third in a sequence).
		CA CC.3.Rinf.10	By the end of the year, read and comprehend informational texts, including history/social studies, science, and technical texts, at the high end of the grades 2–3 text complexity band independently and proficiently.
422	**Selection 1:** Set a Purpose		Read with sufficient accuracy and fluency to support comprehension.
		CA CC.3.Rfou.4.a	Read on-level text with purpose and understanding.
425	**Selection 1:** Before You Move On	CA CC.3.Rlit.1	Ask and answer questions to demonstrate understanding of a text, referring explicitly to the text as the basis for the answers.
	Selection 1: Before You Move On: Draw Conclusions	CA CC.3.Rlit.2	Recount stories, including fables, folktales, and myths from diverse cultures; determine the central message, lesson, or moral and explain how it is conveyed through key details in the text.
	Selection 1: Before You Move On: Draw Conclusions	CA CC.3.Rlit.5	Refer to parts of stories, dramas, and poems when writing or speaking about a text, using terms such as chapter, scene, and stanza; describe how each successive part builds on earlier sections.
426	**Selection 1:** Predict	CA CC.3.Rlit.1	Ask and answer questions to demonstrate understanding of a text, referring explicitly to the text as the basis for the answers.
		CA CC.3.Rlit.5	Refer to parts of stories, dramas, and poems when writing or speaking about a text, using terms such as chapter, scene, and stanza; describe how each successive part builds on earlier sections.
429	**Selection 1:** Before You Move On	CA CC.3.Rlit.1	Ask and answer questions to demonstrate understanding of a text, referring explicitly to the text as the basis for the answers.
	Selection 1: Before You Move On: Visualize	CA CC.3.Rlit.7	Explain how specific aspects of a text's illustrations contribute to what is conveyed by the words in a story (e.g., create mood, emphasize aspects of a character or setting).

SE Pages	Lesson	Code	Standard
430	**Selection 1:** Predict	CA CC.3.Rlit.1	Ask and answer questions to demonstrate understanding of a text, referring explicitly to the text as the basis for the answers.
	Selection 1: Predict	CA CC.3.Rlit.5	Refer to parts of stories, dramas, and poems when writing or speaking about a text, using terms such as chapter, scene, and stanza; describe how each successive part builds on earlier sections.
433	**Selection 1:** Before You Move On: Confirm Prediction	CA CC.3.Rlit.1	Ask and answer questions to demonstrate understanding of a text, referring explicitly to the text as the basis for the answers.
434	**Think and Respond:** Talk About It	CA CC.3.Rlit.1	Ask and answer questions to demonstrate understanding of a text, referring explicitly to the text as the basis for the answers.
		CA CC.3.Rlit.10	By the end of the year, read and comprehend literature, including stories, dramas, and poetry, at the high end of the grades 2–3 text complexity band independently and proficiently.
		CA CC.3.L.6	Acquire and use accurately grade-appropriate conversational, general academic, and domain-specific words and phrases, including those that signal spatial and temporal relationships (e.g., *After dinner that night we went looking for them*).
	Think and Respond: Write About It	CA CC.3.W.10	Write routinely over extended time frames (time for research, reflection, and revision) and shorter time frames (a single sitting or a day or two) for a range of discipline-specific tasks, purposes, and audiences.
435	**Reread and Retell** Imagery	CA CC.3.Rlit.5	Refer to parts of stories, dramas, and poems when writing or speaking about a text, using terms such as chapter, scene, and stanza; describe how each successive part builds on earlier sections.
		CA CC.3.Rlit.10	By the end of the year, read and comprehend literature, including stories, dramas, and poetry, at the high end of the grades 2–3 text complexity band independently and proficiently.
	Reread and Retell Fluency	CA CC.3.Rfou.4	Read with sufficient accuracy and fluency to support comprehension.
		CA CC.3.Rfou.4.b	Read on-level prose and poetry orally with accuracy, appropriate rate, and expression on successive readings.
	Reread and Retell Talk Together	CA CC.3.SL.2	Determine the main ideas and supporting details of a text read aloud or information presented in diverse media and formats, including visually, quantitatively, and orally.
			Engage effectively in a range of collaborative discussions (one-on-one, in groups, and teacher-led) with diverse partners on *grade 3 topics and texts,* building on others' ideas and expressing their own clearly.
		CA CC.3.L.6	Acquire and use accurately grade-appropriate conversational, general academic, and domain-specific words and phrases, including those that signal spatial and temporal relationships (e.g., *After dinner that night we went looking for them*).
436	**Word Work:** Greek and Latin Roots		Determine or clarify the meaning of unknown and multiple-meaning word and phrases based on *grade 3 reading and content*, choosing flexibly from a range of strategies.
		CA CC.3.L.4.c	Use a known root word as a clue to the meaning of an unknown word with the same root (e.g., *company, companion*).

California Common Core State Standards, continued

SE Pages	Lesson	Code	Standard
437	**Selection 2:** Before You Move On	CA CC.3.Rinf.1	Ask and answer questions to demonstrate understanding of a text, referring explicitly to the text as the basis for the answers.
	Selection 2: Before You Move On: Use Text Features	CA CC.3.Rinf.5	Use text features and search tools (e.g., key words, sidebars, hyperlinks) to locate information relevant to a given topic efficiently.
		CA CC.3.Rinf.7	Use information gained from illustrations (e.g., maps, photographs) and the words in a text to demonstrate understanding of the text (e.g., where, when, why, and how key events occur).
439	**Selection 2:** Before You Move On	CA CC.3.Rinf.1	Ask and answer questions to demonstrate understanding of a text, referring explicitly to the text as the basis for the answers.
	Selection 2: Before You Move On: Use Text Features	CA CC.3.Rinf.5	Use text features and search tools (e.g., key words, sidebars, hyperlinks) to locate information relevant to a given topic efficiently.
	Selection 2: Before You Move On: Evaluate	CA CC.3.Rinf.3	Describe the relationship between a series of historical events, scientific ideas or concepts, or steps in technical procedures in a text, using language that pertains to time, sequence, and cause/effect.
		CA CC.3.Rinf.8	Describe the logical connection between particular sentences and paragraphs in a text (e.g., comparison, cause/effect, first/second/third in a sequence).
441	**Selection 2:** Before You Move On: Details	CA CC.3.Rinf.1	Ask and answer questions to demonstrate understanding of a text, referring explicitly to the text as the basis for the answers.
		CA CC.3.Rinf.2	Determine the main idea of a text; recount the key details and explain how they support the main idea.
	Selection 2: Before You Move On: Imagery	CA CC.3.Rinf.4	Determine the meaning of general academic and domain-specific words and phrases in a text relevant to a *grade 3 topic or subject area.* **(See grade 3 Language standards 4–6 for additional expectations.) CA**
		CA CC.3.L.6	Acquire and use accurately grade-appropriate conversational, general academic, and domain-specific words and phrases, including those that signal spatial and temporal relationships (e.g., *After dinner that night we went looking for them*).
442	**Respond and Extend:** Compare Texts	CA CC.3.Rinf.9	Compare and contrast the most important points and key details presented in two texts on the same topic.
		CA CC.3.Rinf.10	By the end of the year, read and comprehend informational texts, including history/social studies, science, and technical texts, at the high end of the grades 2–3 text complexity band independently and proficiently.
443	**Grammar and Spelling:** Adverbs	CA CC.3.L.1	Demonstrate command of the conventions of standard English grammar and usage when writing or speaking.
		CA CC.3.L.1.a	Explain the function of nouns, pronouns, verbs, adjectives, and adverbs in general and their functions in particular sentences.
		CA CC.3.L.1.g	Form and use comparative and superlative adjectives and adverbs, and choose between them depending on what is to be modified.

SE Pages	Lesson	Code	Standard
444	**Part 2:** Language: Express Opinions and Ideas		Engage effectively in a range of collaborative discussions (one-on-one, in groups, and teacher-led) with diverse partners on *grade 3 topics and texts,* building on others' ideas and expressing their own clearly.
		CA CC.3.SL.1.d	Explain their own ideas and understanding in light of the discussion.
445	**Science Vocabulary:** Key Words	CA CC.3.Rinf.4	Determine the meaning of general academic and domain-specific words and phrases in a text relevant to a *grade 3 topic or subject area.* **(See grade 3 Language standards 4–6 for additional expectations.) CA**
		CA CC.3.Rlit.4	Determine the meaning of words and phrases as they are used in a text, distinguishing literal from nonliteral language. **(See grade 3 Language standards 4–6 for additional expectations.) CA**
		CA CC.3.L.6	Acquire and use accurately grade-appropriate conversational, general academic, and domain-specific words and phrases, including those that signal spatial and temporal relationships (e.g., *After dinner that night we went looking for them*).
446	**Thinking Map:** Cause and Effect	CA CC.3.Rinf.3	Describe the relationship between a series of historical events, scientific ideas or concepts, or steps in technical procedures in a text, using language that pertains to time, sequence, and cause/effect.
447	**Academic Vocabulary:** More Key Words	CA CC.3.Rinf.4	Determine the meaning of general academic and domain-specific words and phrases in a text relevant to a *grade 3 topic or subject area.* **(See grade 3 Language standards 4–6 for additional expectations.) CA**
	Academic Vocabulary: More Key Words	CA CC.3.Rlit.4	Determine the meaning of words and phrases as they are used in a text, distinguishing literal from nonliteral language. **(See grade 3 Language standards 4–6 for additional expectations.) CA**
		CA CC.3.SL.6	Speak in complete sentences when appropriate to task and situation in order to provide requested detail or clarification. (See grade 3 Language standards 1 and 3 for specific expectations.)
448	**Strategic Reading:** Learn to Synthesize	CA CC.3.Rinf.10	By the end of the year, read and comprehend informational texts, including history/social studies, science, and technical texts, at the high end of the grades 2–3 text complexity band independently and proficiently.
452	**Selection 1:** Set a Purpose		Read with sufficient accuracy and fluency to support comprehension.
		CA CC.3.Rfou.4.a	Read on-level text with purpose and understanding.
455	**Selection 1:** Before You Move On	CA CC.3.Rlit.1	Ask and answer questions to demonstrate understanding of a text, referring explicitly to the text as the basis for the answers.
		CA CC.3.Rlit.3	Describe characters in a story (e.g., their traits, motivations, or feelings) and explain how their actions contribute to the sequence of events.
	Selection 1: Before You Move On: Cause/Effect	CA CC.3.Rlit.5	Refer to parts of stories, dramas, and poems when writing or speaking about a text, using terms such as chapter, scene, and stanza; describe how each successive part builds on earlier sections.

California Common Core State Standards, continued

SE Pages	Lesson	Code	Standard
456	**Selection 1:** Predict	CA CC.3.Rlit.1	Ask and answer questions to demonstrate understanding of a text, referring explicitly to the text as the basis for the answers.
		CA CC.3.Rlit.3	Describe characters in a story (e.g., their traits, motivations, or feelings) and explain how their actions contribute to the sequence of events.
459	**Selection 1:** Before You Move On	CA CC.3.Rlit.1	Ask and answer questions to demonstrate understanding of a text, referring explicitly to the text as the basis for the answers.
		CA CC.3.Rlit.3	Describe characters in a story (e.g., their traits, motivations, or feelings) and explain how their actions contribute to the sequence of events.
460	**Selection 1:** Predict	CA CC.3.Rlit.5	Refer to parts of stories, dramas, and poems when writing or speaking about a text, using terms such as chapter, scene, and stanza; describe how each successive part builds on earlier sections.
462	**Selection 1:** Before You Move On	CA CC.3.Rlit.3	Describe characters in a story (e.g., their traits, motivations, or feelings) and explain how their actions contribute to the sequence of events.
463	**Meet the Illustrator**	CA CC.3.Rlit.7	Explain how specific aspects of a text's illustrations contribute to what is conveyed by the words in a story (e.g., create mood, emphasize aspects of a character or setting).
464	**Think and Respond:** Talk About It	CA CC.3.Rlit.10	By the end of the year, read and comprehend literature, including stories, dramas, and poetry, at the high end of the grades 2–3 text complexity band independently and proficiently.
			Engage effectively in a range of collaborative discussions (one-on-one, in groups, and teacher-led) with diverse partners on *grade 3 topics and texts,* building on others' ideas and expressing their own clearly.
	Think and Respond: Write About It	CA CC.3.W.10	Write routinely over extended time frames (time for research, reflection, and revision) and shorter time frames (a single sitting or a day or two) for a range of discipline-specific tasks, purposes, and audiences.
465	**Reread and Summarize** Cause and Effect	CA CC.3.Rlit.5	Refer to parts of stories, dramas, and poems when writing or speaking about a text, using terms such as chapter, scene, and stanza; describe how each successive part builds on earlier sections.
		CA CC.3.Rlit.10	By the end of the year, read and comprehend literature, including stories, dramas, and poetry, at the high end of the grades 2–3 text complexity band independently and proficiently.
		CA CC.3.L.6	Acquire and use accurately grade-appropriate conversational, general academic, and domain-specific words and phrases, including those that signal spatial and temporal relationships (e.g., *After dinner that night we went looking for them*).
	Reread and Summarize Fluency	CA CC.3.Rfou.4	Read with sufficient accuracy and fluency to support comprehension.
		CA CC.3.Rfou.4.b	Read on-level prose and poetry orally with accuracy, appropriate rate, and expression on successive readings.

SE Pages	Lesson	Code	Standard
	Reread and Summarize Talk Together	CA CC.3.W.3	Write narratives to develop real or imagined experiences or events using effective technique, descriptive details, and clear event sequences.
		CA CC.3.W.3.b	Use dialogue and descriptions of actions, thoughts, and feelings to develop experiences and events or show the response of characters to situations.
466	**Word Work:** Compound Words		Determine or clarify the meaning of unknown and multiple-meaning word and phrases based on *grade 3 reading and content,* choosing flexibly from a range of strategies.
		CA CC.3.L.4.a	Use sentence-level context as a clue to the meaning of a word or phrase.
		CA CC.3.L.5	Demonstrate understanding of word relationships and nuances in word meanings.
467	**Selection 2 Opener:** Before You Move On: Main Idea	CA CC.3.Rinf.2	Determine the main idea of a text; recount the key details and explain how they support the main idea.
		CA CC.3.Rinf.3	Describe the relationship between a series of historical events, scientific ideas or concepts, or steps in technical procedures in a text, using language that pertains to time, sequence, and cause/effect.
	Selection 2 Opener: Before You Move On: Cause/Effect	CA CC.3.Rinf.3	Describe the relationship between a series of historical events, scientific ideas or concepts, or steps in technical procedures in a text, using language that pertains to time, sequence, and cause/effect.
469	**Selection 2:** Before You Move On: Form Generalizations	CA CC.3.Rinf.2	Determine the main idea of a text; recount the key details and explain how they support the main idea.
	Selection 2: Before You Move On: Cause/Effect	CA CC.3.Rinf.1	Ask and answer questions to demonstrate understanding of a text, referring explicitly to the text as the basis for the answers.
		CA CC.3.Rinf.3	Describe the relationship between a series of historical events, scientific ideas or concepts, or steps in technical procedures in a text, using language that pertains to time, sequence, and cause/effect.
471	**Selection 2:** Before You Move On: Use Text Features	CA CC.3.Rinf.3	Describe the relationship between a series of historical events, scientific ideas or concepts, or steps in technical procedures in a text, using language that pertains to time, sequence, and cause/effect.
		CA CC.3.Rinf.5	Use text features and search tools (e.g., key words, sidebars, hyperlinks) to locate information relevant to a given topic efficiently.
	Selection 2: Before You Move On: Make Inferences	CA CC.3.Rinf.1	Ask and answer questions to demonstrate understanding of a text, referring explicitly to the text as the basis for the answers.
472	**Respond and Extend:** Compare Texts	CA CC.3.Rinf.9	Compare and contrast the most important points and key details presented in two texts on the same topic.

California Common Core State Standards, continued

SE Pages	Lesson	Code	Standard
	Respond and Extend: Talk Together	CA CC.3.Rinf.10	By the end of the year, read and comprehend informational texts, including history/social studies, science, and technical texts, at the high end of the grades 2–3 text complexity band independently and proficiently.
		CA CC.3.SL.4	Report on a topic or text, tell a story, or recount an experience with appropriate facts and relevant, descriptive details, speaking clearly at an understandable pace.
		CA CC.3.L.6	Acquire and use accurately grade-appropriate conversational, general academic, and domain-specific words and phrases, including those that signal spatial and temporal relationships (e.g., *After dinner that night we went looking for them*).
473	**Grammar:** Prepositional Phrases	CA CC.3.L.1	Demonstrate command of the conventions of standard English grammar and usage when writing or speaking.
		CA CC.3.L.3	Use knowledge of language and its conventions when writing, speaking, reading, or listening.
		CA CC.3.L.6	Acquire and use accurately grade-appropriate conversational, general academic, and domain-specific words and phrases, including those that signal spatial and temporal relationships (e.g., *After dinner that night we went looking for them*).
474–476	**Writing Project:** Research Report Study a Model Prewrite	CA CC.3.W.2	Write informative/explanatory texts to examine a topic and convey ideas and information clearly.
		CA CC.3.W.2.a	Introduce a topic and group related information together; include illustrations when useful to aiding comprehension.
		CA CC.3.W.2.b	Develop the topic with facts, definitions, and details.
477	**Writing Project:** Gather Information	CA CC.3.W.8	Recall information from experiences or gather information from print and digital sources; take brief notes on sources and sort evidence into provided categories.
478	**Writing Project:** Get Organized/Draft	CA CC.3.W.2	Write informative/explanatory texts to examine a topic and convey ideas and information clearly.
		CA CC.3.W.2.a	Introduce a topic and group related information together; include illustrations when useful to aiding comprehension.
		CA CC.3.W.2.b	Develop the topic with facts, definitions, and details.
		CA CC.3.W.4	With guidance and support from adults, produce writing in which the development and organization are appropriate to task and purpose. (Grade-specific expectations for writing types are defined in standards 1–3 above.)
		CA CC.3.W.5	With guidance and support from peers and adults, develop and strengthen writing as needed by planning, revising, and editing. (Editing for conventions should demonstrate command of Language standards 1–3 up to and including grade 3.)

SE Pages	Lesson	Code	Standard
479	**Writing Project:** Revise/Edit and Proofread/ Publish	CA CC.3.W.4	With guidance and support from adults, produce writing in which the development and organization are appropriate to task and purpose. (Grade-specific expectations for writing types are defined in standards 1–3 above.)
		CA CC.3.W.5	With guidance and support from peers and adults, develop and strengthen writing as needed by planning, revising, and editing. (Editing for conventions should demonstrate command of Language standards 1–3 up to and including grade 3.)
		CA CC.3.W.6	With guidance and support from adults, use technology to produce and publish writing (using keyboarding skills) as well as to interact and collaborate with others.
480	**Talk Together** **Write a Fact Sheet**	CA CC.3.W.10	Write routinely over extended time frames (time for research, reflection, and revision) and shorter time frames (a single sitting or a day or two) for a range of discipline-specific tasks, purposes, and audiences.
		CA CC.3.SL.4	Report on a topic or text, tell a story, or recount an experience with appropriate facts and relevant, descriptive details, speaking clearly at an understandable pace.
		CA CC.3.SL.4.a	Plan and deliver an informative/explanatory presentation on a topic that: organizes ideas around major points of information, follows a logical sequence, includes supporting details, uses clear and specific vocabulary, and provides a strong conclusion. CA
481	**Unit Wrap-Up:** Share Your Ideas	CA CC.3.W.10	Write routinely over extended time frames (time for research, reflection, and revision) and shorter time frames (a single sitting or a day or two) for a range of discipline-specific tasks, purposes, and audiences.
		CA CC.3SL.1.b	Engage effectively in a range of collaborative discussions (one-on-one, in groups, and teacher-led) with diverse partners on *grade 3 topics and texts*, building on other's ideas and expressing their own clearly.
			Follow agreed-upon rules for discussions (e.g., gaining the floor in respectful ways, listening to others with care, speaking one at a time about the topics and texts under discussion).

California Common Core State Standards, continued

SE Pages	Lesson	Code	Standard
483	**Unit Launch:** Share What You Know	CA CC.3.W.10	Write routinely over extended time frames (time for research, reflection, and revision) and shorter time frames (a single sitting or a day or two) for a range of discipline-specific tasks, purposes, and audiences.
		CA CC.3.SL.1	Engage effectively in a range of collaborative discussions (one-on-one, in groups, and teacher-led) with diverse partners on *grade 3 topics and texts,* building on others' ideas and expressing their own clearly.
		CA CC.3.SL.1.a	Come to discussions prepared, having read or studied required material; explicitly draw on that preparation and other information known about the topic to explore ideas under discussion.
484	**Part 1: Language:** Ask for and Give Advice	CA CC.3.SL.3	Ask and answer questions about information from a speaker, offering appropriate elaboration and detail.
485	**Math Vocabulary:** Key Words	CA CC.3.Rlit.4	Determine the meaning of words and phrases as they are used in a text, distinguishing literal from nonliteral language. **(See grade 3 Language standards 4–6 for additional expectations.) CA**
		CA CC.3.L.6	Acquire and use accurately grade-appropriate conversational, general academic, and domain-specific words and phrases, including those that signal spatial and temporal relationships (e.g., *After dinner that night we went looking for them*).
486	**Thinking Map:** Goal and Outcome	CA CC.3.RL.10	By the end of the year, read and comprehend literature, including stories, dramas, and poetry, at the high end of the grades 2–3 text complexity band independently and proficiently.
487	**Academic Vocabulary:** More Key Words	CA CC.3.Rlit.4	Determine the meaning of words and phrases as they are used in a text, distinguishing literal from nonliteral language. (See grade 3 Language standards 4–6 for additional expectations.) CA
		CA CC.3.L.6	Acquire and use accurately grade-appropriate conversational, general academic, and domain-specific words and phrases, including those that signal spatial and temporal relationships (e.g., *After dinner that night we went looking for them*).
488	**Strategic Reading:** Choose Reading Strategies	CA CC.3.Rlit.10	By the end of the year, read and comprehend literature, including stories, dramas, and poetry, at the high end of the grades 2–3 text complexity band independently and proficiently.
492	**Selection 1:** Set a Purpose		Read with sufficient accuracy and fluency to support comprehension.
		CA CC.3.Rfou.4.a	Read on-level text with purpose and understanding.
497	**Selection 1:** Before You Move On	CA CC.3.Rlit.1	Ask and answer questions to demonstrate understanding of a text, referring explicitly to the text as the basis for the answers.
	Selection 1: Before You Move On: Character's Motive	CA CC.3.Rlit.3	Describe characters in a story (e.g., their traits, motivations, or feelings) and explain how their actions contribute to the sequence of events.
	Selection 1: Before You Move On: Make Inferences	CA CC.3.Rlit.3	Describe characters in a story (e.g., their traits, motivations, or feelings) and explain how their actions contribute to the sequence of events.
498	**Selection 1:** Predict	CA CC.3.Rlit.1	Ask and answer questions to demonstrate understanding of a text, referring explicitly to the text as the basis for the answers.

SE Pages	Lesson	Code	Standard
501	**Selection 1:** Before You Move On	CA CC.3.Rlit.1	Ask and answer questions to demonstrate understanding of a text, referring explicitly to the text as the basis for the answers.
	Selection 1: Before You Move On	CA CC.3.Rlit.3	Describe characters in a story (e.g., their traits, motivations, or feelings) and explain how their actions contribute to the sequence of events.
502	**Selection 1:** Predict	CA CC.3.Rlit.1	Ask and answer questions to demonstrate understanding of a text, referring explicitly to the text as the basis for the answers.
504	**Selection 1:** Before You Move On	CA CC.3.Rlit.1	Ask and answer questions to demonstrate understanding of a text, referring explicitly to the text as the basis for the answers.
		CA CC.3.Rlit.2	Recount stories, including fables, folktales, and myths from diverse cultures; determine the central message, lesson, or moral and explain how it is conveyed through key details in the text.
505	**Meet the Author:** Writer's Craft	CA. CC.3.W.3.b	Use dialogue and descriptions of actions, thoughts, and feelings to develop experiences and events or show the response of characters to situations.
		CA CC.3.W.10	Write routinely over extended time frames (time for research, reflection, and revision) and shorter time frames (a single sitting or a day or two) for a range of discipline-specific tasks, purposes, and audiences.
506	**Think and Respond:** Talk About It	CA CC.3.Rlit.2	Recount stories, including fables, folktales, and myths from diverse cultures; determine the central message, lesson, or moral and explain how it is conveyed through key details in the text.
		CA CC.3.Rlit.3	Describe characters in a story (e.g., their traits, motivations, or feelings) and explain how their actions contribute to the sequence of events.
		CA. CC.3.Rlit.5	Refer to parts of stories, dramas, and poems when writing or speaking about a text, using terms such as chapter, scene, and stanza; describe how each successive part builds on earlier sections.
		CA CC.3.Rlit.10	By the end of the year, read and comprehend literature, including stories, dramas, and poetry, at the high end of the grades 2–3 text complexity band independently and proficiently.
		CA CC.3.L.6	Acquire and use accurately grade-appropriate conversational, general academic, and domain-specific words and phrases, including those that signal spatial and temporal relationships (e.g., *After dinner that night we went looking for them*).
506	**Think and Respond:** Write About It	CA CC.3.W.10	Write routinely over extended time frames (time for research, reflection, and revision) and shorter time frames (a single sitting or a day or two) for a range of discipline-specific tasks, purposes, and audiences.
507	**Reread and Summarize** Goal and Outcome	CA CC.3.Rlit.3	Describe characters in a story (e.g., their traits, motivations, or feelings) and explain how their actions contribute to the sequence of events.
		CA CC.3.Rlit.5	Refer to parts of stories, dramas, and poems when writing or speaking about a text, using terms such as chapter, scene, and stanza; describe how each successive part builds on earlier sections.

California Common Core State Standards, continued

SE Pages	Lesson	Code	Standard
507	**Reread and Summarize** Fluency	CA CC.3.Rfou.4	Read with sufficient accuracy and fluency to support comprehension.
		CA CC.3.Rfou.4.b	Read on-level prose and poetry orally with accuracy, appropriate rate, and expression on successive readings.
507	**Reread and Summarize** Talk Together	CA CC.3.Rlit.2	Recount stories, including fables, folktales, and myths from diverse cultures; determine the central message, lesson, or moral and explain how it is conveyed through key details in the text.
			Engage effectively in a range of collaborative discussions (one-on-one, in groups, and teacher-led) with diverse partners on *grade 3 topics and texts,* building on others' ideas and expressing their own clearly.
508	**Word Work:** Word Categories	CA CC.3.L.5	Demonstrate understanding of word relationships and nuances in word meanings.
		CA CC.3.L.6	Acquire and use accurately grade-appropriate conversational, general academic, and domain-specific words and phrases, including those that signal spatial and temporal relationships (e.g., *After dinner that night we went looking for them*).
509	**Selection 2:** Before You Move On: Preview and Predict	CA CC.3.Rlit.1	Ask and answer questions to demonstrate understanding of a text, referring explicitly to the text as the basis for the answers.
	Selection 2: Before You Move On: Genre	CA CC.3.Rlit.2	Recount stories, including fables, folktales, and myths from diverse cultures; determine the central message, lesson, or moral and explain how it is conveyed through key details in the text.
511	**Selection 2:** Before You Move On	CA CC.3.Rlit.1	Ask and answer questions to demonstrate understanding of a text, referring explicitly to the text as the basis for the answers.
	Selection 2: Before You Move On: Character's Motive	CA CC.3.Rlit.3	Describe characters in a story (e.g., their traits, motivations, or feelings) and explain how their actions contribute to the sequence of events.
513	**Selection 2:** Before You Move On	CA CC.3.Rlit.1	Ask and answer questions to demonstrate understanding of a text, referring explicitly to the text as the basis for the answers.
	Selection 2: Before You Move On: **Visualize**	CA CC.3.Rlit.4	Determine the meaning of words and phrases as they are used in a text, distinguishing literal from nonliteral language. **(See grade 3 Language standards 4–6 for additional expectations.) CA**
	Selection 2: Before You Move On: Goal/Outcome	CA CC.3.L.4	Determine or clarify the meaning of unknown and multiple-meaning word and phrases based on *grade 3 reading and content,* choosing flexibly from a range of strategies.
		CA CC.3.L.4.a	Use sentence-level context as a clue to the meaning of a word or phrase.
515	**Selection 2:** Before You Move On: Character's Motive	CA CC.3.Rlit.3	Describe characters in a story (e.g., their traits, motivations, or feelings) and explain how their actions contribute to the sequence of events.
	Selection 2: Before You Move On: Ask Questions	CA CC.3.Rlit.1	Ask and answer questions to demonstrate understanding of a text, referring explicitly to the text as the basis for the answers.

SE Pages	Lesson	Code	Standard
517	**Selection 2:** Before You Move On	CA CC.3.Rlit.3	Describe characters in a story (e.g., their traits, motivations, or feelings) and explain how their actions contribute to the sequence of events.
	Selection 2: Before You Move On: Clarify	CA CC.3.Rlit.5	Refer to parts of stories, dramas, and poems when writing or speaking about a text, using terms such as chapter, scene, and stanza; describe how each successive part builds on earlier sections.
518	**Respond and Extend:** Compare Settings	CA CC.3.Rlit.2	Recount stories, including fables, folktales, and myths from diverse cultures; determine the central message, lesson, or moral and explain how it is conveyed through key details in the text.
		CA CC.3.Rlit.5	Refer to parts of stories, dramas, and poems when writing or speaking about a text, using terms such as chapter, scene, and stanza; describe how each successive part builds on earlier sections.
		CA CC.3.Rlit.10	By the end of the year, read and comprehend literature, including stories, dramas, and poetry, at the high end of the grades 2–3 text complexity band independently and proficiently.
		CA CC.3.SL.1	Engage effectively in a range of collaborative discussions (one-on-one, in groups, and teacher-led) with diverse partners on *grade 3 topics and texts,* building on others' ideas and expressing their own clearly.
		CA CC.3.SL.1.d	Explain their own ideas and understanding in light of the discussion.
		CA CC.3.L.6	Acquire and use accurately grade-appropriate conversational, general academic, and domain-specific words and phrases, including those that signal spatial and temporal relationships (e.g., *After dinner that night we went looking for them*).
519	**Grammar and Spelling: Past Tense**	CA CC.3.W.10	Write routinely over extended time frames (time for research, reflection, and revision) and shorter time frames (a single sitting or a day or two) for a range of discipline-specific tasks, purposes, and audiences.
		CA CC.3.L.1	Demonstrate command of the conventions of standard English grammar and usage when writing or speaking.
		CA CC.3.L.1.d	Form and use regular and irregular verbs.
		CA CC.3.L.1.e	Form and use the simple (e.g., *I walked; I walk; I will walk*) verb tenses.
520	**Part 2: Language:** Express Intentions	CA. CC.3.SL.1	Engage effectively in a range of collaborative discussions (one-on-one, in groups, and teacher-led) with diverse partners on *grade 3 topics and texts,* building on others' ideas and expressing their own clearly.
		CA. CC.3.SL.6	Speak in complete sentences when appropriate to task and situation in order to provide requested detail or clarification. (See grade 3 Language standards 1 and 3 for specific expectations.)

California Common Core State Standards, continued

SE Pages	Lesson	Code	Standard
521	**Social Studies Vocabulary:** Key Words	CA CC.3.Rinf.4	Determine the meaning of general academic and domain-specific words and phrases in a text relevant to a *grade 3 topic or subject area.* **(See grade 3 Language standards 4–6 for additional expectations.) CA**
		CA CC.3.Rlit.4	Determine the meaning of words and phrases as they are used in a text, distinguishing literal from nonliteral language. **(See grade 3 Language standards 4–6 for additional expectations.) CA**
		CA CC.3.L.6	Acquire and use accurately grade-appropriate conversational, general academic, and domain-specific words and phrases, including those that signal spatial and temporal relationships (e.g., *After dinner that night we went looking for them*).
522	**Thinking Map:** Main Idea and Details	CA CC.3.Rinf.2	Determine the main idea of a text; recount the key details and explain how they support the main idea.
523	**Academic Vocabulary:** More Key Words	CA CC.3.SL.6	
		CA CC.3.L.4	Determine or clarify the meaning of unknown and multiple-meaning word and phrases based on *grade 3 reading and content,* choosing flexibly from a range of strategies.
		CA CC.3.L.6	Acquire and use accurately grade-appropriate conversational, general academic, and domain-specific words and phrases, including those that signal spatial and temporal relationships (e.g., *After dinner that night we went looking for them*).
524	**Strategic Reading:** Use Reading Strategies	CA CC.3.Rinf.10	By the end of the year, read and comprehend informational texts, including history/social studies, science, and technical texts, at the high end of the grades 2–3 text complexity band independently and proficiently.
528	**Selection 1:** Set a Purpose		Read with sufficient accuracy and fluency to support comprehension.
		CA CC.3.Rfou.4.a	Read on-level text with purpose and understanding.
529	**Selection 1:** Before You Move On: Classify	CA CC.3.Rinf.1	Ask and answer questions to demonstrate understanding of a text, referring explicitly to the text as the basis for the answers.
		CA CC.3.Rinf.2	Determine the main idea of a text; recount the key details and explain how they support the main idea.
	Selection 1: Before You Move On: Make Inferences	CA CC.3.Rinf.3	Describe the relationship between a series of historical events, scientific ideas or concepts, or steps in technical procedures in a text, using language that pertains to time, sequence, and cause/effect.
		CA CC.3.Rinf.6	Distinguish their own point of view from that of the author of a text.
		CA CC.3.Rinf.8	Describe the logical connection between particular sentences and paragraphs in a text (e.g., comparison, cause/effect, first/second/third in a sequence).
531	**Selection 1:** Before You Move On: Sequence	CA CC.3.Rinf.1	Ask and answer questions to demonstrate understanding of a text, referring explicitly to the text as the basis for the answers.

SE Pages	Lesson	Code	Standard
		CA CC.3.Rinf.3	Describe the relationship between a series of historical events, scientific ideas or concepts, or steps in technical procedures in a text, using language that pertains to time, sequence, and cause/effect.
		CA CC.3.Rinf.8	Describe the logical connection between particular sentences and paragraphs in a text (e.g., comparison, cause/effect, first/second/third in a sequence).
	Selection 1: Before You Move On: Use Text Features	CA CC.3.Rinf.7	Use information gained from illustrations (e.g., maps, photographs) and the words in a text to demonstrate understanding of the text (e.g., where, when, why, and how key events occur).
533	Selection 1: Before You Move On: Visualize	CA CC.3.Rinf.1	Ask and answer questions to demonstrate understanding of a text, referring explicitly to the text as the basis for the answers.
	Selection 1: Before You Move On: Use Text Features	CA CC.3.Rinf.5	Use text features and search tools (e.g., key words, sidebars, hyperlinks) to locate information relevant to a given topic efficiently.
535	Selection 1: Before You Move On	CA CC.3.Rinf.1	Ask and answer questions to demonstrate understanding of a text, referring explicitly to the text as the basis for the answers.
	Selection 1: Before You Move On: Generalize	CA CC.3.Rinf.2	Determine the main idea of a text; recount the key details and explain how they support the main idea.
		CA CC.3.Rinf.3	Describe the relationship between a series of historical events, scientific ideas or concepts, or steps in technical procedures in a text, using language that pertains to time, sequence, and cause/effect.
537	Selection 1: Before You Move On	CA CC.3.Rinf.1	Ask and answer questions to demonstrate understanding of a text, referring explicitly to the text as the basis for the answers.
	Selection 1: Before You Move On: Main Idea	CA CC.3.Rinf.2	Determine the main idea of a text; recount the key details and explain how they support the main idea.
538	Think and Respond: Talk About It	CA CC.3.Rinf.2	Determine the main idea of a text; recount the key details and explain how they support the main idea.
		CA CC.3.Rinf.5	Use text features and search tools (e.g., key words, sidebars, hyperlinks) to locate information relevant to a given topic efficiently.
		CA CC.3.Rinf.10	By the end of the year, read and comprehend informational texts, including history/social studies, science, and technical texts, at the high end of the grades 2–3 text complexity band independently and proficiently.
			Engage effectively in a range of collaborative discussions (one-on-one, in groups, and teacher-led) with diverse partners on *grade 3 topics and texts,* building on others' ideas and expressing their own clearly.
		CA CC.3.SL.1.a	Come to discussions prepared, having read or studied required material; explicitly draw on that preparation and other information known about the topic to explore ideas under discussion.

California Common Core State Standards, continued

SE Pages	Lesson	Code	Standard
	Think and Respond: Write About It	CA CC.3.SL.2	Determine the main ideas and supporting details of a text read aloud or information presented in diverse media and formats, including visually, quantitatively, and orally.
		CA CC.3.W.10	Write routinely over extended time frames (time for research, reflection, and revision) and shorter time frames (a single sitting or a day or two) for a range of discipline-specific tasks, purposes, and audiences.
539	**Reread and Summarize** Main Idea and Details	CA CC.3.Rinf.2	Determine the main idea of a text; recount the key details and explain how they support the main idea.
		CA CC.3.Rinf.3	Describe the relationship between a series of historical events, scientific ideas or concepts, or steps in technical procedures in a text, using language that pertains to time, sequence, and cause/effect.
		CA CC.3.SL.2	Determine the main ideas and supporting details of a text read aloud or information presented in diverse media and formats, including visually, quantitatively, and orally.
	Reread and Summarize Fluency	CA CC.3.Rfou.4	Read with sufficient accuracy and fluency to support comprehension.
		CA CC.3.Rfou.4.b	Read on-level prose and poetry orally with accuracy, appropriate rate, and expression on successive readings.
	Read and Summarize Talk Together	CA CC.3.Rinf.7	Use information gained from illustrations (e.g., maps, photographs) and the words in a text to demonstrate understanding of the text (e.g., where, when, why, and how key events occur).
		CA CC.3.SL.2	Determine the main ideas and supporting details of a text read aloud or information presented in diverse media and formats, including visually, quantitatively, and orally.
540	**Word Work:** Homographs		Determine or clarify the meaning of unknown and multiple-meaning word and phrases based on grade 3 reading and content, choosing flexibly from a range of strategies.
		CA CC.3.L.4.a	Use sentence-level context as a clue to the meaning of a word or phrase.
541	**Selection 2 Opener:** Before You Move On: Make Inferences	CA CC.3.Rinf.1	Ask and answer questions to demonstrate understanding of a text, referring explicitly to the text as the basis for the answers.
	Selection 2 Opener: Before You Move On: Main Idea and Details	CA CC.3.Rinf.2	Determine the main idea of a text; recount the key details and explain how they support the main idea.
		CA CC.3.SL.2	Determine the main ideas and supporting details of a text read aloud or information presented in diverse media and formats, including visually, quantitatively, and orally.
543	**Selection 2 Opener:** Before You Move On: Ask Questions	CA CC.3.Rinf.1	Ask and answer questions to demonstrate understanding of a text, referring explicitly to the text as the basis for the answers.

SE Pages	Lesson	Code	Standard
	Selection 2: Before You Move On: Form Generalizations	CA CC.3.Rinf.3	Describe the relationship between a series of historical events, scientific ideas or concepts, or steps in technical procedures in a text, using language that pertains to time, sequence, and cause/effect.
545	**Selection 2:** Before You Move On	CA CC.3.Rinf.1	Ask and answer questions to demonstrate understanding of a text, referring explicitly to the text as the basis for the answers.
	Selection 2: Before You Move On: Summarize	CA CC.3.Rinf.2	Determine the main idea of a text; recount the key details and explain how they support the main idea.
546	**Respond and Extend:** Compare Causes	CA CC.3.Rinf.9	Compare and contrast the most important points and key details presented in two texts on the same topic.
		CA CC.3.Rinf.10	By the end of the year, read and comprehend informational texts, including history/social studies, science, and technical texts, at the high end of the grades 2–3 text complexity band independently and proficiently.
		CA CC.3.L.6	Acquire and use accurately grade-appropriate conversational, general academic, and domain-specific words and phrases, including those that signal spatial and temporal relationships (e.g., *After dinner that night we went looking for them*).
547	**Grammar:** Future Tense	CA CC.3.L.1	Demonstrate command of the conventions of standard English grammar and usage when writing or speaking.
		CA CC.3.L.1.e	Form and use the simple (e.g., *I walked; I walk; I will walk*) verb tenses.
549	**Writing Project:** Story Study a Model Prewrite Draft	CA CC.3.W.3	Write narratives to develop real or imagined experiences or events using effective technique, descriptive details, and clear event sequences.
		CA CC.3.W.3.a	Establish a situation and introduce a narrator and/or characters; organize an event sequence that unfolds naturally.
		CA CC.3.W.3.b	Use dialogue and descriptions of actions, thoughts, and feelings to develop experiences and events or show the response of characters to situations.
		CA CC.3.W.3.d	Provide a sense of closure.
550	**Writing Project:** Revise	CA CC.3.W.4	With guidance and support from adults, produce writing in which the development and organization are appropriate to task and purpose. (Grade-specific expectations for writing types are defined in standards 1–3 above.)
		CA CC.3.W.5	With guidance and support from peers and adults, develop and strengthen writing as needed by planning, revising, and editing. (Editing for conventions should demonstrate command of Language standards 1–3 up to and including grade 3.)

California Common Core State Standards, continued

SE Pages	Lesson	Code	Standard
551	**Writing Project:** Edit and Proofread	CA CC.3.W.5	With guidance and support from peers and adults, develop and strengthen writing as needed by planning, revising, and editing. (Editing for conventions should demonstrate command of Language standards 1–3 up to and including grade 3.)
	Writing Project: Publish	CA CC.3.W.6	With guidance and support from adults, use technology to produce and publish writing (using keyboarding skills) as well as to interact and collaborate with others.
			Report on a topic or text, tell a story, or recount an experience with appropriate facts and relevant, descriptive details, speaking clearly at an understandable pace.
		CA CC.3.SL.4.a	Plan and deliver an informative/explanatory presentation on a topic that: organizes ideas around major points of information, follows a logical sequence, includes supporting details, uses clear and specific vocabulary, and provides a strong conclusion. CA
552	**Talk Together** **Write a Story**	CA CC.3.W.3	Write narratives to develop real or imagined experiences or events using effective technique, descriptive details, and clear event sequences.
		CA CC.3.W.2.a	Introduce a topic and group related information together; include illustrations when useful to aiding comprehension.
		CA CC.3.W.3.b	Use dialogue and descriptions of actions, thoughts, and feelings to develop experiences and events or show the response of characters to situations.
		CA CC.3.W.10	Write routinely over extended time frames (time for research, reflection, and revision) and shorter time frames (a single sitting or a day or two) for a range of discipline-specific tasks, purposes, and audiences.
		CA CC.3.SL.1	Engage effectively in a range of collaborative discussions (one-on-one, in groups, and teacher-led) with diverse partners on *grade 3 topics and texts,* building on others' ideas and expressing their own clearly.
		CA CC.3.SL.1.a	Come to discussions prepared, having read or studied required material; explicitly draw on that preparation and other information known about the topic to explore ideas under discussion.
553	**Unit Wrap-Up:** Share Your Ideas	CA CC.3.W.10	Write routinely over extended time frames (time for research, reflection, and revision) and shorter time frames (a single sitting or a day or two) for a range of discipline-specific tasks, purposes, and audiences.
		CA CC.3.SL.1.b	Engage effectively in a range of collaborative discussions (one-on-one, in groups, and teacher-led) with diverse partners on grade 3 topics and texts, building on other's ideas and expressing their own clearly.
			Follow agreed-upon rules for discussions (e.g., gaining the floor in respectful ways, listening to others with care, speaking one at a time about the topics and texts under discussion).